A TASTE FOR OPPRESSION

ANTHROPOLOGY OF EUROPE

General Editors:
Monica Heintz, University of Paris Nanterre
Patrick Heady, Max Planck Institute for Social Anthropology

Europe, a region characterized by its diversity and speed of change, is the latest area to attract current anthropological research and scholarship that challenges the prevailing views of classical anthropology. Situated at the frontier of the social sciences and humanities, the anthropology of Europe is born out of traditional ethnology, anthropology, folklore, and cultural studies, but engages in innovative interdisciplinary approaches.

Anthropology of Europe publishes fieldwork monographs by young and established scholars, as well as edited volumes on particular regions or aspects of European society. The series pays special attention to studies with a strong comparative component, addressing theoretical questions of interest to both anthropologists and other scholars working in related fields.

Volume 6
A Taste for Oppression
A Political Ethnography of Everyday Life in Belarus
Ronan Hervouet

Volume 5
Punks and Skins United
Identity, Class and the Economics of an Eastern German Subculture
Aimar Ventsel

Volume 4
In Pursuit of Belonging
Forging an Ethical Life in European-Turkish Spaces
Susan Beth Rottmann

Volume 3
All or None
Cooperation and Sustainability in Italy's Red Belt
Alison Sánchez Hall

Volume 2
European Anthropologies
Edited by Andrés Barrera-González, Monica Heintz, and Anna Horolets

Volume 1
The France of the Little-Middles
A Suburban Housing Development in Greater Paris
Marie Cartier, Isabelle Coutant, Olivier Masclet, and Yasmine Siblot

A TASTE FOR OPPRESSION
A Political Ethnography of Everyday Life in Belarus

Ronan Hervouet

Translated by Dean Frances

berghahn
NEW YORK • OXFORD
www.berghahnbooks.com

Published in 2021 by
Berghahn Books
www.berghahnbooks.com

© 2021, 2024 Ronan Hervouet
First paperback edition published in 2024

The book was originally published in French
by Le Bord de l'eau under the title *Le Goût Des Tyrans.
Une Ethnographie Politique Du Quotidien En Biélorussie*
© 2020 Le Bord de l'eau.

All rights reserved. Except for the quotation of short passages
for the purposes of criticism and review, no part of this book
may be reproduced in any form or by any means, electronic or
mechanical, including photocopying, recording, or any information
storage and retrieval system now known or to be invented,
without written permission of the publisher.

Library of Congress Cataloging-in-Publication Data

Names: Hervouet, Ronan, author. | Frances, Dean, translator.
Title: A Taste for Oppression: A Political Ethnography of Everyday Life in
  Belarus / Ronan Hervouet; translated by Dean Frances.
Description: New York: Berghahn, 2021. | Series: Anthropology of Europe;
  volume 6 | Includes bibliographical references and index.
Identifiers: LCCN 2020058138 (print) | LCCN 2020058139 (ebook) |
  ISBN 9781800730250 (hardback) | ISBN 9781800730267 (ebook)
Subjects: LCSH: Collectivization of agriculture—Belarus. | Authoritarianism—
  Belarus. | Politics and culture—Belarus. | Political sociology—Belarus. |
  Belarus—Social conditions—1991– | Belarus—Rural conditions. | Belarus—
  Politics and government—1991–
Classification: LCC HN530.7.A8 H47 2021 (print) | LCC HN530.7.A8 (ebook)
  | DDC 306.09478—dc23
LC record available at https://lccn.loc.gov/2020058138
LC ebook record available at https://lccn.loc.gov/2020058139

British Library Cataloguing in Publication Data

A catalogue record for this book is available from the British Library

ISBN 978-1-80073-025-0 hardback
ISBN 978-1-80539-307-8 paperback
ISBN 978-1-80539-421-1 epub
ISBN 978-1-80073-026-7 web pdf

https://doi.org/10.3167/9781800730250

The love of order is cofounded with a taste for oppression.
—Alexis de Tocqueville, *Democracy in America*, 1835

CONTENTS

Acknowledgments	viii
Notes on Text	ix
Introduction	1
Chapter 1. Government of Rural Areas	10
Chapter 2. A Discrete Ethnography	26
Chapter 3. Authorized Resources	48
Chapter 4. Illegalisms	70
Chapter 5. Interdependencies	91
Chapter 6. Life Horizons	111
Chapter 7. Solidarity	133
Chapter 8. Dignity	157
Chapter 9. The Fragility of the World	179
Chapter 10. Levels of Social Order	203
Conclusion	222
References	232
Index	255

ACKNOWLEDGMENTS

I would like to thank all the Belarusians who welcomed me into their homes, in rural and urban areas, for their hospitality and kindness; Sasha for his friendship and indispensable help, without which this research would probably never have been successful; my friends in Minsk who helped me organize my field studies and find new contacts, and those who were present on a daily basis during my stays in Belarus (Ales, Andrei, Diana, Kyril, Roman, Said, Vadim, Vladik, Yves, and Zoya); Florence Weber for agreeing to sponsor my HDR (higher doctorate with accreditation to supervise research) and also for her support and the trust she has placed in me; the members of my HDR jury (Boris Pétric, Jessica Pisano, Antoine Roger, Jay Rowell, and Olivier Schwartz) for their advice, remarks and encouragement; colleagues at my laboratory in Bordeaux (France)—Centre Émile Durkheim (UMR 5116)—which provides an invaluable working environment; Dean Frances at The Home of Translation in Bordeaux (France), who translated the manuscript from French into English with careful consideration of all my remarks and suggestions; colleagues and friends who have allowed me to discuss my current work and/or who have encouraged me during these years of research (notably Élisabeth Anstett, Emmanuel Blanchard, Caroline Dufy, Alexandre Gofman, Glenn Mainguy, Pascal Ragouet, Andy Smith, Ioulia Shukan, and Joël Zaffran); and colleagues, friends, and relatives who had the patience to reread part or all of the final text (Charles-Henry Cuin, François Dubet, Jean Harambat, Michel Hervouet, Xabier Itçaina, Marion Noguès, and Patrick Rödel).

The translation was made possible thanks to the support of the Centre Émile Durkheim (UMR 5116).

This book is dedicated to Marion.

NOTES ON TEXT

In this work, Russian words have been transcribed according to the ISO 9 standard. However, for proper nouns (Lukashenko, Brezhnev, etc.), first names (Sasha, etc.), and the names of cities (Mogilev, Babruysk, etc.), the common transcriptions, as used in the press, atlases, and literature, have been adopted.

Some of the cited authors use transliterations from Belarusian, which explains certain spelling variations in the manuscript. For example, in certain quotations, Lukashenko may also be spelled Lukashenka.

To guarantee their anonymity, all surnames and first names of the persons met in the field and cited in the manuscript have been changed, along with most of the names of the villages and towns in which they reside. The only exception is in chapter 10.

INTRODUCTION

THE LAST DICTATORSHIP IN EUROPE

Belarus has emerged from communism in a unique manner in Europe. Today, it is described by many analysts as the "last dictatorship in Europe" (Benett 2011; Wilson 2011). Its recent history can be condensed into several key dates. On 25 August 1991, the Supreme Soviet of Belarus voted for independence. This was a major turning point. Indeed, the territory currently occupied by Belarus was incorporated into Russia at the end of the eighteenth century and the USSR in the twentieth century, with part of the country absorbed by Poland under its Second Republic (Snyder 2003). In fact, until 1991, Belarus had enjoyed only a very short period of independence. Proclaimed under German occupation on 25 March 1918, the Belarusian National Republic was very short-lived (Wilson 2011: 94), ending on 1 January 1919. It was replaced by the Socialist Soviet Republic of Byelorussia (SSRB), which was incorporated into the USSR three years later. The dissolution of the USSR was declared on 8 December 1991. After a period in which the political elite sought to make quite a radical break with the Soviet past, Alexander Lukashenko embarked on a "conservative revolution" in the country. After becoming the democratically elected president of the country in 1994, he established an authoritarian regime (Linz 2000) in 1996, proudly asserting the Soviet legacy and reviving certain ideological precepts and some of the interventionist administrative and policing practices of the defunct empire (Lallemand and Symaniec 2007). "Everything [occurred] almost as if Sovietism had survived without the Communist Party" (Marcou and Pankovski 2003: 18). First, Lukashenko promoted a "socially oriented market economy" (Lallemand 2006: 203) that was largely collectivized. Second, he established strong continuity with the Soviet past. In May 1995, for example, he secured approval, by referendum, to abandon the red and white national flag and reintroduce the red and green Soviet banner, but this time without the hammer and sickle. The authorities reintroduced emblems similar to those in force during the Soviet era. The Bolshevik Revolution continued to be commemorated on 7 November, and the KGB kept its name. Felix Dzerzhinsky (cf. pp. 60, 87), founder of the Cheka, was personally respected and glorified to the point that a bust of the secret police chief still stands in the city center. In 2004, a new museum dedicated to his memory was inaugurated on Belarusian soil. Last, the elections that have punctuated the country's history since the start of Lukashenko's presidency have been marked by repeated challenges from civil society and international organizations such as the Organization for Security and Co-operation in Europe (OSCE), but also by systematic repression.

The workings of this regime are traditionally described, by scholars and the media, as being based on a "vertical power structure," whose implementation is based on a strictly controlled administration and a powerful police system that represses opponents. Consequently, the academic literature analyzes the authoritarian functioning of the regime (McMahon 1997; Eke and Kuzio 2000; Goujon 2002; Karbalévitch 2012; Hervouet 2013c) and the characteristics of the "state ideology" (Lallemand 2006; Leshchenko 2008), as well as the forms of opposition (Shukan 2008; Goujon 2009) and dissidence (Symaniec 2006; Perchoc 2006; Bigday 2017; Kryzhanouski 2017). The regime is also thought to remain in power thanks to its populist social policy, based on subsidizing often-inefficient economic sectors with the aim of securing the loyalty of a large proportion of the population, and in this way, to a certain extent, "buying" its submission (Wilson 2011).

Without underestimating these essential characteristics of the political machinery in present-day Belarus, my research focuses on practices "seen from below" in order to show, based on the analysis of a singular case, how an authoritarian regime relies on forces other than police violence and redistribution, and permits a form of permeability in its ideology that is capable of absorbing different types of messages in order to perpetuate the political and social order. If we consider, in accordance with Max Weber (2019: 109), that order remains unstable if it is based solely on fear or on "purposively rational motives," we can seek to identify other forms and degrees of legitimation employed by the regime in order to remain in power since 1996. The focus of my research is encapsulated by the following question: how can a system, while broadly imposing severe constraints, produce—sometimes simultaneously but indirectly and unintentionally—acceptable or even desirable forms of life and resulting modes of attachment to the authoritarian regime? It entails approaching "politics from below" (Bayart 1985: 345) based on an ethnographic approach. The aim is therefore to contribute to renewing the approach to analyzing the reasons for the perpetuation of an authoritarian regime (Hibou 2017) by shifting the focus from its institutional and policing operations toward everyday practices.

OPEN INTERPRETATIONS OF CLOSED SOCIETIES

This investigation is consistent with certain trends that have developed since the 1970s in the historiography of communist regimes in Europe. These reflections examine and criticize the "totalitarian paradigm" (Studer 2004: 40) that formerly prevailed, with a view to understanding how societies function. This approach, initially inspired by political philosophy (Arendt 1951) and political science (Friedrich and Brzezinski 1961), is advocated by certain historians who place the emphasis on the "ideocratic" dimension of these regimes and who set out to "reassert the primacy of ideology and politics over social and economic forces in understanding the Soviet phenomenon" (Malia 1994: 8, 16). This approach to totalitarian regimes considers the forces behind their perpetuation by focusing on how the power is disseminated downward from the top to the bottom like a machine activating its "cogs" (Heller 1988). It examines the omnipotence of the one-party state, its institutions, and its ideologies, while assuming them to have performative power. It also investigates the propaganda and indoctrination employed to make the population docile, in addition to the omnipresence of policing organizations, violence, and terror on an everyday basis (Werth 1999b: 85).

Two historiographical schools of thought challenge this approach by putting into perspective the heuristic scope of the notion of totalitarianism (Traverso 2001), perceived as an "obsolete model" (Rowell 1999: 150) or a "masking concept" (Pudal 2009: 164). On the one hand, the American school, described as "revisionist," advocates a social history "seen from below," which is partially exempt from political and ideological determinisms (Werth 2001a), with a particular focus on "everyday Stalinism" (Fitzpatrick 1999). On the other hand, certain German historians of the German Democratic Republic (GDR), operating from the perspective of *Alltagsgeschichte*, have set out to "put the people, the 'ordinary' individuals, the 'little guys' (*die kleinen Leute*), back at the heart of history; i.e., to represent or study them as players in their own right and not just consider them as the silent victims of major changes or structures" (Kott 2002: 226). In this way, both these streams of research examine "everyday life under communism" (Zakharova 2013) and "everyday life in dictatorships" (Lüdtke 2000). In France, these approaches resonate particularly strongly in the research on "a social history of power in communist Europe" (Kott 2002a). They focus in particular on "the social history of the Soviet dictatorship" (Depretto 2001), and on "day-to-day" communism (Kott 2014) or "concrete manifestations of totalitarianism" (Rowell 2006) in the GDR. This historiographic sensitivity, which places the emphasis on "minuscule lives" (Lagrave 2011: 12) and ordinary personal experiences in communist societies, has informed a diverse range of works on the links between daily life and power in the communist societies of Europe (Bertaux, Thompson, and Rotkirch 2005; Neculau 2008; Koleva 2012). They sometimes explore specific spheres of activity such as consumption (Ragaru and Capelle-Pogăcean 2010), cultural practices (Yurchak 2006) such as rock music (Zaytseva 2008), education (Droit 2009), inhabited areas (Crowley and Reid 2002), the relationship with time (Krakovský 2018), and recreational activities (Giustino, Plum, and Vari 2013). In this manner, they implicitly examine the idea of the blurring of the distinction between the public and private spheres in this type of regime (Field 2007; Christian and Kott 2009). These approaches to the social and political dynamics of Eastern European societies are echoed in the "anthropology of socialism" (Sampson 1991) documented in areas situated behind the Iron Curtain, as in Hungary (Hann 1980; Lampland 1991; Burawoy and Lukács 1992), Poland (Hann 1985; Wedel 1986), Romania (Kideckel 1993; Verdery 1996), Bulgaria (Creed 1998), and the USSR (Humphrey 2001; Ries 1997). These anthropological works offer "a valuable contribution in undermining common assumptions about passive, cowed, inert populations at the whim of communist powerholders" (Hann 1994: 235).

Extending the Weberian tradition that distinguishes between power (*Macht*) and domination (*Herrschaft*) (Kott 2014: 261), these historical and anthropological studies show that although the government's power and influence in the communist societies of Europe permeate into the heart of everyday life, it neither determines nor controls it totally. "The authorities are omnipresent but not necessarily effective" (Kott 2002a: 11). In order to analyze the relationships of individuals with the authorities, these perspectives first invite researchers to move beyond the "use of binary categories" (Yurchak 2006: 5) and the "problematic dichotomy" (Lüdtke 1990: 13) contrasting oppression with resistance, and the guilty with the victims. Second, they encourage a departure from "Manichean antitheses" that consider the stability of these regimes to be maintained either by violence, "by guns and tanks," or by successful indoctrination manifested by "forms of collaboration and acceptance, or even of acknowledged support for the regime" (Lüdtke 1998: 7–8). These historical and anthropological studies show that in the communist societies of Europe, there is an extended array of attitudes that reveal "the complex entanglement of consent and dissatisfaction, adherence and refusal, compromise and passive resistance" (Werth 1999b: 90), "behaviors of inertia, avoidance and nonconformity" (Werth 2001a: 128), the joint existence "of situations of hope and despair, uncertainty and relaxation" (Lüdtke 1998: 8), and "multiple types of reactions, [ranging] from deliberate cooperation and unquestioning identification to resistance and opposition, including opportunistic adaptation, apathy and withdrawal into the private sphere" (Kocka 1995: 84).

These studies propose an "open interpretation of closed societies" (Lagrave 2011: 13). They place the emphasis on the "'privatization' of the instruments of coercion" via denunciations, negotiations within enterprises, local arrangements concerning the implementation of directives imposed "from above," and the detachment of individuals from discourses legitimizing the regime (Verdery 1991: 426–428). They insist on the arrangements, the room for maneuvering, the permeable aspects of the system, and the ambivalences in the different types of actions, without evading the forms of supervision, control, and regression that are characteristic of these regimes. Therefore, as in the East German context analyzed by Konrad Jarausch, the common pattern for these studies is to "criticize, in uncompromising terms, the very real inhumanity of the regime while *simultaneously* formulating a differentiated analysis of the partly 'normal' ordinary existence that was possible" in these societies. "This is the condition under which the individual experiences and structural explanations can be unified in one common general interpretation" (Jarausch 2003: 94).

My research is consistent with this movement. Although these different works focus on the communist era, they are also enlightening when investigating a postcommunist context presenting significant forms of analogies and continuities with the Soviet past. More broadly, my thinking on the forces behind the perpetuation of the authoritarian regime in Belarus builds on the questions recently raised by the "political anatomy of domination" that is attentive to the "subtleties of the mechanisms of legitimation."

> The legitimacy granted is never complete and obviously has to compromise with discontent, worry, partial rejections and recriminations; it is less synonymous with adhesion, support and active participation than with accommodation; it primarily reflects a relative and intermittent judgement because individuals do not constantly ask themselves whether the state or the government are legitimate and because the rules by which they assess normality can be plural and refer to different (even contradictory) hierarchies of values. (Hibou 2017: 3)

A POLITICAL ETHNOGRAPHY OF RURAL BELARUS

What sphere would lend itself to reflection on everyday life under the authoritarian Belarusian regime? My previous research on dachas led me to contemplate the different ways in which ordinary citizens create relatively acceptable or even desirable worlds in an economic, political, and cultural environment characterized by very strong constraints (Hervouet 2009a).

In it, I showed how ordinary city dwellers, by putting their energies into the tending of vegetable gardens, put their "desire for happiness" (*volonté de bonheur*; Castel 1968: 21) into practice by loosening the shackles of the system without actually breaking them. I then turned my attentions toward a more paradigmatic sphere than the vegetable gardens tended by city dwellers. Indeed, the kolkhozes and rural communities in general are particularly relevant to an analysis of everyday life under the authoritarian Belarusian regime. Even though they differ from the French situation in many respects, rural Belarusian worlds can also be characterized by the superimposition of professional and domestic scenes, closer mutual-acquaintance relationships than in towns and cities, and domination based on personal relationships (Mischi and Renahy 2008: 17–18). In Belarus, rural areas have remained collectivized and are governed by systematic policies of control. Viewed from outside, the collectivist system can be defined by political constraint, social discipline, and economic control. The Soviet-type collectivist model was abandoned throughout the European postcommunist area, except in Belarus. Indeed, after 1989, the collectivist Eastern European and then Soviet agricultural systems were reformed in different ways (Dufy and Hervouet 2017). The maintenance of this model in Belarus is a little-known aspect of European societies, as illustrated in the following statement by Jean-Louis Chaléard (2010: 31), a geographer specializing in rural communities, who declares that "the collectivist system has disappeared almost everywhere," except "in Cuba, despite recent measures, and in North Korea." This vestige of the past, which is perceived as destined to disappear, has not been the subject of detailed political and sociological analyses. There is practically no mention of rural areas in publications devoted to Belarus, especially in economic analyses. In this academic context, I considered Belarus to be a living laboratory for the analysis of everyday life under dictatorship in the collectivized rural world.

Kolkhozians and countryfolk in general are subject to a hierarchy in the economic and social world, which is also a political and cultural hierarchy. At first sight, they appear to have absolutely no room to maneuver or influence their own destiny. From a "*misérabiliste*" perspective (Grignon and Passeron 1989), kolkhozians could be seen as the paradigmatic product of domination. Scorned by the city dwellers and controlled by the authorities, they are characterized by their humble social standing, their meager economic resources, and their silent and passive acceptance of their situation. In addition to being economically exploited, they could also be considered culturally alienated due to their defense of their own oppressor. Indeed, the countryfolk are often perceived as the propagators of a conservative culture (Goujon 2009: 178) and the president's natural supporters. From this perspective, countryfolk would be characterized only in a negative manner, due to their lack of economic resources, pride, self-sufficiency, practical know-how, and dignity. In this way, my ideas run counter to this top-down approach while avoiding the pitfalls of "populism" (Grignon and Passeron 1989). I am seeking to understand the forms of life that occur in rural areas, from the inside, without assuming my contacts to be motivated solely by the power of a hegemonic domination. I therefore focused on practices aiming toward "self-ownership" (*propriété de soi*; Castel and Haroche 2001) employed by people who, because they are never encountered and because their worlds remain unobserved, are denied any power to define their own projects or appropriate their own existences. These means of self-reappropriation are always fragile, however, and we should not remain silent about the social structure that shapes them. Indeed, they form part of social configurations that are objectively marked by forms of material, statutory, cultural, political, and symbolic domination.

This approach requires an examination of the authoritarian regime at the "grass-roots" level (*au ras du sol*; Revel 1989), and the development of a "political anatomy of detail" (Hibou 2017: 2). It justifies the adoption of an ethnographic approach. This direct survey method is based on traditional observational, interview, and case-study methods, but differs by placing the researcher in long-term, mutual-acquaintance contexts "in which the investigator can develop personal relationships with the interviewees who have also forged personal relationships with each other" (F. Weber 2009b: 5). I spent five years living in Belarus, between 1999 and 2013. This long presence in the country enabled me to build friendships with people who subsequently became strategic allies in my search for interviewees living in rural areas. These allies therefore put me in contact with their family members living in rural communities or in small towns surrounded by kolkhozes. The fact that I was introduced to them by known people allowed me to gain the trust of my interviewees and operate in different regions of Belarus. The interviews were occasionally conducted in a structured manner, using a tape recorder, but were usually carried out informally. I initiated discussions about kolkhozes and rural communities, not only in formal face-to-face settings with interviewees chatting to the sociologist about a subject that had been clearly defined in advance, but also in numerous everyday situations (family meals, discussions about someone's working day, comments about the neighborhood, chats over a shared bottle of homemade wine or vodka, while relaxing in a *bania*—a Russian sauna—etc.), when I latched onto discourses about everyday life in rural areas as they arose, and sought to steer these discussions, to the best of my ability, in the direction I wanted. Between 2006 and 2013, I conducted around forty interviews in different parts of Belarus, with younger and older people, working and retired people, kolkhozians, self-employed people, and teachers in agricultural high schools. The robustness and depth of the material collected enabled me to describe kolkhozes and rural areas as viewed from within. I set out to understand how people in these places constructed worlds that they considered acceptable, without these actions and desires being merely a reflection of the power structure.

It is first a question of an economic ethnography. Considering that "concrete economic practices play an active part in power struggles and power relations" (Hibou 2017: xiv), there was a need to understand "how the most banal economic dispositifs and economic functioning of everyday life simultaneously involve mechanisms of domination" (Hibou 2017: xii). To this end, the survey needed to be painstakingly based on material aspects (budgets, domestic chores, job requirements, timetables, family schedules, etc.) and then related to other spheres of activity (family and neighborhood relationships, organizational hierarchies, relationships with the government), while placing them, via a biographical approach, in a broader temporal context. Examining the rural condition in terms of "interconnected worlds" (*mondes imbriqués*; Dufy and Weber 2007: 19), my approach is therefore situated at the confluence of an economic sociology, a sociology of work, a rural sociology, a sociology of the family and kinship, a sociology of the lower classes and even a sociology of the collective memory. But the aim is also to understand, from this microscopic perspective, the ordinary attitudes to politics and the potential forms of attachment to the authoritarian regime. This ethnography is therefore also a political ethnography (Katz 2009). The thoughts and representations of my contacts are rooted in the daily practices that are an integral part of domestic, professional, and village life. As in the analysis of northern French workers' attitudes to politics by Olivier Schwarz (1991: 79), my approach sets out to obtain "a very indirect 'knowledge,' revealed by traces, which focuses less on positions and attitudes than on underlying forms of *rapport* with politics, as can be inferred from materials which are all-too-often abstruse and incomplete." I perceived the influence of politics in behaviors and discourses that, in isolation, bear no relation to it, but that, when combined and interconnected, may reveal coherent conceptions of what is fair and unfair and of the power struggles within society. I collected concrete accounts of life situations, life stories, complaints, criticisms, and judgments on social organization. I needed to find ways to bring out indigenous and uncensored comments about life in the kolkhoz, to consider them as "symptoms" (Schwartz 1991: 79), and then to infer—from fragments, contextualized, and sometimes very down-to-earth descriptions—representations of the world which are seldom verbalized and rarely systematized in reflexive discourses. To address political issues, I reflected on the nature and meaning of practices at grass-roots level, considering that the political horizon of these practices could be glimpsed through everyday utterances and acts that, at first sight, are far-removed from politics: the cultivation of vegetable gardens, shady dealings at work, family discussions, neighborhood tensions, working conditions, etc. I raised the subject of politics (almost) without talking about politics.

This book revolves around the following reasoning. First, I address rural communities "viewed from above" by analyzing the methods of governing the collectivized countryside in contemporary Belarus (chapter 1). Then, by adopting the methodology of multisite ethnographic sociology (chapter 2), I turn my attention toward practices "viewed from below." I describe the different types of available resources (chapters 3 and 4), followed by exchanges and interdependencies (chapter 5) that enable these worlds to be envisaged as systems. I then analyze how these configurations produce acceptable or even desirable forms of life, based on the satisfaction of material needs (chapter 6), membership of supportive groups (chapter 7) and the defense of dignified ways of living (chapter 8). These forms of life, indirectly produced by the economic and political constraints imposed by the authorities, ultimately echo the expectations and practices of the regime itself. They generate a specific moral economy and expectations of the authorities, which must protect—by violent means if necessary—the fragile rural worlds from certain threats embodied by the figures of the profiteers, idlers, and moralists (chapter 9). In this way, the local aspiration for order converges with the governing power's desire to perpetuate the system (chapter 10).

CHAPTER

1

GOVERNMENT OF RURAL AREAS

Belarus plotted an original course after the collapse of the USSR.[1] Following a period of liberalization, similar in many respects to the situation in other postcommunist countries, Belarus returned to principles of government that are more consistent with the doctrine of the Soviet regime. Since Alexander Lukashenko came to power in 1994, 70 percent of the Belarusian State economy has been administered and nationalized according to five-year plans (EBRD 2013: 13). This reorientation draws on the Soviet model, which is considered to be efficient and modernizing, while adopting innovative forms borrowed from the market economy and made necessary by the end of the division of labor that formerly existed in the Eastern bloc. Lukashenko himself describes this economic, social, and political system as "market socialism" (Hervouet 2013b). This expression echoes a theoretical model developed in 1936–1937 by the Pole Oskar Lange, who sought to link Marxist economic analysis to the neoclassical economy, and combine socialism (i.e., state ownership) with market mechanisms (Desreumaux 2013). The idea of market socialism has inspired reforms in various communist countries, such as China in the 1970s (Amin 2004), Vietnam in the 1980s (Beresford 2008), and, more recently, Cuba (Wilkinson 2012). While the common denominator of these reforms is the quest to maintain a balance between profit and social policies, the methods used to implement market socialism have differed (Batisse and Sélim 2008).

How is this idea of market socialism interpreted and presented in the Belarusian context? According to Lukashenko, the market introduces competition and economic efficiency, while the intervention of a strong state, in the form of various taxes, government-regulated wage scales and prices,[2] and subsidized rental prices (rents, gas, and electricity) ensures social justice since it enables everyone to benefit from the wealth produced, and because it prevents profits from being appropriated by a small minority. Criticizing the Russian liberalization of the 1990s, but also the market economy model promoted by the European Union authorities, among others, he defends the idea that only a strong state can steer the national economy properly. In this respect, he is consistent with the Soviet heritage, to which he openly lays claim, and supports the development of a renewed socialist model, drawing particular inspiration from the Chinese model promoted by Deng Xiaoping (Medvedev 2010). He believes that the market enables the creation of wealth more efficiently than traditional Soviet collectivism, but with the state guaranteeing the "socialist" character of this market by controlling certain functional processes, especially the mechanisms for distributing the wealth that is produced. In the end, Lukashenko presents this Belarusian economic, social, and political system as a model that is not only fairer but also more effective in enabling former USSR countries to emerge from communism.

This representation of the economy has guided the policy applied to rural areas of Belarus. After a dramatic drop in production in the early 1990s, the agricultural sector gradually improved its performance and started achieving results that were lauded by the authorities: increased production, slowdown in rural-to-urban migration, improved living conditions, and political stability in the rural worlds. These objectives were achieved by adopting the Soviet model of a "collectivized countryside" (Maurel 1980), which makes the Belarusian case a notable singularity in postcommunist agricultural and rural developments in Europe. The government presents these results as the product of the state's proactive actions. In ideological terms, the rural world provides the foundations for the staging of power, and is used to justify the adoption of "market socialism." Contrary to the worker-oriented emphasis of the political culture promoted during the Soviet era, the current Belarusian regime mainly promotes itself in rural areas.

This chapter sets out to understand rural government in Belarus from the economic, political, administrative, social, and symbolic perspectives, but also through the prism of its ideological references, with a view to understanding how rural worlds are controlled "from above." Economic dirigisme, disciplinary measures, material improvements, political rituals of legitimization, and paternalistic moralization mechanisms form a system of government that seeks to steer the development of rural areas. Kolkhozes thus emerge as places in which a specific policy of economic, social, and political management is deployed with several closely articulated strands, demonstrating the coherence of the mechanisms of power implemented in contemporary Belarus.

COLLECTIVISM

Industrialization of Agriculture

In the last days of the Soviet Union, agriculture was a major economic sector in Belarus, but it has declined considerably in importance over the past twenty-five years. Indeed, agriculture accounted for 22.7 percent of GNP in 1990 but just 7.9 percent in 2012 (National Statistical Committee 2014). This is also reflected by a decline in the rural population, which represented one-third of the total population (34 percent) in 1990; today, it amounts to barely a quarter (23 percent) (National Statistical Committee 2014). The proportion of the labor force currently working in the agricultural sector is less than one person in ten (8 percent) (National Statistical Committee 2014), compared to almost one in five (19.1 percent) in 1995 (*Selk'skoe hozâjstvo* 2015: 5). In 1995 there were 843,500 people working on collective farms, but by 2014 there were only 324,000 (*Selk'skoe hozâjstvo* 2015: 5). This relative contraction of the agricultural sector in the structure of the Belarusian economy should not detract attention from its recent growth. According to official statistics, the performance of Belarusian agriculture has recovered compared with the situation just before the nation became independent. This is reflected by the agricultural production index, which stood at 100 in 1990, fell to 77 in 1994, but climbed to 118 in 2011 (*Belarus' Segodnâ* 2012).

One of the regime's stated objectives was to ensure food self-sufficiency and thus strengthen the sovereignty of the young state. The goal of food security is now said to have been achieved. Imports account for only 10 percent of the food consumed. Although the trade balance for agricultural products remained negative in 2005 (-$376 million), it was positive by 2014 ($745.2 million) (*Belarus' Segodnâ* 2012). In addition, the relative share of agricultural products in overall exports is rising, standing at 9 percent in 2005 and 15.5 percent in 2013 (National Statistical Committee 2014). The agricultural sector has therefore benefited from the relative openness of the Belarusian economy (Mourão 2015). The biggest-selling products are butter (Belarus is the world's third-largest exporter), milk, cheese, and flax (the country accounts for 16 percent of areas sown with this crop worldwide) (Gusakov 2014: 6).

These successes are based on a productivist model in which the size of farms must enable economies of scale to be achieved. In 2014, there were 1,462 collective farms, with each farm cultivating 5,134 hectares, on average;[3] in 1995, there had been 2,553 collective farms cultivating just 3,037 hectares (*Selk'skoe hozâjstvo* 2015: 5). In the wake of the Soviet model, the authorities opted for a "generalized industrialization of agriculture," with large farms organized along the lines of rural factories, involving a division of labor in terms of the specialization of tasks—tractor drivers, milkers, zootechnicians, agricultural engineers, laborers, etc. (Maurel 1980: 17; Pouliquen 1982: 11–15). This choice is currently being reinforced by certain trends in Belarusian industry (manufacture of tractors and agricultural machinery, potash mining), which enable certain domestic agricultural needs to be met directly, without relying on imports. The aim is to increase productivity, and production quality is not considered a crucial issue. It should also be noted that land contaminated by the Chernobyl disaster has been "remediated" (Kasperski 2020), which has increased the available production areas. This concerned 1,009,900 hectares of land in 2011 (Republic of Belarus 2011: 50–51). As in the Soviet era (Maurel 1985), individual plots of land also contribute to agricultural production in the country. Today, private individuals can own up to 0.15 hectare of private property for their homes and up to one hectare for their vegetable gardens (*Kodeks* 2008). The private sector has remained very small. Today, a private "farmer" (*fermer* in Russian) has the right to rent up to 100 hectares of land. There were about 2,500 farmers in the country in 2016. In 2014, 76.4 percent of agricultural production came from the various public collective farms, 1.5 percent from small farmers, and 22.1 percent from private individuals' vegetable gardens. In 2005, the breakdown was as follows: 61.3 percent from collective farms, 0.7 percent from small farmers, 38 percent from vegetable gardens (National Statistical Committee 2014). This shows that state-run farms are accounting for an increasing proportion of production. The recovery of collectivized agriculture since the mid-1990s has been partly due to significant public investment. Indeed, the authorities have been spending 12 percent of the state budget on rural development.[4]

Chronic Difficulties

While the Soviet-type industrial model remains the benchmark for public policy in the Belarusian countryside, the problems inherent to the collectivized agricultural sector of the 1970s and 1980s also continue today. In the Soviet context, physical and technical infrastructures were beset by chronic organizational difficulties manifested by the struggle to retain qualified personnel (Maurel 1980: 17). These historical problems persist today (Richard 2002: 168). Recurrent topics raised in the interviews conducted in rural areas include problems encountered with tractors and combine harvesters, the question of the management's agronomic and logistical expertise, the shortage of labor and the obligation to employ inefficient "alcoholics." Wages also remain low. The average wage on collective farms was 68 percent of the average wage in 2009, and 74.8 percent in 2013 (National Statistical Committee 2014).

These difficulties could explain why the investments have not fully borne fruit, despite the government's State Program for Rural Revival and Development launched in 2005. According to the Belarusian political scientist Valeri Karbalévitch (2012: 276), "The kolkhozes—renamed 'agri-food cooperatives'—have not become more profitable." In addition, the investments made in the form of loans to collective farms, as part of the policy of modernizing agriculture and its technologies, have increased these farms' debts to private banks and the state, which exceeded $680 million in March 2014 (Volkova 2014). In this context, it is difficult for the managers of collective farms to motivate their employees. As a result, the countryside is perceived as unattractive, and rural enterprises struggle to retain qualified workers. According to a survey carried out in 2007 by the Academy of Science, only 20.3 percent of the young people questioned wanted to live and work in the countryside at the end of their studies, while 46.1 percent wanted to leave their village (Smirnova 2009: 149).

How are the chronic difficulties of agriculture being addressed by the political authorities? President Lukashenko's public speeches provide some indications. For example, in his address to the Fifth Belarusian People's Assembly on 22 June 2016, Lukashenko announced that despite $50 billion being invested since he came to power, certain problems remained. The cost of agricultural production in Belarus currently remains one and a half times higher than in Western European countries. The agricultural system is struggling to modernize its technologies. Discipline at work remains poor. Consequently, despite the extent of the public investments, Belarusian collective farms have failed to conquer new markets and have continued, as in the past, to export to the Russian market—an outlet they are likely to lose in the near future due to the rapid development of agriculture in Russia (Lukashenko 2016).

DISCIPLINE

Administrative Pressure

Reforming the system, however, is inconceivable for the authorities. The challenges of the collectivized countryside go far beyond economic issues. As in the Soviet era, this is an inherently political system. Power must also be deployed in rural areas, where the collectivist system is particularly adapted to the exercise of strong political control. In the rural world, the verticality of power—with the president personally appointing the heads of local executive committees, who are, in turn, responsible for the appointment of kolkhoz directors—ensures the loyalty of state machinery at different levels of the territory, as well as close economic, administrative, and political coverage of the country (Karbalévitch 2012: 227, 275). However, Lukashenko sees this system as suboptimal, primarily because of the people who implement it. It can function only if discipline is maintained. To improve the situation, there is no need to change the rules of the game, but to control, monitor, and threaten workers and the people in charge of them. The country's modernization is thought to depend on the president's ability to maintain sufficient "administrative pressure"—a favorite expression used repeatedly in his different interviews. These measures are based on the threat hanging over kolkhoz directors, direct coercion of the workforce, and administrative measures to support struggling regions.

Kolkhoz directors must be effective. If the results of their operations are disappointing, they will be held personally responsible. The authorities use threats to "motivate" these directors. They risk being transferred to difficult posts and are publicly denounced as inefficient. They may even be prosecuted. Moreover, while directors need to be efficient, they must also be loyal and refrain from calling into question the foundations of the political and economic system. Preference for liberal reforms can lead to the imprisonment of kolkhoz directors (Karbalévitch 2012: 246, 263) or senior officials in the sector—such as Vasilii Leonov, minister of agriculture from 1994 to 1997 (Matsuzato 2004: 248).

Administrative measures are sometimes adopted to support struggling kolkhozes. The authorities may order a factory to support a loss-making kolkhoz (Karbalévitch 2012: 276). For example, in 2007, accompanied by a Belarusian friend, I met the director of a kolkhoz covering six villages, with 843 inhabitants and 320 employees. He explained that his collective farm had been associated with Belaz, a truck-manufacturing plant. His organization had to supply agricultural products to the Belaz canteen, while, in return, the factory provided him with equipment, spare parts, machinery, and help with their maintenance. This type of patronage is consistent with practices adopted in communist Europe (Kott 2014: 65–68).

Control of the Workforce

To overcome the difficulties inherent to the system, the authorities do not settle for simply targeting the directors of agricultural structures. As in the Soviet era (Sapir 1984), they adopt coercive measures designed to bring the behavior of the workforce into line with the administration's expectations.

This control concerns the entire workforce on the labor market. Different measures have been adopted to this end. On 5 July 2002, for example, a presidential decree ended the existence of permanent contracts in favor of fixed-term and variable-term contracts lasting from a minimum of one year to a maximum of five years.[5] This rule was inspired by neoliberal principles and marks a break with Soviet legacies, enabling the management to subject employees to a productivist logic. It also helps to ensure the political loyalty of employees. For this reason, it is considered by opposition groups and analysts of the Belarusian system as "machinery of political blackmail against the country's employees" (Lallemand and Symaniec 2007: 108). This control of the workforce takes on particularly systematic, authoritarian, and dirigiste accents in rural areas. For example, at the end of their studies, students who have received government scholarships—in line with Soviet practices—are assigned a "compulsory job" lasting two years, very often in the rural world. Young university graduates who start working for a collective farm often face the same difficulties: low wages, poor-quality housing, the obligation to use agricultural equipment and machinery that are often in a deplorable state, the brutality of kolkhoz directors, and a lack of motivation among local employees (Borovoj 2013). However, the system of compulsory employment for grant-holding students is not the only way of mobilizing labor for kolkhozes that need it. As in the Soviet era, students, grant-holders, and army soldiers are regularly mobilized to provide assistance for collective enterprises at harvest time. Certain convicted offenders may also be mobilized.[6]

Disciplinary measures can be implemented by decree in an ad hoc manner, to enable the attainment of targets set by the government. In 2007, the Belarusian Ministry of Forestry launched a program to modernize this sector and increase the production of the nine wood processing companies. The state invested approximately $980 million. In theory, these companies were supposed to achieve the expected results by 2009, but in 2012 only a single site—Ivacevici, not far from Brest—was making a profit. With working conditions deteriorating, workers in this sector were tempted to seek employment elsewhere. Lukashenko then decided to employ coercive measures. A few weeks before the publication of Presidential Decree No. 9—"On additional measures for the development of the wood processing industry"—on 7 December 2012, he announced, "Resignation will be strictly prohibited until the modernization of wood processing companies has been completed. Workers will not go anywhere without their manager's approval. If he lets you go, then leave. Otherwise, get back to work" (Levšina and Pul'ša 2012). In total, nearly ten thousand workers were covered by this new law (Preiherman 2012).

PATERNALISM

Agri-towns

These coercive measures are combined with policies relating to a form of paternalism interpreted as a "system governing all relations between the employer and the employees *of the enterprise as a whole* .... It originates in the world of work but aims to incorporate and thus protect people before, during and afterwards, on a daily, weekly, yearly, and lifelong basis" (Gueslin 1992: 201, italics in the original). These policies focus primarily on the production of public goods and the improvement of lifestyles, particularly through regional planning operations designed to slow down rural-to-urban migration. This is how the agri-town development policy, initiated by Nikita Khrushchev when he was secretary general of the Communist Party of the Soviet Union (Kerblay 1985), was brought up to date by Lukashenko.[7] In line with the Soviet rationale, an agri-town is defined as an "urban-type rural center with high-quality social infrastructure and production structures, whose residents, along with the inhabitants of neighboring villages, benefit from conditions conforming to the main social standards" (*Belaâ Rus'* 2008).

During the 2000s, several five-year plans for the countryside were implemented, including the Revitalization and Development of the Rural World plan for the 2005–2010 period. As part of this program, 1,481 agri-towns were established in the following regions: Vitebsk (254), Grodno (239), Brest (222), Gomel (238), Mogilev (203), and Minsk (325). Nearly $16 billion was invested (Rusyj 2011). While the agri-towns are presented as a new type of rural center, which could imply that they were created ex nihilo, in practice, this has simply been a process of transforming pre-existing municipalities with populations ranging from 300 to 1,500 inhabitants. The state has defined forty-three social standards that are supposed to ensure a quality of life approaching the standard observed in cities. New housing built under this policy must therefore be equipped with gas and water supplies and a central heating system. These standards also concern the condition of roads and public transport services (with daily connections to the nearest urban centers); the presence of stores; access to medicine, nurseries, and schools; the establishment of a post office with a telephone communications department; and the existence of banking and notarial services. Agri-towns must also include a dry-cleaning service, sports facilities, a fire station, a hotel in some cases, a discothèque, a café, and cultural institutions such as a cultural center or a library.[8]

Consequently, rural government aims not only to modernize productive structures but more broadly to improve infrastructures in order to create desirable lifestyles, retain the rural population, and ensure forms of stability and social integration in the countryside. These policies thus prevent the "proletarianization" (Allina-Pisano 2008: 189) of rural areas observed in other post-Soviet countries, where the adopted reforms have radically transformed lifestyles inherited from the Soviet era, plunging rural populations into situations of great "social insecurity" (Castel 2003). The official discourse concludes that the rural modernization program has been a success, based on positive feedback from rural populations (Kozlovič 2013) and the interest that the agri-town policy has aroused in neighboring Russia, where it has been exported to the Russian regions of Leningrad, Kaliningrad, and the island of Sakhalin (*Sahalin i Kurily* 2016). However, this policy is struggling to stem the rural exodus. Young people still seem to prefer the city to the countryside. Higher education is the main vector of social advancement and rural-to-urban migration. Only young grant-holders working for collective farms return to their villages, bound by their prior commitment to spend five years working for them at the end of their studies. The vast majority of the young grant-holding specialists in the Belarusian State (doctors, teachers, or agricultural engineers), who are assigned to their posts by the government for two years, return to the city afterward.

Agrarian Festivals

The rural authorities also strive to raise the moral standards of workers. This policy is implemented nationwide, and comes to the fore in the organization of *Dožinki*. *Dožinki* are the nationally important agricultural festivals organized by the public authorities under Lukashenko's control and with his participation. In its current form, this festival has existed since 1996, but its roots can be traced back to both traditional peasant culture and Soviet traditions. In 1984, Stolin—a city in southern Belarus close to the Ukrainian border—organized an agricultural festival called the Polesia Fair (Polesskij kirmaš'). The festival set out to celebrate the work of Soviet farm workers but also to present the economic results of farms in the border regions of Belarus and the Ukraine. This annual festival continued until the end of the 1980s. At the start of the 1990s, nobody thought of continuing this event, as it was considered too costly and too "Soviet." In 1994, the first presidential elections held in independent Belarus were won by Alexander Lukashenko. In the spirit of this new state ideology, the national radio and TV company Belteleradiokompaniâ organized the first *Dožinki* festival of folklore on 7 and 8 September 1996, along the lines of the Polesia Fair. According to the organizers and participants, the first *Dožinki* in 1996 were a resounding success among kolkhozians and the region's inhabitants. The authorities therefore decided to organize *Dožinki* annually in September in one of the country's 118 districts. Originally local festivals concerning a specific sector, the *Dožinki* were rapidly transformed into a phenomenon of national importance.

In 1997, the festivals' organization was placed under the direct control of the head of state. The *Dožinki* have since become a showcase for the success of Belarusian agriculture with the mission of manifesting the regime's ability to transform society by modernizing its territory. Each year, a *Dožinki* is organized in a new region of Belarus.[9] The festival is hosted by a town chosen by the government as soon as the previous edition ends. Preference is given to district capitals with more than 12,500 inhabitants. In his opening speech for the 2012 *Dožinki*, President Lukashenko declared that the choice of the town is influenced by the economic performance of the district in which it is located. In fact, the authorities often opt for a town that requires extensive modernization. In this manner, the festival budget is also used to speed up the development of a number of small provincial municipalities (Sturejko 2012). At the start of this century, the growing public investment in the *Dožinki* was used to finance vast reconstruction and restoration programs for historic buildings and monuments. For example, $135 million was invested in the 2013 *Dožinki* organized in Žlobin (80,000 inhabitants), where almost 300 sites and buildings were rebuilt and 196 restored at their proprietors' expense, as requested by the public authorities (Proleskovskij 2013). Therefore, the *Dožinki* have often been identified by those living in or around the host town as the "third birth" of their town, after its foundation and reconstruction following the destruction wrought by the Great Patriotic War (Sturejko 2012). These improvement works, like the agri-town policy, follow a standardized program that includes the modernization of infrastructure (roads, pipelines, telephone lines, etc.), the reconstruction of railway stations and hotels, the construction of stadiums (often ice rinks), the creation of pedestrianized streets in the town center, and, finally, the restoration of historic buildings together with the creation or reconstruction of monuments (Vodolažskaâ 2012). These large-scale public works gradually became a burden on the state budget. For this reason, in March 2014, during the economic crisis, Lukashenko announced his decision to reform the *Dožinki*, which would now be organized at the local level.

The festival program is identical from one year to the next, with the *Dožinki* taking place over a weekend, and everything happening on an open-air stage installed in the main square of the town. The festivities begin with the opening speech by President Lukashenko, who provides a reminder of agriculture's importance to the national economy and reports on the year's harvest. Next, the president awards the prizes for the best workers and enterprises competing in the Republican Agricultural Production Competition. The tradition of holding this competition began in the USSR during Stalin's era. In the absence of the competitive mechanisms that characterize market economies, socialist economic competitions for industrial and farm workers were invented to encourage productivity (Werth 2012: 243–244). This practice of "socialist emulation" remains unchanged in contemporary Belarus, where the agricultural sector remains largely dependent on state subsidies. The ceremony ends with a grand concert given in the guests' honor. For the rest of the weekend, the festival is given over to the all-Belarus crafts fair and different cultural manifestations conforming to public tastes (various concerts, tastings of traditional dishes, beauty contests, etc.). Each of these events must be formally authorized by the authorities.

These festivals are influenced by politics on three different levels. First, like the agri-town program, they are used to modernize infrastructure and channel investments into struggling rural areas. They are a sign of the regime's capacity, in spite of its neopatrimonialist tendencies, to successfully implement policies designed to enhance public assets (Hervouet 2013b). Next, they embody a shift in the way power is staged and orchestrated by the authorities (Lapatniova 2013). The emphasis is placed on the agricultural roots of the regime, which lauds its successes in rural areas. In 2003, President Lukashenko made the following declaration: "We (Belarusians) all come from villages. Our Belarus is a country of small farmers" (Zadora 2015: 183). These festivals are therefore events in a political agenda that forms part of the Soviet tradition, on the one hand, and introduces a number of innovations, on the other. Soviet society, like the communist world in general (Krakovsky 2014), was indeed regulated by a schedule of specific festivals designed to encourage social integration and the emergence of a specific society. Like the French republican festivals analyzed by Olivier Ihl (1996: 259), these manifestations constituted "rituals of representation" that set out to reveal consent and legitimize political authority. The *Dožinki* are directly inspired by Soviet-type festivals in which the regime's achievements were carefully promoted and exemplary workers rewarded. By reviving rituals such as the *Dožinki* or the days of voluntary work called *subbotniki*, as in Lenin's time (Hervouet and Kurilo 2010; also see chapter 7), the regime portrays national history as an extension of the Soviet past. At the same time, these *Dožinki*, in contrast to *subbotniki*, did not exist per se before 1991. President Lukashenko has transformed them into a full-blown national festival encapsulating the ideology of the newly independent republic. The festival is based on asserting the value of local skills, costumes, farming techniques, and customs—in short, Belarusian folklore—which is used to promote a new national consciousness and thus helps to legitimize the newborn nation. Therefore, the *Dožinki* seem to precisely match the criteria of "invented tradition" described by the British historian Eric Hobsbawn (2000: 1). It should also be noted that this promotion of traditional rural folklore is currently a constituent part of a self-promoting, outwardly oriented diplomacy (Vanderhill 2013). For example, when the French actor Gérard Depardieu met Lukashenko, the president was in a field cutting hay in the traditional manner (*Le Figaro* 2015). Finally, the *Dožinki* are also a public, media-driven manifestation of paternalist practices encouraged by the regime. Awarding prizes to the best workers perpetuates the practice of awarding labor medals, *gramota* (diploma of honor), and other rewards seen during the Soviet period.

Moralization Devices

This dignifying of exemplary workers, raising of moral standards in professional and social life, and folklorization of the rural world can be observed at the local level.[10] It was witnessed in practices I recorded on a kolkhoz in the Minsk region in 2007. These moralization devices are based on the valorization of tradition, the civilizing control exercised by the authorities, the promotion of disciplined bodies, and reputation, exemplarity, and punishment.

In our conversations, when referring to workers on the collective farm, the director does not use the term "kolkhozians," which in the Russian language and inherited from the century of sovietization often equates to morons lacking any interest in their work. He refers to them as "countryfolk" (*krest'ânin*), to place the emphasis on the tradition to which they belong. He deplores the loss of the traditional skills and know-how possessed by their forebears, which are denigrated by the kolkhozians themselves. "People immediately reject anything related to the old ways of life," he says. Therefore, no one knows how to weave or work with flax anymore, which used to be common practices throughout Belarus. The director promotes the transmission of this age-old expertise. One senior farm manager mentions an old woman who was the only person in the village still capable of creating a traditional haycock. The management of the kolkhoz asked her to share her experience with the younger ones. It has taken steps to preserve and perpetuate Belarusian culture. This cultural promotion takes center stage at receptions for delegations, for example. Young women are obliged to wear traditional dress when greeting guests, but this embarrasses them and makes them feel ill at ease. The management lectures them and threatens them with financial penalties—non payment of bonuses—if they refuse to play the game.

According to the director with whom I spoke, the kolkhoz also tries to influence the workers' behavior by steering them away from alcohol consumption by promoting sports or other various leisure activities deemed to be healthy, such as kitchen gardening or approved forms of culture. Efforts are made to occupy the workers during their free time. As an initial step in this direction, they are allowed to use sports facilities originally intended for passing tourists. Next in the agri-town development program come plans to develop cultural activities in rural areas. Plans to open a cultural center were announced. Finally, excursions were also organized. In the 2000s, for example, workers were invited to the Logojsk ski resort, where they met Irina Rodnina, the three-times Olympic figure skating champion and ten-times World Champion. The president himself attended this event. According to a kolkhoz manager, these excursions make the workers feel more included in society. These activities also keep people busy and leave them no time to think about drinking. "Skiing gives you the same adrenaline as when you down 150 grams of vodka," says the manager. Kolkhoz workers are even obliged to take part in these activities outside working hours. For example, the kolkhoz director ordered all workers to become members of the new National Library, inaugurated in 2006, and sent a student delegation to visit it.

The kolkhoz introduced new ways of collectively valorizing certain attributes—the sense of endeavor and perfectionism apparent in beautiful formal gardens and kitchen gardens with their plentiful crops—which simultaneously deprecate idleness and laziness. On the kolkhoz, competitions were organized and prizes given for the "best kitchen garden," the "best garden," the "best home interior," the "best entrance hall," the "best fence," the "best house," and so on. Prize winners received 200,000 rubles, or around $80 at a time when the average wage in Belarus was $350. In this way, the authorities promote logics of competition or emulation, not only economic, but also social and symbolic. The kolkhoz also holds up a number of local figures with solid reputations as examples to be followed. The director himself must appear to be irreproachable, humble, and devoted to his duties. During the *Dožinki*, the director has been on the stage to receive prizes from President Lukashenko on two occasions. Upon his return to the kolkhoz, he donated one of his two prizes to the community, to finance the upkeep of the sports complex. One worker followed his example in order to steer his three children away from the temptation of drinking.

Finally, the kolkhoz can use different forms of constraint or even sanctions to force its employees to work, especially those designated as "alcoholics." These employees may be laid off for a number of days, although the shortage of labor means they must be subsequently rehired; their bonuses can be withheld; they can be excluded from the many benefits associated with membership of local interdependence networks, such as access to a tractor, and the various gifts distributed by the kolkhoz. Local stores are prohibited from selling them alcohol, and they are threatened with expulsion from their apartments provided by the kolkhoz almost free of charge. The police raid workplaces in order to monitor employees' blood alcohol levels. Children are taken away from the homes of alcoholic parents, and employees can also be forced seek treatment by being referred to doctors who may use "coding" therapy (*kodirovanie*) to cure them of their pathology. This "therapeutic coding" consists of a series of psychological methods used to instill the fear of death in alcoholics if they subsequently consume alcohol. These techniques are not recognized by mainstream medicine and are practiced in different private centers. Three main methods are used: hypnosis, introducing a "capsule"—in reality, a placebo—into the patient's body, which is supposed to kill him or her if alcohol is consumed, and treatment by different magnetic "waves" emitted by special devices (Kuzina 2015).

Overall, according to the testimonies gathered, these efforts are considered to have increased the productivity of this kolkhoz. People are said to be more motivated than before. In addition, the governor of a Russian administrative region had heard about the practices introduced in order to raise moral standards on this kolkhoz through an article published in the magazine *Sel'skaâ žizn'* [Rural Life]. He sent a delegation to visit and expressed his desire to institute similar practices in his *oblast'*, where seven thousand former collective farm workers had lost their jobs and turned to the bottle. However, the people interviewed concede that younger people are not always enthusiastic. They often take correspondence courses in the hope of one day leaving the countryside.

These analyses indicate that the implementation of market socialism in Belarus has promoted a top-down approach to rural governance. The authorities implement agricultural policies, adopt administrative measures, and undertake to modernize the countryside according to standard plans. The impetus for any change or economic momentum can only come from the highest level of the state. It is also said that Lukashenko, to ensure this manifestation of order and monitor the efforts made to cultivate and develop rural areas, flies over the territory by helicopter, thus exercising his power through airborne "spatial acts" (Cohen 2012: 638). The societal paradigm promoted is that of "socialist paternalism" as defined by the American anthropologist Katherine Verdery (1996: 63): "Subjects were presumed . . . to be grateful recipients—like small children in a family—of benefits their rulers decided upon for them." The state defines the needs of rural populations (types of housing, leisure, etc.) and provides for their satisfaction. The "normal," acceptable, and desirable life is defined by the state. Consequently, in this conception, market socialism is seen not only as a socioeconomic model, but also as the guarantee of democracy. Indeed, in Lukashenko's discourse, democracy is defined not in relation to institutional guarantees or the protection of individual freedoms, but in terms of meeting the basic needs of the entire population. "Market socialism" is thus claimed to embody the traits of the Belarusian national character based on egalitarianism and collectivism, and opposed to the Western values of materialism, individualism, and egocentrism (Leshschenko 2008: 1421–1423). Disciplinary measures, which reflect the authoritarian dimension of the regime, are therefore presented as measures required to reform the antisocial behavior of certain people who are accused of not fully appreciating the different material and symbolic rewards provided by the authorities in an effort to engage workers, and of being largely to blame for the country's agricultural difficulties. Great continuity can therefore be observed with Soviet practices that came to the fore during the Yuri Andropov era (Graziosi 2010: 316), but also through certain innovations, such as the *Dožinki*: economic difficulties are attributed to the moral failings of those who do not recognize the regime's supposed material and symbolic benefits, which must be corrected by coercive measures. This is how the different dimensions—economic collectivism, "administrative pressure," the modernization of lifestyles, and paternalistic practices on which the concrete implementation of Belarusian market socialism is based—form a system.

In return, rural populations are expected to be accountable, loyal, docile, and obedient. How do countryfolk themselves react to these forms of governance? How do they judge the collectivist system? Different surveys conducted in rural areas by Belarusian researchers point toward the people's attachment to kolkhozes, their rejection of the market economy (Zlotnikov 2006: 86–87), and their strong reservations about the expected benefits of the privatization of land. In 2009, of the people living in rural areas, 61.6 percent were said to oppose the private ownership of land (Smirnova 2009: 343–349). These ideas corroborate the conclusions reached in political analyses, which describe the rural population as conservative (Goujon 2009: 178; Karbalévitch 2012: 264; Zadora 2015: 187). Moreover, the regime appears to be widely supported by these populations. Independent surveys found that in 2001, the president was supported by 41.6 percent of the Minsk population and 72.4 percent of people in rural areas (Ioffe 2014: 221); in 2010, these figures had dropped to 32.1 percent and 50 percent, respectively (Wilson 2011: 257). This attachment to the regime and the figure of Lukashenko can be interpreted as a direct result of the effectiveness of the resources deployed by the authorities. This top-down view of the system assumes more than demonstrates that the official discourse has a performative dimension. Performing an ethnographic analysis of the dictatorship corresponds to focusing on practices at the lowest levels of society and endeavoring to understand the links between these practices and the aims of the regime. This means investigating the forces behind the legitimacy of such a regime, without automatically accepting the effectiveness of the messages and policies handed down from the upper echelons of the state.

NOTES

1. This chapter partially reproduces the contents of the following articles: Hervouet and Kurilo 2016; Hervouet, Kurilo, and Shukan 2017. I would like to thank Alexandre Kurilo and Ioulia Shukan for their permission to include this material.
2. The economic difficulties encountered from 2009 onwards led the government to reduce the list of products with regulated or subsidized prices. This practice was abandoned in January 2016 (*BT* 2016).
3. One hectare equals 10,000 square meters, or approximately 2.47 acres.
4. However, a recent reduction in public subsidies for agriculture in Belarus can be noted (Lukashenko 2015). According to Valeri Karbalévitch (2012: 276), this figure does not exceed 3 to 4 percent in developed countries.
5. Since the implementation of the system, nearly 90 percent of public workers/employees have been hired on fixed-term contracts (*Naviny.by* 2013).
6. In relation to the Soviet era, reference should be made to Andrei Amalrik's (1970) exile to Siberia in 1965, where he worked as a dogsbody on a kolkhoz.
7. In addition to the agri-town policy, the authorities have recently promoted another project designed to improve the lives of kolkhozians and modernize the countryside by developing agritourism and ecotourism. In 2018, more than two thousand locations in Belarus offered this type of service. Economic operators in this field benefit from tax exemptions and pay a special tax of just $12 per year. The Official Website of Belarus explains this issue: http://www.belarus.by/ru/travel/agri tourism-in-belarus.
8. The Belarusian press regularly publishes photographs of agri-towns showing residential buildings and those housing local services (Kozlovič 2013). For a highly detailed description of an agri-town, see Hervouet, Kurilo, and Shukan 2017: 101–105.
9. In Belarus, there are six administrative regions divided into districts.
10. A monograph on a village in northern Belarus (Hervouet 2014) shows how these paternalistic moralization policies are sometimes based on religious institutions. See chapter 10 of this volume.

CHAPTER

2

A DISCRETE ETHNOGRAPHY

How can we elicit a spontaneous indigenous conversation about an authoritarian regime characterized by its desire to exert total control over its population? How can we examine the political aspects and the dictatorship without (hardly) any reference to politics and despotism? This was the major methodological difficulty concerning my work in Belarus between 2006 and 2013. This chapter[1] is presented in the form of a reflexive look back at a field experiment conducted between 2006 and 2013, entailing trial and experimentation that gradually, over the years, generated sufficiently robust material to propose a reflection on the everyday life under the dictatorship. When conducting my research on the dachas and vegetable gardens of city dwellers between 1999 and 2003, I had no particular difficulties in meeting interlocutors or entering into discussions with them in the form of recorded interviews. In this way, I showed how ordinary city dwellers, by putting their energies into the tending of vegetable gardens, put their "desire for happiness" (*volonté de bonheur*; Castel 1968: 21) into practice by loosening the shackles of the system without actually breaking them (Hervouet 2009a). This field was accessible for two reasons. On the one hand, in people's imaginations and local representations, the question of dachas seems remote from any kind of political issues and tends to be more associated with nonproblematical agricultural and cultural practices. I was perceived as a strange French folklorist who was solely interested in an ordinary, and ultimately not very serious, activity. My work had also attracted the attention of journalists with varied links to the government who treated me as an exotic curiosity (Tkačenko 2002; Šanski 2003). On the other hand, the political regime has become more repressive over the years, and its authoritarian dimension has become more burdensome in daily life.

The methodological difficulties therefore appeared at a later date, when I entered a new field of research in 2006. I wanted to shed light on the various ways in which people in rural areas can, without fully and positively adhering to the existing regime, take ownership of its rules and consent to them. While the questions about the everyday life under the dictatorship were an extension of my previous work on dachas, there was a major difference concerning the field of study. Indeed, the collectivist mode of government in rural areas takes on a crucial political importance for the regime, as Lukashenko's remarks at a 1998 meeting in Grodno demonstrate:

> Why must we keep the collective farms, which are in reality state farms? It's because the kolkhoz and the sovkhoz are not just ways of organizing agricultural production . . . . If they cease to exist, the state will be unable to implement its policies in rural areas efficiently. The kolkhoz and the sovkhoz, with their administrative apparatus, their specialists, and their leaders, are the cornerstone of the state's power in rural areas. This concerns half of our population, which ensures the stability of our society. (Quoted in Karbalévitch 2012: 275–276)

In this context, the project to conduct an ethnographic survey of rural areas in Belarus runs into three difficulties: conducting a survey primarily among the working classes, for which the primary problems facing the ethnographer have been highlighted in the literature (e.g., Mauger 1991); carrying out this ethnographic study in an environment—rural areas—in which the state, via its economic and administrative structures, is omnipresent, and in which there is particularly strong control over the people; and studying politics in a regime inherited from the Soviet Union, which does not tolerate any challenges to its authority or critical debate. Consequently, the authoritarian nature of the regime had a decisive impact on how I was able to conduct my survey. I will start by analyzing the existing constraints on access to research fields in present-day Belarus, while pondering the continuities and differences in relation to the work carried out by Western anthropologists during the Iron Curtain era. I will then examine the special conditions concerning field surveys, necessitating certain compromises with the precepts of sociological ethnography, and requiring the practice of a "discrete" form of ethnography (*ethnographie en pointillés*). Lastly, I will clearly explain the "tricks" (Becker 1998) and maneuvers employed to successfully build up a sufficiently robust body of material to construct an analysis, in spite of these constraints.

SURVEILLANCE

Legacy

Despite the great difficulties associated with conducting field surveys during the communist era, several Western researchers have carried out research of an ethnographic nature in Eastern European countries (Hann 1994). In these closely monitored societies, they have had to overcome different types of obstacles. Without claiming to present an exhaustive list, I will now mention some of these studies, paying particular attention to those focusing on rural communities. To access the sites for their research, these anthropologists had to obtain special authorizations. On this subject, Katherine Verdery (2013) recounts the institutional context of her first visit to Romania in 1973. She obtained a grant in the framework of a partnership between IREX (International Research and Exchanges Board) and the Romanian Academy of Social Science. "Without one of these exchange grants, it was very difficult for U.S. citizens to work in Romania" (Verdery 2013: 40). In 1966–1967, Caroline Humphrey (2001) was a beneficiary of exchange agreements between the British Council and the Chair of Ethnography at the State University of Moscow. These arrival contexts influenced the definition of their research subjects. The Romanian sociologist Mihail Cerna, who had encouraged Katherine Verdery to study Romania, had explained to her before her departure that she "clearly must not submit a project that directly or indirectly concerns the functioning of the socialist system, but rather that [she should] choose a topic that interests the authorities, such as folklore" (Verdery and Faure 2011: 202). Indeed, "scientists in Central and Eastern Europe ... were in a quest to find the 'people,' in their desire to build a nation and reveal its original nature. To this end, they did not require comparisons or theories, but instead they needed to accurately describe the local traditions" (Verdery and Faure 2011: 207).

In 1967, Caroline Humphrey was supposed to be working on kinship in Buryatia, by outwardly adopting an approach that conformed to the Soviet principles of *etnografiâ*, which is similar to folklore studies (Gessat-Anstett 2001: 66), but which was far removed from the perspectives of Western social anthropology. These activities could not therefore openly appear to be focused on the socialist system in force.[2] Researchers from other disciplines could collaborate with local teams to analyze the operation of collectivized agriculture, but field visits were short and very closely supervised (Maurel 1980: 19–20). In this regard, the French geographers Joseph Casas and François Labouesse (1983: 1) wrote, in 1983, "Until then, none of the 150 missions conducted in the USSR since 1970 in the framework of the official agreement between INRA and VASKhNIL[3] (including ours) had included visits lasting more than a few hours!"

For researchers who had access to the field, the practice of ethnographic work was closely supervised. Katherine Verdery (2013: 37) lived in a village but could not study how the collective farm operated. She therefore wrote a social history of a Romanian village spanning three centuries with barely a mention of the situation in communist Romania (Verdery 1983). After consulting *Securitate* reports to which she eventually gained access in 2008, she finally understood the extent to which she had been under surveillance (Verdery 2018). This explains her difficulties in finding face-to-face contacts in the villages and why she was compelled to focus her research on subjects relying on access to available sources in libraries or on interviews conducted with city-dwelling intellectuals. Caroline Humphrey managed to reside in Buryatia by focusing her work on kinship systems and beliefs—particularly Shamanism. It was only tangentially that she managed to collect a substantial body of new material on the functioning of collective farms. Although surveillance and mistrust were apparent—some considered her to be a spy (Humphrey 2001: xix)—there appears to have been a lower level of control than in the context described by Katherine Verdery. Verdery (2013: 41) describes a final constraint. Could the dissemination of scientific texts that were considered harmful to the image of the regime pose a threat to the subjects of the survey? This uncertainty caused certain researchers to wait until after the collapse of the Berlin Wall to publish their analyses of life under socialism (Kideckel 1993; Verdery 1996).

Dead Ends

In the post-Soviet context, it was not strictly necessary for me to adhere to institutional procedures in order to obtain a visa, travel to Belarus, and move around the country. This is a key difference in relation to the communist period. In addition, I could choose whether to collaborate with Belarusian colleagues or work alone. It seems to me that the constraints of scientific cooperation are likely to resemble those encountered by anthropologists in the 1970s and 1980s. I have doubts about the expediency of turning toward ethnologists. For example, the research conducted in villages of Western Belarus by a Polish anthropologist (Engelking 2002), in collaboration with Belarusian researchers, very closely resembles the practice of descriptive and folklore-oriented Eastern European ethnography (Alymov 2011). The rare studies by Belarusian sociologists on the collectivized rural world are based on descriptions and opinion surveys (Smirnova 2009). Despite their interest, they share the common characteristic—as in the Soviet era (Bikbov 2009: 124, 130)—of not proposing a critical analysis of political dimensions and refraining from any reflection on modes of domination and power. To this risk of misunderstanding, related to the divergent histories of our disciplines in both countries, is added my wariness toward the academic world, which is likely to be subjected to a specific type of control by the regime.

At this point, I should mention my previous experiences in Belarus and recount certain events that reflect the hold of the surveillance system over citizens in Belarus. From 1999 to 2001, I was employed by the Cultural Department of the French Embassy in Belarus, where my main function was teaching economic and social science at the Franco-Belarusian Faculty of Political Science and European Studies, a department of the European Humanities University, which was independent of the authorities. When I began my research on dachas in Belarus, I immediately discussed it with my students, who were important allies in my fieldwork. Pressure from the authorities forced this university to close in 2004, and it was relocated from Minsk to Vilnius (Rennes 2006). I could therefore no longer rely on this institution to help me find partners. I started by conducting three initial field missions in rural areas of Belarus, in 2006, 2007, and 2008, outside any institutional framework. I then spent three full years in Belarus, from 2009 to 2012, where I held the post of codirector of the Franco-Belarusian Center of Political Science and European Studies (CFB), while also remaining on the French Embassy's staff. On an exceptional basis, given the tensions prevailing in the country and the pressures exerted on certain members of other embassies (*Naviny.by* 2006; Taras 2011), my family and I held diplomatic passports. During these three years, I put my surveys on hold, in compliance with the duty of confidentiality required by my superiors at the French Embassy, but different events that occurred between 2006 and 2012 prompted me to proceed with caution once I resumed my field studies in 2012 and 2013.[4] Here is one such example.

In principle, an opportunity arose to establish links and collaborations with colleagues at the Faculty of Philosophy and Social Science at the State University of Belarus. As codirector of the CFB, I organized a conference to be presented by a French anthropologist at the Faculty of Philosophy and Social Science. On the day in question, a Belarusian colleague, the speaker at the conference, and I were summoned to the dean's office, along with several lecturers from the Faculty. Another person, who was not a member of the teaching staff, was also present and was introduced to us by the dean as someone who "dealt with international relations." The discussion revolved around the subject of the conference ("Transformations in Marriage in Europe") and the riots that had occurred in France in 2005. During the discussion, the "international relations representative" asked specific questions to determine the statuses of the different people present and insisted on seeing our visitor cards while attempting to find out whether there were any reasons, other than academic, for our presence. He did not seem to belong to our host community and was treated with particular respect by the dean.

While searching on the Internet a few days later, a colleague could find no trace of this person in the university's organizational structure. He was only mentioned in an article stating that he had accompanied a Belarusian delegation to China. My colleague considered that this information pointed toward him being an informant for, or even a member of, the KGB. This suspicion of the academic world being subject to surveillance slowed my progress.

However, I initially decided to continue along this path. In this way, during my years spent there, I gradually forged ties with a renowned Belarusian sociologist who has been published abroad. When, a few weeks before the end of my contract at the French Embassy, I told her about the possibility of setting up a research project on rural areas, she immediately replied, "It's not in vogue." She was much more interested in other proposals I put to her, such as working on gender issues. Was she concerned that a project on rural areas—providers of essential support for the regime—would attract the authorities' attention? Or did she really think that there was nothing to be gained by exploring rural worlds? Perhaps she thought that performing a survey of rural worlds would not be a very strategic choice when it came to attracting sources of Western funding. My lack of proximity to this colleague prevented me from taking this discussion any further. The fact was that she categorically refused my proposal to work on the practice and customs of sociology under the authoritarian Belarusian regime.

In the end, I decided not to embark on any academic collaboration, considering it to be too complicated. I was concerned about running into indifference, mistrust, or incomprehension. I therefore addressed the issue of "everyday life under the dictatorship" without institutional support for accessing the field.

The second type of approach to gaining access to the field in rural areas consists in directly contacting the directors of kolkhozes through official channels. Two interrelated obstacles then become apparent. In principle, as there is no tradition of social anthropology, but definitely a tradition of close surveillance of economic and social activities, the directors prefer to avoid this type of contact. They consider any interest in their kolkhoz to be suspicious, as they believe that there is nothing exceptional about their work. Why talk about banalities? The response of the deputy director of a kolkhoz, contacted by telephone in April 2006, is very revealing: "I'm very busy at the moment. I don't have time to meet you. Our kolkhoz is very ordinary. It is devoid of any interest. You'd be better off visiting Snov. Have you been to Snov? It would be better if you went there rather than visiting us."

Furthermore, as a rule, you must also complete the necessary formalities and obtain an administrative authorization before being able to meet with these directors. I have avoided this approach. Indeed, I prefer to remain discreet in my dealings with the administration to prevent any misinterpretation of my work as a researcher. I practice sociology, but I do not hand out any questionnaires or produce any statistics. It could be considered that I practice an unauthorized form of journalism, for example. Any mistrust could be reinforced by the fact that I spent five years working for the French Embassy (1999–2001 and 2009–2012). Moreover, I assume that if I went through an authorized channel, the director would only give me stock statements. Incidentally, a colleague who was allowed to accompany a delegation of French farmers during an official visit to kolkhozes and agri-food production sites in Belarus told me how only the successes and efficient aspects of the system were shown, while any complications were kept out of sight. Finally, there is little likelihood that I would receive such an authorization quickly. In this regard, the following comment by *Le Monde* reporter Piotr Smolar (2012) is highly revealing:

> We wanted to closely examine one of Alexander Lukashenko's flagship projects: the *agro gorodki*—agricultural villages. The aim is for the state to create and support villages in order to revitalize rural areas. Mr. Lukashenko wants to build 1,500 of them, so that 30 percent of the population can continue to live in rural areas. To visit Juravliny, in the western region of Brest, you must seek permission from the management of the collective farm of the same name, which encompasses three villages. There are three schools, two kindergartens, three "cultural centers," two clinics and three Orthodox churches, according to its website. Happiness in a healthy environment. Problem: to witness this happiness, as the collective farm's lawyer explains by email, you have to obtain permission from the district's Department for Ideological Work . . . which will never be granted.

All in all, it seemed inadvisable for me to use the official institutional channels and pass through formal procedures to gain access to the field in rural areas of Belarus.

Suspicion

The dramatic changes in modes of travel between the East and West enabled me to circumvent the first difficulty encountered by anthropologists seeking to work behind the Iron Curtain: entering the country. As I did not need to obtain researcher status to cross the border and travel around Belarus, I ultimately decided to work alone. Nevertheless, I was still faced with another difficulty similar to that encountered by anthropologists during the communist era: coping with the surveillance system. My approach posed two types of risks. The first was a personal risk. As I carried out my research work without links to a Belarusian institution, I could be subject to different forms of harassment. In Belarus, I was often told in informal discussions that anything that is not clearly permitted is prohibited, and there is no law stipulating that questioning kolkhozians about their everyday lives is permitted. A risk, however minor, would therefore appear to exist. This could lead to the subsequent rejection of a visa application and the inability to continue my survey. This circumspection is not unjustified in light of the fact that the Russian authorities have recently made life difficult for Western researchers and have not hesitated to expel some of them (Schreck 2015).

The second risk was to my contacts. As in the Soviet era, the authorities were careful to avoid tarnishing the image of the regime. In 2005, a law was adopted on untruthful and defamatory information given to foreigners, for which criminal sanctions apply (Nečapajka 2005). I did not want my contacts to be associated with me and to be accused of criticizing the regime. I was also conscious of the fact that while I personally have little to fear, these people could think that they were taking a risk by agreeing to cooperate with me. Indeed, the presence of what my contacts called the "services" (meaning the security services) was a recurrent topic in everyday conversations, like the "eccentric" neighbor who listened to the dissident radio station *Svaboda* and thought he was being monitored by KGB agents, and the employee of a private company who told me that to be awarded a particular public contract, you had to "grease the palm" of a KGB officer.

The functioning of the regime is intrinsically linked to the power of the security services and police (Hervouet 2013b). This is reflected in a latent suspicion that permeates everyday relationships, and it prompted me to adopt a cautious approach to my work with the people I interviewed. The manifestation of control by the authorities is based on suppositions, conjecture, and speculation, giving free rein to the most paranoid interpretations. In his review of a novel by a young Belarusian intellectual—a story of love and crime set in Minsk and aptly entitled *Paranoia* (Martinovich 2010)—the American historian Timothy Snyder (2010b: 34) writes,

> To travel to or from Belarus is to become acquainted with the KGB. At the European airport from which you depart from Minsk, a functionary, likely female and seemingly harmless, patrols the gate area. At a certain point she asks each passenger for his or her passport, although on what authority is a bit unclear. At the Minsk airport, as you depart Belarus, an obvious KGB functionary checks your documents one last time before you board the plane. Then he boards the plane with you. The KGB officer is probably accompanying a Belarusian official on a journey abroad since Belarusians of any significance cannot travel without a political chaperone. But perhaps he is also watching you. As soon as you have that thought, you've entered the world of paranoia that is Martinovich's subject.

It is in the interest of such a regime to make people believe that everything is under surveillance. Indeed, different events do suggest that, potentially, everything may be monitored. Incidentally, I can recount only certain anecdotes about this subject because the people who are associated with them to a greater or lesser extent, and who were asked for permission to include their accounts in a publication, preferred that I refrain from doing so. They were worried about KGB members reading my book and reaching them in this way.

Here are a few meager illustrations of this unusual context. At the embassy, we were warned that we were probably under electronic surveillance. A colleague told me how, when driving around town earlier than usual one morning, he went around a roundabout twice and became certain that he was being followed. I also recall how, a few days before my departure from Belarus in 2001, I noticed that the front door of my apartment appeared to be locked, but that a magnetic device had been inserted into the lock, which made it possible to enter without the key . . . and nothing had been taken from the apartment. A Belarusian friend with whom I discuss my research asks me to write to him via a specific email account that he consults only during his trips abroad.

These local situations need to be interpreted in a context of omnipresent state-sponsored violence. Here are several events that occurred during my stay in Minsk, between 2009 and 2012. On 3 September 2010, Oleg Bebenine, founder of the information website Charter97.org and an ally of the dissident Andrei Sannikov, was found hanged in his dacha (Harris 2010). The presidential election took place on 19 December 2010. Thousands of people flooded into the center of Minsk to protest the results. They met with fierce repression. Hundreds of people were roughed up and arrested. Convictions followed. Several opposition candidates were imprisoned. Following the protests, the television channels broadcast recorded conversations of people at the scene of the events or nearby, suggesting that the entire city-center population was under electronic surveillance (April 2010). Several weeks later, I found out that one of my eighteen-year-old students had been arrested for challenging the legitimacy of Andrei Sannikov's detention (Plaschinsky 2012) and that she had spent the night in a Belarusian jail. At around 6:00 PM on 11 April 2011, a bomb exploded at Oktyabrskaâ—the only station at which Minsk's two underground rail lines intersect. Over three hundred people were injured, and fifteen people were killed in the explosion. It was rush hour, and above all the time when students at the Franco-Belarusian Center of Political Science and European Studies were heading toward the building in which we were working, close to this station. An anguished wait then followed before we learned that none of our students were among the casualties. In the following days, the two alleged perpetrators were arrested. They were tried, condemned to death, and executed by a bullet to the back of the head on 18 March 2012 (Bohdan 2011). The Belarusian authorities gave no explanations for these acts. Analysts interpret them as the result of a struggle between groups linked to the security services, or as a settling of scores by a foreign force in retribution for the Belarusian authorities' failure to honor an agreement (Bohdan 2011).

In the summer of 2011, several peaceful demonstrations were organized through social networks, attracting several thousand young participants. They took place just a few hundred yards from where I was living and working. There were no slogans, and nothing was planned. People simply gathered from time to time, applauding in unison. Then silence returned before, once again, the crowd started clapping. The repression was severe (Leshchenko 2011). Online, I saw students being manhandled not only by clearly recognizable law enforcement officers but also by a number of people in civilian clothing and obviously determined to use force to quell the unrest.

On 20 December 2011, three Ukrainian activists belonging to FEMEN protested in front of the KGB headquarters in Minsk to mark the first anniversary of Lukashenko's re-election. On the evening of their action, at Minsk station, as they were about to board a train to Kiev, they were kidnapped "by police officers and KGB agents"—according to a statement by Inna Shevchenko published on the FEMEN website. The law enforcement officers blindfolded the three activists and threw them into a bus that drove all night to a forest in the Gomel region, 320 km southeast of Minsk. Forced to undress in the middle of the woods in temperatures close to zero, they were reportedly covered with oil by their attackers, who then threatened to burn them alive, before abandoning them to their sad fate. They eventually returned to Ukraine on foot (Barthet 2012).

On 14 April 2012, Andrei Sannikov, a dissident and candidate for the presidential election of December 2010, was released from prison. He had been beaten and arrested on 19 December 2010, when thousands of people had challenged the authorities in the center of Minsk. Sentenced to five years of imprisonment on 14 May 2011, he explained that he had asked for a presidential pardon after being tortured (Agence France Presse 2012).

Although I am aware that it is possible and even probable that my attitude is excessively cautious, this context prompted me to adopt a specific approach to conducting my surveys in the field.

STRATAGEMS

Prudence

When making contact with people, I adopt two attitudes. The first, of lesser importance, is to assume the role of a French teacher, an erudite tourist interested in the traditions and customs of Belarus. I introduce myself in a not untruthful but abbreviated manner. The aim is to communicate with public figures or officials without formalizing the encounter and without publicizing my status as a researcher. In this way, I met with the priest of a small Belarusian parish, the founder of a temperance museum. A few weeks after our meeting, however, he was accused by the Lithuanian authorities of having participated in the execution of several Lithuanian anti-Soviet partisans after the Great Patriotic War. This made it difficult to pursue my work and, incidentally, the priest died a few months later (Hervouet 2014; also see chapter 10 in this volume).

In this way, I also met a kolkhoz director and his colleague in charge of ecotourism. Here is how this visit unfolded. In November 2007, I visited a kolkhoz that had diversified its activities by developing agritourism. I was accompanied by a friend who had read about this kolkhoz in the press and had called to make an appointment for our visit. We arrived there one morning at around 8:00 AM. The manager appointed to greet us—a woman in her fifties—had forgotten about us. She turned up late. I told her that I was interested in tourism and agriculture. She decided to take us to meet the director. We waited thirty minutes for him to receive us. His office was large and fully refurbished. He was about forty years old, with light-colored eyes and an athletic appearance; he came from the village we were visiting. He talked about his education, his thesis in economics that he had just completed, his trips abroad—three days in France, including one at Disneyland, and his stays in Germany, Sweden, Japan, and Italy. The telephone kept ringing throughout our interview. This young director came across as modern and enlightened, far from the clichéd tales about kolkhozes told in the city. But it was difficult to obtain anything other than the general information that was available in the press, even though he deigned to share certain secrets in a somewhat secretive tone:

> People here don't want freedom. They are not used to it. They expect to be told what to do; they don't want to be autonomous. Old Lenin did a good job rewiring their brains [a small laugh]. If they had freedom, only ten of them would cope with it successfully. (Unrecorded interview, 31 October 2007)

At the end of the conversation, I asked whether my friend could take a photograph of the director and me standing side-by-side. He agreed but shifted the position of his desk so that the diplomas and awards associated with the activities of the kolkhoz appeared in the background, rather than the portrait of A. Lukashenko. As we were leaving, he demanded that I send him any texts prior to their publication—an eventuality that had not even been discussed with him. He was concerned about any deformation of his carefully controlled statements, and reminded us that not everything he had said could be written down, as this could cause him problems. Although I managed to collect some interesting information, the director made it clear to me that he was not fooled, and that he was therefore closely controlling everything I was told.

Consequently, this method proved to be very risky and only moderately productive as it did not enable me to obtain spontaneous comments, which are the only way for me to investigate "everyday life under the dictatorship." How should I proceed? I had no plan, no program, no timetable, and few specific ideas about how I would approach working in the field. I refused to develop an excessively narrow form of questioning that could lead me, without proper consideration, to dismiss comments that might be legitimate, interesting, and worthy of inclusion, along with any other findings. I decided to embark on this ethnographic adventure by allowing myself to follow any byroads that seemed relevant to my work, in the hope of managing, slowly but surely, to collect interpretable material. Incidentally, with regard to his fieldwork carried out among employees of the RATP (Paris public transport operator), starting in 1992, Olivier Schwartz (1998: 6) writes,

> Convinced that the conditions for the success of an ethnographic survey are much less dependent on the interest of the "subjects" than on the quality of the "fields," and that whoever is fortunate enough to have access to a "field" will, sooner or later, find a subject, I had embarked on this adventure without a precise idea, at the outset, of what I might find there, or of what I should even look for.

To access the field, I made up my mind to meet people whom I could trust and who could trust me. I mobilized my network of close and not-so-close contacts that I had been developing in Minsk since 1999. Because bonds had been established between us, these people made an effort to act as intermediaries and sometimes to make contact with old acquaintances. The political conditions specific to this regime therefore led me to meet people known primarily via chains of mutual acquaintants. I stayed clear of official messages and institutional channels, preferring to gather—directly or indirectly—the comments and actions of kolkhozians and countryfolk.

Two new difficulties faced me. Firstly, it was hard to limit my field to a clearly defined geographical area. This was partly due to the surveillance system in force. If I wanted to remain discreet and travel freely without official researcher status, I would need to avoid lengthy stays in one place in order to maintain a low profile. One long stay in a village without authorization could appear suspicious, whereas frequent travel should appear normal for a foreigner visiting the country. Consequently, my inability to remain in one place for a lengthy period meant that the environment I was investigating was partially fragmented, and if I tried to situate my contacts in local configurations, I was not always able to correlate information by gathering other people's points of view. Therefore, the understanding of mutual acquaintance environments often remained patchy. If mutual acquaintance, reflexivity, and long timeframes are the three key ingredients required for ethnographic surveys (Beaud and Weber 2010: 278), then my approach needed to find ways of accommodating these methodological requirements without following them to the letter, but also without automatically invalidating the substance of the material collected.

Silences

The second difficulty pertained to the fact that many of the people I met were unwilling to enter into discussion. I encountered varied situations. I addressed the issue of everyday life in rural areas by collecting life stories. I introduced myself as a French teacher who had published a book on dachas in Belarus and was preparing for a new work on everyday life in the country. While my aim was to produce a political ethnography of an authoritarian regime, it was impossible to present it to my contacts in this way without running the risk of being denied access to them. Some of them trusted me immediately and were forthcoming, but in most cases, the people I met were reticent about responding, or even totally uncommunicative. This reserve in the discussions can be explained by two intertwined characteristics of the survey situation: the survey was being conducted both under an authoritarian regime and in a working-class environment.

My contacts clearly seemed afraid. As the people I met had been contacted through acquaintances, they usually trusted me. But sometimes they were afraid to talk to me. They were probably worried about the consequences of their comments if the administration found out about them. In March 2008, a Belarusian friend and I were received by a family I had previously met in a village during the previous year. He was a driver for the kolkhoz, while she was employed by a small private company. Their neighbors then joined us. The woman was a senior kolkhoz official. The man was the deputy director of the kolkhoz and head of the local executive committee in charge of agricultural issues before becoming the director of the office of the president of the district's executive committee. We drank, he talked to me about the riots in France, made fiery comments about immigrants living in France, and then we drank some more. Despite the drunken ambiance, there was a certain restraint. He mentioned that "he couldn't talk about everything, for obvious reasons" and that he therefore preferred "not to talk about anything." He nonetheless managed to slip into the conversation that he did not agree with the centralized system in agriculture, and that he would have preferred greater autonomy, as in France. At that very moment, his wife interrupted, stating that she did not want to talk about politics and stressed on several occasions during the meal that people live well on the kolkhoz, repeating herself with so much insistence that she seemed to be making a show of her loyalty toward the regime—perhaps she suspected me, my Belarusian friend whom she did not know, or maybe her neighbors. On another occasion, in November 2012, I had a conversation with an elderly woman in an isolated village. I had met her through a friend who had found this contact for me through a close relation, who had contacted someone living in the country who knew this woman. She was living very modestly and received me with kindness but also with reserve. As she spoke, she rubbed her hands together feverishly and could not hide the anxiety she was feeling as she began telling me about conflicts on the kolkhoz in a very distant manner, and was clearly apprehensive about the consequences of her comments.

I was confronted with a "self-evident fact" (*état de fait*; Lahire 2019: 25–27): nobody talks about what everyone knows and what everyone has learned to keep quiet about. People have learned to be very discreet. Family stories are sometimes repeated as a reminder of foolish, loose-tongued people who would not have been deported if only they had kept quiet, like the uncle who spent five years in a prison camp for joking about Stalin just after the Great Patriotic War (Applebaum 2003). This automatic suspicion of people from outside one's own world is not unique to Belarus and is observed in other regions of the former USSR. For example, Jessica Pisano mentions it in relation to her own surveys in rural Ukraine (Allina-Pisano 2008: xxi).

However, my contacts' reticence cannot be solely explained by their fear of the police. Another obstacle is posed by the sense of social inferiority felt by the people I met. This difficulty is not specific to the authoritarian nature of the regime (Bourdieu 2008: 36). This feeling of being ashamed of themselves originates from the condescending and scornful attitude adopted by city dwellers toward people who live in the country. In the cities, one frequently hears remarks tinged with scorn about rural communities, which reflect a form of class-based racism (Lapatniova 2001: 60). Kolkhozians are associated with negative qualities: they are seen as narrow-minded, easily pleased, and uneducated; they have a reputation for drinking too much and for supporting a political regime that prevents the country from entering the modern era.

I was also refused contact on several occasions, sometimes even by close relations of people I had known for several years and who trusted me completely. They did not dare to meet me, through embarrassment, fear, or timidity. This is what my allies told me about their contacts: "They're worried about saying something stupid"; "They don't have time to tidy up their home"; "A Frenchman deserves a better welcome than I can give him"; "They think they've got nothing worth talking to you about," etc. This is what I wrote in my field journal on 16 April 2006:

Vova's mother called the former kolkhoz director whom she knows. He refused to meet me because the apartment needed to be made presentable. You don't receive a Frenchman like that. What's more, it's Easter. Preparations must be made to welcome family members. In the same way, Vova's wife's aunt, who lives in a village in Western Belarus was reluctant to receive a Frenchman.

On 2 November 2007, I finally met Alexander, who is a teacher in an agricultural high school. Vova's mother-in-law had been organizing this visit for several days. Alexander rejected the first proposal to meet. We then decided to meet after one of his classes. He specified that he had only "twenty or thirty minutes" to spare. In the end, we talked at length—in reality, he had no pressing engagement. After more than an hour of conversation, he said, "I hope I didn't say anything stupid, but I've stated things honestly and truthfully."

My interlocutors' reticence cannot be explained solely by a form of self-censorship related to fear or internalized social shame. It also a product of specific forms of sociability, which could mean that volubility is frowned upon. In local settings, one cannot overtly say what one thinks. This would amount to claiming a sort of special status—a lofty attitude which could be perceived as the manifestation of a haughty nature. Untoward comments about other people, if passed on, could be harmful to the person who made them and result, for example, in their exclusion from mutual assistance systems operating within mutual acquaintance networks.

The final obstacle is linked in equal measure to the functioning of the authoritarian system and the codes of conduct governing working-class environments. The people I met seemed to be afraid of tarnishing their image. Bearing witness to problems with the functioning of the system to which one belongs means giving cause for criticism of the world to which one is functionally and emotionally attached and, in a certain manner, giving rise to a judgment about one's own self. Moreover, informal practices based on wily resourcefulness and "getting around" the system are considered morally acceptable and altruistic when they are personally used to benefit one's close relations, but they are frowned upon when used by other people (Ledeneva 1998). When dealing with a foreigner, who is not supposed to comprehend the ethical nuances of these underground forms of life, people will probably prefer not to mention them at all. To save face, certain contacts decide to remain silent.

Also, and most frequently, critical views of the world are revealed by fleeting gestures or words that are retracted, by occurrences of stereotyped comments and formulations that must be painstakingly compiled. Moral sentiments (A. Smith 1976) are often condensed into sparse formulas lacking clear explanation. The sociologist's work therefore consists in bringing to light, from varied and heterogeneous discursive environments (when people are talking about their neighbors, children, colleagues, holidays, potatoes, etc.), interiorized forms of subjectivity that are resistant to semantic elucidation.

Privacy

Consequently, when I managed to gain access to villages and to meet people who were not opposed to the idea of speaking to me, I needed to use a range of ploys to create situations that would encourage them to make precise and personal comments. As an outsider on two levels—as a Frenchman and an academic—I had to take steps to reduce the social distance that separated me from my interviewees. With hindsight, I consider that my behavior in the field was guided by three principles: the "deceremonialization" of the survey situation, the familiarization with the subjects of the survey, and the symmetrization of relationships by self-exposition.

First, it was desirable to minimize the academic connotations of the survey situation. Like other researchers in the post-Soviet regions (Gessat-Anstett 2007: 13; Allina-Pisano 2008: xxii), I soon abandoned the Dictaphone that I had used to record my interviews on dachas between 2000 and 2003. People are wary of leaving traces that could be transformed into incriminating evidence. When Svetlana, a pensioner, mentioned the carrots she had purloined during a *subbotnik*—a "voluntary" day of labor (Hervouet and Kurilo 2010)—organized on the neighboring kolkhoz, her son jokingly reminded her that her comments were punishable under the law on untruthful and defamatory information given to foreigners. Svetlana, initially quite hesitant, ended up saying, "In any case, it isn't recorded." The Dictaphone also reinforces the ceremonial and academic nature of the meeting. I sometimes took notes during the discussions; however, slowly but surely, due to the misunderstanding of the nature of my work and the mistrust it arouses, I acquired the habit of not transcribing conversations until I returned home. In addition, when I started, I used a very general and adaptable interview guide to orient my first biographical interviews. This formalization of the discussion was sometimes perceived as artificial and abnormal. Since then, I very often improvised according to the contexts of my encounters—over a cup of tea, during a meal, or in the vegetable garden—with a view to asking questions that related to the discussion in progress. The information gathered was scattered and fragmented. I then had to record it in a field survey log. The benefit of this is the fact that the discussion took the form of friendly and innocuous dialogs resembling the exchanges one might have with a newcomer to one's neighborhood or within an extended circle of friends. It formally excluded the creation of a survey situation. This manner of flitting freely around the social world I was studying required me to be satisfied with blending into the background in scenes of everyday life without outwardly exerting any influence on how they unfolded. Undeniably, this facilitated the gathering of everyday comments that might have been made in my absence, but it sometimes made it difficult to go deeper into certain questions. In these interviews, I needed to bring out my contacts' experience and wait for them to take the initiative to talk about what they were unhappy with. A Belarusian friend who knows these communities because he grew up in them and continues to live in them helped me with these ideas. An example is recorded in my field survey log entry for 4 March 2008:

> To prepare for the interview with Andrei Petrovich [a former director of a kolkhoz and currently a teacher in an agricultural high school], I discuss my ideas with my friend. For example, I am thinking about asking why young people would settle in rural areas if they are poorly paid. My friend's reaction is immediate. You must not talk about negative things. My contact must mention them spontaneously, otherwise he will clam up.

I therefore needed to adopt a patient approach and wait for situations to arise that were sometimes impossible to trigger. I sometimes returned from long days almost empty-handed. But that is the price I had to pay to have a hope of being told some privileged information next year.

Indeed, the second general principle I have adopted has been, whenever possible, to revisit the same people every few years. Familiarity and trust develop throughout the duration of the relationship. The primary benefit of this approach is the respect one inspires by returning to the same places on a regular basis. At first sight, it could seem surprising—or even suspicious—to some of my contacts that I would like to see them again. I also try to find excuses to contact them again and maintain links over the years. For example, I pass on presents to and from a family in a Belarusian village whose daughter lives in France. Another technique consists in bringing a gift with me on my next year's visit that makes reference to the discussions we had together the year before—like honey or wine. These tiny services, resembling a kind of gift and passing of debts from one side to the other, facilitate the maintenance of fragile links. The other tactic used to this end consists in sending people a few photos of the moments we spent together, accompanied by a short message, a few months after the event. People sometimes mention this to me on subsequent meetings. These tactics help to create a form of ordinary routine and provide evidence of our relationship.

These techniques for "deceremonializing" the survey relationship and creating familiarity have sometimes been supported by practices designed to eradicate social distance, with a view to generating contexts that are propitious to the production of noncontrolled comments. It is an established fact that "a part of the investigator's expertise relates to the art of camouflage" (Mauger 1991: 127). However, this strategy of blending into the background does not lead to the adoption of a casual attitude or a bird's-eye view that implicitly requires contacts to behave as if the investigator were not there. On the contrary, it relies on making an active contributor to the interactions, in which I have developed an understanding of certain rules during the course of my experience, which bring into play certain facets of my personality as an academic, a Frenchman, and an urbanite, who is also a man—presumably with manly qualities—as well as a husband and a father. I use certain ploys to conceal the first three characteristics, which generate intimidation and reticence, while emphasizing the last three, which I often share with my contacts. Conforming to the desired and expected norms for masculine behavior first implies adhering to the standards for alcohol consumption. On many occasions, I have been welcomed to a table laden with food. The meal and the discussion are punctuated by relatively codified toasts ("To our meeting," "To friendship," "To love and women," "To family," "For the road," etc.), which are intended to lead to a controlled form of drunkenness among men (Pesmen 1995). This collective drunkenness is a way to slip out of one's social roles and show one's true nature, without disguise. Synonymous with virility and honesty, it takes place in front of the women, who encourage it as long as it remains governed by ceremonial rules of shared hospitality and commensality. In this way, a trusting relationship sometimes develops, based on the sharing of vodka or its home-made equivalent, *samogon*. This vodka strips me of the social power with which I am associated because I become weak. I accept the risk of being unable to control myself, physically and verbally—the alcohol thickens my tongue and sometimes makes my pronunciation imprecise. My long stays in Minsk have taught me to drink sodas and eat fatty foods during these meals to absorb the vodka and keep face. In this horizontal world that vodka creates, discussions flow more easily. It becomes possible to talk about the neighbor—the director of a kolkhoz—whose lover committed suicide, or bookkeeping ruses used to misappropriate goods, the price of the new car belonging to the head of the local executive committee, and so on. I must focus my efforts on avoiding passing out before my hosts and on taming the vodka's fire. The difficulty lies not only in following the gist of the conversation and asking the questions I need to pose at the right time, but also in remembering the answers that are given to them. Perhaps the reason why people speak to me so openly is because they assume that, due to the drunkenness, I will forget everything that is said. In these situations, the presence of an accompanying Belarusian friend is a precious aid. He is the designated driver of the car and, in this capacity, does not drink a drop of alcohol. As he remains sober, he can remain attentive to all details given during the discussion. Also, during these meals, while I am trying to cope with my weakened mind and body, my ally remains clearheaded, which facilitates the subsequent transcription of the conversations.

I have also used a second method to quickly develop a trusting relationship. The *bania*—or Russian sauna—is the other masculine world in which confidences can be shared. In November 2012, I visited a small village where I met Maksim, a carpenter with whom I got along well. In the evening, he invited two friends, one of whom was a young mechanic working on the neighboring kolkhoz, to meet at the *bania*. The meeting took place, but this time without consuming vodka, as Maksim is a recovering alcoholic. For several hours, I took part in the everyday conversations, without managing to talk to the mechanic about his work. It was only later—in the *bania*—that he told me about the director of the kolkhoz with whom he did not get along, his pitiful wage, and his desire to leave. We were all naked in the *bania*, sweating, whacking ourselves with birch branches, and stripped of the vestimentary indications of our social attributes. That was when he confided in me. Once out of the sauna, the discussion turned toward subjects other than the kolkhoz and its injustices. Lastly, I sometimes put my own family to service in the field, bringing my family status to the fore in an attempt to divert attention away from my other social characteristics. The presence of my French partner, who learned Russian at school, sometimes accompanied by our young sons, contributes to the symmetrization of relationships. It brings my own private life out into the open and encourages my hosts to share details of their own.

My survey was conducted between 2006 and 2013. I met current and retired kolkhozians, male and female, who occupy, or used to occupy, a range of different posts: directors, milkers, drivers of tractors and other vehicles, mechanics, veterinarians, etc. I also interviewed self-employed craftsmen living and working in villages (a carpenter and a glassblower), teachers at agricultural high schools collaborating with collective farms, and academics whose families live in rural areas. I conducted around forty interviews in total and took part in many everyday events (Easter and birthday celebrations, family meals, working on personal plots of land, etc.), while carrying out a form of multi-integrative ethnography, defined as "this series of partial totalizations which attempts to describe the groups to which people belong, social scenes and personal histories" (Beaud and Weber 2010: 294). Over the years, chance and uncertain encounters with people—some relatively forthcoming, others almost totally uncommunicative—have been a source of heterogeneous material that has gradually acquired a certain robustness. In this article, I have explained the difficulties and obstacles that I have endeavored to overcome in my efforts to build up a sufficiently substantial body of material on which to base my analysis. To examine the rural working classes in an authoritarian context, I adopted, sometimes with certain adaptations, the techniques and tactics used in the traditional French approach to sociological ethnography—as in the work by Olivier Schwartz (1990), Florence Weber (2009a) and Nicolas Renahy (2005)—which set out to build relationships based on trust and familiarity in mutual-acquaintance contexts in order to comprehend the varied dimensions of the spheres investigated (domestic, family, professional, and neighborhood, and in relationships with the government and bureaucracy). Despite the "literary narcissism," the "self-promoting dimension," and the "exaltation of subjectivity" (Olivier de Sardan 2000) that such an explanation of my work could have implied, I nevertheless wrote this text and did so for different reasons.

Due to the division of the scientific work on "area studies" in France, numerous specialists in Eastern European countries are neither sociologists nor anthropologists, and some of them are unaware of, or do not necessarily recognize, the soundness and legitimacy of ethnographic knowledge based on a long tradition of research (Céfaï 2003). Consequently, a colleague who specializes in dissidence in the USSR saw my work on dachas as nothing more than a series of relatively naive accounts and the evocation of a limited impressionistic experience, suggesting that my arguments boiled down to a few moderately amusing anecdotes. She wrote,

> After setting off to teach in Belarus in 1999, Ronan Hervouet discovered a society which he examined with a sociologist's eye, but also from the perspective of Candide.... From time to time, the reader may be troubled or charmed by the repeated use of "I," which sometimes transforms this work into a series of reminiscences about his travels. The same characters—members of the circle of friends—are often encountered. (Vaissié 2010)

Here, I have shown that the nature of the material collected cannot be reduced to that found in a personal diary or travel journal. My reflexive methodological approach is consistent with "informed empiricism" (*empirisme instruit*; Schwartz 1993: 305). It cannot be assimilated to a subjective posture recounting an intimate adventure. Instead, armed with the knowledge of tools developed throughout the history of the discipline, it is designed to produce a sufficiently robust corpus of material to envisage the proposal of general statements of an objective nature.

I have then shown that the conditions for research under an authoritarian regime invalidate the precepts of ethnographic methodology. Indeed, it is risky to settle in a single area for too long without running the risk of attracting the attention of the authorities and therefore potentially bringing the investigator and the survey subjects to the attention of the police state. Although it is inadvisable to remain in the same place for a lengthy period, the ethnographer has the ability, by different means, to maintain links with the survey subjects and to return to the same places every few years. Although it might not be possible to perform an in-depth analysis of specific cases in singular areas in absolute compliance with textbook survey techniques, one can multiply the number of geographical points of access to the field and correlate information about these widely scattered "minor cases." Although it is difficult to talk about politics directly, it is possible to make deductions based on behaviors, comments, and situations in direct relation to the everyday activities of the survey subjects. This discrete and "impure" ethnography (Schwartz 1993: 266) is neither patchy nor botched. It cannot be reduced to a flat description of singularities, and it aspires, by patiently building up material, to become increasingly generalized. Although it makes compromises with the traditional requirements for field surveys, it still seeks to propose a robust approach in compliance with the epistemological requirements of the discipline. Such an ethnography may be undertaken if the survey is designed to be conducted over a long period, on the one hand, and if there is a refusal to conform to overly prescriptive and restricting research protocols, on the other. Despite being uncomfortable, this approach has proven to be heuristic.

This reflexive exercise urges a reappraisal of the question of social distance and trust in survey relationships. Admittedly, social distance is not an obstacle and trust is not a necessity in every type of ethnographic survey (Bonnet 2008). However, in a working-class environment, trust may be considered desirable for gaining access to comments and enabling discussion (Mauger 1991: 126–127). In working-class environments that are also under an authoritarian regime, it seems to be a necessity. Several stratagems designed to gain the subjects' trust have been proposed. These ruses, aiming to facilitate deceremonialization, familiarization, and the symmetrization of relationships through the investigator's self-exposition, neutralize—at least partially and temporarily—this social distance and enable the creation of conditions of possibility that are sufficient for the utterance of spontaneous comments in the investigator's presence. Only the establishment of trust and forms of intimacy can prevent the encounter from becoming a series of excessively banal, insignificant, and repetitive exchanges.

Lastly, the description of the concrete aspects of such work could contribute to the debate on the transformations of the modus operandi for research, a consequence of which is to direct researchers toward protocols that are "not excessively time-consuming" (Lahire 2012: 344) and to encourage "inter-team collaboration" and "loose groupings of teams or laboratories" (Lahire 2019: ix). However, I have shown how my customized small-scale approach to sociology, which is characteristic of other surveys in "difficult settings" (Boumaza and Campana 2007: 9), would have been difficult to duplicate within overly prescriptive collective research protocols. This open-ended approach to scientific work is ill-suited to certain requirements of funding bodies in terms of the programming of activities and of the quantitative objectives to be attained (e.g., number of interviews, observations, future publications). I have experimented with the adoption of a highly specific approach to research time, in which I focused on the long term without a clear idea of where the paths I was following would lead me.

NOTES

1. This chapter was previously published, in part, as an article (Hervouet 2019).
2. This does not mean that it had been impossible to carry out any research that expressly aimed to study the functioning of socialism beyond the Iron Curtain. But it does mean that it was conducted under very specific circumstances. For example, Michael Burawoy was authorized to work in a Hungarian factory in 1984, but this was only because his Hungarian colleague János Lukács had contacted an acquaintance and member of the Central Committee of the Hungarian Communist Party, who pleaded in their favor with a senior civil servant in the Ministry of the Interior (Burawoy and Lukács 1992: 7).
3. INRA = Institut national de la recherche agronomique (French National Institute for Agricultural Research). VASKhNIL = Lenin All-Union Academy of Agricultural Sciences of the Soviet Union.
4. Between 2012 and 2016, I received funding from the *Conseil Régional d'Aquitaine* (Aquitaine Regional Council) for a collective survey that I was coordinating. The research was titled "The production and expression of moral sentiments in a context of radical social change. An analysis of rural experiments in three post-communist countries (Russia, Belarus and Romania)."

CHAPTER

3

AUTHORIZED RESOURCES

A "top-down" perspective on rural areas reveals the political, administrative, and moral injunctions that govern rural worlds. An ethnographic posture provides an insight into the practices adopted in this universe characterized by powerful economic, legal, and technical constraints. First of all, fieldwork enables the description and situation of multiple and diverse resources that are relatively visible to an observer and mobilized in daily practices, but remain virtually absent from a "top-down" description of rural government. A distinction can be made between the mobilization of authorized resources (chapter 3) and the use of illegalisms (chapter 4), even if the boundary between the legal and the illegal, the official and the unofficial, is porous and shifting. The aim is to identify the nature of the potential resources, not to measure them. The different resources identified are of different quantitative importance. Once described, the question of their frequency and unequal distribution will be discussed. First, it is important to understand that the manner in which rural worlds are perceived via institutions and modes of government leads to the representation of a heteronomous universe. We will see that a detailed description of the mobilizable resources observed reveals a world in which modalities of action are not inevitably dictated by the regime.

OWN CONSUMPTION

The Personal Plot of Land

The current resources of rural households are largely similar in nature to those available during the Soviet era. Employment on the kolkhoz provides a minimum set of resources: a salary, access to housing, public services (electricity, school, post office, etc.), and the promise of a future pension. Today, working on the kolkhoz is particularly important in that it puts a roof over people's heads at a time of high urban real estate prices. Indeed, "agritown" development policies are designed to consolidate and modernize this system inherited from the Soviet era.

> For housing, it is either the family home . . . or it is the kolkhoz that provides housing. If the latter applies, you have the right to live in it, for a ten-year period. At least one of the spouses must work on the kolkhoz. After ten years, the kolkhoz no longer has the right to reclaim this dwelling, but that does not give the occupant any right of ownership. After thirty years, you get the right of private ownership of this house. These are small, humble houses but they have everything you need. Kolkhozians who obtain these houses have to pay something to the kolkhoz but not very much. It's like a kind of loan but over thirty years, which is quite easy for the kolkhozians to pay. (Alexei, principal of a technical high school, who is around thirty years old, and his father-in-law, a veterinarian, who is in his seventies. Interview recorded on 14 April 2006)

In addition to these benefits, different types of donations may be made to workers who are considered worthy. Their portraits are often displayed in the administrative center of the kolkhoz, as in Soviet times. They may receive gifts during festivities organized at the local or national level. During the *Dožinki*, for example, the best workers are offered not only *gramata*—certificates praising the qualities of good workers—but also various goods, such as televisions, or bonuses in monetary form. However, despite these different benefits and donations, employees' salaries and elderly people's pensions make it difficult for them to get by. "The poorest get $200 or $300 [per month], the others $400 or $500. Pensions are $150 to $200" (Svetlana, an engineer nearing retirement living in Minsk, who spends all her free time in a village in Northern Belarus. Unrecorded interview, 29 October 2013).

Consequently, the cultivation of personal plots of land remains a widespread practice and the food products consumed by households are largely self-produced. The kolkhozian's life is divided between working on the kolkhoz and working on the personal plot. Villagers have access to a personal plot of land, which is a tradition dating back to the period of rural collectivization. The 1935 Artel Statute grants kolkhozians the right to cultivate a small plot of land.[1] This right was confirmed by the 1936 Constitution. Article 7 states that

> in addition to its basic income from the public, collective-farm enterprise, every household in a collective farm has for its personal use a small plot of land attached to the dwelling and, as its personal property, a subsidiary establishment on the plot, a dwelling house, livestock, poultry and minor agricultural implements—in accordance with the statutes of the agricultural artel.

The attitudes of the party and government toward personal holdings varied in the decades following their authorization, alternating between "a policy of encouragement or tacit acceptance during certain periods (food shortages)" and "a policy of discouragement or repression during other periods" (Nacou 1958: 151). Contemporary practices are similar to those described in the USSR of the 1980s. The geographer Marie-Claude Maurel (1985: 160) referred to these practices revolving around small personal plots of land as "small-scale agriculture" (*petite agriculture*), which she defined in the following manner:

> The expression "small-scale agriculture" applies to the scale of the subsidiary economic means, to the small size of the cultivated plots—generally occupying a few hundred acres, to the limited number of livestock—just a few animals, and to the division of production into small quantities. The term "small-scale" also refers to the technical and socioeconomic characteristics of this form of agricultural activity. It applies to the modest means and methods employed, but also to the organization of work, which is carried out by different family members on a part-time basis. The mode of production characterizing small-scale agriculture forms part of the domestic economy.

Production

Today, this plot of land surrounding the house remains the focus of everyone's attention. As in Soviet times, its surface area ranges from 0.25 to 0.5 hectare. Nowadays, however, people wishing to farm more land can ask the local kolkhoz for permission to cultivate fallow land (Flavier 2017). In a discussion with Ludmilla (the senior manager of a firm in Minsk), her aunt, and her cousin (a construction engineer in Minsk), who grow everything in the garden of their dacha located in a village, Ludmilla's aunt said, "The situation is better now than in Soviet times, of course. Before, we couldn't have that much land. Now, if you ask the kolkhoz, you will be given some" (Unrecorded interview, 27 October 2012). It is where all the fruits and vegetables required for the household's annual consumption are grown. In addition, there is often a barn that enables people to raise a few chickens, rabbits, pigs, and sometimes a cow.

How can one gain an insight into everyday life in rural areas? In their conversations, the kolkhozians I encountered provided fragments of information about their lives, talking about the care given to their cow, the need to harvest the potatoes, or the date set for killing their pig. The self-evident nature of their lives, as they saw it, prevented the production of a discourse on their practices from a bird's-eye perspective. In this respect, my interview with Svetlana proved to be enlightening. She is the mother of a Belarusian friend—Masha—whom I have known since 2000. I had the opportunity to meet Svetlana on several occasions, in Minsk or at her dacha. We arranged to conduct a formal interview in October 2013. I asked her to tell me what she knows about daily life in rural Belarus. At that time, she was about fifty-five years old. She worked in a state-owned company and traveled to Russia once a month for five days at a time. She was a senior manager, made a good living, and drove a four-wheel-drive vehicle. She had an apartment in Minsk, and went to her dacha near Postavy in Northern Belarus every weekend. The house used to belong to her mother, who died in 2010. Svetlana had running water and toilets installed in her home. She was a Communist at the time of the USSR. Her remarks were therefore not immediately critical, unlike the comments made by most of the city-dwellers I met who wanted me to think they were "modern." She sought to demonstrate that this is a coherent way of life, categorizing it in the manner typical of the Soviet managerial class, in terms of the needs to be met and the functionality of the organization of everyday behaviors. In addition, she viewed the kolkhozians' work from a scholastic perspective. She described it as she saw it from the outside, sketching the outlines of a seasonal occupation organized into clearly defined tasks. Svetlana had prepared for this interview. She described people's lives in rural areas in a structured manner, as if she were giving a presentation. She placed the emphasis on the repetition, regularity, similarity, and homogeneity of behaviors.

> There are around four combine harvesters on medium-sized kolkhozes, and ten on the big ones. They make small profits on the village kolkhoz. You have to get up at five in the morning to look after the cows. The women feed them. Then, you have to heat up the stove and prepare breakfast. You cook *blinis* [pancakes] made of flour or potatoes, *salo* [lard], and eggs. You make a meal for the man before he goes to work, consisting of bread, *salo* and cucumbers. And then you take the children to the *sadik* [kindergarten]. If there is no *sadik*, you keep them at home and look after them yourself. In my village, the *sadik* was shut down fifteen years ago. In spring and summer, you have to put the cattle out to pasture. A waiting system [*otchered'*] has been devised for grazing in the village. Everyone takes their turn at grazing their cows. In the morning, they remain in the meadow until 1:00 PM; they then move closer to the village to drink, until 3:00 PM; they are then sent out to graze again until 8:00 PM, before returning closer to the village, at which time the calves are herded into the cowshed. You must also feed your chickens and pigs. You have to milk the cows. In the evening, you dine on milk, bread and *kaša*. . . . In the spring, the soil must be prepared, sometimes with a tractor, but often with a horse-drawn plow. This is how you make the furrows for planting potatoes, in particular. You cultivate thirty to fifty acres. There are around three horses per village, and you pay for the service. You plant cabbages and carrots, as well as tomatoes and cucumbers in greenhouses. Today, to brighten up our meals, we also grow peppers, apricots, and grapes. I personally harvested two bucketsful of grapes this year. I'll make a delicious alcoholic beverage—*nastojka*—with them. In July, you put up hay for the winter. The family mows it by hand and dries it out until the end of August. The land the hay grows on belongs to the kolkhoz, but these fields can be used free of charge. In September, the kolkhoz harvests its crops, particularly

maize. But you have to milk your cow during the lunch break. The children help out during the holidays, and the grandparents also help as much as they can. [Masha, now a producer of TV shows and videos, interrupts at this point by telling me that she, as a child, used to milk the cows in the village to help her grandmother]. From June to September, you collect fruits, berries, and mushrooms from the forest.... This allows you to make jam, which we eat with bread, butter, and tea. You make *pirogi* with the jam and in this way you don't have to spend money in the shops. The mushrooms collected are also prepared, either by drying them or pickling them in jars. A family consumes three pigs per year. You butcher one in the fall, one around the first of the year and one around Easter. You make regular sausages and smoked sausage with the pork. You raise rabbits, especially when it's hard to raise a pig. (Svetlana, unrecorded interview, 29 October 2013)

This description highlights the low level of mechanization, the seasonality of work spread out over the year, and the importance of mutual assistance and exchanges within the "household" (*maisonnée*), defined as a "membership group which brings together people who pool their resources on an everyday basis" (F. Weber 2002: 73), within the village,[2] in addition to the gendered codification of the distribution of domestic and productive tasks. Not only must the women of Belarusian villages work on the kolkhoz, like the men, under physically arduous conditions; they are responsible for numerous tasks in the vegetable garden—upkeep, tending to farm animals—and must also run the household: they cook, serve meals, do the laundry, clean their houses, and look after the children. Some rural households, living in recently built dwellings, benefit from running water, a bathroom, a washing machine, and central heating. However, many people live in traditional houses (*hata* in Belarusian, similar to *isba* in Russian), which lack these different amenities. Therefore, a large number of domestic household tasks must still be carried out manually, as in the Soviet era (Bridger 1987).

How should we refer to these tasks? What terms should be used to describe them? The expression used to designate them in Soviet times—the personal subsidiary economy (*ličnoe podsobnoe hozâjstvo*)—implies that these activities are of secondary importance to the tasks carried out for the kolkhoz. They are considered as extra work. However, some testimonies indicate that the link between work on the kolkhoz and work on the personal plot is less hierarchical, and that the latter sometimes seems to be the household's primary activity.

That's how it was in Soviet times and that's how it remains today.... People work more at home than on the kolkhoz or the sovkhoz. All families have a cow and sometimes even two cows. After that, there may be poultry or other animals. People often have a vegetable garden next to the house and land elsewhere. People who want to live better obviously work harder at home than for their employer. As for the milker's typical workday, let's say that she works on the kolkhoz for a couple of hours in the morning.

After that, she'll work for an hour at noon and two hours in the evening. And for the rest of the time, she doesn't work, she stays at home. The husband and wife have complementary tasks because the wife can work during the day, for example. The husband carries out certain tasks before his working day, if he is a tractor driver, for example. He might cut grass for a couple of hours in the morning. Then his wife will tend to it during the day, in order to produce hay. He'll return home after his working day and continue by gathering the hay into stacks, or he might do something else. (Alexander, a former kolkhoz director attached to the technical high school, now a teacher in this technical high school. Interview recorded on 21 April 2006)

Consequently, this is less a question of extra work or "work on the side" (*travail à-côté*; F. Weber 2009a) than a constituent part of daily activity, overlapping with work on the kolkhoz. These practices form a polyactivity (in terms of tasks, level of mechanization, and type of production) that takes place both on the kolkhoz and on its margins.

However, there is more to rural worlds than the kolkhozes. The people I encountered were also employed as local public servants, teachers, or workers in small production units. They sometimes had plots on which they had built modest houses, which they referred to as their "dachas." This urban use of the countryside is far from unique to Belarus. While dachas are put to varied uses, both in Belarus (Hervouet 2009a) and in the post-Soviet area (Caldwell 2011), the personal plot of land remains an economically important resource (Hervouet 2006; Southworth 2006).

In her presentation, Svetlana focuses on all the resources produced and consumed by the household. Households composed of elderly people, and widows in particular, thus organize their lives around these autarchic practices. Their low pensions, amounting to between $200 and $300 per month, allow them to make a few additional purchases and pay their gas and electricity bills. However, for many other households with greater needs—buying a second-hand car in Poland or Lithuania for $3,000, buying a satellite dish, buying clothes for their children, and sometimes financing their studies in a neighboring city or holidaying in the Crimea or Turkey—other activities can generate additional income.

Real disposable income, estimated on the basis of their wages, vary according to the level of inflation and exchange rates. These incomes may vary significantly from one year another, or even within the space of a few months. At the end of 2010, before the presidential elections, the average monthly salary reached $530, according to official statistics. In 2011, devaluations and high inflation caused the situation to deteriorate, leading to variations of between $135 and $210 over the year (Lashuk 2012). Between 2006 and 2013, discussions with the people I encountered suggested that households of working couples were earning around $400–$800 monthly. These sums are not sufficient to explain the expenditures that I have observed or been told about, and which is far from exceptional. Consequently, even if the fruits of self-production are considered money not spent (F. Weber 1996), in order to understand the structure of domestic budgets, it is necessary to identify the other remunerative activities—in money or in kind—that enable households to increase their resources.

MARKETS

Food Products

Domestic production is primarily intended for self-consumption and redistribution within the household, but, as in the Soviet era, part of the surplus can also be sold, either through a state-run trading network or on the free market (Maurel 1985: 164).

Villagers can sell some of their products to the nearest kolkhoz at a known price that is determined in advance. The enterprise then sells them on an open market. If a market exchange is considered "a transaction on clearly established terms" (Le Velly 2012: 13), the site of this transaction can be designated as an administered market.

> A *telega*[3] comes to collect the milk every morning and delivers it to the sovkhoz, which pays for it at the end of the month. . . . You can also take your mushrooms or berries to the *priomnyj punkt* and sell them. These outlets belong to the *leshoz* [collective forest enterprise]. The mushrooms are then sold in Poland and also in France [Svetlana's daughter, Masha, joins the conversation and points out that one of her Belarusian friends living in Paris had seen *lisički iz Belarusi*—Belarusian chanterelles—on market stalls in the French capital]. (Svetlana, unrecorded interview, 29 October 2013)

Here, people are therefore working for the kolkhoz twice: directly, in exchange for a low wage; and indirectly, by selling their personal production there, for the monetary equivalent of a fixed price.

Villagers can also resort to free markets, just as in the Soviet era when they had access to "kolkhoz markets" and "peasants' markets" (Kerblay 1985: 309–324). They can sell their products directly via these markets, which can be found in all cities. Here, consumers can buy food from different wholesalers, but they can also directly buy the kolkhozians' own production. Several testimonies also indicate that market transactions regularly take place in poorly defined, semi-legal frameworks. In 2006, for example, Mikhail, who teaches in an agricultural high school, was telling me about his passion for mushrooms. He mentions in passing that during perestroika, people were already selling them to the Poles. He adds that even today, Poles still sell them at very high prices to Germans who use them in the pharmaceutical industry. Markets are therefore accessible to anyone with minimal resources—especially a car—and enable them to sell whatever they have produced. Some people develop this polyactivity while continuing to work on the kolkhoz, while others—a minority—start their own businesses and become farmers (*fermery*).

> Maksim tells me about a farmer near Rakov. He has 27 hectares and has planted potatoes and cabbages.... Maksim thinks that 95 percent of countryfolk are happy to settle for a routine existence. Five percent are interested in producing profitable products: turf, strawberries, sausage, and high-quality cheese. The others are afraid of anything new. If you don't drink, you can buy a tractor, a car or a machine to saw wood. Some people have ten jobs at the same time: they grow flowers, they sell on the market.... (Maksim, a self-employed carpenter in a small village 50 kilometers from Minsk, who lives in a hamlet. Unrecorded interview, 2 November 2012)

However, the number of farmers remains very low (see chapter 1). There are onerous administrative constraints. In addition, various reports indicate that the authorities seem to be relatively suspicious of economic independence in rural areas. Maksim tells me that in Ivenec, some farmers cultivate two hectares of strawberries and also have apple orchards. He thinks they make a good living, but when he mentions the self-employed farmer living near his home, he reports the following episode:

> The head of the *ispolkom* [Executive Committee] came to see one farmer near Rakov and reproached him for the furrows in his potato fields not being straight. The farmer replied that he was doing things as he saw fit. The head of the committee retorted that he was not the owner, that he was only renting the land from the state, and this farmer was eventually fined. To increase his production, he had nevertheless hired workers and incurred expenses. In the end, his income is low. The state buys products at very low prices: 800 rubles per kilo of cabbage, for example. (Maksim, unrecorded interview, 2 November 2012)

These activities must therefore remain modest. Individuals are expected to be aware that they depend on the authorities' goodwill.

Urban Uses of Rural Areas

Rural areas of Belarus are not self-contained universes. The villages visited are not cut off from the world, as anthropologists may discover in the vast spaces of Russia (Paxson 2005). What is more, they are extensively appropriated by city dwellers seeking places for both production and recreation.

The tendency toward the acquisition of dachas—the second homes of city dwellers—is long-established, but increased sharply during the 1980s and especially in the 1990s. Dachas are sometimes grouped together in collectives, isolated from the rest of the village, but sometimes, they are also former *isbas*, inherited from parents or purchased from the descendants of deceased villagers. The *dačniki* often build their own houses, or at least partly, and must maintain the adjoining garden, which is used either as a vegetable garden or, for the standardized uses of nature espoused by city-dwellers, as a lawn for relaxation and outdoor family meals of grilled meats and kebabs (Hervouet 2009a). The *dačniki* may ask villagers to perform various tasks for them: watching the house in winter to prevent *bomži* (homeless, vagrants) from moving in, carrying out relatively urgent repairs, cutting wood for the stove when it is cold, assisting them with certain crops, such as potato picking, etc. They can also purchase a little milk, *tvorog*, honey, or meat from the villagers.

The *dačniki* are not only an additional source of income. Sometimes, they are also depicted as people who infringe the local economic regulations. Vova—my friend who was accompanying me in the field on that day—reported the comments of our interlocutor, Alexander, who had previously managed a small collective farm:

> There were lots of *dačniki* and he really hates them . . . [Vova laughs]. They would steal everything they could find [Vova laughs briefly]. They would steal potatoes and apples. . . . They would pay the employees of this collective farm who did odd jobs for them with vodka, which the people would then drink instead of working. They could cause quite a lot of harm to the farm. [Vova laughs briefly]. (Alexander, a former kolkhoz director attached to the technical high school, now a teacher in this technical high school. Interview recorded on 21 April 2006)

City-dwellers spend time at their dachas but also benefit from the different infrastructures developed as part of the agritourism policy. Since the mid-2000s, the authorities have supported the development of urban uses of nature, leading to the emergence of potential new resources in rural areas. This had led to Belarusian and foreign tourists visiting rural areas, although this remains a limited phenomenon. The country attracted 137 thousand foreign tourists in 2013, ranking it in second-to-last position in Europe, ahead of Moldova (Charnysh 2015). Russians are widely represented, accounting for more than 80 percent of the tourists who stay in Belarus. It is not easy to estimate their participation in leisure activities in the country since they may visit for business or family reasons and also engage in tourist activities. In addition, the border between the two countries is not controlled, and Russians can visit Belarus without a visa, which makes it difficult to keep track of their stays. Another source indicates that around 600 thousand Russians may have engaged in tourism-related activities in Belarus in 2011 (Preiherman 2012). The country's authorities thus praise the social virtues as well as the economic benefits of these activities, which are opening up the countryside.

According to the official statistics for 2011, a total of 1,576 agritourism dwellings were identified and 15 percent of their visitors were foreigners (Preiherman 2012). Four different ways of organizing the reception of tourists have been observed in the field, which are differentiated according to the status of the people offering the service: kolkhozians, small private entrepreneurs, private investors, and certain collective farms.

Kolkhozian households can accommodate visiting tourists in their own homes. Green tourism organizations and associations collect the offerings and publish them online on dedicated websites. In 2011, my partner, our two children, and I thus chose to stay in a modest residence near Lida, in Western Belarus. In a small village, a couple of somewhat cash-poor kolkhozians had divided their home into two parts and were renting out one half of it to visiting tourists for around $50 a night. The comfort provided was rudimentary, but the additional income was substantial for a family of kolkhozians. It is difficult to assess the frequency of such initiatives. It should be noted that this couple in their fifties with whom we stayed did not grow up in the village and appeared to be atypical. Originally from a mining area in Northern Russia, they had to leave their region after the husband had an occupational accident, which coincided with the collapse of the Soviet Union. They settled in various parts of the crumbling empire before taking refuge with distant relatives in this village in the early 2000s.

Some self-employed people, sometimes from cities, have seen agritourism as an economic opportunity, such as Marat, with whom we have stayed on three occasions in his home on the banks of River Berezina. We found his details on an ecotourism website. Marat is an urbanite and lives in the neighboring town of Borisov. Residents of Minsk, as well as Muscovites, come to stay in the house that he built entirely by himself in the early 2000s. We spent time with him, fishing in the marshes, cooking, walking in the forest to find traces of beavers, smoking, and drinking coffee. An understanding and familiarity developed between us. He then told me about his life course and his reasons for spending much of his time in the countryside. He clearly expressed an entrepreneurial logic.

> Marat, who's in his early fifties, tells me that he ran Komsomols in the Murmansk region until the early 1990s. He was in charge of several hundred people. He then started a small business that lasted two or three years. He used to buy *Luč* watches in Minsk for a dollar apiece and then sell them for $10 in India, where he would then buy t-shirts, which he would sell upon his return to Belarus, at the large Dynamo market in the center of the capital, where he managed two stalls. From his initial outlay of one dollar, he would end up earning $100, but he was only allowed to travel to India once every six months. Then the Poles and residents of the Baltic States entered this business and it became less and less profitable. Marat thought he had set aside enough money for the rest of his life, but then the cost of living went up. He had to pay bribes

to customs officers. He then got into agritourism, building a large wooden house and its *bania* on the banks of the Berezina River, rented out for $100 a night for four people—plus $60 for each additional person. Marat acts as a fishing guide for tourists, offers a *bania* service, and serves food on demand—a supplement is charged for most of these extras. He tells me that he makes $3,000 dollars per month. He is saving up to pay for his son's college education. (Field survey log, review of the 3–5 August 2010 period)

Certain private investors carry out larger-scale projects, building full-fledged resorts, which compete with the networks of sanatoriums and rest homes inherited from the Soviet era. In November 2012, friends from Minsk took me to visit the immense *kotedži* near Ivenec, built by an acquaintance of theirs who had done "very well in business." The manager greeted us. He was a native of the area. The buildings were new, made of solid timber logs, with large indoor fireplaces and skylights on their sloping roofs. Around the *kotedži*, there was a pond and a small wooden bridge. Further on, a modern *bania* had been built. The huge chalet sleeps around thirty people. Each guest has to pay $100 a day. Belarusian or foreign tourists come here to relax with their families, to party with members of their work council, or to hunt.

The organization of tours for foreign hunters—from Italy, Russia, Poland, the Czech Republic, and Belgium—is constantly developing. Forests cover 40 percent of the land in Belarus. Companies offer three-day hunting trips priced at $1,200, including a license to bring your own firearm, accommodation, meals, a hunting permit, transport from the airport to the hunting grounds, an interpreter, and a guide. For an additional charge, hunting trophies can be prepared and shipped to the hunters' countries of origin. The prices of the prey vary, starting at $12,000 for a European bison, between $120 and $700 for a wild boar, $800 to $5,200 for a moose, and between $800 and $4,000 for a red stag, with the prices governed largely by the size of the animal and its horns. It also costs hunters $12 to shoot a partridge, a waterfowl, or a woodcock, and up to $600 for a capercaillie (Smok 2015). This range of services is provided by both collective forest enterprises (*leshozy*) and private entrepreneurs.

Over the past fifteen years, the country's authorities have been developing legislation, focusing particularly on taxation, in order to promote ecotourism activities and give inhabitants of rural Belarus other potential sources of income. Certain private operators have seized this opportunity. Directors of kolkhozes are also seeking to invest in agritourism in order to boost the economic activity of struggling farms. The following observations highlight the importance of certain managers' initiatives to diversify kolkhozians' sources of income. In October 2007, Vova and I visited a kolkhoz that is developing agritourism activities. This context allowed me to present myself as a French tourist eager to discover this type of infrastructure in Belarus. We met the young director, who was not yet forty years old, and whose speech, postures, and style of dress present a modern image. He lived in Minsk. Four years earlier, he came up with the idea of developing green tourism in order to boost the moribund economy of the kolkhoz he was running. What were the origins of the project? One day, a friend called him to see if he could meet members of an American delegation who were interested in all aspects of Belarus, Chernobyl, and agriculture. This group visited the kolkhoz. These visitors thought that Belarusian villagers still wore clogs and continued to mow by hand. The director was proud to show them the mechanization of agricultural production inherited from the Soviets in the twentieth century, but the Americans were more interested in watching an old man drawing water from a well for his sheep. When he started drinking from the same bucket, the Americans were astonished. The director explained to them that it was very pure spring water. He also drank some. The members of the delegation asked if they could do the same and take photographs of this exceptional moment. The director replied jokingly: "Give the old man five dollars and drink away!" He was taken at his word. This gave him the idea of developing agritourism. As a graduate in agronomy and international economics, he had been able to anticipate the transformations of the Belarusian economy and the development of the service sector.

Consequently, he decided to focus on this ecotourism development project. While he did not hide his regrets because his ambitions had not been realized two years later, due to a lack of support from the national authorities and local government elites, numerous infrastructures have nonetheless been created. After our meeting with the manager, an employee took us on a tour of the complex, which included a floodlit soccer field for use at night, a riding club, a *bania* with room for twelve people at a rate of $70 for three hours, a fitness room, another room with a table-tennis table and a pool table, a hunting lodge, and a life-size reproduction of an underground hideout for partisans combating the Nazi invaders during the Great Patriotic War. Representatives of the armed forces hold formal talks here. Recently, 180 people had held a celebration here. Our guide added that local youths appreciate these facilities, which they can use when they are not booked by guests. A hamlet with four houses intended for green tourism uses had also been developed. One house was inhabited by a kolkhoz employee (who looked after the cattle), another was occupied by a 78-year-old woman who had been a widow for thirty years, and who had "lived there forever," the third was inhabited by a woman in her thirties and her father, a cabinetmaker, both of whom managed the site, and, finally, the last one was used to accommodate visiting tourists. This hamlet was also commercially productive with thirty-six beehives and several fruit trees on the site. A vast traditional barn, looking out onto the gardens, was being built and would also be a pleasant location for drinks. The base of the building resembled a beehive, and the building had already been named the "House of Honey." A little farther away stood the workshop of a woodcarver who showed us his creations, which reflected a highly inventive spirit and manifested technical expertise, far from the "crude products" purportedly sold to tourists in the capital. The hamlet covered 9.5 hectares. A kitchen garden, containing vegetables and aromatic plants, had been created there, and a few rabbits were also raised in this area. Just outside the hamlet, cows were grazing in a field. The authorities considered this to be an exemplary site. As we were waiting to meet the director after our arrival at the kolkhoz in the morning, we leafed through the guest book set out in front of his office. It contained words of thanks from the ambassadors of Cuba and Vietnam, and their wives. We were later told of the enthusiasm displayed by the Venezuelan ambassador, who was always eager to help chop wood or taste traditional dishes.

Finally, it is worth noting that certain historic sites located in the countryside are on the itinerary of tours organized for tourists and supplement these small local economies. For example, in October 2012, one of my former students and I visited the Dzerzhinsky Museum, built in the heart of a forest west of Minsk. In 1957, a first museum had been created in the village of Ivenec, near the place where the founder of the Cheka was born and raised. At the beginning of the 1990s, this institution was struggling to survive on very meager financial resources. The election of Alexander Lukashenko heralded a return to favor of the Soviet legacy. A project to build a new museum from the ruins of the house in which the chief of the political police had been born was therefore launched. It opened in 2004. Our guide told us that it receives three thousand visitors each year. These include many schoolchildren, but also members of official delegations of the security services, both Belarusian, which have kept the acronym KGB, and Russian, the FSB.

The description of these activities related to urban uses of the countryside is enlightening. The direct beneficiaries of these infrastructures are primarily city-dwellers (small-scale entrepreneurs or bigger investors) and the state-owned companies that are developing this new economic sector. However, inhabitants of neighboring villages can also derive economic benefits from these activities. They can rent out part of their home, although this is a rare practice. The *dačniki* and tourists can also pay them, formally or informally, to perform various services. Countryfolk can sell some of their products, such as jams, fresh *tvorog*, or honey, directly to them, and they can also provide certain services (for example, looking after their homes or chopping firewood). In this way, different markets for goods and services develop in rural areas, albeit on different scales and in a fragmentary manner. Such transactions promote the circulation of money in these areas.

Exchange Rates

Lastly, I have identified how certain inhabitants of rural areas manage to tap into flows that extend beyond their locality's borders. They do this by exploiting financial processes for their own ends. The exchange rate of the Belarusian ruble has varied greatly since its introduction in 1991. Between 2001 and 2015, it suffered a fifteen-fold depreciation in its value against the United States dollar. From 2009 to 2015, the country endured three sharp and unexpected devaluations. In January 2009, the ruble was devalued by 20 percent. In 2011, despite repeated promises that the authorities would not devalue the currency, there were three devaluations in the space of a few months, while prices doubled in that same year. On 27 December 2014, the Belarusian ruble was also devalued, just a few weeks after the 30 percent devaluation of the Russian ruble against the dollar. During 2015, the exchange rate of the Belarusian ruble was more than halved against the United States dollar (Alachnovič 2015). The following narrative shows how, in certain specific configurations, this uncertainty can sometimes be exploited and used to one's advantage.

Marat was a city-dweller who chose to rent out his comfortable country house located on the banks of the River Berezina as his main economic activity. I met him for the second time in the summer of 2011. We had first met a year earlier, and I noticed that he had changed his car. This scene occurred a few weeks after the devaluation of the national currency. Faced with the severe financial crisis affecting the country's accounts, the Central Bank had decided to devalue the Belarusian ruble by 36 percent at the end of May 2011. The objective was to align the different rates in force in an attempt to halt the decline in the country's foreign exchange reserves. In response to the widening trade deficit, the authorities had already eased their exchange rate policy several times since January 2011, effectively triggering uncontrolled devaluation and creating several different exchange rates within the country. But let us return to Marat. During that summer day, we first engaged in small talk before he explained how he bought his car. Prior to the devaluation, he had borrowed the equivalent of $4,500 in rubles from the bank. He had changed the rubles into dollars at a time when it was still possible, because in the midst of a crisis, it is almost impossible to buy foreign currency. Marat bought his car for $3,000. This therefore left him with about $1,500. The ruble was then devalued by three times its value, so he changed his dollars back into rubles, and this amount was nominally equivalent to the amount he had borrowed. He then repaid his bank loan, which had been defined in rubles. In short, at the end of these transactions, he got his car for free and had spent nothing. Marat is neither an oligarch nor a high-ranking official. As he was organizing hunting and fishing trips for people who sometimes occupy senior government positions, he had heard rumors about the possibility of an imminent devaluation, despite official announcements to the contrary made repeatedly over a period of several weeks. Marat exploited this information and took a "gamble" that paid off. If he had been certain of the veracity of these unofficial mentions of devaluation, he could even have bought a new Porsche rather than a secondhand Peugeot. He did not remain passive in relation to the crisis, and he grasped economic phenomena that are not easy to understand. This fact, picked up during an informal discussion with a person to whom I had already spoken a year earlier and who knew that I would not reveal his secret, shows that certain social positions in the countryside—involving formal and, especially, informal relations with senior government officials or even well-informed local banking staff—enable people to slot into national or international financial processes.

A few years earlier, in 2006, Mikhail, who is in his sixties and teaches mechanical engineering in an agricultural high school, had told me the following story. Due to high inflation in the early 1990s, he and his wife lost all their savings. Some people, who were "well connected" at that time, obtained bank loans and were thus able to build large houses for what were ultimately modest amounts. Depending on their connections, personal networks, and ability to glean information or forge links with key players in the rural world, particularly in banking institutions, certain inhabitants may thus possess significant resources.

INTERNATIONAL MOVEMENTS

Other resources came to light during my conversations. Far from being totally cut off from broader dynamics, rural areas should actually be thought of as offering resources connected to international flows, which might not be revealed by a cursory examination. These remarks prompt us to consider that these universes are linked to transnational processes, in line with Boris Pétric's (2015) approach to rural areas in the Kyrgyz Republic.

Cross-Border Activities

One day in November 2013, I met an old friend, Yuri. Like me, he was close to forty years old. It was a Sunday. We were waiting to catch a bus. I had watched his son growing up over the past fifteen years. He told me about his recent divorce and about his new wife. We traveled to the site of the house he was building on the outskirts of Minsk. After a few hours of work, we headed off to eat at his parents-in-law's apartment, located in a dilapidated building on the outskirts of the capital. Yuri gave up his academic career more than ten years ago to pursue a career as an opposition activist. His parents were retired kolkhozians. Yuri grew up in the countryside, often visited his parents, uncles, and cousins, and had an insider's understanding of the rural world. I told him about my book project and solicited his reactions to my theses and hypotheses. He mentioned certain practices barely glimpsed on my travels around the countryside, and which were poorly identified in my field notes.

> There are various opportunities. In the east, people travel to Russian cities for seasonal work. Moscow is one big construction site. In the west, we can trade with Poland. Forty thousand Belarusians have a "Pole card" [long-term Polish visa]. If you are of Polish origin, you can get a five-year visa, and can easily go to work in Poland. (Yuri, unrecorded interview, 2 November 2013)

In border areas, city-dwellers and certain villagers travel abroad for seasonal work. Belarusians can work in Russia without a visa or any kind of authorization, for example (Plaschinsky 2012). In 2008, the Polish government adopted a law allowing them to issue a "Pole card," giving free long-term visas to inhabitants of areas formerly under Polish control between 1921 and 1939 but which are now part of Belarus, Ukraine, or Lithuania. To obtain this visa, applicants must prove that their forebears lived in Poland between 1921 and 1939, or that they perform important services for that country. In addition, they must also master the language and be familiar with the country's culture. The card is reserved for citizens of the former USSR. In 2013, the Polish authorities declared that they had awarded cards to 42 thousand Belarusian citizens during that year. They do not publicly announce the total number of holders as this issue is a source of diplomatic tensions with the Belarusian Ministry of Foreign Affairs. Some estimates put the number of Belarusian recipients of Pole cards at 70 thousand (Smok 2016). Yuri told me that this opportunity allows certain residents to cross the border regularly to work in Poland before returning to Belarus. It can be assumed that this practice is more widespread in border regions, where I have not done any specific field work.

Cross-border travel also allows Belarusians to buy high-quality consumer goods at lower prices in Lithuania or Poland. Customs duties on products imported into Belarus are high. Therefore, if you want to buy a foreign-branded TV or washing machine, or even shampoo or jeans, it is worth traveling to Vilnius, Bialystok, or Warsaw. In 2013, Belarusians spent approximately $3 billion, or 4 percent of GDP, on consumption abroad (Alachnovič 2015). Lithuania is a favorite destination. Approximately 400 thousand Belarusians stayed there in 2012. Vilnius is located about 200 kilometers from Minsk. It is cheaper to shop in this capital, despite the cost of visas and transport, than to buy products imported into Belarus and subject to high customs duties. In some of Vilnius's shopping centers, 20 to 30 percent of sales are to Belarusians. They buy clothes, food, household equipment, children's goods, and cosmetics (Astapenia 2013). Lithuania has become less attractive since 2015 because prices have tended to rise due to the adoption of the euro. Poland is another popular destination. Two million Belarusians visited the country in 2012. The reason for visiting given by 73 percent of these people was "shopping" (*šoping* in Russian; Borowska 2013). The Polish government has introduced a special type of Schengen visa for Belarusians, which allows them to visit for *šoping* purposes. This first short-term visa issued for consumption is free of charge, but it is subject to the obligation to spend between $70 and $100 on miscellaneous purchases. Thereafter, it is easy to obtain another visa for subsequent shopping trips to Poland (Alachnovič 2015). Some analysts mention that it is not only border residents who benefit, but also "people from all over Belarus," who go there on tours organized by travel agencies and self-employed individuals (Smok 2014). Russia is also an attractive destination for Belarusian consumers. In January 2014, the Russian ruble was devalued by 45 percent. The Belarusian ruble was also devalued, but at a later date. Consequently, for a few weeks, it was possible for Belarusians to buy cars in Russia as the price differences amounted to thousands of dollars for the same cars, and tens of thousands for luxury goods (Smok 2014).

These practices are an additional new resource for rural households, as they enable them to save money. I remember the young vice principal of an agricultural high school rejoicing at the flat-screen television he had been able to afford when he went to a Polish supermarket near the border, acquired at a much lower price than could be found in stores in Minsk. I also recall the shopping trip planned by a self-employed carpenter from a small village near Minsk, who was intending to spend a few hundred patiently saved dollars to buy goods that had long remained beyond his means. If residents of rural areas are unable to travel to Poland or Lithuania in person, it remains possible, in many cases, for their relatives—city-dwellers or countryfolk—to buy goods for them. Some people also seem to take advantage of these price differences to resell products acquired abroad to people who struggle to travel there in person. To encourage purchases on Belarusian soil and curb the flight of currency abroad, the Belarusian government introduced new restrictions on imports of goods by individuals on 10 March 2015. Since then, people who have bought microwave ovens, refrigerators, washing machines, and computers abroad must prove that these items were purchased for personal use (Alachnovič 2015). The authorities are also combating smuggling across the borders. While large-scale scale smuggling is carried out by organized networks seeking to take advantage of the differences between cigarette and diesel prices in Poland and Lithuania, on the one hand, and Belarus, on the other, small-scale smuggling is also carried out by relatively poor individuals making a profit from cross-border trade (Kachurka 2014). These activities seem to be particularly widespread in the Grodno region, where there are fewer job opportunities than in other regions of Belarus (Smok 2015).

Humanitarian Aid

Villagers may benefit from programs proposed by humanitarian aid networks. After 1991, various international nonprofit projects with ambivalent effects (Rausing 1998) were carried out in the former USSR to support impoverished households and promote the "transition." Belarus continues to benefit from such programs. I was able to observe a local example of some of their effects. In October 2012, I visited a village near Slutsk with Andrei, a Belarusian friend and photographer. Once there, I met Ludmilla through a retired French teacher, who was also my children's babysitter. Ludmilla was around fifty years old. She lived in Minsk but often traveled to this village where her aunt resided for most of the year. On that day, Ludmilla's sister had also come from the capital to visit their relative. The house was a traditional *isba* that Ludmilla's extended family, who lived in the city, used as a dacha. Relatives had been coming to it regularly for many years. Her aunt had integrated into this village and knew her neighbors well. Over tea, we started discussing the history of the place. They eventually told me about Sasha, who was a forest ranger (*lesnik*) for a nearby collective forest enterprise (*leshoz*) and who lived with his family in a house previously occupied by a relative of Ludmilla, now deceased. We left the *isba* and went to visit Sasha with whom my hosts seemed to have a good relationship. His imposing wife, Evgenia, who was about thirty-five years old, opened the door smiling. She proudly showed us around her house, in which we found running water and toilets—remarkable luxuries for an old *isba*, which are normally equipped with latrines consisting of a hole at the bottom of the garden surrounded by a fragile wooden structure. I was then shown a washing machine, a computer connected to the Internet with a flat screen, and a television made by the Belarusian brand Horizont, complete with a DVD player. In the garage, Sasha showed me his Volkswagen Passat—a model that Andrei said is very "fashionable" in rural areas—and a Minsk motorcycle. In short, all the attributes of modern comfort were apparent under one roof. Moreover, Ludmilla struggled to hide a hint of jealousy in her comments. The couple had two daughters who were around ten years old. They also looked after three children, placed with them by the social services, whose parents had either died or were in prison. Evgenia earned an income for this activity. Ludmilla told me that this is a fairly common practice in rural areas. Her remarks were tinged with suspicion about the couple's possible motives for becoming a foster family, with the implication that they might have been driven by greed rather than altruism. We stayed there for a short while, chatting about one thing and another, while the children enjoyed the caramels I had brought. Evgenia told me that her daughters did not speak French but that they could speak English and had recently been to Ireland. When we returned to their house, the three women told me that the couple's two daughters took the places of the other three foster children in the family's care when they visited the United Kingdom on European Catholic programs intended for orphans. It was made clear to me that under the circumstances, this subject could not be discussed any further. However, it became apparent that this use of a humanitarian program—which in this case was not intended for them—constituted a household resource. It enabled the two girls to participate in a foreign visit that helped them linguistically, and which their parents did not have to pay for. In addition, these children's trips to Western Europe have given their families an opportunity to buy products—especially hi-tech goods—that are cheaper abroad than in Belarus, where high customs tariffs are in force. Finally, Western host families often show their generosity toward these children with uncertain futures by offering them gifts that may sometimes benefit entire families.

Over the past fifteen years, for example, I have witnessed groups of "Chernobyl children" at Paris or Frankfurt airports returning to Belarus laden with suitcases and other oversize parcels. About 70 percent of the radioactive fallout from the Chernobyl explosion landed in Belarus. Cesium deposits alone were over three hundred times higher than the levels recorded after Hiroshima (Ackerman 2006). A quarter of Belarus is contaminated. This mainly concerns the Mogilev and Gomel regions in the south and east of the country. Approximately two million people, including 500 thousand children, now live there and are exposed to the health-related impacts of the disaster (Petryna 2002). Between 1990 and 2015, programs intended for children growing up in contaminated regions enabled the organization of one million stays lasting several weeks in more than thirty destinations, with Italy alone hosting nearly half of these children. This aid began to decline in 2004. Nevertheless, in 2015, a dozen countries hosted 16,500 visiting children (Gubarevich 2016). During my five years spent teaching in Belarus, I met several students from contaminated areas—excellent speakers of French or Italian—who had a "second family" in the West with whom they stayed on a regular basis. In regions that were economically devastated by the Chernobyl accident and its consequences, these international humanitarian networks have unquestionably been an important resource for certain households.

Transnational Marriages

On several occasions during my travels, it became apparent that the daughter, granddaughter, niece, or cousin of the person talking to me was married to a Frenchman, an Italian, a German, or an American. Studies of the "mail-order bride industry" have shown that, since the 1990s, the new conditions for East-West mobility and technological innovations have facilitated the growth of matrimonial matchmaking, which has become quite a significant phenomenon in quantitative terms. In the early 2000s, at least 80 of the 200 to 250 international matrimonial agencies operating in the United States specialized in women from the former USSR. In Russia, there are 400 matchmaking agencies for Russians and Americans (Visson 2001: 206; Luehrmann 2004). This places Russia second, behind the Philippines, in the number of "fiancée visas" granted by the United States immigration services (Visson 2001: 205; Yvert-Jalu 2007: 275). Although Russian immigration, which has been increasing since the collapse of the USSR, remains relatively limited in France (Tinguy 2004: 294–317), currently standing at nearly sixty thousand individuals, it has distinct characteristics (Hervouet and Schiff 2017: 96). Compared to immigrants from other parts of the world, Russian immigrants stand out for being both predominantly female and highly educated. Indeed, in 2012, 64 percent of immigrants born in Russia and living in France were women. More than half of Russians entering France have a higher education degree. This is a form of immigration whose primary motivation is probably not access to the labor market, since, unlike European trends, less than 20 percent of Russian migrants are employed in the first year of their residence in France (Brutel 2014). They—mostly women—initially come for other reasons: studies, internships, to work as au pairs or to join a spouse (Hervouet and Schiff 2017). It is worth noting that, on average, 95 percent of Franco-Russian marriages involve a French husband and a Russian wife (Giabiconi 2005).

While it is difficult to document the Belarusian case precisely, these matrimonial dynamics were indeed mentioned several times in my fields of investigation. For example, friends from Minsk introduced me to an acquaintance of an acquaintance who lives in a small village near Rakov. The person I met was a woman about seventy years old. She lived in a very modest *isba*. She was uneasy and did not understand what I expected from her. She talked mainly about collectivization, war, her neighbors from the city, and environmental activists, and carefully avoided talking about the kolkhozes, which "pay you nothing." She then mentioned her family. She had two sons and a daughter. One of the sons went to university and worked for the railways. The other worked as a laborer in Minsk. They helped their mother by coming to work in the vegetable garden every weekend. Her daughter graduated from a technical school and spent two years in Minsk, followed by two years at the Technical Institute in Gomel. She then married a German. This child from a very poor family had acquired the ultimate status of being married to a foreigner. The babushka added nothing more, and the interview took place in such a tense atmosphere that I felt compelled to end it prematurely in order to spare my interlocutor any further anxiety. Nevertheless, through these few snatches of information disclosed in passing, she revealed that her daughter had succeeded in life.

Several years earlier, in 2007, a French friend who knew that I was looking for contacts in the Belarusian countryside told me that he had met a doctoral student at a party in Paris whose brother had just married a young Belarusian woman. My friend helped me find the necessary information. I then called this person who was married to a Frenchman. She told me how to contact her family, who lived on a kolkhoz in Western Belarus. Accompanied by my friend Vova, I finally met her parents in November 2007. Ekaterina, her mother, used to work in the village grocery store; her stepfather was a driver for a kolkhoz director, and her brother was a tractor driver. Their village was poor. The meal that I was served reflected the household's limited resources. Only one bottle of vodka was opened and very quickly emptied, followed by some cheaper *samogon*. Ekaterina was full of life. She told me she went to France for her daughter's wedding. Her husband did not start talking until we had drunk several glasses of alcohol. He was a reserved man and seemed intimidated by the situation. He did not attend the wedding, either due to a lack of financial resources or because he was worried that his presence—as a simple Belarusian kolkhozian—would embarrass his stepdaughter. But he was delighted that I drank more than his French son-in-law, who paid them a visit a few weeks earlier. Indeed, as I learned during the discussion, it was thanks to the latter that the house was now equipped with a hot-water tank and a water-heater, which made it possible to take a shower in the bathroom. Ekaterina's husband was also very proud of his second-hand Renault Laguna, bought with the help of his stepdaughter's new family. These small details reveal the importance of the resources that such a marriage can provide for the household, enabling family members to be invited abroad, obtain a visa, purchase a few goods in the West, receive occasional gifts, and above all, to be spared from worrying about their child's future. Parents take comfort from this upward mobility, which gives meaning to their efforts to properly educate their offspring in this harsh and trying world.

NOTES

1. An artel is a cooperative society in which ownership is collective.
2. I will return to this point in chapter 5, on interdependencies.
3. A *telega* is a four-wheeled horse-drawn cart used in Russia.

CHAPTER

4

ILLEGALISMS

The resources observed in rural Belarus originate not only in the authorized ways described in the previous chapter, but also from illegal practices, transgressions, and a variety of fraudulent schemes. These practices are partly consistent with those described by analysts of the Soviet world. Since the publications by Aron Katsenelinboigen (1977) and Gregory Grossman (1977), the literature on the "second economy" in the USSR and Eastern Europe has grown considerably (Sampson 1987; Favarel-Garrigues 2007: 31–48). As an "integral part of everyday life in all the socialist societies" (Sampson 1987: 121), it takes on a systemic dimension in the operation of shortage economies. The practices encompassed by this term are very diverse. Steven Sampson (1987: 124) states that they cover what is "unplanned, unregulated, unreported, privatized, and/or illegal." These practices differ across economic sectors and throughout regions and countries. The aim here is to highlight how this "second economy" offers opportunities to ease economic constraints. These are illicit practices, but they are not systematically sanctioned. They can also be classified as "illegalisms." This term, coined by Michel Foucault (1995), makes it possible to "move beyond a normative vision of offences and illegalisms, because the distinction between offences and illegalisms enables one to question the relativity of the criminal penalty, i.e. the chances of escaping it" (Favarel-Garrigues 2007: 46–47).

THE ILLICIT USE OF COLLECTIVE RESOURCES

Petty Theft

"There are different ways to get by." This frequently heard phrase reflects the difficulty of getting people to talk about these illicit practices. People who agree to discuss them seek to maintain a positive self-image. In our discussions, I assiduously refrain from passing any judgment. I try to reinforce my interlocutors' positive perceptions of themselves and their life worlds. At the local level, everyone knows about these practices, but nobody mentions them. They are routine and self-evident. Everyone is involved in them, but nobody boasts about it. In local settings, reputations are based on the recognition of people's honesty. Everyone believes that one can be both honest and use illegal methods to achieve one's goals. Indeed, no one has a choice. However, what is known and understood from within may be perceived, from an external perspective, as the manifestation of moral defects. Consequently, people use the "language of denial" (Bourdieu 1998: 98). My interlocutors avoided explaining the different practices they use to get by in life. Whenever I asked for details or examples, the answers I received were evasive. My interlocutors used circumlocutions or vague formulations, suggesting that these fragments of information were sufficient for me to understand the social logics at work. They resorted to "practical euphemisms" (Bourdieu 1998: 98). It should also be noted that academic studies of the collectivized countryside in the USSR do not specifically elaborate upon these various forms of illegalisms, which nevertheless constitute elementary forms of the rural economy (Maurel 1980; Casas and Labouesse 1983).

However, immersion in the field and contact with people who trusted me enabled me, little by little, to collect some significant material, but under specific conditions. Indeed, these practices were mainly revealed by discourses relating to others rather than about oneself. For example, Ludmilla, her cousin, and her aunt explained the success of their neighbor Sasha, a forest ranger, in terms of his illicit activities:

> In fact, instead of carrying out the tasks he is supposed to perform (clearing out dead wood, maintaining roads, looking after the wildlife, etc.), he spends part of his time felling trees, damaging the forest in the process, and then selling these logs to private customers. (Ludmilla, a senior manager in a company in Minsk; her aunt; and her cousin, construction engineer in Minsk. They grow everything in the garden of their dacha located in a village. Unrecorded interview, 27 October 2012)

While such denunciatory comments are informative, they are hard to verify and are sometimes nothing more than rumors. Meeting Maksim was therefore a boon to my research. He was one of the few characters I met who actually wanted to speak freely about these practices. Maksim was the same age as me—thirty-six years old—when we first met in October 2012. He came from the city of Babruysk and had held a variety of different jobs. He was a physical education teacher, served in the army, and worked on construction sites before deciding to move out to the countryside. He was now a self-employed carpenter in a village near the hamlet where he lived, and made artistic items—sculptures, shelters, etc.—from materials he found in the surrounding forest. Maksim was close to the world of the kolkhozes as he dealt with them every day. He knew the leading local players, with whom he forged working relationships; but he was also outside this world, which perceived him as a person apart, who did not drink, and who built cabins in the trees. He was an eccentric and a dreamer, but at the same time a formidable worker. I met him through friends from Minsk. It was a Sunday and our mutual friends were present. Maksim told me about his life course, talked generally about the kolkhozes, and took me to interview his retired neighbor. I did not rush our discussions. I seized on the information he was willing to share with me during that day. In the evening, as I was leaving, he invited me to return a few days later, alone. I accepted. On the day in question, he met me at the bus station in the neighboring village and drove me to his friend's house, who was a glassblower and criticized Lukashenko, whereas Maksim, adopting a proactive stance, defended him. Then he asked me, "What do you want to know about the kolkhozes?" I told him that I would like to identify the informal practices that are the only way to understand how these worlds operate, and later that day wrote about our conversation:

> [Maksim said,] The tractor driver earns $8 to $10 a day and has to work weekends. He earns a small wage plus some bonuses at the end of the season. In stores, he buys on credit, which he repays when he has money coming in. How does he manage to get by? He says the machine is broken, pretends to repair it and sets aside some diesel fuel. He sells twenty liters of diesel for 100,000 rubles—twelve dollars—and for that he only works 5 minutes. The boss does the same thing. He receives two tons of diesel, keeps one for himself and sells it to the locals. I mention to him that the management still has an obligation to achieve results. Maksim and his friend respond by telling me that the results are only what is written down, what everyone is happy to write. On the kolkhoz, everyone steals. Since everyone steals, anyone can also control anyone else. People steal fuel, but they also steal seeds. (Unrecorded interview with Maksim and his friend from Minsk, 1 November 2012)

After this discussion, we left the glassblower and went to Maksim's house. He was preparing a *bania* for his friends who were due to visit that evening. One was in the car parts trade. The other one—Vladimir—was a mechanic for a collective farm, and Maksim said that he would be able to tell me everything I needed to know about kolkhozes. His friends arrived. All three engaged in a voluble discussion. Then our host invited us to take our places in the *bania*. Naked, we sat in the stifling heat, sweating, and started chatting about one thing and another. The *bania* is a place for discussion (Pesmen 2000: 95–112). Time passed. We slapped ourselves with birch branches. Then Vladimir suddenly turned to me and started telling me about the kolkhoz, without any prompting on my part. My notes:

> He is a 22-year-old mechanic and works on the kolkhoz. He tells me that the director of the SPK (an *agrokombinat* consisting of four kolkhozes and an agri-food factory) officially earns several thousand dollars a month. That is the official salary. He has also bought a $14,000 Jeep, which proves that his income is not limited to his official salary. I ask him how one becomes a director, what training is needed. He immediately answers: "*po blatu*" [through relations]. In the *bania*, as we are doing at this moment, people discuss and assign different posts. He talks about the agricultural machinery on the kolkhoz where he works. As a mechanic, he is up to date with all the news. The kolkhoz has purchased Belarusian machines. They are guaranteed for two years. At the end of this period, they no longer work but the loans must still be repaid. If the boss steals, everyone steals. "Why bother working if you can make a living by stealing? You're better off stealing, especially fuel; if you don't, you're stupid." (Unrecorded interview with Maksim and Vladimir, 1 November 2012)

In March 2008, during a conversation with Alexander, a teacher in a technical high school and former director of a small kolkhoz, he told me that pensioners can participate in work on the kolkhoz for a low wage. What is more, people turn a blind eye to them pilfering a few agricultural products that they can then sell to market traders and in this way earn a little money.

These heterogeneous practices, regularly reported in various discussions with people from different backgrounds, are widespread. They seem to be considered self-evident in the discourses. They reflect attitudes to the workplace that were generalized in the Soviet Union and Eastern European countries, where—not only in the countryside (Humphrey 2001: 254), but also in the factory (Haraszti 1977)—collective resources were used and misappropriated for personal purposes (Verdery 1996: 51).

Time

The anthropologist Katherine Verdery (1996: 39–57) refers to the "etatization of time" as one dimension of life forms in communist regimes. She shows how, in communist Romania in the 1980s, intentional devices, on the one hand, and the effects of the functioning of a shortage economy, on the other, caused the system to make extraordinary demands on personal time. She lists queuing, irregular work patterns due to the erratic distribution of essential production resources, interruptions to domestic routines due to water and power cuts, personal plans constrained by pro-natalist policies, time wasted on crowded or delayed public transport, unpredictable government bans on road traffic, mandatory mobilizations during political rituals for national celebrations or visits by government officials, and the haphazard periodicity of secular political rituals whose dates changed each year. Time was characterized by arrhythmia and uncertainty. People suffered from their inability to control their environment and their powerlessness to act. However, Romanian anthropologist Vintilă Mihăilescu has pointed out that although the state dispossessed Romanian citizens of their ability to exercise control over daily routines, these people would then, in return, steal time from the Romanian State, by taking time off work, for example; by analogy with the principle of gifts and counter-gifts described by Mauss (2002), he mentions the principle of "theft and counter-theft," which would appear to have been at the heart of social dynamics in the Romania of the 1980s.[1]

The forms of time deprivation in post-Soviet Belarus are greatly reduced in relation to the Romanian context of the 1980s, but this phenomenon still exists—in cities (Hervouet 2009a: 27–45) as well as in the countryside. The time constraints for salaried work, particularly on collective farms, are particularly burdensome. Nonworking time is also subject to various obligations: invitations to participate in tasks that are, in principle, voluntary during *subbotniki* (see chapter 7 of this volume); time spent repairing one's car under the constraints imposed by an inefficient parts distribution system, particularly in the countryside; time spent on daily administrative procedures, and so on. However, kolkhozians and villagers must also free themselves from these constraints in order to engage in self-production and polyactivity, such as selling their self-grown production at markets or engaging in another activity alongside their salaried employment. As kolkhozians earn very low salaries and may feel somewhat cheated by their hierarchy, they do not hesitate, in return, to carry out their personal activities during time that is supposedly reserved for their official work. This is mentioned in several interviews.

> Currently, the working day is from 6:00 AM to 10:00 PM, at this time of the year. The employees eat in the fields, without going home. The kolkhoz picks up the bill. In livestock rearing, the women work from 6:00 AM till noon. After that, there's a break between noon and 2:00 PM. Work resumes from 2:00 PM to 4:00 PM, followed by a break until 8:00 PM. The cows need milking three times a day. People's hours of work during the day, are therefore dictated by the animals' needs. . . .
>
> *They work from 6:00 AM to 10:00 PM for the kolkhoz. But don't the kolkhozians also have a plot of land?*

During the working day, they can also do their own work, at the same time. They are not under scrutiny every minute of the day. The kolkhoz's management turns a blind eye if a tractor driver wants to do something for himself during the working day because the managers understand the people's situation. In families, there are other people who are not of working age. Grandparents and children can work on personal plots during busy periods when there is also work to be done on the kolkhoz. There are different ways to get by. (Alexei, principal of a technical high school, who is around thirty years old, and his father-in-law, a veterinarian, who is in his seventies. Interview recorded on 14 April 2006)

From the elliptical comments made by Vladimir the mechanic, I learned the following:

> He completed an advanced technical training program. As he benefited from free higher education, he owes the state two years' work and was sent to the local kolkhoz. He earns 2,250,000 rubles, or €200 [$230] per month. Maksim had introduced him to me as the "chief engineer" [*glavnij inžener*], responsible for 10,000 hectares. The small kolkhozes manage about 4,000–5,000 hectares of land. This young mechanic also works for the carpenter as an unskilled laborer, earning $35 a day, while the carpenter earns $60–$70. Consequently, the young kolkhozian pretends to earn his living working on the kolkhoz. He goes there in the morning, issues a few recommendations, and then goes to work for Maksim. (Unrecorded interview with Maksim and Vladimir, 1 November 2012)

In this way, misappropriations of time are a resource that is difficult to detect, hard to measure, and rarely mentioned. However, this practice reflects rural people's ability to seize opportunities to act upon their environment. Working time can, to a certain extent, be transformed into time for one's own activities.

Bookkeeping

When, in April 2006, I asked Mikhail, a retired technical high school teacher, the question "How do kolkhoz directors line their pockets?," he answered,

> The state promotes collaboration between kolkhozes. In fact, exchanges are made officially, and then materials or a proportion of the crops disappear. The books can also be cooked. Only one in three cows may be counted. All the kolkhoz's equipment and crops are at the director's disposal. (Mikhail, retired mechanical engineering teacher in an agricultural high school, about sixty years old. Unrecorded interview, 15 April 2006)

In November 2007, I met Alexei, another technical high school teacher, and his father-in-law, a retired veterinarian for a kolkhoz. They explained to me that more collective resources are misappropriated today than during

Soviet times. They described an example of fraud. Cows that have already given birth to calves are entered in the accounts as cows that do not give milk. The volumes obtained from milking them are added to the total production of the kolkhoz, which is then presented as evidence that the kolkhoz's milk production has increased.

During the following year, another discussion with Alexei revealed a different practice:

> I ask him whether the increase in milk prices has had a positive impact on the farm run by the technical school where he works. He smiles. He tells me about the state's systematic demands, passed on by the Executive Committee, for ever-increasing production and productivity. He then explains how the management of this farm massages the figures. It informs the authorities that the farm has increased its production, and that these additional volumes have been purchased by local government staff for their own consumption, with their own money. In fact, the farm's management has, informally, "reimbursed" these local government staff via a fund intended for the payment of bonuses. The milk disappears because, supposedly, it has been consumed by the local government employees. The money goes around and the extra milk, recorded in the accounts, never actually existed. (Unrecorded interview, 2 March 2008)

Yuri, an opposition activist, is an old friend. His parents are retired kolkhozians. He is familiar with this world, but has moved away from it over time. Although he fully understands the processes governing its operation, he struggled to give me concrete and situated examples. However, he did mention a remarkable recent practice:

> Accountants are central figures on the kolkhoz. The director must trust them because there are always abuses. For example, the kolkhoz director and his family decide to go to Turkey, but they buy a sightseeing tour from a company based in Moscow or Vilnius. That way, money transfers can be concealed. In Belarus, agencies complain that they have little business, but there are rumors about them giving information to the tax authorities. As a result, people turn to foreign operators who are paid with money embezzled by cooking the books. (Unrecorded interview with Yuri, around age forty, 2 November 2013)

These discourses directly echo testimonies collected during the Soviet era, reflecting a remarkable continuity of practices. In a letter addressed to *Pravda* on 6 June 1979, for example, the following episode was reported:

> The investigation conducted in response to an anonymous letter showed that two tractors which had not been entered on the balance sheets were indeed operating in the mechanized detachment of the district's Selhoztehnika branch. One of them had been deleted from the lists, but had not been scrapped; the other had been assembled on site from parts and other equipment. As a result, the average yield of the detachment's tractors increased by 320 hectares in conventional units. (Revuz 1980: 38–39)

In her monograph on two collective farms in Buryatia, Caroline Humphrey (2011) presents an in-depth analysis of these accounting practices, which she describes as "manipulable resources" and which consist in "producing more goods than are entered in the accounts." These goods are then available for sale on various semilegal, or totally illegal, markets. They may be appropriated by certain company executives, or used to remunerate and motivate kolkhoz workers in an attempt to achieve the targets set in the plan (Humphrey 2011: 221).

This may lead to kolkhozians not working, stealing the kolkhoz's products (potatoes, carrots, wood, etc.), either directly or by massaging the accounts (underestimating the weight of the meat produced and pocketing the difference for personal consumption, etc.), pilfering the kolkhoz's resources (diesel, spare parts, construction materials, etc.), or borrowing machines without paying for their use (tractors to plough kolkhozians' own plots or harvest their own potato crop, etc.). Descriptions of these little-mentioned practices show that, as in the Soviet era, restrictive work organization systems are accompanied by different ways of misappropriating collective resources in order to improve one's own situation.

ALCOHOL

Codes

Patterns of vodka consumption in the Soviet and post-Soviet world were analyzed by anthropologist Myriam Hivon (1994), whose research was carried out in a small village in northern European Russia between July 1992 and October 1993. Vodka consumption marks major life-cycle events such as birthdays, weddings, and funerals. Significant volumes may be drunk. Hivon notes that for a wedding attended by about a hundred guests, 142 half-liter bottles had been purchased, and some guests were still worried about running out of alcohol (Hivon 1998a: 522). She also reports her observations made at a villager's funeral:

> An enormous amount of vodka is also required for funerals. Indeed, it is traditional for the deceased's family to serve a glass of vodka to everyone who comes to present their condolences at the family's home or in the cemetery. The importance of this tradition is reflected by the fact that the state grants 12,000 rubles in compensation to the families concerned. We had an opportunity to attend a villager's funeral, and we found that most of that money had been spent on drink. Indeed, the tombstone had been made by the deceased person's sons, the grave dug by relatives and friends, and the prayers recited by other villagers. No priest was present. Therefore, this event had required minimal expenditure, except for the vodka: a truck laden with bottles

followed the procession to the cemetery where a glass of vodka was offered to a hundred or so people with close or distant ties to the deceased, who were then invited to prolong the event at the deceased's home. In addition, the grieving family is expected to commemorate the third, fifth and fortieth days of the death by inviting all friends and relatives who were at the funeral to join them, thus ensuring that the deceased will rest in peace. Vodka is served on each of these occasions. (Hivon 1998a: 522)

The anthropologist also points out that religious holidays, such as Easter or Christmas, and holidays inherited from the Soviet tradition, such as Revolution Day (November 7), Red Army Day (February 23), Women's Day (March 8), Workers' Day (May 1) and Victory Day (May 9), are opportunities to share vodka. Lastly, she mentions other occasions that are conducive to alcohol consumption. For example, at the end of a working day, villagers happily serve a glass to anyone who has helped them to sow seed, harvest crops, or make hay.

These codified uses of vodka imply that all rural people must always have a few bottles at hand. This explains its continued use in social exchanges. This drink is a nonperishable commodity that can be stored and consumed periodically for different festivities. Someone who provides a service will be satisfied if he is paid in rubles or in "liquid" form. In the context of hyperinflation in Russia during the 1990s, people often even preferred to be paid directly in vodka (Hivon 1998a: 518–519). These small payments in kind previously existed in the Soviet Union when it could be hard to find well-stocked grocery stores. Alcohol was often used as a reward for the varied services that kolkhozians performed for each other, such as cutting and sawing wood or haymaking for a neighbor. For example, old women who live alone in their *isbas* have often told me that they ask "locals" or "alcoholics" to cut firewood for them for the winter in exchange for a few bottles of vodka. This makes vodka an important resource to possess, as it may be used directly as currency in local trading channels.

Alcoholics

In all my interviews and discussions conducted since the beginning of my research, a standard character—referred to as the "alcoholic"—tends to crop up in conversations. The volumes of alcohol consumed in the country are remarkable. In 2000, it was observed that Belarusians drink more than Russians, and that, on average, 11 liters of vodka are consumed per person each year (*Belarus Today* 2000). In 2012, an official survey indicated that one in five Belarusian men regularly indulge in excessive alcohol consumption (Ânuševskaâ 2012). This high consumption appears to be promoted by health policies that fail to take the issue very seriously (Zajac and Jakaulieu 2012) and by low prices—in 2011, a half-liter bottle of vodka cost $3.00 when the average salary was $200.00 (Kryvoi 2011). Excessive alcohol consumption is not a recent phenomenon in these regions, and the Soviet authorities began to seek ways to control it in the 1980s (White 1996). The collapse of the USSR was accompanied by catastrophic biographical disruptions that were sometimes accompanied by a descent into alcoholism (Pesmen 2000: 170). Studies of alcohol consumption analyze the ritual, controlled, domestic, and masculine dimensions of drinking (Pesmen 1995). In such cases, there is no mechanical association between alcohol and alcoholism. The literature also highlights the devastating consequences of regular and excessive alcohol consumption on family life and its links to domestic violence. For example, this constant threat was a recurrent theme in the diary kept for twenty years by Evguenia Kisseliova (2000), a Russian working-class woman who was born in 1916 and died in 1991, and in Svetlana A. Alexievich's (2017b) polyphonic work on "Soviet civilization":

> Tamara Sukhovei, waitress, 29 years old.
>
> Life's a bitch! I can tell you ... it's no picnic. I've never seen anything good or beautiful in this life. I can't think a single thing ... It's been like this since I was little: There's nothing but vodka in the fridge. In our village, everyone over the age of twelve drinks. Good vodka is expensive, so people drink moonshine and cologne, glass cleaner and acetone. They make vodka out of the shoe polish and glue. Many young men die—from that vodka, of course—it's toxic. I remember how one of our neighbors used to get drunk and fire birdshot at the apple trees. Call his whole household to arms .... Our grandfather also drank into old age. At seventy, he could put away two bottles in a single night. And he was proud of it, too. He'd returned from the war covered in medals—a hero! For a long time, he'd just parade around in his army jacket, drinking, carousing, having a gay old time. While my grandmother worked. Because Grandpa was a hero .... He would beat my grandmother half to death. I'd crawl around on my knees in front of him begging him to not lay his hands on her. He chased us around the house with an axe .... We'd sleep at the neighbors'. In their barn. He hacked the dog to pieces. My grandpa made me hate all men. I was planning on staying single. (Alexievich 2017b: 403–404)

These testimonies highlight the destructive dimension of alcoholism without addressing the ways in which people labeled as alcoholics are qualified or their status in the social worlds to which they belong. Yet, the "alcoholic" is a recurrent figure in the discourses and relates to characteristics that remain implicit but seem widely shared. Here is how they are gradually outlined in the discourses, starting with a typical first allusion to this issue.

> There are 6 to 8 alcoholics in the village. Their parents are usually dead. You become an alcoholic when no one takes care of you, when no one pays attention to you. The villagers use alcohol to pay people to do odd jobs for them. The price of vodka is rising. A liter costs at least 40 to 45,000 rubles—about $5. (Svetlana, an engineer nearing

retirement, who spends all her free time in a village in Northern Belarus. Unrecorded interview, 29 October 2013)

As soon as they earn a few rubles, these people buy vodka or the heavy and very sweet 18 percent wine. Alcoholics may be local people or come from elsewhere. Sometimes known to the local community, they may also be spectral figures of unknown origin.

> Ludmilla is telling me about general movements and mobility. Some of the newcomers are retired people who have given their apartments in the city to their children and decided to move out to the country. Others—some of them alcoholics—have sold their apartments in the city and can move to the village. Many of them struggle to rent an apartment in Minsk, it is too expensive. (Ludmilla, manager in a company based in Minsk who visits the family dacha situated in a village on a very regular basis. Unrecorded interview, 27 October 2012)

I have not found any documented work on this social universe with its porous boundaries, which is almost inaccessible. I therefore propose certain interpretations based on sparse, scanty, and fragmentary materials, in order to characterize this inescapable figure.

On my first visit to a kolkhoz on the outskirts of Minsk in April 2006, accompanied by my friend Vova, we were greeted by the veterinarian. His name was Vasily. He criticized the management and seemed to be highly involved in managing the kolkhoz, mobilizing workers, and issuing instructions to various people as we talked about village life. Aged around forty, his face was red and swollen, a sign of excessive and regular vodka consumption. Furthermore, on that morning, he was exuding the aromas of recently ingested alcohol. It was mid-morning. He mentioned his trajectory. He came from the Gomel region and his parents were sovkhozians. When he was five years old, he lost his father, who was unintentionally killed by a villager and drowned. His mother raised her three children on seventy rubles a month. He was the only one who ended up with a career. He briefly mentioned one of his brothers, who looked after livestock and became homeless a few years ago. Vasily started working on a kolkhoz in the Gomel region, but there were major conflicts with certain colleagues, and he decided to leave. One summer, while he was recovering in a sanatorium close to the village where he was currently working, he heard that the neighboring kolkhoz was looking for a veterinarian. He turned up there and was hired. He found an old *isba* of just 28 square meters, without running water or sanitary facilities. Seven people still lived there with him: his mother, his brother, his mother-in-law, his wife, and their three children. Thanks to his income, he was able to save the life of his third child, who was born prematurely after seven months of pregnancy. He then told us about the kolkhoz and the problems that have to be overcome every day for the collective farm to function properly. He mentioned how hard it is to get the employees to work. "There are alcoholics and layabouts." For example, the kolkhoz had allocated an apartment to two families, but their members did not work and did not look after the dwelling. The veterinarian suggested that the director organize a Review Board, in accordance with the law—he specified that President A. Lukashenko had approved the confiscation of apartments occupied by people who damaged them—in order to examine the state of the housing, with the aim of evicting these people, renovating the apartments, and publishing an advertisement in the newspaper. The kolkhoz could then hire two new families to work as livestock keepers. The renovated apartment could be allocated to them. But the director refused.

Our interlocutor interrupted the conversation to talk to a thin workman with a bony face and a somewhat ghostly appearance, whose movements were hesitant. He was between forty and forty-five years old and had lost some of his incisors and eyeteeth. A tobacco-stained mustache brushed his chin. He was a cattleman on the kolkhoz. He exchanged a few words with the veterinarian, then Vasily dialed a number on his personal cellphone and handed it to the kolkhozian. Our interlocutor rejoined us a few minutes later. He explained that this person was an alcoholic, came from a family of alcoholics, and wanted to call his sister, who was hospitalized in an intensive care unit. "But is he capable of working if he is an alcoholic?" I asked. The veterinarian explained that every morning, he had to be served a glass (*stakan*) containing 250 grams of vodka, and after drinking that, he could work efficiently for a few hours at a stretch. This alcoholic used to work on a nearby kolkhoz. One day, he punched his manager and was fired. Since then, he had been taken on here.

In the evening, we visited Vova's parents, who lived nearby. When Vova told his mother about our meeting with Vasily, she told us that his wife was "a bit of a drunkard" and that she only had children for the social security benefits. The next day, when talking to my friend about the veterinarian, I expressed surprise at the latter describing the cattleman as an alcoholic when he himself, as evidenced by his glassy stare, seemed fairly intoxicated. On the one hand, Vova was an academic with detailed knowledge of the sociological literature. On the other hand, he was raised and continued to live in a town of a few thousand inhabitants. His family trajectory meant that he was deeply familiar with the rural worlds of Belarus. Vova told me that people are only alcoholics because they are labeled as such. It is not a medical definition. They are described as alcoholics once they start selling their belongings to buy vodka. In his opinion, that was why the veterinarian was so insistent on the fact that he was feeding his children and offering them a decent life. He was not like the alcoholics who work on the kolkhoz. He was someone, even though he and his wife were regular vodka drinkers.

In this way, the ordinary modes of categorization distinguish between drinkers and alcoholics. This echoes sociological studies of the working classes in France, which clearly differentiate between drinking-related practices and alcoholism-related practices (Merle and Le Beau 2004). In an ethnographic study of a car factory, Michel Pialoux (1992: 102, 107) highlights the multiple facets and ambivalences of alcohol consumption, fluctuating between, on the one hand, the affirmation of a "fraternal and virile world" and, on the other hand, the manifestation of "a potential loss of self-control, risk of destabilization, disruption to collective life, interactions, personal life, as well as—from a more distant perspective—a risk of forfeiture, self-destruction, complete exclusion and death." In the context of the lives of dockworkers in Le Havre studied by Jean-Pierre Castelain (1989: 8, 66, 9), the first extreme relates to a "codified consumption of alcohol" consistent with "looking after one's body, sharing, friendship, and of course, celebrations that justify intoxicating or high-quality drinks, consumed at celebrations of family and community life," while the second extreme relates to "drinking for the wrong reasons [*mal boire*], [to] drunkards who become unbearable due to their violence toward their families, and their inability to work or interact with their colleagues." Alcoholism is therefore not defined in a quantitative manner, on the basis of excessive alcohol consumption. It is defined by a specific way of drinking. "Social abnormality" is embodied by "the person who drinks too much and for the wrong reasons (alone), breaching the principle of the circulation of pleasure" (Castelain 1989: 69). On the kolkhoz, the difference between the veterinarian's drinking and the cattleman's alcoholism does not reside in the volume of alcohol consumed or in its regularity, but rather in the visible consequences of excess. Being described as an alcoholic relates to the existence of a specific biographical breakdown. An alcoholic is not someone who drinks but rather someone who ends up selling his or her belongings to buy alcohol. Therefore, the problem is not the addiction itself but that fact that it prevents people from living autonomously.

People labeled as "alcoholics" occupy various positions in the local social sphere, working intermittently for the kolkhoz, selling their labor to villagers who pay them to do odd jobs, or committing petty theft in homes to obtain a few rubles from the sale of stolen property. These diverse occupations seem to form a continuum that enables people to occupy different positions successively. One day you might work on the kolkhoz; the next day you might chop wood for a babushka; and on the third day you might commit a robbery or two. However, certain alcoholics seem to gravitate toward a third extreme, in which case they join a specific category: *bomži* (*Bez Opredelennogo Mesta Žitelstva*)—meaning "people without any specific place of residence"—a phrase originating from official Soviet police documents of the

1970s (Ryabchuk 2010: 353), which can be translated as "homeless people" or "vagrants." The *bomži*, in the native language, are necessarily alcoholics and are usually homeless. They are no longer able to work regularly on the kolkhoz, either because they have been driven away from there or because they are physically unable to do so. They no longer have access to the different markets described previously. They can no longer be integrated into networks enabling the use of collective resources because they are no longer trustworthy. So they are often obliged to sell their labor on a daily basis in order to earn a few rubles, by digging the garden of a *dačnik*, or by cutting wood for a villager who is too old to do the job herself. Their other option is to steal. The term *bomži* is used in discourses with reference to their petty theft, which the community considers to be intolerable. They move into empty houses, especially dachas reserved for summer vacations. From cellars, they steal canned food, patiently cooked by the property owners during the summer. They steal fruits and vegetables from kolkhoz fields or private gardens. They collect metal in order to sell it. The press is full of news items implicating these *bomži*. Moreover, some of them whom I managed to meet and with whom I exchanged a few words bore prison tattoos, a sign that they had spent time in Belarusian jails. One babushka, born in 1930, described their misdeeds with compassion:

> Today, there are a few alcoholics in the village. They will do anything to buy themselves a drink. They are paid 25,000 rubles to cut wood. But once, the alcoholic I hired was too drunk to cut any. He wanted to drink before he started work. I refused, and he left without doing the job. On another occasion, the same alcoholic saw that I was in the *bania*. He came into my house to steal a brand-new switch which he must then have sold. I think that he also stole some plates and an aluminum container from me. I don't have any proof, but I know it was him. But I didn't want to go to the police. Before, I used to leave different objects out in the yard, but now I bring everything inside. This alcoholic had a sister. She died. "Work and don't steal," she used to tell him. The babushka says that this alcoholic knows how to work but does not want to. Even his sister, before she died, could not convince him. Under such conditions, no one can help him. (Ossip's great-aunt, a retired kolkhozian, in a village near Vitebsk. Unrecorded interview, 26 October 2013)

She mentioned another alcoholic who used to steal vegetables, strawberries, cabbages, and beets. He was run over by a car. "God saw him do it," she finally said, claiming death was his punishment for stealing a few fruits and vegetables from the village.

In this way, it became apparent that the presence of these "alcoholics" is a resource for the villagers. They give elderly people who are no longer able to perform grueling tasks—cutting wood, plowing their land, etc.—the opportunity to pay someone else to carry out these essential tasks for them, in vodka or in rubles. This makes the production of alcohol all the more important because it allows anyone with a stock of *samogon* to ensure the maintenance of the vegetable gardens that are essential to the domestic economy.

Distillation

In his *Involuntary Journey to Siberia*, Andrei Amalrik (1970: 175) provides a detailed account of the methods used to produce the homemade alcohol consumed in rural areas:

> Ordinary vodka bought in the village store was kept for special occasions; they usually drank the home-distilled variety. Made from rye, this is singularly unpleasant to the taste, muddy green in color, and about 70 proof. Not every villager has his own still. In preparation for a holiday or to repay a neighbor for some good turn people borrowed a still from someone and made an extra supply. Homemade beer, on the other hand, was brewed by everybody and all year round. Boiled water is poured into a bucket, six—or, if the brewer is mean, four or five—pounds of sugar are added; yeasts is put in when the water has cooled, and sometimes tea for coloring and hops for taste. Hops are always added if the beer is going to be offered to guests, so they should get drunk quickly and drink less: a characteristic feature of village hospitality. The beer must ferment for at least three or four days and after that it still goes on getting stronger and stronger. Three mugs of beer are enough to knock a man out, so the peasants find it cheaper to brew a bucketful of beer than to buy a pint of vodka in the store. Illicit brewing is an offense punishable at the very least by a fine of one hundred rubles, but it can also lead to forced labor for several years. Many of the villagers had paid fines, and one had spent a year in camp, but this deterred no one.

I met several people who produced their own vodka. I personally took part in the distillation of a type of homemade vodka called *samogon* in a forest in Northern Belarus (Hervouet 2009a: 86–88). The person supervising the process was a police officer in a neighboring village who knew trustworthy people who would warn him if the police were alerted by their informants and were planning a raid. On that day, we distilled ninety-five liters of *samogon*. Since then, this activity has become too dangerous. The officer's brother, whom I saw again years later, explained to me that the risk had become too great and that they had been forced to stop producing such quantities of *samogon*. In the end, it was the policeman's father, a retired kolkhozian, who finally resumed production in his garage, out of sight. But the quantities distilled are much smaller and intended only for household consumption or as gifts for friends.

In October 2013, I also met an amazing character in a village near Orsha. She was the great-aunt of Ossip, one of my students when I was teaching at the European University of Humanities in Minsk at the end of the 1990s. She was about eighty years old and lived alone. She was married twice, and both her husbands died of heart attacks. At the funeral of her second husband, she cursed God, and people thought she must have been a sinner to suffer so much misery. Ossip greatly admired her freedom of thought, her independence, and her indifference to what people say. Not only did she blaspheme publicly, she also gave her cow an obscene nickname that shocked the neighborhood. Despite being arrested twice for illegally growing poppies, she continued to do so in order to cook a famous *blini* dish according to a recipe she learned from her mother. Lastly, she boldly insulted her son's lover, which led to her being brought before the judge. This eccentric character lived in a state of near autarchy.

> In Soviet times, I had a plot of fifty ares [*sotok*; 100 square meters]. I grew cereals, potatoes . . . I also raised calves, sheep and pigs. Raising calves was profitable; I sold them to the neighboring sovkhoz. Today, I continue to cultivate my plot. Members of my family help me. I now cultivate twenty ares. I pay people from the kolkhoz to plow it with a tractor. Today, I'm self-sufficient in fruits and vegetables, and I raise hens. There's currently a ban on raising pigs for health reasons [at the time of the interview, an outbreak of swine influenza was sweeping through the country]. Alcoholics are paid to do odd jobs, like chopping wood. In the area, there's a gang of alcoholics who have a leader. You can get them to harvest your potatoes or build a house and you'll pay less than you would through the official channels. I pay them in vodka. (Ossip's great-aunt, unrecorded interview, 26 October 2013)

She produced a bottle of *samogon* so that we could drink a toast to our meeting, and then explained how she distills it herself. She called her bottle of *samogon* "my darling." I pointed out to her that it is rare to see women drinking and distilling, and asked, "How did it start?" She said her mother taught her. She added that it was cheaper than buying bottles of spirits at the grocery store. She distilled it at home.

Maksim, an independent carpenter, told me about another way to make vodka.

> He bought ten liters of *spirt* from guys in Minsk, which is enough to produce fifty liters of vodka. People in Babruysk steal *spirt* from the factory and sell or exchange it elsewhere. Maksim bought it from people who work at the Bulbaš factory, and they may have stolen it. When a few youths brought him some tree trunks, he paid them in *spirt*. (Maksim, unrecorded interview, 1 November 2012)

The production of homemade vodka could be viewed as money not spent, which amounts to saving a sum of money that, without this personal production, would have been used to buy alcohol for consumption during the festivities that mark the year. Vodka can also be used as a trading currency. In both cases, vodka is a resource that enables people to improve their daily lives.

ON THE MARGINS

Poaching

I remember a friend's uncle whom I had met in the Orsha region in 2000 when I was investigating dachas in Belarus. Originally from a village devastated by the Chernobyl disaster, then rehoused in various regions of Belarus, the different members of this extended family, whom I had met in Molodechno, Minsk, and Orsha, often talked nostalgically about their home region and the beauty of its landscapes, rendered uninhabitable by the invisible radiation. On this particular day, he greeted me by showing me some beautiful freshly caught fish. I asked him where he had caught them. He smiled and answered, "In the River Pripiat." This river originates in the far northwest corner of Ukraine, crosses the Belarusian border south of the city of Pinsk, and then, at the end of its journey through Belarus, heads toward Ukraine and crosses the thirty-kilometer zone around the Chernobyl nuclear power plant. This river gave its name to the town of Pripiat, located below the power plant and built in 1970 to accommodate workers at Chernobyl. Deserted and abandoned since 1986, Pripiat has become the "Soviet Pompei" (Ackerman 2016: 15) and a favorite nuclear tourism destination. Radioisotopes have leached into the river and continue to do so. "It's forbidden to fish in it," he continued, "but I still go there; I know the area well." At the same time, Belarusian friends—students and French-speakers—were sometimes spending weekends or university holidays following groups of Belgian hunters in the forests of Belarus. In this way, the issue of hunting and poaching arose incidentally in my field studies. The wild animals living in Belarus's vast forests are a resource for some people, either by poaching or by selling prestigious prey for premium prices, even if it means circumventing or violating regulations.

Woods and forests cover 40 percent of Belarus. Vadzim Smok, the author of an article providing valuable information on this subject (Smok 2015), indicates, albeit without further elaboration, that many Belarusians hunt in violation of the legislation in force, despite increasingly severe penalties and fines. Forest workers, forest rangers, and *leshoz* employees may track down a few animals for their meat or fur. For a fee, they may also guide hunting enthusiasts in search of prey to shoot. This gives lowly employees of forestry organizations another way to make ends meet. When the hunters require greater guarantees, and/or when protected species are being hunted, environmental protection agencies and the police themselves may be bribed. They may even supply the poachers themselves. For example, in December 2014, the KGB arrested a group of ten hunters in the Gomel region, within the area irradiated by Chernobyl. Wilderness protection officers and members of the police formed part of this group. They organized hunts for Russians living near the border, and also sold meat from illegal hunts to local inhabitants. They were sentenced to four years in prison. In this way, residents, local authorities, and foresters conspire to organize illegal poaching practices. Official declarations confirm the extent of these practices. In 2013, Lukashenko declared that he was astonished at the quantities of equipment and game seized from poachers: a thousand guns, 300 kilometers of fishing nets, and dozens of tons of meat and fish.

In the 1990s and 2000s, Belarus remained a little-known hunting destination, but the number of foreign hunters rose in the 2010s. The high prices of prey compared to average incomes in rural Belarus encourage new forms of poaching of prestigious game. For a fee, local environmental protection officials cover up hunts for rich foreigners. In 2012, for example, a Russian citizen killed one bison and wounded another in the district of Valožyn, while Lithuanians killed three more in the district of Hojniki. In 2009, an Italian was arrested in the Belovežskaâ Puŝa primary forest, a national park in which hunting is prohibited. A local forester had been his guide in this protected area where he had killed a female bison.

Prostitution

The activities described so far are illegal. However, provided that they remain limited—with the definition of "limitation" being informally stabilized in unwritten rules that are implicitly understood by participants in the local social game—they are tolerated not only by the hierarchy and police but also by the village community, which, far from regarding them as scandalous, perceives them as a simple adaptation to needs. However, there are other equally illegal practices that are reprehensible from the perspective of local morality and repressed by the police. Studies of the sex trade in Eastern Europe analyze "prostitutional trajectories" (Darley 2007: 287) and the "trafficking of women" in a migratory context (Braux 2015). In Belarus, while analysts point to the risk of this phenomenon developing in connection with the country's organization of international events such as the 2014 World Hockey Cup (Preiherman 2012), they also highlight the successes of the government's fight against modern forms of slavery and "human trafficking" (Smok 2015). The fragile and fragmentary evidence collected in the fields of study provides further indications of the existence of irregular and poorly organized prostitution practices.

At the end of October 2012, I traveled with Anton, one of my students in Minsk, to the Dzerzhinsky Museum, located in the forest around the city of Dzerzhinsk, west of Minsk. We took the bus from Minsk and arrived at a stop a few kilometers from the museum. The manager of a hunting lodge was waiting for us there. Nikolai was an acquaintance of Anton's father, who worked in timber construction and had professional connections with several *leshozy* in the region. Our host was very talkative in the car. He was forty-three years old and appeared to have been drinking. He complained about Lukashenko, "who is crazy." He showed me all the land adjacent to the road we were on and told me that the tractor driver who works from 6:00 AM until midnight earned 4 million rubles a month, or $500, that he personally earned just 2.5 million rubles, and that his wife—a physics and mathematics teacher—brought home 3 million rubles a month. He gave me a detailed description of the exhausting work carried out by a milker on the kolkhoz, who was paid 1.5 million rubles per month. I asked him how people managed to live. Nikolai told me they have no choice. I asked him if they complain. He replied that if they are not happy, they can go elsewhere, collect empty bottles and return them for the deposit. Then he told me about the hunting lodge where I could stay with my family and children. He told me the price for foreign tourists: $50 a day and per person. For local people, the price is one million rubles a day, and up to ten people can stay. I said I found this expensive. He asked me how much I earned, how much my wife earned and how much I paid for rent. He saw me smoking a cigarillo and asked me for one. Very quickly, we started confiding in each other as we talked about politics, money, and tobacco. He then told me about his current work. Previously, Nikolai was an ordinary forest ranger [*lesnik*], before becoming the driver for the head *lesnik*, with whom he was on good terms. The latter's brother was subsequently appointed to a very high-ranking post in the country's government. The head *lesnik* then became head of the *leshoz* and appointed his former driver as manager of the hunting lodge. His boss, whom he described as his friend, was around thirty-five years old and, like Nikolai, loved women. Moreover, while Nikolai was driving the car one day, his friend was having sex with a fleeting conquest in the back seat. In fact, he gleefully told me that he organizes meetings with women in the hunting lodge. He told me about the Czechs who visited as part of a delegation working with the *leshoz* authorities. After drinking, they went to the *bania*. He brought them two girls, he told me, but specified that the girls did not get paid and they were simply happy to be part of this festive evening. Some Germans also came and said they could not sleep if there were no girls. Why, when we barely knew each other, was he talking to me so freely? Clearly, he felt protected because he was the friend of a senior government official's brother. In fact, the people who talked to me were generally those with a sound reputation because they were good workers, and sometimes devout people who had a sense of dignity. The people who liked to drink, who were not exemplary vis-à-vis the shared morality, did not want to meet me. Our driver on this day was therefore an exception. Perhaps he also imagined that, as a thirty-five-year-old Frenchman who had been coming to Belarus for fifteen years, I must share his taste for the famously beautiful Belarusian women. When we arrived at our bus stop, however, he apologized twice, implicitly mentioning the bawdy subjects discussed and his frequent cursing. This exchange avoided the issue of prostitution. The driver specified that the girls had not been paid, but from the moment he started talking about these escapades, what else could he do but deny the commercial dimension of the sexual exchanges in question? It is not unreasonable to presume that this curious narrative implicitly referred to existing practices in which certain women may sell sexual services. Moreover, this discourse echoed others, heard more than ten years ago, from student friends who worked as interpreters for Belgian hunters who came to Belarus to shoot big game. There, too, they were told about the need to find girls in order to round off successful hunting trips in the forest. A friend who lived near the agricultural high school in a rural town surrounded by fields also told me about cars with Minsk license plates that drove around the school at nightfall. Rumor had it that certain female students were paid for their services in cars, with their headlights off, in out-of-the-way areas a few hundred meters from their student residence. These reported comments seem to indicate that certain women use their bodies to obtain resources that supplement their meager incomes. In the different cases mentioned, there did not seem to be any organization managing these services. The transactions would appear to be rather occasional, linked to fluctuating economic needs, and irregular.

The kolkhozes are clearly paradoxical in that they are a controlled but uncertain world. The survey shows that, far from being an inert and passive universe, governed by routines of habit and hardship, these rural areas are home to multiple practices intended to increase people's resources and protect them from uncertainty. To understand how villagers perceive, judge, and assess the political system, it is important to understand the different parameters that define their worlds, which are governed not only by prescriptive, administrative, bureaucratic, economic, and political rules imposed from "above," but also by less visible, rarely verbalized behaviors brought to light by an ethnographic approach that focuses on the details of axiomatic daily lives. The actions of countryfolk are therefore not simply the product of rules imposed from outside, from the hierarchy, from the state apparatus. They reflect the existence of diverse and fragmented opportunities with a more or less random distribution. The presence of these resources implies some room for maneuver in relation to the official line. People and groups do not act mechanically in relation to what is expected of them, but operate in gray areas characterized by indeterminacy and uncertainty. These observations are consistent with Katherine Verdery's (1991: 427) remarks about "real socialism" in Eastern Europe: "Policies may be made at the center, but they are implemented in local settings, where those entrusted with them may ignore, corrupt, over-execute, or otherwise adulterate them." To analyze how inhabitants of rural worlds relate to politics, we first need to understand how they act. What they do cannot be reduced to expectations imposed from above since various kinds of resources can be mobilized in their environment. This implies a power to act that is missing from the conception of a repressive and coercive state in which ordinary citizens are defined as the "powerless ones," whose existence is governed by "such intricate and well-developed mechanisms for the direct and indirect manipulation of the entire population that, as a physical power base, it represents something radically new" (Havel 1985: 26). From this perspective, power is reified and conceptualized as an attribute, as something that is imposed on external actors. We will now analyze the methods used to mobilize the identified resources and show that they reveal relationships of dependencies and interdependencies emphasizing a conception of power as a "relationship" (Crozier and Friedberg 1977: 26). In fact, power in the Belarusian regime must be analyzed in terms of the vertical control mechanisms monopolized by the authorities, while also considering the relationships of dependencies and interdependencies in which the different social groups governed by the authoritarian government are embedded. We will thus see, from a configurational perspective, that "while different degrees of independence—or to express it differently, of power—can be observed in the relations of people to each other, there is no absolute zero-point of one or the other" (Elias 2006: 156–157). By taking account of these power relationships (chapter 5), we can then comprehend the moral feelings that structure these worlds (chapters 6 to 8), and the subsequent relationships with politics that they imply (chapter 9).

NOTE

1. Vintilă Mihăilescu raised these issues at a conference given at the invitation of Pierre Bidart at Université Victor Segalen Bordeaux 2, at the beginning of the 2000s.

CHAPTER

5

INTERDEPENDENCIES

In the preceding two chapters, I have listed the different resources mobilized by rural inhabitants seeking to ease the powerful material constraints imposed by the official functioning of the kolkhozes. Here I analyze how these potentially accessible resources are actually appropriated and implemented in personal projects. They involve relationships between people, who are the sole guarantors of the movement of the goods and services in question, and concern different types of dependencies and obligations.

ECONOMY OF OBLIGATION

Domestic Economy

The academic literature highlights the importance of family exchanges to overcome difficulties due to the shortage economy, both in the Soviet era and in the post-Soviet world. For example, Elisabeth Gessat-Anstett (2001a) describes the family's involvement in residential strategies, in making optimal use of living space, in the construction or acquisition of new housing, in vegetable gardening, cutting wood, watering, canning, curing, and jam making, and so on. Different terms are given to this mobilization of kinship in the literature. Gessat-Anstett (2001a: 124) refers to the links between blood ties and marriage ties on the one hand, and exchanges of goods and services on the other, as the "kinship network" (*réseau de parenté*). She borrows this expression from Georges Augustins (1998), who defines the notion in the following way:

> A kinship network is none other than a set of more or less long-term, durable, and more or less binding personal ties that must, in order to exist, be legitimized (by a reference to a common ancestry) and activated (by an exchange of reciprocal services).... A network is interpreted as a set of relationships between individuals with a specific basis (economic, parental, emotional). (Augustins 1998: 18)

Glenn Mainguy (2016), in his analysis of the everyday economy in the post-Soviet Russian rural world, borrows the idea of "practical kinship" (*parenté pratique*) proposed by Florence Weber (2002), mobilized in the form of a "household" (*maisonnée*), which is defined as "the basic unit of practical kinship in which a variable part of the daily tasks necessary for the material survival of its members is carried out" (F. Weber 2002: 89). Mobilizing the household is essential to the functioning of the domestic economy. Maintaining the personal plot of land and vegetable garden, raising domestic animals (hens, rabbits, a cow, and sometimes a horse), doing the housework, dealing with the administration, etc. require help from relatives. While the Russian situation in the 2010s differed from the Belarusian collectivist context, the forms of exchanges seem to follow the same logic. Mainguy identifies two types of processes. The mutual assistance process (*logique de l'entraide*) focuses on nondaily activities, such as the planting and harvesting of potatoes or haymaking. A principle of reciprocity prevails in the provision of mutual assistance: "Individuals agree to help other individuals since they know that they will then be in a position to request a service that cannot be refused" (Mainguy 2016: 69). People work for others who will in turn be available to work for them. The cooperation process (*logique de la coopération*) is based on daily activities—tending to the vegetable garden, watering vegetables, or putting animals out to pasture. The principle of mutualization is fundamental to cooperation, driven by "a group of actors maintaining relationships that are governed by the principles of co-production, joint management of production and collective administration of the wealth produced" (Mainguy 2016: 81). People are no longer working *for* another person but rather *with* them.

According to Mainguy, the first process is limited to the household, but the second surpasses it. However, mutual assistance processes sometimes extend beyond the household context. For example, coworkers and/or neighbors may sometimes provide occasional assistance. In addition, in the observations made in Belarus, these mutual assistance processes did not seem to be limited to nondaily activities, as they are also occasionally mobilized in daily activities. Maksim, for example, was a self-employed carpenter in a village. He cultivated a vegetable garden, hunted, did odd jobs, and was proud to lead an almost autarchic life, but although he provided assistance to neighbors, particularly the elderly babushka who lived in the *hata*—a traditional house—located about fifty meters from his own, he also received help. Sometimes, when he was working in the village, he asked his neighbors to take care of his horse. But these mutual assistance processes have their limitations. It is not possible to ask for too much help on a daily basis. This makes it difficult to ask other people to look after one's cows, as they have to be milked every day. Consequently, only people who do not work on the kolkhoz—usually pensioners or kolkhozians' wives—can look after them. In certain villages suffering from depopulation, people are finding it hard to keep raising cows. In Maksim's village, there are fewer and fewer of them: fourteen in 2008, eight in 2009, four in 2010, and only one remaining in 2012.

However, mobilizing the household and horizontal social networks is not sufficient. To obtain a tractor or livestock feed at reasonable prices and, more generally, to gain access to the collective resources used for personal purposes, people must make sure they remain on good terms with the kolkhoz hierarchy—and sometimes with the local government or the police. This brings to mind the definition of dependency proposed by Albert Memmi (1993: 32): "Dependency is a binding, more or less accepted relationship with a person, an object, a group or an institution—real or ideal—and which relates to the satisfaction of a need." Countryfolk therefore depend on their superiors to develop their worlds. For all that, are they dominated and subordinated, subject to the goodwill of their hierarchy? In fact, while employees are dependent on their hierarchy, the latter also depends on their work and commitment. The social system in rural Belarus can be considered as a series of mutual dependencies that force people to meet other people's expectations. In this respect, these worlds form part of processes pertaining to what Gilles Laferté (2010), in his study of credit and debt, calls the "economy of obligation."[1] Here, people are less bound by credits and debts than by favors (monetary rewards, tolerance towards illegalisms, services rendered, commitment to work) and debts. "Thus there is a double system of dependance in the [collective] farm: the ordinary working people are always finding themselves in circumstances where they need an official to make an exception in their favour, while the officials need to win support, i.e. honest labor, from the workers in order to maintain their positions" (Humphrey 2001: 11). The economy of obligation thus enables managers to control their kolkhozes and establish their "power over the people" (Laferté 2010: 63), while employees consent to their subjection in order to control their domestic economies.

Kolkhoz Economy

To understand the kolkhoz directors' guiding principles, it is necessary to examine their social and professional trajectories. The successful management of a kolkhoz can act as a springboard toward high-ranking positions in government organizations. The trajectory of President Alexander Lukashenko, a former sovkhoz director during the Soviet era, bears witness to this. Yuri, whose parents are kolkhozians, is a trained politician and an opposition activist. He gave me a structured analysis of the principles governing the trajectories of local agricultural elites, which I sketched out in my field notes:

> What training have kolkhoz directors received? At the start, they are often young specialists—mainly agronomists or zootechnicans. They then become directors. In the USSR, some of them made careers in the basic Party structures. If they demonstrated particular intellectual qualities, they could be promoted. The director's position was, and still is, a very important means of social advancement. Agricultural work was glorified, and still is to some extent. It is therefore a means of upward mobility and professional advancement. There were three levels in the Party's organizational structure. First: kolkhoz director and then instructor of the District Party Committee. Second: Second Party Secretary in charge of agriculture. Third: First Party Secretary. Alternatively, and at the same time, people could climb the ranks of the Executive Committee. However, in Soviet times, the head of the Executive Committee was often the local Party leader. As a result, when the country became independent, a large proportion of Members of Parliament came from the agricultural sector. The last director of the sovkhoz in which Yuri's father worked was a member of the Supreme Council for the second assembly of 1990–1995. Today, it is still possible for people who start out as kolkhoz directors to move on to careers in state organizations. (Yuri, around forty years old, son of retired kolkhozians, and an opposition activist. Unrecorded interview, 2 November 2013)

Conversely, if a manager fails to mobilize the workforce, he or she could be sent to a more minor kolkhoz with fewer career development opportunities.

Directors have targets that must be attained in terms of production and the development of agricultural and village infrastructures. However, they face a variety of problems, including defective machines, absenteeism, alcoholism, labor shortages, climate-related uncertainties, and guidelines for production choices that are sometimes out of step with locally available resources. To overcome these difficulties, they have to find ways of motivating employees despite the poor working conditions and remuneration. The available resources have limited effects. First, the bonuses permitted by the official compensation system remain low and are not sufficient to motivate staff throughout the year. Second, the threat of dismissal has limited effect. As rural areas suffer from labor shortages, it is difficult to replace the people who are dismissed. As a result, managers are regularly obliged to use undisciplined workers, including those considered "alcoholics," to carry out various tasks on the kolkhoz. Last, the use of physical force to control behavior was mentioned in several interviews, but only in reference to the Soviet period. At this time, directors could indeed beat a kolkhozian to death without fear of retribution (Humphrey 2001: 123). In addition, Lukashenko himself, who had been a sovkhoz director during the Soviet era, is said to have used physical force on his workers (Karbalévitch 2012: 47). How can kolkhozians be encouraged to work today? How can they be motivated? How is trust developed?

Reciprocities

Formally or informally, the kolkhoz provides resources that enable households to function. For example, countryfolk need a horse or tractor to plow the personal plots of land on which they grow potatoes. The kolkhoz offers this service at fixed rates. In 2006, a veterinarian told me how this works. The collective farm possesses five horses that are used to help people who work there or those living in the surrounding villages. The prices are low: 1,000 rubles a day for the farm's employees, and 3,000 rubles for *dačniki*. To reward certain workers or thank them for their loyalty and commitment, the prices may be even lower. Whenever possible, the management allocates resources at the best rates in order to build loyalty, not only among employees, but also among retirees or other workers with relatives working on the kolkhoz. It can then count on their support at key periods of the agricultural production cycle. Alexander—currently a teacher in a technical high school—recalled his time as the director of a small collective farm in the early 1990s in the interview below, in which he first refers to the official rule governing the use of kolkhoz resources, before mentioning the spirit in which it was applied:

> The kolkhozians, for example, had priority over villagers who did not work on the kolkhoz. They might need a horse to cultivate their plot of land, for example. A similar principle applies to land. Kolkhozians had the right to rent between forty-five and sixty ares of land from the kolkhoz. People who didn't work on the kolkhoz could only rent fifteen ares. People who didn't work on the kolkhoz also had to pay for services that were provided by the kolkhoz. If they took their cows to graze in the kolkhoz's fields, they had to pay—not much—but they still had to pay. It was the same for the machines. They had to pay the kolkhoz for their use. It was simply because these people had more time, and sometimes earned more than the kolkhozians. So I think it was right that they had to pay the kolkhoz for the use of these different resources.
>
> *Okay, but you couldn't control everything. . . . If the tractor driver helps a person he knows, a cousin for example . . . maybe he won't charge him.*

That would happen, and you could even say that these forms of work were actually authorized. . . . Sometimes, we personally allocated the tractors. The directors themselves offered them to people because these people would then work better on the farm. If you let them work for neighbors or people they know, if you gave them the right to do so, the people who rendered these services would be given things in return, and then the employees would be more motivated to work on the kolkhoz. We set a small symbolic price, just so that it wasn't free, to improve people's motivation. (Alexander, about fifty years old, former director of a small collective farm, now a teacher in a technical high school. Interview recorded on Friday 21 April 2006)

In the same way, help can be given to people who are not employed by the kolkhoz. For example, the livestock, such as pigs and cows, raised by countryfolk sometimes require medical intervention. In April 2006, a veterinarian told me that he looks after animals belonging to villagers living around the collective farm. To buy certain medicines, he had recently sold a calf belonging to the kolkhoz. "I make do by using the company's property to meet some of the inhabitants' needs," he said.

In this way, if the management gains a reputation for taking good care of its workers—the term used in the discussions is *zabota*—it can expect employees to work properly in return. It will also be able to mobilize their family members, including pensioners, for very low wages at crucial periods of the agricultural production cycle, especially harvest time. The narratives I collected highlight the compromises made vis-à-vis the official, recognized, and regulated practices. However, lengthy immersion in the field has revealed that these compromises also revolve around illegalisms that allow kolkhozians to carry out their work "on the side." As they feel indebted, they then commit themselves wholeheartedly to their salaried tasks.

Yuri explained to me the role of koklhoz directors in this given and take:

What makes a good director? Well-regarded directors are those who let people make a little more money. You can use what belongs to the kolkhoz to a certain extent, but you can't overdo it. Take what is grown for the kolkhoz, for example. If you're in charge of the potatoes, you can take a few bags home with you. *Vsë vokrug kolhoznoe, vsë vokrug mojo* [everything around here belongs to the kolkhoz, everything around here is mine]. . . . The kolkhozians are dependent on the farm for the tractor, for harvesting the wheat. The machines are used for personal purposes. You must always strike a balance. As my father used to say: "I survived five sovkhoz directors." . . . But what does "let the people make more money" mean? Using the kolkhoz's tractor, renting out the combine harvester for a low price, obtaining seed that is "donated" by the farm. My father was in charge of a group that grew potatoes. He would bring sacks home on a regular basis. A stupid director could control everything, but a smart one would cut people some slack. (Unrecorded interview on 2 November 2013)

Directors can also use collective resources for their own personal benefit. The construction—for themselves or a member of their family—of a house, a *bania*, or a garage sometimes requires the mobilization of labor. They may also want to render service to a person to whom they are indebted, such as an accountant with bookkeeping expertise. Rather than using an independent contractor whom he would have to pay, the director can incorporate this request into the underground system of transactions binding the different members of the collective farm. In this way, directors and kolkhozians depend on each other both contractually—first, to make sure that the work is done, and second, to ensure that salaries are paid properly and working conditions are adapted to the kolkhozians' constraints—and privately.

The structural nature of these arrangements is all the more apparent in situations when the circulation of favors and debts is interrupted. When the terms of the "economy of obligation" are not respected—that is, when the management does not feel sufficiently beholden towards it employees—the latter will no longer consider themselves indebted and will become less committed to their work. The business will then suffer as a consequence. In fact, this system of interdependencies between the directors and kolkhozians is in a fragile state of equilibrium and depends on the local economic situation. If their kolkhoz is powerful, directors will have everything to lose by alienating themselves from the workers and losing their trust, as the economic performance of the kolkhoz is likely to deteriorate. In return, the workers have everything to gain by establishing trusting relationships with the director. They can earn good wages, work under satisfactory conditions, and benefit from the farm's extensive resources. If their kolkhoz is weak, however, directors know from the outset that the authorities expect little from them. The workers will then know that there is little point in working too hard on the kolkhoz, because everything is already dysfunctional and they will have nothing to gain, at least in the short term. The nature of mutual dependencies thus depends on the local situation and its fragile equilibrium inherited from the past.

Structurally, the organization of official work can therefore function only if these minor illegalisms are tolerated. The director thus integrates these constraints into the management of the organization's production. The rule to be followed therefore consists in the systematic nonapplication of the written rule. Vova, an academic from Minsk who lives in a village of five thousand inhabitants near the capital, told me, "Belarusian society is like an iceberg. There are visible rules that are ultimately very unimportant for the functioning of Belarusian society, and there are underground or informal aspects" (Field survey log, 27 October 2007). This economic and social system is not unique to contemporary Belarus but is directly derived from the collectivist nature of agricultural production, as anthropologists who have studied rural areas governed by socialist systems have pointed out. Indeed, Caroline Humphrey (2001: 225–226, 265–266, 305–306) described similar practices in Buryatia in the 1960s and 1970s, as did Gerald Creed (1998: 184–218) in Bulgaria in the 1980s, who refers to "informal proliferations," and David Kideckel (1993: 101–137, here 102) in communist Romania, who postulates that based on the objectives pursued by the state on the one hand and rural households on the other, "socialist labor must be understood as the product of the attempts of each to control and manipulate the other," adding, "At the same time, the struggle also produced accommodation and interdependence."

LEVELS OF POWER

Verticality of Power

The economic and social system in operation in the countryside involves mutual dependencies between kolkhoz employees, their families, and the senior managers of these collective farms, who must also mobilize other forms of support in local or regional government in order to manage and develop the kolkhoz's economic activity. To understand these forms of interdependencies within elites, we can examine the logic that applies at the national level,[2] and then try to understand how it is applied at the local level.

Lukashenko uses the expression "verticality of power"[3] to state that no authority should compete with central government, whose decisions must be strictly applied at all levels of political, economic, and administrative life. Since the early years of Lukashenko's regime, the power of the state has been asserted to counter the centrifugal tendencies that tended to appropriate public, administrative, and economic resources. In 1993, a year before the presidential elections, he was elected to parliament as president of the Anti-Corruption Commission. While Boris Yeltsin in Russia was seeking the support of regional clans and powerful oligarchs linked to finance and the media in order to ensure his victory in the presidential elections, Lukashenko was making significant efforts to undermine the economic and administrative elites. After seizing full powers through the revised constitution of 1996, he indicted and prosecuted high-ranking players in government and economic spheres, effectively eliminating any competing authority in the country. For example, charges of corruption were used in the high-profile trial of Vasily Leonov, the former minister of agriculture who disagreed with Lukashenko on reforms to be adopted in the rural world, and against Yuri Feoktistov, director of the country's largest metal works in Žlobin (Matsuzato 2004: 244). This monopolistic ambition has been accompanied by a takeover of regional policy, with the president—following the decrees of 20 January 1995 and 18 March 1996—now being able to appoint all local executive leaders. He has since sought to appoint officials to posts located outside their places of origin in order to avoid the development of regional clans (Matsuzato 2004: 251). He also took on the criminal worlds that became increasingly important during the 1990s, resorting to physical eliminations without trial: he had truck robbers executed on the Brest-Minsk highway, and a mafia character named "Shchavlik" suffered the same fate (Karbalévitch 2012: 220).

Finally, to maintain firm control over the administrative and economic spheres, the authorities conduct regular campaigns involving "purges" (Lallemand and Symaniec 2007: 111), often in the form of anti-corruption measures. In this context, Belarus has lacked forces sufficiently powerful to compete with the president's personal power. In contrast to Russia, there are no oligarchs controlling sufficient resources "to influence national policy" (Guriev and Rachninsky 2005: 132). In Belarus, the important businessmen are replaceable managers who must show complete loyalty to the president if they want to remain in their posts. This explains why they have little influence on political life in Belarus, and why Andrew Wilson (2011: 243) refers to them as "*minigarchs*" who are aware that they run real risks of dismissal and prosecution. Heads roll on a regular basis, sending out a signal that the political powers are capable of making but also destroying these businessmen's fortunes. However, it does remain possible to enrich oneself discreetly and to avoid challenging the idea of an egalitarian society promoted by the authorities. In this way, Wilson (2011: 243) refers to "underground millionaires." Since the protection of private property is subject to the politician's goodwill, these people know that everything can disappear if they fall from favor. The regime therefore claims to be independent of the "clans" that are said to run politics in neighboring countries, to the detriment of the population's wellbeing, even though it can also be noted that the president maintains or has maintained close links with certain Russian oligarchs, such as the late Boris Berezovski (Wilson 2011: 244). The country's strong man has thus built "a regime of personal power" and possesses "absolute power" (Karbalévitch 2012: 412), practicing a form of "sultanic presidentialism" (Goujon 2009: 169)[4] in which his decisions prevail over those of any other institution (Eke and Kuzio 2000: 531). Consequently, in Belarus, he is sometimes respectfully, reservedly, or scathingly referred to as *Batka*—"father" in Belarusian—a term reflecting the control he exercises from above and the position of supreme authority he occupies in popular representations.[5] His power is based not only on his capacity to exploit violence and coercion but also on his ability to redistribute resources (Shukan 2005). He is not just a "strong man"; he is also a "big man" (Médard 1992).

In fact, state control of the economy is a configuration in which bribery can flourish (Bafoil 2014: 41). The discretionary power of bureaucrats in regulating the economy creates significant opportunities for the misappropriation of public funds. The opacity of corporate accounting practices enables the misappropriation of public resources for personal purposes. The most seriously affected sectors are trade, industry, and agriculture (Silitski and Pikulik 2011: 120). The government regularly stage-manages arrests of corrupt civil servants and senior officials. In fact, Lukashenko monopolizes the distribution of kickbacks and only allows certain loyal servants, including members of the security services, to enjoy these privileges, provided that this phenomenon remains discreet and limited.

The president personally claims to live modestly. In 2005, for example, he stated in an interview, "I don't have an apartment or any savings" (Karbalévitch 2012: 150). In fact, he is probably the biggest personal beneficiary of the system.[6] According to the Wikileaks revelations, the US diplomatic services in Belarus estimate Lukashenko's fortune at $9 billion (Elder and Harding 2010). These personal profits are probably channeled through the Directorate of Presidential Affairs (Upravlenie Delami Prezidenta—UDP), created by decree in August 1994 and placed under his direct authority. This structure is considered "an instrument of administrative expropriation of public property for the President's benefit" (Lallemand and Symaniec 2007: 109). It manages state-owned real estate and enjoys preferential conditions for the management of some of the lucrative sectors it oversees, such as hotels and tourist complexes, the timber industry, alcohol importation, tobacco, cars, and more. The profits can be paid into a special presidential fund that is kept separate from the state budget and is totally confidential and opaque. This privatization of the public sphere extends into the president's nepotistic practices. His personal physician, Irina Abelskaya, who is also his lover and the mother of his youngest son, Kolya, has been appointed as chief medical officer of the state hospital attached to the Directorate of Presidential Affairs, a post normally reserved for members of the senior nomenklatura. His eldest son, Viktor, was named as the president's national security aide in 2005 (Bohdan 2012), a post that gives him a variety of opportunities to increase his personal wealth. The president has even adopted an ambiguous stance concerning his dynastic ambitions in recent years by involving his son Kolya—still a child—in the management of state affairs. The political scientist Karbalévitch (2012: 223) deems that, in this way, Lukashenko has "privatized" the Belarusian State: "The country has become the fiefdom of one person and the institutions are now his private property."

Lukashenko has been able to establish himself as head of state thanks to the support of the security services, which also benefit from the system. In Belarus, eight bodies are currently authorized to carry out investigative and surveillance activities, and are in competition with each other: the KGB, the Ministry of the Interior, the Public Prosecutor's Office, the Presidential Security Service, the State Control Committee, and the Analytical and Operational Center, as well as Ministry of Defense units and the Border Guard. In 2011, Lukashenko granted more power to the KGB, enabling it to control different government bodies, such as the Directorate of Presidential Affairs (*Charter'97* 2012a), but also other bodies responsible for exercising control, such as the Public Prosecutor's Office (Silitsky and Pikulik 2011: 121). Today, the KGB appears to play a leading role in these structures, and the kickbacks attached to major economic transactions seem to be mainly granted at its discretion. However, to prevent this organization from becoming a closed environment working to further its own interests rather than those of the president, Lukashenko has forced several KGB directors to resign because he questioned their loyalty, and his decision therefore prevails over that of the security services (*Belorusskij Partizan* 2012). This enables him to wage a very selective war on corruption, turning a blind eye to the different abuses of members of his entourage and intervening only if they go beyond the boundaries he has defined for them. It would therefore seem appropriate to describe this regime as a system of "patronal presidentialism," which is not fundamentally different from the systems observed in other countries of the former USSR (Stewart et al. 2012: 6; Laruelle 2012: 309–310). His power is based on "patrimonial administration" since the bureaucrats' loyalty is based on their personal relationships with the leader (Guliyev 2011: 583), sustained by both fear and rewards.

What is the extent of these practices? According to the NGO Transparency International's annual corruption ranking, Belarus was ranked 36th in 2002, 151st (out of 180) in 2008, and 123rd (out of 176) in 2012—the year in which Russia was ranked 133rd and Ukraine 144th (*Charter'97* 2012b). Corruption, nepotistic practices, and the granting of privileges to friends—a characteristic of "crony capitalism"—are therefore features of the Belarusian institutional landscape (Eke and Kuzio 2000: 530, 543). The private and public domains are partially merged, and the boundary between personal wealth and state resources is blurred and porous. Ultimately, however, these misappropriations and practices involving the privatization of the common good have remained limited and controlled. This is partly due to the use of intimidation and force, enabling the system to redistribute some of the wealth produced in the country through housing, rural modernization, education, and health policies. Although, as other analysts have pointed out, this is indeed a patrimonial system (Eke and Kuzio 2000: 543; Ambrosio 2006: 423), or more precisely a neopatrimonial system (Bach 2012), it should be specified that it is a question of neopatrimonialism within the state rather than a state policy of neopatrimonialism. Here, state capture by disparate centrifugal forces does not seem to have occurred, since neopatrimonial practices have not prevented the implementation of public policies or the country's economic development.

Local Power Structure

Academic studies analyze the structuring of power at the national level, but do not describe it at the local level. The testimonies provide an understanding of the organizational fulcrums of local power, first at the village or town level, and second at the district level—that is, the intermediate level between the regions and municipalities. This power structure is neatly analyzed by Yuri, an opposition activist.

> In villages, there are several positions of institutional or moral authority: the director of the kolkhoz, the officially elected leader of the *sel'soviet* [town hall], the school principal, and sometimes, in certain villages, the religious authority embodied by the priest. (Yuri, around forty years old, the son of retired kolkhozians, and an opposition activist. Unrecorded interview, 2 November 2013)

The local power structure thus differs in some respects from the situation during the Soviet era. On the one hand, the role of the Communist Party—fundamental before 1991 (Humphrey 2001: 119)—has disappeared. On the other hand, the importance of support from local religious authorities appears to be a new phenomenon. Indeed, a monograph on a Belarusian village (Hervouet 2014) mentions the existence of links between the economic, administrative, and religious authorities. In some areas, the church acts in the interest of the administration and the leadership of the kolkhoz. The priest contributes to the moralization of social life by combating alcoholism and promoting a spirit of discipline and obedience toward the authorities. He thus encourages people to work honestly—that is, in accordance with the expectations of the collective farm's leadership. He helps to build reputations, which can potentially aid social advancement.

> Religion sometimes plays an economic role at the local level. Churches are sometimes built in villages. In some cases, there are interactions between the church and "businessmen" who launder money. The "businessman" pays the church, in the form of a donation, and in this way gains the institution's favors. The priest can also introduce the businessman into power structures by saying: "Look, this man is helping us." (Yuri, unrecorded interview, 2 November 2013)

In return, the priest can benefit by having churches built, the roads leading to them paved, and the church's architectural heritage enhanced, all of which will increase his standing. Senior figures in the local economy may need to use the local Executive Committee's administrative resources, particularly for mobilizing labor at harvest time, as explained by the former director of a collective farm. As it is not possible to rely on assistance from a seasonal labor force from other countries to support the kolkhoz's year-round workforce, high-school or university students are frequently mobilized. Arrangements are made with the education authorities to mobilize student labor, and a blind eye will be turned to any illegalisms committed by these temporary workers in order to ensure that the required work is properly performed.

> Students are sent to places with little mechanization of labor. They are sent to harvest carrots, beets and onions. Cabbages are too valuable, and the risk of theft is too high. There are machines for harvesting potatoes. This labor force often works in the morning and then has to be fed in the canteen. For five mornings worked, a student receives about 20,000 rubles [less than $10]. Students are also sometimes sent to distant kolkhozes for two-week periods. In this case, they are fed and housed on site. These benefits are deducted from their wages. Students generally steal very little. They are lazy. In addition, their parents often live in rural areas and have no need for stolen vegetables. For the most part, the teachers are the ones who steal the most. The bus arrives in the fields empty but will be overloaded when it leaves, with vegetables even transported on the vehicle's roof. The kolkhoz authorities do not object because the kolkhoz produces too much and the prices of the products, set by the state, are not high. What's more, much of the production rots away in warehouses and some of the carrots are used to feed the cattle. (Mikhail, a retired teacher of mechanical engineering in an agricultural high school, about sixty years old. Unrecorded interview, 28 October 2007)

These local authorities are accountable to the next level of the administrative hierarchy, which is the district level.

> The key positions at the district level are as follows: Head of the KGB, Chief of Police, Head of the Executive Committee, Head of the Prosecutor's Office. Each position is managed as a specific domain. There is another powerful position: the local bank manager, who can grant loans, and in exchange obtain various favors. These loans are precious, for the interest rates that can be charged, but also because 80 percent of kolkhozes are not profitable and need loans, especially to pay wages. The local elites perpetuate themselves. They make room for their sons-in-law, nephews, etc. (Yuri, unrecorded interview, 2 November 2013)

Rendering service to government or police officials at the local or district level may be rewarded by the bestowal of valuable protection by the recipients of these services.

> Running a kolkhoz can have its advantages. If you're on good terms with the local police chief and you break the speed limit, you can arrange to pay a fine and avoid having your license revoked. You can also come to arrangements with the judge and prosecutor. You can protect others, especially members of your family (your own children if they do something stupid). (Yuri, unrecorded interview, 2 November 2013)

Indirectly, this may also enable certain types of protection to be given to kolkhoz employees, who would then be in the director's debt. The police may also show leniency and not report people who make *samogon* on a small scale, without making a business of it. In this way, it can be seen that the system of mutual dependencies extends beyond relationships between employees and kolkhoz directors. The latter must deal with the local, regional, or even national administrative, political, and sometimes religious authorities in order to run the collective farm under their responsibility. However, while the economy of obligation seems to operate according to stabilized norms and expectations that are universally understood, the ways in which the ties between members of the elites are mobilized seem much more unstable. This means that kolkhoz directors must rely on the powerful esprit de corps that is said to exist within their community, in order to remain in their posts.

Esprit de Corps

The relationships between the various local authorities are marked by uncertainty. Since the central authorities refuse to authorize the creation of stabilized networks, which could break away from presidential authority or distance themselves from it, local elites are required to innovate and also to develop their territories, but they are unsure of whom they can count on, over time, to carry out their projects.

The following narrative sheds light on this issue. In November 2007, I traveled with Vova, a Belarusian colleague, to a kolkhoz that had diversified its activities, particularly by deciding to embrace agritourism.[7] The director, who was in his forties, greeted us and told us about his plans. Two years earlier, representatives of the Ministry of Agriculture had visited the site and encouraged him: "That's good, you need to carry on like this." He invested $4 million of the kolkhoz's disposable assets in his project, which was included in the National Agritourism Development Program (2006–2010). Firmly believing that there were real economic opportunities to be exploited, he launched the construction of a complex consisting of a hotel, a restaurant, and a conference room on a very accessible site close to the Brest-Moscow highway. He expected this to create sixty jobs. He also had houses built to encourage young people to stay and work on the kolkhoz. But he had to interrupt the project. Another million dollars were required to finish the work. He jokingly asked me if any French investors might be interested. The Ministry of Tourism and Sport was not providing any real support for what he was doing. Its representatives asked him to draw up a business plan for the future development of the site. He did as he was told. His efforts were also appreciated by the prime minister, who promised that he would receive funding from the loans granted to Belarus by the Chinese, but he had never had any concrete responses. "There is no money in the country, nothing ever happens," he said. Other local tensions were mentioned by his colleague. Loans were being granted to the area as part of the "agritown" development policy.

Local authorities used these funds and could give advisory opinions. The kolkhoz offered training courses for tour guides and bartenders at the local high school, but the Executive Committee refused to create these programs on the pretext that there were no development prospects. The director was now pessimistic. He used to believe in his project's potential. It was promising. Now the resources had run out. He was discouraged. Under the current conditions, agricultural enterprises could not be profitable. Food prices were fixed, while fuel, energy, and spare parts prices were rising. No one wanted to invest because afterwards, he said, because *"Batka* could visit, simply point to the place and require the building to be demolished." This account is revealing in that it reflects the regional development initiatives adopted and the difficulty of succeeding without strong administrative and political backing.

Instability is sometimes exacerbated by injunctions from the national authorities. For example, the "twinning" operations between kolkhozes and urban factories, which were imposed by the state in the early 2000s, were unpopular with local administrative officials. This complicated the rules of the game and increased the sources of uncertainty.

> My friend and I went to the principal town of the region in which I live in order to register with the authorities. We were accompanied by a neighbor from the apartment building of the friend with whom I was staying. She works in human resources at a technical high school. She explained that the *ispolkom* [Executive Committee] frowns upon links between kolkhozes and factories because it loses some of its control over the kolkhozes. Executive Committees like to keep kolkhozes under their control. In this way, they can benefit from the resources and are therefore unhappy to see links being established between agricultural enterprises and large factories in the city, but they cannot oppose decisions made at the highest level of the State. (Field survey log, 23 November 2007)

These remarks about the precarious nature of economic, administrative, and political configurations are recurrent in the interviews. Alexei, the principal of an agricultural high school, explained to me that "tensions between the leadership of the kolkhozes and local authorities are the norm" and told me an anecdote:

> A kolkhoz director had developed activities related to agri-tourism, but he was too independent; he talked too much. His wife had studied in the United States. He was relieved of his duties. In the end, he set up a small rural tourism business on a self-employed basis. (Alexei, about thirty years old. Unrecorded interview, 3 November 2007)

In the end, the directors' struggles to stabilize their institutional environment may thwart their plans. However, they can be severely sanctioned if their results are disappointing. These sanctions are based on what my interlocutors generically termed "administrative pressures" and are similar to those prevailing in the Soviet era (Urban 1989: 108–115). These sanctions consist first of all in making the management's incompetence public, which Alexander, a former kolkhoz director, mentioned in an interview:

> In the 1990s, when I was running the farm, the most effective strategy was the moral pressure exerted on the managers. The main results were made public quickly and by different means. They were posted everywhere, published in the press, and at all the meetings it was announced that specific kolkhozes had failed to meet the requirements. Of course, on the financial level, a portion of the bonuses was withheld, but not the entire amount. This took a far greater toll on the spirit than on the wallet. It was something of a disgrace. (Alexander, interview recorded on 21 April 2006)

Tensions with local or regional administrative authorities can lead to dismissal. Indeed, kolkhoz directors are actually appointed by the administrative hierarchy even if, officially, the kolkhozians themselves participate in the decision-making. Alexei and his father-in-law explained:

> Officially, it is decided at a meeting of the kolkhozians. But the administration usually makes a proposal. The District Executive Committee submits two or three nominations. Among these applications, there may be one from this farm and another from who knows where. Afterwards, the kolkhozians hold a meeting. . . . They vote. People are used to voting for the nominations submitted by the Executive Committee, because they are used to believing in the authorities and they often don't even know the person who gets the job. It's the head of the Executive Committee who makes the proposal and the kolkhozians sincerely support this nomination. (Alexei, principal of a technical high school, who is around thirty years old, and his father-in-law, a veterinarian, who is in his seventies. Interview recorded on 14 April 2006)

Not only might people's reputation be sullied, they could be assigned to a weak kolkhoz in a struggling region, or dismissed, but they also risk being sued for misuse of corporate assets or embezzlement of public funds. Yuri explained:

> Why are people put on trial? How do you know which limits cannot be overstepped? A director might not have shared [resources] with the head of the police, the KGB chief or the Executive Committee. You have to develop your network and know this network's ground rules. You have to avoid getting into direct conflict with important networks. (Yuri, unrecorded interview, 2 November 2013)

What steps can people take, in this context, to maintain or strengthen their position? First of all, they must demonstrate their political loyalty, or at least abstain from displaying suspicious orientations. Yuri gave me an example of someone who would not be considered:

I have a friend who works on a kolkhoz. He is responsible for commercial matters and supplies—he is responsible for the delivery of spare parts for machines, for example. He studied at the State Economic University. If he had been politically loyal, he would have been a kolkhoz director. He is involved in the Belarusian Popular Front [BNF, a nationalist opposition party], like his father, and he speaks Belarusian. It is harder for him to use the Belarusian language than for me, as I live in the city. (Yuri, unrecorded interview, 2 November 2013)[8]

Those who want to maintain or strengthen their position can then seek to comply with administrative injunctions, even if they seem to be suboptimal from an economic standpoint. Vasily gave me an example:

The director is not an expert in the agricultural field. I gave him an ultimatum. If the cleaning machines for the pig shed were not replaced over the summer, I would resign in the autumn. Let's take the example of a five-hectare field that could be used as pasture for the cows. If the director had decided to convert these five hectares of land into cow pasture, milk production would have increased. We could have had 5,000 liters of milk per year per cow, no problem. This is the target set for the district's farms. The director didn't make these five hectares available. In fact, he had been criticized by the leadership of the *ispolkom* [Executive Committee] for growing too little wheat. He therefore decided to use these five hectares for wheat. This was ridiculous because five hectares more or less doesn't make much of a difference for wheat, whereas they would have made an important difference to milk production. The manager doesn't even know exactly when to cut the grass for haymaking. (Vasily, about forty years old, a veterinarian on the farm attached to a technical high school in the Minsk region. Unrecorded interview, 16 April 2006)

Kolkhoz directors must therefore maneuver to obtain protection from the regional, or even national, government bodies. Discourses on this subject are recurrent, but elliptical. I asked Maksim how one becomes a kolkhoz director and what qualifications one needs to obtain. He told me that one needs to study economics and agronomy, but what one needs most are contacts and protection (Unrecorded interview, 31 October 2012).

Lastly, kolkhoz directors, who are subject to similar injunctions and tensions, seem to develop an esprit de corps that gives them a certain stability. As they are all in the same structural position, they are also encouraged to maintain good relations and help each other when necessary. Alexander shared examples from his experience:

Solidarity between kolkhoz directors, in the form of exchanges and mutual aid, has always existed. There are current examples of this. Here at my agricultural school, a machine that is used to cultivate the land on the farm adjoining the school recently broke down. The neighboring kolkhoz helped us out. And likewise, if they are having problems with one of their machines, the technical school will send them the same type of machine, because the sowing period is very short. You have to do everything on time, you can't wait. Otherwise, you'll never get by. This relationship must be very close. If there were ever any disagreements between the presidents of kolkhozes, the kolkhoz would face immediate problems. (Alexander, interview recorded on 21 April 2006)

This system produces strong interdependencies, which generate solidarity among elites, linking the local levels to the national levels. My notes from a conversation with Mikhail and Elena point to this:

> Everyone steals because it's not private property. Basically, everyone controls everyone else, asymmetrically, but there are some resources for everyone. Mikhail insists that directors stick together. Not all of them have the same training, even if today most of them come from the Academy under the President. But Mikhail explains that in fact, they are regularly brought before the Executive Committee, are slapped on the wrists, and show strong solidarity with each other. (Mikhail, a retired teacher of mechanical engineering in an agricultural high school, about sixty years old, and Elena, a teacher of biology and botanical science in the same agricultural high school, who is also about sixty. Unrecorded interview, 16 April 2006)

This esprit de corps seems to allow them to avoid certain legal proceedings.

> Mikhail talks about kolkhoz directors in the region who were arrested. They were looking to sell state-owned land. The supposed purchasers were in fact agents of the state. He then mentions kolkhoz directors who, at the time of perestroika, had built large *kotedži* and bought apartments in Minsk. I ask if they had been arrested. Today, they are running new kolkhozes. He thinks that one of the main reasons for this is the great solidarity within the network of kolkhoz leaders. However, the penalties inflicted upon kolkhozians who commit offenses are very severe, even for stealing potatoes. (Mikhail and Elena, unrecorded interview, 16 April 2006)

For those who are adept at maneuvering, there are many benefits. First, they are assured of comfortable incomes compared to the average in rural areas. The authorities deliberately remain vague, or even opaque, about the distribution of revenues, which enables them to distribute bonuses freely according to the economic situation and the need to reinforce local loyalties according to the circumstances. Estimates vary in the interviews. For example, Yuri told me a kolkhoz manager earns, officially, €700 to €1,000, which corresponds to eight to twelve million rubles, and a kolkhozian earns around two million rubles—between €200 and €300 (Unrecorded interview, 2 November 2013). For the director of a kolkhoz in Northern Belarus, however, the earnings mentioned are very different:

> The director of the kolkhoz to which my village belongs studied in Vitebsk. He knows the place well. He probably studied at the University of Management. He does not earn more than four million [in October 2013, one euro was exchanged for 12,600

Belarusian rubles]. The difference between this director and the others is that he owns two or three cows, four pigs and two calves; he has a large estate. (Svetlana, mother of Masha, an engineer nearing retirement, who spends all her free time in a village in Northern Belarus. Unrecorded interview, 29 October 2013)

This enables people to increase their informal income without anyone asking questions. When the loyalty of local elites and kolkhoz employees is guaranteed, people can raise their standard of living, to a certain extent, without any trouble. They can even protect their family members through their contacts with the local police. Nevertheless, this art of maneuvering seems to have a significant psychological cost. Contradictory injunctions often have to be dealt with. Administrative pressures appear to be unevenly applied throughout the territory, but they are particularly strong in the kolkhozes, which are of major political importance. Maksim mentions these pressures and their effects:

> Nearby, there is an *agrokompleks* called Peršaj 2000. It sets the benchmark. In the regions or possibly on smaller scales, there are model complexes. They attract money, lots of money. The president travels to Peršaj by helicopter, for example. I have heard that the bosses and managers there are sick and afraid—under great pressure. Everything there is tightly controlled. Journalists and diplomats are invited to this type of kolkhoz. (Maksim, a self-employed carpenter living in a hamlet fifty kilometers from Minsk. Unrecorded interview, 2 November 2013)

The description of the effective functioning of the kolkhoz and, more broadly, of the relationships and interdependencies in rural worlds, paints a picture of the social world in the countryside that contrasts with the representations presented by the media and politicians. Consent is seen as the product of discipline imposed from above. Lukashenko claims to govern machinery that functions automatically if the directives handed down from the topmost decision-making body are properly transmitted down through the ranks to the most localized actions. Media and academic discourses place the emphasis on coercion, fear, and violence to explain the workings of a system that manages to perpetuate itself despite the harsh working conditions and faint hopes of economic success. This conception of society as a machine prevents us from understanding the multiple networks of exchange—formal and informal—that govern the regulation of these worlds. Anthropologists who studied rural life in communist Europe at local levels have previously identified this pitfall. Steven Sampson (1984: 288), when pointing out that local groups and individuals potentially had more power than most observers of socialist regimes realized, suggests that socialist Romania was "a society with a plan, but not a planned society." Far from being concentrated at the top of an institutional pyramid, power is disseminated and mobilized in a fragmentary and tenuous manner in multiple areas of the social space. The kolkhozes form a world reflecting aspects of a configuration structured by complex systems of interdependencies, hovering between different states of unstable "balances" (Elias 1978: 75). These systems of interdependencies paint a picture of a society moving like a Calder mobile.

NOTES

1. Laferté borrows this expression from Craig Muldrew (1998).
2. In the following pages, I revisit some of the elements developed in Hervouet 2013b.
3. Medvedev (2010) cites a speech given to students in 2008, for example, in which the head of state explicitly associates the definition of the "Belarusian model" with the "verticality of power." Lukashenko has been using this concept since the mid-1990s. It is worth noting that Putin takes up this expression in the early 2000s, often associating it with the "dictatorship of law" (Vitkine 2007).
4. Grigory Ioffe (2004 : 100) objects to this reference to sultanism, which he describes as "journalistic hyperbole."
5. In the Kremlin's "soft-power" strategy of discrediting Lukashenko in the run-up to the presidential elections in December 2010, the Russian media even described the Belarusian president as a "godfather" (Marin 2010).
6. Brian M. Bennett (2011: 281), the United Kingdom's ambassador to Belarus from 2003 to 2007, nevertheless gives credence to the argument that Lukashenko is not likely to have increased his personal wealth.
7. The meeting is mentioned in chapter 2.
8. The use of literary Belarusian in social relations often manifests itself in the proximity of the speaker to the ideas of the nationalist opposition to the regime. Further details are given in this book in chapter 9.

CHAPTER

6

LIFE HORIZONS

So far, I have shown what resources have been mobilized by the actors, and how their use has resulted from strong forms of interdependence, from local to regional or even national levels. I would now like to focus on how these practices are perceived and evaluated. They entail specific ways of thinking and considerations of what is fair and unfair—in short, moral sentiments. These practices, embedded in specific configurations partly determined by structural constraints arising from the country's political, economic, and social organizational structures and history, generate specific expectations and particular projections into the future. They provide an insight into what is considered honest and dishonest, great and insignificant, glorious and wretched, legitimate and illegitimate.

First, we will see that these practices enable people to create their own worlds, which they perceive as desirable. Indeed, the use of formal and informal resources, based on the mobilization of forms of solidarity, enables people to satisfy material expectations and attain life horizons that are defined as desirable. However, these goals can be understood only if such practices are firmly rooted in biographical histories. Indeed, taking account of the past helps us to develop a general understanding of what people consider to be legitimately expected of the economic and political system. The forms of material stability and protection from social insecurity generated by the above-mentioned configurations often seem legitimate in the collected discourses. The extent to which the past exerts a "regulative force" (*puissance régulatrice*; Durkheim 2002: 209) over life's desires cannot be understood unless these forms of legitimacy are embedded in the individual and social histories of the Belarusian and Soviet century.

ASCETICISM

Limitation of Desires

The everyday lives of some of the people I met revolve around satisfying basic needs and possibly acquiring meager surpluses, which enable them to look beyond the mere physical reproduction of their worlds and toward the creation of possible futures for themselves. Elderly people, born before the Great Patriotic War, live their lives in an extraordinarily frugal manner that could even be considered ascetic.

In October 2013, I traveled with Ossip—one of my former students—to a small village near Vitebsk, where we met his great-aunt, Maria, born in 1930. She lived in a very modest house; the interior was partly dilapidated, and the fleurs-de-lis-patterned wallpaper was torn. The babushka was now very old: her fingers were gnarled; she was toothless; she had a heart attack two years ago. She lived with her cats. Two of them were wandering around her bedroom. When we arrived, she was getting out of the *bania*. Her daughter-in-law was with her, accompanied by one of her sons, to help her get around. Maria said that since her heart attack she had lost her faculties—she could barely walk. As the discussion progressed, she cheered up and started talking about herself. She still grew food crops on her personal plot of land, but had had to stop raising animals because of her declining health. The kolkhoz did not give her any particular help. She hired someone to plow her land with a horse. For six furrows, she paid 20,000 rubles, which was just under $3. She had three children but one of her sons had died. She had six grandchildren—"May God keep them healthy"—who, for the most part, worked in the city, but they did not enjoy their work because there was no money in it. When we talked about her pension, she said that it was enough for her to get by on—"*mne hvataet.*" She received 2,850,000 rubles per month, the equivalent of $300. She pointed out that the country's president increased the pensions by 5 percent in January 2013. She gave 150,000 rubles a month, or just over $12, to her granddaughter who had just given birth and was on maternity leave. She talked about the rising prices of products. The pension she received increased with age, which allowed her to buy certain medicines. She said that the state is supportive, that if she is worried about her health, she can call the doctor who will come an hour or two after her call. Her friends were dead, but she did not feel lonely. Maria gave as much money as she could afford to her grandchildren. She came back to this subject several times. Her pension—the fruit of her labor—not only put food on her table, it also allowed her to give to others, which established her place in a broader entity: her family and her descendants. In this way, her life, reduced to the reproduction of material conditions revolving around her plot of land, was not doomed to a form of social nonexistence. Her declaration of satisfaction contrasted sharply with the miserable living environment, her extremely difficult material conditions, the very basic comfort, the monotony of her diet, and an existence with no apparent horizon. But Maria was typical of the elderly people I met, for whom the payment of even a small pension seemed to satisfy their expectation of what they believed the state should legitimately provide. This income enabled them to pay a few very small bills and, in the testimonies gathered, most babushkas prided themselves on managing to build up savings from these tiny sums. The savings set aside allowed them to buy a few treats for their grandchildren and, when viewed in light of their own past, they saw these situations as the realization of unhoped-for childhood wishes. Despite the feeble level of social protection it provides, the state enables them to consult doctors, to be hospitalized if necessary, and to buy certain medicines. The very idea of buying a car, traveling, or buying things—except for a few pictures of saints—does not seem to even cross their minds. They cannot even imagine having running water and a toilet in their *isba*. The most important thing is being able to eat meals that never change: potatoes, bread, a few jars of pickles and tomatoes in vinegar, *kaša*, jam, apples, sausage and sometimes a little chicken. Their world is Durkheimian in the sense that they have very limited desires and that the political, economic, and social structure allows them to satisfy expectations which they consider to be legitimate (Durkheim 2002: 209–210; Cuin 1991).

These expectations are reiterated by the current political authorities. In 2001, President Alexander Lukashenko declared, "The democracy we need is when a man works and earns a wage, no matter how much, so that he can buy a small amount of bread, a little milk, some fresh cream, a little *tvorog* [a type of cottage cheese], and sometimes a little meat, to give to his child, etc. But as far as meat's concerned, let's not eat too much of it in summer" (quoted in the opposition newspaper *Naša svoboda*, 10 April 2001). Ridiculed by the opposition press, this declaration makes sense to these people, not because they are alienated by the state propaganda whose discourse might hold more performative power over them than the educated city dwellers, but because it directly echoes their own personal histories. Indeed, to understand their adherence to this norm of frugality and asceticism, we need to be aware of the history of these generations born before the Great Patriotic War. Only then does it become possible to understand how past experiences have shaped particular dispositions that define the horizons of a world which, in the eyes of these individuals, appear to be desirable and emancipating, when they may seem extremely limited to individuals socialized in subsequent generations.

Lands of Violence

To situate these individual histories in the collective history, it is important to recall certain facts about the tragic events that affected this region throughout the twentieth century. The historian Timothy Snyder (2010a) refers to the territory extending from central Poland into Russia, and taking in Ukraine, Belarus, and the Baltic States, as the "bloodlands." This was where, between 1933 and 1945, the Nazi and Soviet regimes murdered around fourteen million people. "These people were all victims of murderous policy rather than casualties of war" (Snyder 2010a: 10). The testimonies collected in rural Belarus today refer to two major events: collectivization and the Nazi invasion.

The forced collectivization of the countryside was accompanied by harassment, confiscations, deportations, and executions. Between 1929 and 1933, approximately three million peasants from the Soviet Union—supposedly *kulaks*—were deported to the Urals, Siberia, Kazakhstan, and northern Russia (Mondon 2004: 15). The part of current Belarusian territory that then belonged to the USSR was affected by this policy, even if the pace of collectivization was slower there than in the other republics. In 1934, throughout the USSR as a whole, 71.4 percent of farms were collectivized. This proportion did not exceed 55.3 percent in Belarus (Drweski 1993: 83) despite the systematic use of violence, as the following letter shows. This was a plea sent to the "All-Russia *Starost*,"[1] Mikhail Ivanovich Kalinin, by Piotr Leonidovich Herman of the hamlet of Babich-Liad in the borough of Babruysk, situated in the district of the same name, in the rural soviet of Borovichi, on 4 April 1930. Kalinin, who came from peasant stock, was then head of the Soviet state[2] and claimed to oppose any form of violence against the peasantry.

> I hereby appeal to you for clemency.
>
> I was deported from my country of origin with my sick wife, Anna, 40, and my children, Maria, 8 years old, Piotr, 6, Pavel, 3 and Elena, 2, to the Siberian taiga, which means certain death for me and my family, all because, this year, I paid the individual tax that was wrongly levied.
>
> I had two horses, two cows, five sheep. How can the Soviet authorities mete out such inhuman treatment to people who have done nothing to deserve it?

> My wife and I are farm workers; we have worked all hours to pay off the debt on the land my father had purchased. I bought these fifteen dessiatins [around 40 acres] through my own labor. I was a shepherd for four years. Is it my fault that my father bought some land? For that, do I deserve to be sent straight to my death with my family? Is it my fault if, in our rural soviet, 50 percent of the people have been deported on the strength of denunciations alone?
>
> This year, I was charged 185 rubles in individual taxation. I paid this sum, and then everything was confiscated from me—all my belongings—the whole caboodle. If only it had stopped there! But no, they had to deport us too! What kind of criminal am I? Let the Soviet authorities come and take my children from me right now, they're all bloated with hunger! My wife and I are going to die, just because we wanted to help consolidate Soviet power. (Mondon 2004: 135–136)

The policy of repression was stepped up in 1937. Joseph Stalin and Nikolai Yezhov, head of the NKVD (People's Commissariat for Internal Affairs) from September 1936 to November 1938, planned the "direct physical liquidation of the entire counter-revolution." Moscow sent revised quotas to the regions under Order 00447 of 30 July 1937, titled "On the Operations to Repress Former Kulaks, Criminals, and Other Anti-Soviet Elements" (Snyder 2010a: 81). The NKVD carried out "mass killings" intended to bring about the "deliberate destruction of the educated representatives of Belarusian national culture" (Snyder 2010a: 98), particularly in the Kurapaty forest (Marples 1994; Goujon 2008). The terror unleashed in rural areas was accompanied by the use of torture.

> Confessions were elicited by torture. The NKVD police organs applied the "conveyer method," which meant uninterrupted questioning, day and night. This was complemented by the "standing method," in which suspects were forced to stand in a line near a wall, and beaten if they touched it or fell asleep. Under time pressure to make quotas, officers often simply beat prisoners until they confessed. Stalin authorized this on 21 July 1937. In Soviet Belarus, interrogating officers would hold prisoners' heads down in the latrine and then beat them when they tried to rise. Some interrogators carried with them draft confessions, and simply filled in the prisoner's personal details and changed an item here or there by hand. Others simply forced prisoners to sign blanks pages and then filled them in later at leisure. In this way Soviet organs "unmasked" the "enemy," delivering his "thoughts" to the files. (Snyder 2010a: 82)

The obstacles to collectivization were then removed, since in Belarus, 96.2 percent of the land was collectivized in 1937 (Drweski 1993: 83).

Following the Soviet-German nonaggression pact of 23 August 1939, the Soviet invasion of eastern Poland beginning on 17 September and its subsequent annexation into western Belarus were also marked by mass deportations and executions (Snyder 2010a: 128–130). Operation Barbarossa, launched on 22 June 1941, and the eastward progression of German forces were accompanied by the systematic extermination of Jews, carried out between 22 June 1941 and September and October of that year, especially by the Einsatzgruppen, whose members committed one murder per day, on average (Ingrao 2013: 104). In the regions that came under German civil administration in Belarus and Ukraine at the end of 1941 (White Ruthenia, Volhynia-Podolia, Zhytomyr, Kiev, and Nikolaev), only 1 percent to 5 percent of the one million Jews who had lived in these regions in 1939 remained alive (Dean 2000: 168–169). In *The Complete Black Book of Russian Jewry*, Ilya Ehrenburg and Vasily Grossman (2009: 158–159) recount the events that unfolded in the Belarusian village of Gory in 1941:

> Many Jews lived in the town of Gory: workers, lumberjacks, artisans, craftsmen, and farmers from the Cherny Styag farm. Their blacksmiths, boot makers, and village tailors were known far and wide. Who did not know the blacksmith Abram Altshuler? In Gory there was a high school, a library, a large club, a hospital, and a cultured park where people could relax.
>
> In the summer the linden trees were in bloom. In the autumn the dahlias turned red in the front gardens.
>
> On 19 October 1941, early in the morning, the Germans surrounded the village. A German broke into the home of the eighty-year-old Efros. The old man begged. The German grabbed him by the arm and shouted, "Come on!" Efros replied, "Don't touch me! I have enough strength to go to my grave." The Germans drove the invalid Gurevich from the house next door; his wife Mirra was crying. Gurevich said, "Mirra, you mustn't cry." The Jews were taken to the factory. There a huge grave had been dug. An old woman named Rakhlev yelled, "Not a drop of blood will be forgotten! You will pay for all of this . . . ." She was the first one they killed. The Jews undressed. "I'm cold," little children cried out. Khana Gurevich screamed, "I won't let these reptiles mock my little boy." The aged Efros was the last to be murdered.
>
> On 21 March 1944 the Red Army liberated the village of Gory. They dug up the grave near the factory and discovered a horrible sight. Here a woman with a child in her arms; there a little boy hugging an old woman around the neck, apparently his grandmother. Hundreds of bodies.

The partisan movement was formed during the winter of 1941–1942 (Cerovic 2018). It developed and gathered momentum throughout 1942, through "a patient labor of coordination, organization, and command unification of those troops" (Ingrao 2013: 15). It was accompanied, on the one hand, by repeated pressures on rural people to support the resistance movement and by raids on villages, with the primary aim of killing inhabitants who had collaborated (Sumpf 2013: 637–638), and, on the other hand, by retaliatory measures and "murderous predatory raids against the local peasantry" (Ingrao 2013: 22) conducted by the Nazis. Jews who had managed to flee into the forests also joined the partisan movement, as evidenced by the Bielski network (Dean 2000: 126–127). From the beginning of 1942, the occupying forces launched a veritable "war on Russian peasants and Jews" (Ingrao 2013: 22), leading to acts of mass violence. This took the form of a cynegetic war led by the Dirlewanger unit, in which human beings found in the region were considered "game" (Ingrao 2013: 23). This commando group, initially consisting of eighty men, began operating in Belarus in February 1942. Increasing in size to eventually become a battalion of 750 soldiers, it would remain in place until the collapse of the Center Army Group in the summer of 1944. At the outset, all members of this unit were hunters and poachers, soon joined by men who had served long prison sentences for offenses against people and property. During their time in Belarus, they participated in around fifty "search-and-destroy" operations. They operated with brutality and cruelty, committing many atrocities. Some examples:

> The *Sondereinheit* established, in the summer of 1943, a "method" that was widely copied.... What von Gottberg meant by "mine detector" was to round up the Russians inhabitants of local villages and make them walk in close order in front of the troops in order to detonate any mines, the justification being the presumed complicity of these populations with the partisans.
>
> ... In February 1943, for example, it burned no fewer than ten villages. The exhumation report of the Soviet investigating commission mentions, besides the number of villages and the number killed in each, that neither cartridges nor projectiles were found, and it concluded that the two thousand victims had been burned alive in barns. A witness to the massacres, Alexander Mironov, saw a man, laughing, throw a fourteen-year-old child into a bonfire. (Ingrao 2013: 113)

On 22 March 1943, the Dirlewanger Brigade burned down the village of Khatyn and massacred its 149 inhabitants. Only one man and three children survived (Rudling 2012). This village has since become a symbol of the atrocities committed by Nazi invaders on the civilian population in Belarus. In 1969, a memorial complex erected in Khatyn was inaugurated to commemorate the victims of Nazi barbarism in Belarus (Goujon 2011; Moine and Angell 2011). Between 1941 and 1945, 209 towns out of a total of 270 and 9,200 villages were destroyed (Drweski 1993: 103), with 2,230,000 Belarusian inhabitants losing their lives (Rudling 2012: 29). According to official estimates, the Byelorussian Soviet Socialist Republic lost more than a third of its population. Civilian casualties in Belarus during the Great Patriotic War were among the highest in Europe. "This was a demographic catastrophe of the first order, comparable in historical terms only with events such as the 'Black Death' or the Thirty Years War" (Dean 2000: 119).

Anamnesis

In the post-Soviet context, memories of the Stalinist period are often recounted with reluctance (Bertaux et al. 2005: 8), restraint, and reserve (Gessat-Anstett 2007: 14–15), with significant use of euphemisms (Duprat-Kushtanina 2013: 227). They bring to light discrepancies and distortions between the official, "supervised" memories (Pollack 1993: 30) and individual memories (Figes 2007: 597–656). Similarly, the suffering during the war (Alexievich 2017a) is not necessarily consistent with the glorifying narrative promoted by the Soviet and post-Soviet authorities (Goujon 2010). Many similar accounts have been collected in Belarus, and biographies are seemingly marked by tragedies and traumas. Indeed, it was a struggle to survive in Stalin's time, when members of one's family were deported. It was a struggle to survive during the Great Patriotic War, when the Nazi invader killed and burned nearly everything in his path, and the partisans threatened you to ensure their own survival. This private memory of events relating to these acts of mass violence is an "underground memory" (*mémoire souterraine*; Pollack 1993: 20), which is suppressed, held back, kept quiet. Unspoken memories may "not only be the effect of interdictions from above, they can also stem from the internalization of feelings of inferiority and shame, or the anticipation of discrimination" (Pollack 1993: 22). This private memory sometimes surfaces in terse and concise comments, and sometimes in descriptions relating to a familiar event, a burnt-out house, a confiscated plow, or murdered brothers (Hervouet 2007). Practical knowledge of the authorized discursive forms prompts my interviewees to speak in elliptical terms, and causes them to display physical manifestations—trembling, wringing of hands, watery eyes—of sorrows suddenly recollected from their past.

In October 2012, the carpenter Maksim knocked on the door of his neighbor, Valentina, who asked us to come in. I asked her to tell me about her life on the kolkhoz, and that was virtually the only question I needed to ask. Sitting on the edge of her bed, stroking the cat lying on her lap, she started talking almost uninterruptedly, speaking in Trasânka, a mixture of Russian and Belarusian. Zoya and her husband, friends from Minsk, were with me. Zoya translated into Russian and English for me as the account progressed, switching from chronological milestones to brief comments about key events in her existence. Here are her experiences as she recounted them (via Zoya) that day.

Valentina was seven years old in 1943. She has two sisters. One was born in 1932, the other in 1940—the latter has been paralyzed for several years. She now lives alone in her sister's house. Her story begins during the war. The partisans would come each night, but sometimes "bandits" came too.

They took everything away, even women's underwear. Her father died in 1943. Her mother died in 1950. She had to start working after her father died. They had twenty hectares of land. Her father was a carpenter. The family owned eleven hectares of forest, three cows, two horses, goats, pigs, etc. She then talked about collectivization. In this part of Belarus, which had been Polish before the war, collectivization occurred in 1949–1950. There was no question of complaining. Who would have dared to say no to the authorities? To Stalin? Everything had to be given away—land, tools, animals. As an orphan, she had to work hard. Then, the villagers were able to cultivate a personal plot of twenty-five *sotok* (ares) of land on the kolkhoz. The house she used to live in with her sisters was built between 1960 and 1963. In 1963, she watched helplessly as the *isba* burned down. The women gathered in a circle around the burning house, carrying icons and praying that the wind would change direction and spare the other houses. The wind did indeed change direction and only their house was destroyed by the flames. After the fire, the director of the kolkhoz asked her to leave, but she refused. She was afraid to move to the town and wanted to stay on the kolkhoz. She told us about the *trudodni* (workdays, basis for pay computation). The work was very hard, and you only got paid at the end of the year. You had to provide 250 bucket-loads of food for the animals three times a day. The young pigs would eat 520 grams (1.15 pounds) of food per day. She used to feed 420 pigs. She achieved good results. She was rewarded by the union. The first combine harvester (*kombajn*) appeared in the 1950s, but most of the tasks were carried out by hand. The kolkhoz director was very strict. If potatoes were left in the furrows after the harvest, people were not paid. He was the one who gave permission to leave the kolkhoz and move to the city. Young people would go to Minsk, perhaps for training, but they would subsequently return to the village. Then, in the 1980s, other, younger, directors were sent to the kolkhoz. In 1991, Valentina lost all her savings, which amounted to 7,000 rubles. That was a significant amount of money at the time, equivalent to the price of an ordinary car, such as a Moskvich. Her life story unfolds as a series of losses. Valentina lost her father, then her mother, then her house, and then her savings. She does not want young people to experience what she has been through. She does not want to share that with anyone. She has nephews who have all worked as senior managers in different companies based in cities. They grew up in the village but managed to benefit from higher education and leave the kolkhoz. She receives a pension of two million rubles, or $200. That is enough for her to live on because, as she says, she does not drink. Now, there is no longer any doubt about the course of events to come. She expects nothing better than what fate has in store for her in her old age. Today's difficulties are assessed in light of the terrible situations she experienced before.

It was very cold in the house. The roof was not insulated. At the end of the discussion, as we are left the room, she remained seated, wrapped up in several coats and stroking the cat lying on her lap.

A few days later, in November 2012, accompanied by Zoya and her husband, I met another babushka, Anna, in a village fifty kilometers from Minsk. Anna seemed worried as she greeted me. I explained to her that I was collecting testimonies about life in rural Belarus in the twentieth century. Then Anna commenced telling her story.

During the war, the Germans burned down all the houses in the village, she said. Only the one she still lives in today was spared. Her expression then hinted at the suspicions the family had to endure during and after the war. The countryside was collectivized in 1951. Her parents owned two cows. When she talked about collectivization, about everything that had to be handed over to the kolkhoz, she wept. She remained silent for a long time. Then she talked about the horse they took from her family. One day, when her father was returning from the field in which he had been working with the animal, he was told, "That's the last time you use it; tomorrow you'll have to give it to us." Personally, Anna did not want to join the kolkhoz and work for nothing. But sometimes she was forced to do so, and she concentrated on growing flax. Her stepfather had four brothers. Two of them were sent to Germany. After the war, one of them remained there and then emigrated to Ireland. He became rich. Now he was dead. Anna returned to the subject of the misery of life on the kolkhoz. The people in charge paid you nothing, she said. She referred to the register in which the days worked were recorded, with subsequent payments based on the *trudodien* principle. She talked about her children, two sons and a daughter. One son works on the railways, he has had a higher education. The other works as a laborer in Minsk. They visit every weekend to help their mother by working in the vegetable garden. Her daughter graduated from a technical school, spent two years in Minsk, two years at the Technical Institute in Gomel and then married a German. She lives in Germany. The school is located eleven kilometers away. Until 1985, the bus passed through the village. After that, you had to catch it at a stop three kilometers away. She used to accompany her daughter and went to meet her every day. Today she does not receive a pension because she didn't work on the kolkhoz for long enough. She receives her deceased husband's pension, which amounts to less than $120 per month. She also receives a small amount from the *sel'soviet* but nothing at all from the kolkhoz. "Life goes on" (*žizn' prodalžaet'sa*). In her family, they butcher two pigs a year. It costs 1.2 million rubles to buy two piglets—equivalent to a monthly wage. She also keeps beehives. There are no shops in the village. The nearest is three kilometers away. Delivery men (*avto-

lavki) come to the hamlet several times a week. The local kolkhoz is very inefficient and very poor. Her niece works on a kolkhoz; she is in charge of the animals and earns 1,200,000 rubles, just over $120. Her husband is a mechanic. Three poor kolkhozes were joined together but that just created another poor kolkhoz. She doesn't blame the directors. In fact, she doesn't blame anyone.

On Anna's advice, we then went to an eighty-four-year-old neighbor, who helps her to kill her pigs. He did not understand why I was interviewing him. He said that he used to work on the kolkhoz, as if the details were self-evident. He mentioned collectivization and then talked about a village resident who sang a song about Stalin after the war. He was sentenced to seven years in prison for this. Then he was silent. We left.

For kolkhozians born before 1941, the biographical narrative—sometimes disjointed—systematically returns to the periods of collectivization and the Great Patriotic War. Their lives reflect the fact that people had to work hard before gradually emerging from this long process of survival and sometimes managing to build a home, raise their children, and occasionally look after them as adults in search of employment. Women recount the hard work that marked their lives in a postwar USSR bled dry by conflict, "when the female population, in the words of the popular refrain, replaced 'the men, the horses, and the tractors'" (Bertaux and Garros 1998: 11). Work on the kolkhoz, on the orders of sometimes-violent directors, was poorly paid. People could barely get by on the *trudodni* system, introduced as part of the standard kolkhoz status adopted in 1935. Here is the testimony of Lyudmila, "a Russian woman of the [last] century" who explains how the system operated in the postwar period:

> When the calendar year ended, the kolkhoz did its accounts. It first paid its taxes to the state and divided what was left among the kolkhozians, according to the number of daily work units they had completed during the year. These units were ticked off in a ledger. Small lines were placed alongside the names; that's why people would say that they worked for "sticks." But who could make 365 sticks a year? No one! Because you could only make money by mowing and plowing! And even then, they were awarded according to the yield—so it was not easy to earn a "stick" in a day. It all depended on the land to be worked on and your physical condition. Well, let's say that a strong man managed to earn 300 sticks in a year, what could that get him? The kolkhoz would do its accounts . . . it would have a certain amount of money left over . . . so it would set the daily unit at ten kopecks, for example. Ten kopecks, even multiplied by 300, wouldn't pay off the hundreds of rubles owed in taxes! Where would you get this money from? Because for all the rest, the kolkhozian was paid in kind. He might receive three or four sacks of potatoes. He wasn't going to give them back, was he? And in any case, they were hardly worth anything—you were underpaid for everything you delivered to the state! And don't even think about trying to sell your potatoes if

you haven't paid your taxes! You'd be arrested on the spot! Sabotage! Enemy of the people! (Bertaux and Garros 1998: 56–57)

Conditions in rural areas gradually improved, transforming the "second-class citizen status" (Sumpf 2013: 294–300) previously attributed to kolkhozians. In 1966, the *trudodni* system was replaced by guaranteed remuneration on the kolkhozes. In addition, the payment of pensions to the kolkhozians from 1964, along with the granting of various social benefits (health insurance and leave) and the generalized increase in wages and incomes, improved the material living conditions of the majority of rural people (Maurel 1980: 18). In 1976, kolkhozians were also granted domestic passports, and in 1988 they were allowed to leave their kolkhozes with fewer formalities (Eaton 2004: 135–138). Since the promulgation of the Law of 17 March 1933, kolkhozians had been prohibited from leaving the collective structure without a contract from their future employer that was ratified by the administration. As they were also denied domestic passports, they were no longer legally entitled to travel (Bertaux and Garros 1998: 58).

Occasionally, other events crop up in the discourses. Economic difficulties led to particularly acute shortages in the late 1980s, and the disappearance of accumulated savings in the early 1990s. But the period ushered in by the 1970s was synonymous with a departure from past tragedies, and the difficulties that followed are not presented as having a decisive impact on life trajectories. A more recent event that has also been seen as a new tragedy in people's lives is only mentioned by a handful of people: those affected by Chernobyl (Alexievich 2005). In fact, Belarus was hit particularly hard by the disaster. The number of cancers (of the thyroid, rectum, larynx, etc.), diabetes, blood disorders, and birth defects are reported to have increased significantly (Hervouet 2009a: 155–171). Tens of thousands of people have had to be relocated. Their narratives reflect the pain of being uprooted (Kasperski 2020).

For every member of this generation I met, surviving the tragedies of the past and now having a house, a family, and neighbors who can help them take care of their plot when they reach old age seems to embody the life they have long aspired to lead. Their children have been educated, often enjoy upward social mobility, and have jobs. It would be unreasonable to ask for more. These old women tell me they have enough income to live on. They have nothing more to hope for, settling for a stable status. Although they do not claim to be happy, they do not portray themselves as unhappy. Forming part of self-help networks based on the family, the neighborhood, and the resources of the neighboring kolkhoz, they have constructed their lives by being satisfied with their situation.

EASING OF SOCIAL CONSTRAINTS

Upward Mobility

The narratives of interviewees born after the war have a different tone from those of the previous generation (Hervouet 2009b). These people have different expectations. They want to buy a house with modern comforts, a car, and to offer their children good educational opportunities. Their narratives are more troubled but imply that the threat hanging over their destinies after the collapse of the Soviet Union is now behind them. They are familiar with the rules of life on the kolkhoz, whose continued existence in the 1990s enabled these people to mobilize sufficient resources to make plans for their lives, which remain modest. They do not dream of traveling or consuming more than is strictly necessary. Although the system is sometimes criticized—and in the presence of a Western academic, it seems appropriate not to defend a system accused of being outmoded by experts opposed to the regime—it is never radically challenged. For those who know the rules, it has been possible to build a world that meets the material expectations to which they could reasonably aspire.

Mikhail's biographical narrative is revealing. A product of the postwar rural world, he was able to seize the opportunities offered by the Soviet system, which enabled him to climb the social ladder and build a life for himself as an honest man. We will thus see that this generational approach to biographical narratives highlights differentiated ways of periodizing the Soviet era. "Far from the smooth and uniform history imposed by the 'seventy-years of communism' cliché, this approach supports the idea that 'we should talk about Soviet *regimes*'" (Bertaux and Garros 1998: 17).

Born in 1946, Mikhail was a mechanical engineering teacher in a technical high school. He now received his retirement pension but continued to teach. He lived in a village located a few dozen kilometers from Minsk. Accompanied by his son-in-law, who was a friend, I met him for the first time on 13 April 2006. I entered the apartment. Mikhail invited me to take off my coat and sit comfortably in an armchair in front of the table set for dinner. He immediately adopted a warm manner. He served me vodka, told me he supports the French national soccer team and got me to sample his homemade wine. Very quickly, he began telling me about himself. The questions I ask are intended to elicit a name, a date, or a description of a practice. But Mikhail himself dictated the pace, the sequencing, and the time shifts of his discourse. He created a narrative out of his life.

I met Mikhail and his wife on other occasions in 2006, 2007, and 2008. The discussions followed the same course. In these exchanges, several patterns inevitably recurred, structuring his representation of how his existence had unfolded (Hervouet 2009b: 206–210). He often talked about his father who returned from the Great Patriotic War as an invalid. His foot had frozen. Mikhail repeated that his father worked so hard, despite his disability, that "we didn't know when he slept." When he returned from the war, he had to work on the kolkhoz. His retirement and disability pensions were insufficient to live on. Working on the kolkhoz allowed him to graze his cows, receive some support, and cultivate his vegetable garden there. Nevertheless, he decided to leave this organization. He started looking after the livestock personally owned by the kolkhozians who, in return, paid him in cash or in kind, according to their resources. He earned more in this way. The day after his departure from the kolkhoz, a tractor driver came to dig a trench on his personal sixty-are plot of land: the director informed him that he was taking back half of the cultivable land for the kolkhoz. Mikhail's father reacted immediately. He applied to the military commissariat, managed to regain the use of his plot of land and obtained permission to look after the kolkhozians' cows. His work was very arduous. It was hard to look after the livestock herds. The village was surrounded by marshland inhabited by predators, including wolves. Mikhail's father would sometimes spend the entire night looking for cows bogged down in the swamps. All the men in the village then had to be summoned to pull them out.

Mikhail often talked about his poor childhood and, through his personal experiences, recounted the difficult living conditions in the Belarusian countryside after the war, which were then shared by most of the country's inhabitants. Indeed, 27 percent of the country was urbanized in 1956, and 43.4 percent in 1970 (Richard 2002: 130). He shared happy memories of school, which he attended from the age of six or seven. As soon as the snow melted, he would walk there barefoot, but never got sick. The meals always consisted of potatoes, bread, salt, onions, and *kvass,* a Russian drink made from rye. Despite this, like many Soviets from the rural world, he benefited from upward intergenerational mobility (Arutiunian 1973). In this way, his father managed to finance the university studies of his three children. Mikhail trained as an agricultural mechanical engineer at the Belarusian Institute of Mechanization and Agriculture. His grant was enough for him to live on, but his mother gave him five rubles a month from her savings to make sure that he would not go short of anything, and that he would not have to jeopardize his studies by working on construction sites like other students. Mikhail often referred to the improvement in material conditions permitted by the system. The stores were certainly well stocked in the 1960s, but people's pockets were empty. Kolkhozians began to earn more in the 1970s, but shortages became recurrent. However, Mikhail then pointed out that he acquired his apartment at the age of twenty-six. A few years later, thanks to his father's status as a disabled war veteran, he purchased a large bookshelf and then, in 1975, his first car.

Mikhail described the Soviet world as a slow accession to material comfort and social dignity. His father's suffering was not in vain. Despite the physical hardships he endured—losing his foot in the battle against the enemy, his body exhausted by work—and moral tribulations, such as the retaliatory measures employed by the director of the kolkhoz, his children were able to enjoy upward social mobility and then benefit, like many people in this postwar generation, from a certain degree of material comfort (Vichnevski 2000: 100–103; Lewin 2005: 266–268). It should be remembered that "from 1950 to 1970, Soviet per capita food consumption doubled, disposable income quadrupled, the work week was shortened, welfare benefits increased, consumption of soft goods tripled, and purchases of hard goods rose twelve-fold" (H. Smith 1977: 74). In rural areas, the introduction of the telephone, radio, refrigerator, charcoal-free samovar, and the television were viewed as the "concrete manifestation of the benefits of communism," and the possession of these appliances was seen as the "pinnacle of all progress" (Kéhayan and Kéhayan 1978: 112–115). Mikhail mentioned the different possessions his family managed to own, even specifying the dates of these acquisitions as landmark family events that transformed its members' lives. In this way, he personally benefited from the economic development of Belarus, which had become one of the richest republics in the USSR in terms of annual per capita income by the end of the 1980s. In 1990, this income was estimated at US$4,000—one of the highest in Eastern Europe (Livoskaïa 2001: 104). Mikhail, the son of a kolkhozian, also managed to earn a university degree and become a teacher. The Soviet system even gave him the opportunity to contemplate new personal horizons. For example, in his thirties, he was given the opportunity to train tractor drivers in Angola. He refused to do so, even though the proposed pay was very attractive, and he would have gained access to "special stores" known as *beriozka*. He also recalled a trip to the GDR with a delegation from his hometown and the welcome they gave their East German comrades the following year, in 1975. Respected by his pupils and peers, Mikhail enjoyed a certain prestige in the village where he lived, with everyone I met describing him as an exemplary, dynamic, humble, and honest person. His life also embodied a form of Soviet happiness. Moreover, Mikhail confided—sometimes discreetly, as if he were afraid of how I might judge his words—that there were good things in the Soviet system, and that in any case his life had been better than his parents' lives. During a meal in March 2008, he disclosed, "For a long time, I thought that we were happy, as they told us we were."

When he talked about the end of the Soviet system, Mikhail regularly told me about his children's happiness. He often mentioned his son's house, built over a nine-year period from 1994 to 2003. In the early 1990s, he had no money to build it because all his savings—equivalent to the value of an apartment before the crisis—had dwindled away due to inflation. It was a difficult time. The stores were empty. They started from scratch. He could not borrow from the banks since loans were reserved for the "privileged" classes at that time. His daughter-in-law's father, Dimitri, was a veterinarian on a nearby kolkhoz. The number of livestock was constantly declining. The farm's construction projects were also abandoned, and the available equipment had been disposed of to pay its employees. In addition, although there was no money left to pay wages, there was a specific budget line for loans. Dimitri was able to obtain a loan. This enabled Dimitri and Mikhail to build a home for their children.

But Mikhail often returned to his obsession. He feared that he would not be able to "make his dream come true" and offer his daughter a place to live in Minsk. He had been saving up to buy her an apartment for several years. But his income was growing at a slower rate than property prices. What he seemed to fear in this world created after the collapse of the USSR is that he would fall short of the example set by his father. Certainly, despite the end of the communist system, he was able to offer his son a lovely home, thanks to his hard work and *blat*—"the use of personal networks and informal contacts to obtain goods and services in short supply and to find a way around formal procedures" (Ledeneva 1998: 1). But the conditions remained too difficult for him to imagine doing the same for his daughter. He nevertheless was trying to do so, by working full-time at the high school despite his retired status, and cultivating his vegetable garden whenever he had any free time, to save some money and drastically reduce his spending.

The collapse of the communist system did not lead to a dramatic change in Mikhail's status, but it did force him to alter his domestic and professional priorities. Rather than interrupting his biographical journey, these events merely distorted it. However, this collapse had highly symbolic implications. It called into question his sense of achievement as a man and a father. Consequently, on several occasions during our meetings, he muttered to me that he regrets the collapse of the Soviet Union, even though he is secretly aware that if this historic event had not taken place, he would probably have been unable to admit this to me. He concluded by stating that he lives better than his parents did, and than he did as a child. So the system can work, he said; "There are good kolkhozes in operation today, especially in the Minsk region."

Concerns

For members of this generation, life trajectories are seen as an ascension, disrupted by the transformations introduced by perestroika and the transitional period. The discourse of Andrei Petrovich, a former kolkhoz director, reflects the resentment felt against the changes made to a system that was supposed to satisfy everyone's needs. He was now praising Alexander Lukashenko for restoring the rules of a bygone era. On 20 April 2006, I met Andrei, who was nearly eighty years old at the time (Hervouet 2009b: 215–220). Then retired, he had taught in the same agricultural high school as Mikhail, but had also run a sovkhoz in the 1960s. He felt indebted to my friend Vova, who had recently done him a favor, which is why he felt obliged to agree to the invitation to meet me. He gave the impression of wanting to gain the upper hand from the outset. After all, he was dealing with a Frenchman who, as he saw it, must have rejoiced at the collapse of the USSR, and despised the world built by the communists. The context probably favors such an interpretation. My visit took place very shortly after the Belarusian presidential elections. The media coverage and political attitudes abroad were consistent in their criticism of Lukashenko's regime. In the recorded interview, the retiree's discourse seems carefully structured. It is delivered almost uninterruptedly, and lasts for nearly an hour and a half. He knows that I am interested in life on the kolkhozes. In his comments, presented as a defense and an illustration of an economic system to which he has dedicated his life, Andrei Petrovich is highly critical of the historical turning point of perestroika, a policy which he describes as "totally screwed up" (*bardak*).

He began working on kolkhozes, then barely mechanized, as a child. At the end of the war, he qualified as a tractor driver. He then studied agricultural mechanization at a technical college in a small Belarusian town. After graduating with "high honors," he started teaching in a technical college in the mid-1950s. This institution had a remarkable array of resources at its disposal, according to Andrei: "In the early 1960s, we had fifty or so trucks, sixty tractors, around ten combined agricultural machines, many excavators, and carts at our disposal. This was a period of such plenty that the land-improvement agency once gave us fifteen DT-75 caterpillar tractors, for free. These tractors are still operating today." Then, in July 1963, he was appointed director of a kolkhoz, a post he held until to August 1971. In minute detail, he lists the successes achieved while he was running this institution:

> During this eight-year period, the sovkhoz constructed twelve concrete bridges, built two new hog houses, and rebuilt three existing ones. The sovkhoz raised two thousand hogs. We built three cowsheds and rebuilt more than a dozen livestock buildings. These were seventy by nine meters, or seventy by twelve.... We built a sauna, a store, and a two-story building housing a primary school and a middle school. We mechanized all operations related to cattle rearing, such as milking. In the hog house, we also mechanized several operations, such as fodder distribution.... Under my leadership, the sovkhoz built eight water towers. We drained 1,000 hectares of peat bog: 500 hectares using our own resources and 500 hectares funded by a state-run program. When I left the sovkhoz, these 1,000 hectares were being cultivated.

He considers that kolkhozes and sovkhozes with good directors during this period enjoyed real prosperity. In 1971, he returned to teach at the technical high school. He acted as president of the party cell for his institution, while also spending eight years writing a doctoral thesis. According to Andrei, many interesting technical proposals were made in theses defended at that time, but not all of them were put into practice. He tells us that if all these proposals had been adopted, we would now be living in a communist society.

His hopes were dashed by perestroika. He explains:

> After 1985, the efforts made to develop the kolkhozes, sovkhozes, and industry waned. In my view, the leaders at the highest level were responsible for this change, above all Gorbachev and his close collaborators, who invented this famous "reconstruction" [perestroika] that nobody needed.... To accomplish this "reconstruction," they could have simply abolished the Sixth article of our Constitution which stated that the Communist Party was a guiding force for development and led our society. All that was needed was for companies to be managed by specialists rather than by the party, whose members were incapable of running companies. All this, of course, without denying its successes such as the conquest of space and the development of major companies in Russia and Belarus. All this is to the party's credit.... At that time, it was believed that anyone who had studied at the Communist Party University was "czar, God, and Commander-in-Chief." He considered himself sufficiently competent to give orders to scientists and any specialists. He could look down on everyone.... The party [in this way] proved to be incapable of organizing production in enterprises in a profitable way. The party should have been reorganized instead of reorganizing industry and agriculture. In the end, we caused great damage to our state—more important than that caused by the Great Patriotic War. And all this happened in peacetime.

He welcomes the election of Alexander Lukashenko, which put an end to the "totally screwed-up" policy promoted by Mikhail Gorbachev and continued by Boris Yeltsin, with the support of "Belarusian and Ukrainian spongers."

> The collective mode of production is currently the most efficient.... Lukashenko is maintaining this system, which had almost disappeared. But Lukashenko has turned toward the people and begun to protect them. In the last elections, Lukashenko won an absolute majority of votes.[3] Because the people trust him. He protects them, even if he has his problems and faults. Pensions and wages, although modest, are paid on time, while in other former Soviet republics, and even in Russia, this issue has not yet been resolved. In our country, if wages are not paid on time, business leaders can be punished and even dismissed.... Recently, the economic situation in Belarus has improved considerably. Yields have increased. On certain kolkhozes, wheat yields have reached sixty or even ninety quintals per hectare.

Andrei gives his version of Belarusian history since the war, relating it to the stages of his professional career and the institutional transformations undertaken by the country's leaders. In his discursive strategy, he defines his trajectory as a true vocation. He believed deeply in the progress promised by the Soviet authorities; he sought to do his best to bring this expected reality to fruition, and he believed he could see material signs of the dawning of this bright future in the world around him. Consequently, the reforms undertaken during perestroika not only called into question the rules governing the operation of the institutions in which he works, but also cast doubt on the meaning of his existence, based on work and concern for others, at a deeper level. The term used—*bardak*—is used by other people of his generation who view the transition as a breakdown and who also talk about "Gorbachev's damned perestroika," "mishap" or "*der'mokratiia*," combining the pejorative term *der'mo* (shit) with the idea of democracy (Duprat-Kushtanina and Vapné 2015: 7–8). The "totally screwed-up" policy triggered a real "breakdown in intelligibility" (Bensa and Fassin 2002) in the course of his life, which grieves him, not only because others are no longer "protected" and are at the mercy of "profiteers" and "spongers," but because the coherence and legitimacy of the world to which he has devoted his life are suddenly called into question.

A few days after this interview, Vova's mother told us about Andrei Petrovich. She explained to us that after leading the sovkhoz, he was sick for two years and had to be treated with medication. He avoids mentioning this suffering in his narrative, perhaps because it makes sense to him and he considers that one inevitably has to make personal sacrifices to make the world a more prosperous place. Devoted body and soul to this cause, he rises up against those who, through their reforms, have denied any meaning to his pain. These are the terms in which we should interpret the severity of his accusations, comparing perestroika to the Great Patriotic War, in which 26 million Soviets, including 2.2 million people in Belarus, died.

Stringency of Regulation

These biographical narratives show us which events have influenced life trajectories and daily life. The lives of the generation born before the war were marked by collectivization and the Nazi invasion, followed by difficult working conditions until the normalization of the kolkhozian's status, in a manner of speaking, under Leonid Brezhnev. What happened next does not appear to have had a decisive impact on life trajectories. The difficulties of the 1980s and the economic upheavals that have marked Alexander Lukashenko's regime are viewed as minor. The system implemented in the 1960s, which despite certain modifications continues to operate along broadly the same lines today, is considered to have satisfied basic household needs. The life trajectories of the generations born after the war are described as an ascension, disrupted by perestroika, but normalized by Lukashenko's restoration of conservative policies. This world is seen as being capable of satisfying the collective needs of everyone who accepts its rules. Today, while people still show pride in having personally created or produced the things required for their lives, there is also satisfaction in showing the still rare items that can only be bought, and which people have managed to acquire not only because they have enough money, but also because they have found ways of obtaining them—for example, by managing to obtain a Polish visa and crossing the border to buy a large flat-screen television or a washing machine. Since 2010, several people have told me that certain families spend their holidays in Turkey, the popular new holiday destination. Rare items are markers of success, evidence that the rural world offers opportunities—for those who know how to take them—to access lifestyles that are seen as the definition of civilization. The system is described as allowing everyone to satisfy their needs, using the resources provided by collectivist structures. These narratives do not take the form of heroic biographies of the lives of extraordinary individuals. Instead, they recount broadly similar trajectories.

Consequently, for these generations who manage to acquire these desired goods, it may be all the more immoral to complain about the economic situation, the system, or the president, etc., when things are better than they were throughout the twentieth century. Memories of collectivization, the Nazi invasion and occupation, inflation, and the uncertainty of the 1990s remain vivid in people's discourses. In several meetings, the tragic dimension of the Soviet century suddenly came to light. In April 2006, I was in discussion with an agricultural high school teacher who was describing difficulties concerning the transmission of traditional know-how throughout the century, and then started to talk about deportations. At that very moment, his wife interrupted. Her paternal grandfather had been sentenced to several years of detention in the gulag. He was forced to leave his wife and four children, and no one ever heard from him again. On 5 November 2007, Vova told me about a member of his wife's family who had been deported for several years during his youth, after the Great Patriotic War, for telling a joke about Stalin. Ever since, he had refused to discuss politics, either positively or negatively. On 1 November 2012, I met a master glassmaker in a village about a hundred kilometers from Minsk. He told me about his paternal grandfather, who had been deported to Kazakhstan and died there. His son was fourteen years old at the time and had to dig a grave in the frozen soil to bury his father. While I was talking to an enthusiastic teacher at a technical high school about his trajectory, he explained the toponymy of the place he comes from: Klermont. It has had this name since 1812. It is located near Minsk, far from the most contaminated areas of the country. There are now only a few houses left. In 1986, a radioactive cloud passed overhead and burst over the village.

Nobody realized until 1988, and then its inhabitants were evacuated. I asked him: "Did your parents leave their home?" "They died in it," he replied.

The memory of previous disasters and the awareness of a life in which material expectations have been partially satisfied have shaped attitudes, causing judgments to lean toward the defense of the kolkhoz system. This collective, incorporated history also explains what analysts refer to as the patience of these post-Soviet populations (Coenen-Huther 1997). Economic fluctuations accompanied by inflation and devaluations do not cause despair. In October 2012, I asked the carpenter Maksim how people manage financially. Wages had indeed dropped significantly in the months preceding our discussion, from about $400 to $250. He gave me an explanation. High wages are exceptional if they are compared to the average remuneration over the past decade. Consequently, he said, "we're about back to normal." People then put on hold purchases of items that are not considered strictly necessary; they wait for better days to come and resume their routine in the kolkhoz. When I ask another interlocutor the question "Do people complain?," she replies,

> If they are used to it and have a stable family life, they don't complain. They go to Ukraine, take it easy, and have a normal lifestyle. After the collapse of the USSR, no one knew what was going to happen. Then, people's lives calmed down. Before, there was no electricity in the streets. Now, the streets are well lit, and everything works. On the other hand, when people are alcoholics, they don't take care of anything and therefore they complain. (Svetlana, an engineer nearing retirement, who spends all her free time in a village in Northern Belarus. Unrecorded interview, 29 October 2013)

How can you complain when things are better than before? Also, how can you complain when things are worse elsewhere, as the Russian and Belarusian media report on a daily basis? Therefore, this world is far from being an anomic one. The desires and aspirations of life, curbed by an incorporated history, enable the actors to be satisfied with their living conditions.

These analyses should not lead to the assumption that everyone is satisfied with their lot in life. I have heard recriminations on several occasions. At the end of our discussion, Babushka Maria talked to me about the president, which happened very rarely in the interviews I conducted. She told me that her grandchildren blame him a lot. But she thought that he was making an effort, that he was doing the best he could, and that he needed support, with criticisms making his task even harder. This is a rare example, in my interviews, of a criticism of the political sphere. Her daughter-in-law, she said, tells her that Lukashenko is corrupt. Her grandchildren, who live in the city, say they cannot continue to live on the pittance they are paid. These remarks reflect generational divides. When expressing their dissatisfaction, younger people consider that their earnings should enable them to appropriate things—possessions or an urban life. Urbanization, new information technologies, and easier mobility outside the country's borders are leading to the emergence of new desires. In the end, the babushka did not vote for Lukashenko because of her grandchildren. She did not go to the polls on election day.

In rural areas, however, I have observed that expectations remain limited—from ascetic among older people to moderate in the postwar generations. While not everyone's expectations can be met, some people seem to agree on the acceptability of their lot in life. As certain people succeed, many believe that the system as it exists enables you to get by. These discourses therefore leave no legitimate grounds for complaint. The system provides the resources and rules required to build an honorable life for yourself. If you lament your condition, it is because you are unable to take advantage of these situations and lead an honest life. Only the "spongers" and the alcoholics—those immoral characters– can complain. Their inability to take advantage of the system is not blamed on the defects and failures of the economic and social system, but on their own moral shortcomings.

NOTES

1. In imperial Russia, this term refers to the peasant leader of the rural community.
2. Kalinin was president of the Presidium of the Supreme Soviet and hence the *de jure* leader of the Russian Soviet Federative Socialist Republic and subsequently of the Soviet Union from 1919 to 1946.
3. In 2006, seeking a third consecutive term of office as president, Lukashenko claimed to have won 83 percent of the first-round votes. During these elections, fraud was detected by independent observers.

CHAPTER

7

SOLIDARITY

Analyzing the links between collective and individual histories reveals the emergence of certain ways of legitimizing the existing system. The use of authorized resources and illegal practices enables the construction of acceptable or even desirable worlds, with the extent of this desirability only being comprehensible if the narratives are situated in the context of the entire twentieth century. This conclusion echoes the approach based on a "social compromise" (Fehér, Heller, and Márkus 1983: 104, 277–279) or a "social contract" (Kusin 1978: 179), sometimes colorfully referred to as "gulash socialism." This perspective maintains that the legitimacy of the authoritarian Soviet regime is based on a form of contractual exchange by the citizens and authorities, with the former accepting reduced freedoms in exchange for the fulfillment of their material needs (White 1986). It typically explains the fall of communist regimes by their inability to meet the population's consumption needs. This theory has been discussed in the context of communist regimes (Ragaru and Capelle-Pogăcean 2010: 7–47) and with regard to authoritarian regimes in general (Hibou 2017: 233–254). In the Belarusian context, it is sometimes used to explain the perpetuation of Alexander Lukashenko's regime (Gajduk, Rakova, and Silickij 2009). However, this approach does not take account of the moral and symbolic meanings encapsulated in the organizational structure of rural communities.

Based on the analysis of a social and political ritual,[1] I will show that forms of attachment to the system are not limited to the satisfaction of material needs, but are also connected to values promoted by the regime, in this case, solidarity and a sense of community. In this manner, the regime indirectly produces forms of moral satisfaction that give meaning to the citizens' ordinary existences.

A SOVIET RITUAL

Origins

In 1997, Lukashenko restored the tradition of *subbotniki* (Lapatniova 2001: 76), which are a typically Soviet ritual. This term has usually been translated as "Communist Saturdays" (Labica and Bensussan 1982: 805), although this has now been replaced by "days of voluntary work."[2] What do they entail? These are supposedly nonworking days on which people are called upon to donate their labor for free and on a voluntary basis. This voluntary work generally takes place on Saturdays, or occasionally on Sundays, when it is then referred to as *voskresniki* (Kaplan 1965: 31). It should be noted that, by extension, my interviewees in post-Soviet Belarus referred to any "voluntary" work required at places of work or residence as *subbotnik*, even if it did not take place on a Saturday.

The founding moment of this tradition was a clearly defined event. The first *subbotnik* took place in Russia in the context of the civil war. On Saturday, 12 April 1919, thirteen members of the Communist Party and two sympathizers were working together at the Moscow-Sortirovochnaya depot on the Moscow-Kazan line. They repaired three locomotives required for transporting people and equipment to the Eastern front in order to counter the threat posed by Admiral Kolchak's troops. They were working without remuneration (Chase 1989: 111). On 10 May 1919, 205 people took part in a new *subbotnik* on this same line. They worked without remuneration for between three and six hours. According to *Pravda* on 17 May, the productivity of the loading operations was 270 percent higher than that achieved by ordinary workers; all in all, four locomotives and sixteen carriages were returned to service; 9,300 poods[3] were unloaded or loaded (Lenin 1919). The first mass *subbotnik* was organized nationwide throughout Russia on 1 May 1920. Lenin himself helped clean up a construction site in the Kremlin. With others, he carried a tree trunk to Red Square. A photograph of this scene, revisited by numerous Soviet painters and illustrators, became a legendary image familiar to all Soviets.

Lenin's (1919) prose transforms these "Communist Saturdays" into a paradigmatic figure for socialist labor carried out for "society as a whole": they are "extraordinarily valuable as the actual beginning of communism." The work carried out during *subbotniki* is truly free, as it is carried out for its own sake and not to meet a given need. It ceases to be a means to an end and becomes an end in itself, and because it leads to a higher public good, it is carried out with enthusiasm. In his first text devoted to this issue, Lenin cites a long passage from the *Pravda* issue of 17 May 1919 in full, which describes the spontaneous *subbotnik* of 10 May on the Moscow-Kazan railroad line:

> The enthusiasm and team spirit displayed during work were extraordinary. When the workers, clerks and head office employees without even an oath or argument, caught hold of the forty-pood wheel tire of a passenger locomotive and, like industrious ants, rolled it into place, one's heart was filled with fervent joy at the sight of this collective effort, and one's conviction was strengthened that the victory of the working class was unshakable. (Lenin 1919)

This enthusiasm was reflected by the productivity being far higher than that observed for paid labor. Lenin did not hesitate to talk about the participants' "heroism." They were held up as references and tangible proof of the arrival of the "new man." Therefore, these *subbotniki* constitute a core value in his vision of the building of socialism and reflect its superiority over capitalism. According to Lenin (1919),

> the first communist *subbotnik*, organised by the workers of the Moscow-Kazan Railway in Moscow on 10 May 1919, was of greater historical significance than any of the victories of Hindenburg, or of Foch and the British, in the 1914–18 imperialist war. The victories of the imperialists mean the slaughter of millions of workers for the sake of the profits of the Anglo-American and French multimillionaires, they are the atrocities of doomed capitalism, bloated with over-eating and rotting alive. The communist *subbotnik* organised by the workers of the Moscow Kazan Railway is one of the cells of the new, socialist society, which brings to all the peoples of the earth emancipation from the yoke of capital and from wars.

Institutionalization

"We shall work for years and decades practising *subbotnik*s, developing them, spreading them, improving them and converting them into a habit," wrote Lenin (1920). In accordance with Lenin's desire, this practice was institutionalized in the Soviet Union.

What type of work was carried out? The very first *subbotniki* in April and May 1919 were devoted to repairing locomotives and improving traffic on the Moscow-Kazan line in the context of the civil war. It very quickly became possible to participate, even indirectly, in a collective undertaking. Following the creation of a *subbotniki* bureau in September 1920, people could take part by working, as during their normal working hours, at their factory or administration. The salary corresponding to this work was not paid to the participants but deposited in a fund destined for purchasing food for the children and families of Red Army soldiers (Chase 1989: 117). Very soon, universal participation in the enhancement of urban spaces was also promoted. The *subbotnik* of 1 May 1920, mentioned above, in which Lenin helped clean up a construction site in the Kremlin, is one example. Alexandra M. Kollontaj (1978: 236) mentions these same activities in 1921: "The women unload the wood, clear the snow, sew the soldiers' uniforms, clean the hospital and barracks, etc." The template for *subbotniki* was therefore created at the outset.

When were *subbotniki* organized on a USSR-wide scale? In the postwar period, they became an integral part of everyday life. In the book inspired by his popular television program *Namedni*, Leonid Parfionov (2009: 240) dedicated an article to them, in which he stated that Communist Saturdays became a key *topos* in the national consciousness. After 1945, this practice was also exported to different Eastern-Bloc countries, including the GDR (Sommer 2002: 325), Bulgaria (Palairet 1995: 502), and Hungary (Burawoy and Lukács 1992: 46).

The sixty-two-volume *Grand Encyclopedia*, published in Moscow by Terra in 2006, states that "the frequency of the Communist *subbotniki* was never stable. *Subbotniki* were sometimes held every weekend in certain years, and then only sporadically during the following year" (vol. 48: 512). They were often scheduled for dates close to important anniversary celebrations in the national historiography. In 1957, the Soviet leaders decided, as an extension of the policy of de-Stalinization, to replace the Day of Remembrance of Lenin's Death (21 January) with a *subbotnik* on his birthday, in order, in the official terms, to "keep the spirit of Leninism more alive for eternity" (Binns 1980: 172). From the 1970s onward,[4] a Communist Saturday was systematically organized around 22 April, Lenin's birth date. Others were sometimes organized to prepare for commemorations and/or to celebrate other events, such as the fortieth anniversary of the victory of Moscow over the Nazi army (Yurchak 2006: 272), or the fortieth anniversary of the defeat of the Nazis.[5] There was massive participation in these Communist Saturdays. In 1975, for example, according to the sociologist Christel Lane (1981: 119), around 140 million people took part, out of a total population of 240 million inhabitants. Other *subbotniki* were organized at the regional, district, and municipal levels, at workplaces or by residential buildings.

The number of *subbotniki* in which people were expected to participate varied according to their region of residence and the activity sector in which they worked. When they were organized at the local level, their role was often to assemble a labor force in order to perform an urgent task. They were held in this manner to overcome certain difficulties in kolkhozes and sovkhozes. References to them are made in texts recounting daily life in the Soviet Union. For example, in his *Involuntary Journey to Siberia*, the dissident Andrei Amalrik (1970: 286) recounts the follow details about his day in Gourievka on Sunday 24 July 1966: he is at the police station but only finds one officer on duty, who tells him that everyone has gone off to work on the "Communist Sunday." The anthropologist Caroline Humphrey (2001), who carried out a long field survey at two kolkhozes in Buryatia in the early 1980s, notes the frequency of these voluntary days of labor dedicated to urgent agricultural tasks. She mentions a high-school student's description of her activities in a local newspaper in March 1980: "We organize *voskresniki* (Sunday labor-days) for the cleaning out and heating of the cattle-sheds" (Humphrey 2001: 303). She also records the testimony of a kolkhozian from Buryatia, in an interview with the local press on 5 June 1980:

> We started to harvest only on August 20. It was a bit late. At first I thought, "The grass is too thick, we'll never manage to cut it." But it was all right, they helped me. The specialists of the kolkhoz, the director, and the Party Secretary organized a *subbotnik* [labor-day], and we scythed the whole lot by hand. We got it off the fields in time, before the rains. (Humphrey 2001: 257)

Rebirth

Subbotniki-type practices are found in different countries of the former USSR.[6] However, they generally seem to be organized according to local initiatives and there is no national framework to maintain their distinctiveness as a social and political ritual. In Belarus, the national organization of *subbotniki* re-emerged in 1997, and became a focus of the authorities' attentions. A national *subbotnik* is held each year around 22 April, without any specific reference being made to Lenin. Soviet tradition is thereby faithfully incorporated into the Belarusian present.

Each year, the ritual is symbolically assigned to a specific collective endeavor. For example, republican *subbotniki* have been devoted to the building of the National Library (2003), the restoration of the Khatyn memorial (2004)[7] and monuments commemorating Soviet sacrifices during the Great Patriotic War (2005), the construction of the Minsk-Arena sports and cultural complex (2006 and 2008), the renovation of the Zubrenok children's hospital and school buildings and the building of orphanages (2007), and the building of an aquapark in Minsk (2012). Several million participants are mobilized to participate in these days. To this end, according to the official figures reported by the national daily newspaper *Belarus' Segodnâ* on 22 April 2008, more than 3,500,000 people were believed to have taken part in the event on 19 April—out of a population of around ten million inhabitants.

As in the Soviet era, these nationally organized *subbotniki* are accompanied by a significant number of similar events organized at the regional, district, and municipal level, in workplaces or at residential buildings. In 2012, several local *subbotniki* were organized to provide help for the construction of the new Minsk subway line. In this way, the number of events in which citizens are invited to participate varies from year to year and according to the city or professional activity. The majority of the people interviewed declared that, in the 2000s, they participated in two or three days of voluntary labor per year, and no more than five. According to the principal of a technical high school in a small town forty kilometers from Minsk, there was a maximum of four or five per year in the 2000s, peaking at ten or so in 2003, although they could have been more numerous in the 1990s, given the major difficulties affecting the kolkhozes.

In terms of how the work was organized, a great continuity between the *subbotniki* of the Soviet era and those of post-Soviet Belarus can be observed. On these particular days, certain employees work in their factories or administrations but do not receive their wages, which are directly paid into a special fund that is used to finance a specific collective undertaking (National Library, orphanages, etc.). Others are assigned to cleaning up the streets, urban spaces, and workplaces: picking up litter in public parks, repainting benches and fences, liming trees, cleaning monuments, etc. When they are organized at the local level, *subbotniki* may also bring together a labor force to provide support for certain kolkhozes. Finally, the staging of the ritual by the political authorities varies according to whether it is carried out by the national, regional, or local authorities.

As during the Soviet era, the current Belarusian authorities approach these days in the form of a political ritual. On the one hand, the governing powers often put on a performance to mark these occasions, via codified and repeated gestures. Political leaders personally participate in the collective undertakings, like Lenin in the Kremlin or Lukashenko on the National Library construction project. On the other hand, the citizens are supposed to be motivated by the emotional power generated by the proliferation of selfless acts. The manifestation of the altruistic sentiments expected on these days implies a "non-congruence with the everyday experience" and "the expression of mandatory emotional attitudes" (Mariot 1995: 151). In this sense, participation in *subbotniki* has ritual characteristics: it is a "symbolic comportment (whose meaning [goes] beyond the act itself), which [is] socially standardized and repeated regularly" (Kott 2014: 320).

In line with studies on the GDR in particular (e.g., Kott 2014), the approach I have adopted pays less attention to the "rite-makers" than to the practices, discourses, and ordinary representations deployed in these contexts imposed "from above." From this perspective, the contemporary Belarusian situation constitutes an exceptional research setting. The continuity of practices before and after 1991 is clearly apparent, but the opportunities to access the field, conduct interviews, and observe behaviors contrasts strongly with the opportunities available to researchers during the Soviet era. Consequently, Belarus can be regarded as a veritable laboratory for the analysis of certain practices inherited from the Soviet world. The survey on *subbotniki* was conducted between 2006 and 2008 and involved around fifteen interviewees (Hervouet and Kurilo 2010: 91). Rather than inferring the actors' behaviors from the political rhetoric, which was more easily accessible in the USSR, ethnographers can now observe and interpret the interactions in everyday life and, by ceasing to consider isolated individuals confronted with a top-down ideology, they can analyze the interweaving of official postures, practices situated on local social scenes, and the material supports for these behaviors (F. Weber 2001b). Certain studies conducted by Soviet historians and sociologists and their Western counterparts examining the reasons for participation in this ritual in the communist era concluded that the motivation may stem from a "willingness to obey" (M. Weber 2019: 338) shaped by the expectations of the regime, in accordance with its ideology (Lane 1981: 162–163; Chase 1989: 112). The effectiveness of this ritual could reflect the power of the rhetoric delivered from "above" (Lane 1981: 119). With very fragile empirical materials, they conclude that the participants were enthusiastic participants. It could be considered that these researchers, without adopting methodological safeguards, settled for formulating explanations for politics by politics. In his historiographical analysis of political celebrations in France after 1789, Nicolas Mariot (2008: 119) remarks on the same tendency among many historians to "[politicize] behaviors with disconcerting ease." Access to the field in Belarus enables the researcher to examine this dimension of enthusiasm that is supposed to motivate the participants in *subbotniki*. However, it becomes clear that the people interviewed never directly reproduce the official rhetoric. The survey casts doubt on the role of the state ideology as the driving force behind this mobilization. None of the interviewees explained that they participated for the reasons expressed in the political rhetoric. Criticisms are even formulated, which challenge the legitimacy of this ritual. They can be divided into three categories.

IDEOLOGICAL LIMITATIONS

Forced Labor

Subbotniki are sometimes denounced as being a form of forced labor. In principle, sanctions are prohibited because participation is, in theory, voluntary. In reality, testimonies indicate that punitive measures are applied to nonparticipants in an informal manner: disruptions to work schedules, daily harassments, more stringent inspections at work, nonpayment of end-of-month bonuses, etc. In certain very exceptional cases, they may even lead to dismissal. We will now consider three examples. First, the 2004 report by the Committee of Inquiry of the International Labor Office on trade union rights in Belarus mentions the following case concerning two active members of the Free Belarusian Union, an association created after the strikes in April and May 1991. The workers Evgenov and Bugrov claimed to have been dismissed for refusing to work on a Saturday that had been decreed a working day by the director of the factory without the agreement of the workers in question. The Belarus authorities contested this version, mentioning breaches of discipline at work (ILO 2004: 158–159). Second, the human rights advocacy organization Viasna, created in 1996, mentions proceedings launched in April 2003 at the request of the Grodno branch of the Association of Belarusian Students. The national *subbotnik* was scheduled for 19 April. The university's administrative board, as instructed by the vice-chancellor, Maskevich, ordered the deans of each faculty to organize a clean-up of the campus with the students. By refusing to participate, the association was seeking to draw attention to the binding and illegitimate nature of these practices (Krasnova 2003). Third, in an article published in the journal *Naše mnenie*, the Belarusian political scientist Oleg Grablevski (2011) likens participation in these days to a form of "slavery" (*rabstvo*). He refers to the obligation imposed on workers in the energy sector at Mogilev to participate in the *subbotnik* of 25 June 2011. Failing to participate in the *subbotnik* is considered to be an "unjustified absence." To conclude, Valeri Karbalévitch (2012: 251) formulates a similar interpretation, drawing parallels between a state ruling by discipline and participation in this ritual: "Frightened individuals are easy to govern. They are sent to participate in *subbotniki*; they are obliged to vote 'correctly,' to sign fixed-term employment contracts, to make donations to national projects, to join the official unions and approved youth organizations, to subscribe to state media .... And they obey without making any fuss."

This binding dimension was apparent in the very first *subbotniki* to be organized (Kaplan 1965: 37). Lenin (1919) himself wrote that "the great beginning, the 'communist *subbotniks*,' must also be utilised for another purpose, namely, to purge the Party." This threat was made at a time when the "Red Terror" was being rolled out on a massive scale throughout Russia (Werth 1999a: 71–80). Orlando Figes (1997: 726) even considers that, at the start of the 1920s, "not to 'volunteer' for the *subbotnik* was, after all, to invite suspicion and perhaps persecution as a 'counter-revolutionary.'" Cécile Vaissié (1999: 243) states how, a few decades later, dissidents sought to denounce this situation. At the end of 1981, for example, the SMOT (a free, inter-professional workers' union created in 1978) encouraged workers to stop participating in these days: "It is a call for a strike, but a strike that cannot be punished if the authorities want to maintain the myth of the population's spontaneous participation in these days." The ordinary citizens themselves mock the official discourse vaunting the merits of free and voluntary labor. Amandine Regamey (2007: 126) recounts as much in this *anekdot* from the 1970s, when

> young children were brought together to listen to a participant in the first Communist Saturday sharing his memories:
>
> [He said,] "So, with my friend Fedia, we were told to take a break from our machines and were taken to the *subbotnik*. When we got there, we saw a small fellow wearing a cap, who came up to us and with his strange way of pronouncing the letter 'r', he said: 'Pick up this beam, comrades.'[8]
>
> "'Why don't you get lost?' we said to him.
>
> "Well, I never saw Fedia again, and as for me, I've only been out for a month."

Today, the *Grand Encyclopedia* (2006, vol. 48: 512) acknowledges that in the Soviet era, "the rare non-participants were subject to social and even administrative sanctions."

The Profiteering State

A second criticism can be identified. It is not a day dedicated to the attainment of a selfless social objective (celebrating national unity or helping orphans, etc.), but rather a day whose purpose is to extort more money from the people, for the benefit of certain leaders, or to fill the state's coffers. This is what Elena, a biology teacher at a technical high school in a small Belarusian town forty kilometers from Minsk, had to say in a discussion held in October 2007. She recounted that a *subbotnik* had been organized to enable teachers to help out on a kolkhoz. They preferred to give money to the school administration rather than donate their labor. A few days later, they read in the local newspaper that a banquet had been organized for the directors of kolkhozes around the town and that they had received substantial bonuses. The teachers immediately thought that the sums collected during the *subbotniki* had been used for these purposes. They suspected the state of cheating them.

Other testimonies indicate that it is legally possible to avoid attending the *subbotniki* in return for a payment to one's employer. This implies that the main objective is not universal participation in a common undertaking, but rather an opportunity to extort more money from the workers. When I met

Dimitri in 2007, he was around forty years old and a senior manager in a private firm selling household electrical appliances in Minsk. Each year, when a national *subbotnik* is organized, he said, the company transfers an amount equivalent to the daily wages of all employees into the state coffers, but it does not ask them to come and work. From an organizational standpoint, it would be inefficient to mobilize all their staff for an entire day. "And the state takes advantage of this to fill its coffers," Dimitri said, then continued by telling us the following joke. When Lenin carried the tree trunk to Kremlin square, he was helped by so many people that the complete team could have formed a new Communist Party. By attacking the founding myth behind these days, he indicated metonymically that, in his opinion, the *subbotniki* are a front for a vast ideological deception. The reasons for his critical stance can only be understood by analyzing the position he occupies in the Belarusian social context. Private enterprises are frequently inspected and are subject to numerous constraints imposed by the authorities. The payment of what is considered to be an additional tax also slows the firm's growth. Moreover, private-sector employees do not benefit from the services available to those who work for the state (holiday homes, accommodation, etc.). Consequently, we can assume that Dimitri is more loosely connected than others within the interdependency networks embedded in state-managed structures. In utilitarian terms, this day is therefore interpreted as an additional cost. The denunciation of *subbotniki* is then formulated in more general and more moral terms as an absurdity, an anachronism, and a lie by the state. Here, the survey situation only confirms the strength of his beliefs. In conversation with a Frenchman who is immediately assumed to be a supporter of the ideas of the political opposition to Lukashenko's regime, Dimitri portrayed himself as a member of this young generation that is calling for change, and wanted to appear "modern." By laughing at the joke about Lenin, he was highlighting his rejection of the Soviet past and challenging the current regime while scorning such forms of allegiance and the intrusion of politics into social relations. When I finally asked him whether the *subbotniki* should be abolished, he spontaneously replied, "Of course!"

This criticism was also made during the Soviet era. Traces of it can be found in the writings of Hedrick Smith (1977: 380), head of the *New York Times*' Moscow office for more than three years in the early 1970s:

> In spring, people "donate" an unpaid Saturday (a *subbotnik*) to what is theoretically a voluntary mass spring cleanup. In fact, as one Russian friend remarked, most factories, stores and other agencies simply get a day's unpaid work out of their labor force. Indeed, I noticed that in May 1974, *Pravda* happily reported that 138 million people produced nearly 900 million rubles ($1.2 billion) worth of goods and services on the spring *subbotniks*, confirming that cost-free output was the prime interest in preserving this ritual begun by Lenin.

The Interest of Selflessness

A third criticism of *subbotniki* appears in the discourses. In fact, rather than being completely unpaid, there may be opportunities for participants to benefit from certain goods or services in return. These material incentives play a role from the origins of the movement. In consideration for the work carried out, people receive a half-pound of bread (Kaplan 1965: 38) or enough wood to heat their home for several weeks (Chase 1989: 125). Even today, participation in these days enables people to obtain appreciable material resources in an economic context in which budgets are extremely tight. Irina is a retired primary school teacher. Nevertheless, she continues to work at the village school for a few hours because she cannot make ends meet with her meager pension. During a family meal on 28 October 2007, she recounted that a few weeks before, in September, the principal of the school had sent all the teachers out to pick carrots on the kolkhoz one Thursday afternoon, after the last class of the day. This is a common practice. The kolkhozes regularly require additional labor to accomplish certain tasks. She explained:

> When the weather's bad and the kolkhoz has insufficient labor to carry out all the work required quickly, the Executive Committee decides that all administrations must help the kolkhoz. Each of these organizations has a specific task to accomplish, which is coordinated at the district level, where the allocation of specific establishments to particular kolkhozes is decided. The same situation applies to schools. There are pupils who do not have classes and are sent to work at agricultural holdings. If people help out at the kolkhoz when it is not a *subbotnik*, they must be paid.

> *Can you give some examples of specific tasks?*

> [Her husband Vladimir:] Picking up rocks, putting hay in barns, picking vegetables and potatoes when the weather's bad.... You've got to do everything quickly to prevent the vegetables from rotting in the fields.

> *And do you work with the kolkhozians?*

> [Irina:] The kolkhozians work separately, they do other things. The supervisor comes and shows what you have to do, and the group sent from the establishment does what it has been told to do in the fields. The teachers keep an eye on the students while they are working. (Irina, a teacher at a village primary school, around sixty years old, and her husband Vladimir, a retired teacher at an agricultural high school, also around sixty. Interview recorded on 14 April 2006)

On that particular day, the teachers summoned by the principal of the school had to work for three to four hours. Irina said that she went off to do so very happily. In fact, she immediately realized that she would be able to pilfer some carrots. She jokingly said that they put the bad ones in the cart and kept the best for themselves. She collected two big bags of them—that is, forty kilograms. After a few hours' work, the director of the kolkhoz arrived on the site. He was a former pupil of the school. Some of the teachers present had known him since he was a young child. He thanked them very politely and asked them all not to work too hard. Finally, to show that he was beholden to them, as though he were embarrassed by the fact that the teachers had come to work on his farm, he suggested that they take some carrots. But they had already helped themselves without permission.

Participation in the *subbotniki* also helps ease other constraints. Daily life in Belarus is characterized by a series of procedures that deny people control over their own time (Hervouet 2009a: 27–45). This mandatory mobilization is a manifestation of this heteronomy, but it also often holds the promise being able to claw back some time for oneself in the future. Irina recalled the time when she was the principal of the nursery school. "They"—namely the local Executive Committee—used to ask her to ensure the presence of the school's employees at the *subbotniki*. She clearly explained that she had no legal means of forcing them to do so. However, she could compensate them for their participation by granting them days off work on the dates they wanted, in the framework of authorized annual absences. Caroline Humphrey (2001: 305) mentions a similar situation observed in a kolkhoz in Soviet Buryatia: "The difficulty here, where the nearest market is hundreds of kilometers away, is how to get the goods there . . . . The first necessity is to obtain permission from the brigadier for absence from work and authorization to go to the town—perhaps a bottle of vodka, or attendance at a 'voluntary' *subbotnik* might be required."

Participation in the *subbotniki* also opens up other possibilities. On 4 March 2008, I met Irina's sister, Tatiana. Born in 1942, she worked in a factory in Minsk from 1963 to 1996. She began her career as an ordinary worker, but was steadily promoted and rose through the ranks to become an engineer a few years before retiring. She was involved in the factory's trade union and managed the Children's Committee. As such, she was in charge of the young pioneers' camp attached to the factory. For the *subbotniki*, held only once a year around Lenin's birthday in April, some of the factory's employees were instructed to participate in the upkeep of the pioneers' camp (painting, cleaning, sundry repairs). Tatiana was responsible for allocating the tasks. She insisted on the good times enjoyed during these days. When Tatiana was no longer present, her nephew explained that the "good results" achieved on this occasion ensured that her two daughters would benefit from the best possible treatment during the school holidays at this highly reputed pioneers' camp.

These different criticisms could be taken to imply that the *subbotniki* are meaningless. They appear to be neither truly voluntary nor truly selfless undertakings dedicated to serving a collective cause. The criticisms, both scholarly and local, reveal the lack of performativity of the official discourse. They challenge the analyses that assume enthusiastic support for the discourse of the Soviet regime. The first two criticisms see potential punishment as the sole driving force behind the actions of ordinary citizens. The third is based on the premise of unscrupulousness, with people appearing to act as if they adhered to the discourse, while in reality pursuing purely personal goals. The reasoning proposed in these different analyses is dichotomous: either one adheres to the discourse legitimizing the ritual and participates in it enthusiastically, or one does not believe in the discourse and participates in it out of obligation or self-interest, without sharing any of the regime's views. Certain reflections seek to associate these two approaches within a global analysis. On the basis of a survey conducted in the early 2000s on a sample of twenty-six people residing in the Russian town of Kaluga, Vjačeslav Popkov (2004: 171–172) concludes that the youngest interviewees participated in *subbotniki* under constraint, and the oldest due to their "conviction."

PRACTICAL SOLIDARITY

The Circularity of Exchanges

These interpretive frameworks prevent us from understanding the ambivalent ways of appropriating *subbotniki* that are mentioned by ordinary people interviewed in Belarus, and from comprehending the ambiguous forms of attachment and detachment generated by this ritual. The variable nature of the judgments made about these days reflects their contradictory nature. Indeed, despite the imposed constraints, the discourses collected are relatively uncritical and the descriptions imply that it is possible to participate in them without feeling that one is being exploited and forced to do a "chore." As a consequence, radically critical positions appear to be marginal. In general, they seem to be formulated by people situated outside the established social norms, either because they occupy specific positions in the economic sphere (particularly in the private sector) or because they openly challenge the political regime (such as the militant members of the opposition). The vast majority of the people encountered formulate ambivalent criticisms of the *subbotniki* but never forcefully contest their legitimacy.

The insincerity of the governing figures can therefore be criticized. In this respect, Mikhail's position is revealing. When I met him, he was around fifty years old. Born into a poor kolkhozian family, he had improved his social status and become a teacher of mechanical engineering in an agricultural high school. During our numerous meetings, Mikhail often stressed that he had always felt that he had lived well during the Soviet era and that he still shared the values of solidarity and altruism promoted by the authorities at that time. When he talked about the *subbotniki*, he defended their positive aspects, but what he said indicates that although these forms of altruism existed in the communist world, they did not exist *because of* the political regime. For example, he explained that Lenin's Communist Saturday was perceived in a positive light by the population because it corresponded to the cleanup activities traditionally carried out in the villages before Easter. The conversation continued. A little later, his wife Elena, a teacher of agronomy in the same technical high school and a devout member of the Orthodox church, intervened. She mentioned the *talaka* (a Belarusian term), which could be considered the "righteous opposite of the *subbotnik*." She called it the popular and spontaneous version of Communist Saturdays. This term refers to the mutual assistance practices of villagers after the Great Patriotic War. This insistence on the "popular" and "traditional" foundations of solidarity expressed in this manner reflects the fact that this couple considers it important to explain that they are not fooled by the authorities. This form of discourse is frequently expressed by the people interviewed, who mention the importance of the examples of solidarity mobilized on these days but also the lack of sincerity displayed by the authorities, who are accused of being more interested in counting the money collected than with glorifying the collective work accomplished. Therefore, solidarity is not presented as a manifestation of the effectiveness and mechanical performativity of the official discourses.

The second reservation sometimes expressed concerns the efficiency of the work carried out on these days and echoes the criticisms of the bureaucracy frequently expressed in everyday discussions. The tools required to perform the activity in question are sometimes lacking, or the tasks imposed seem absurd. In this regard, Vladimir, who teaches in a technical high school and is married to Irina, wondered why people are asked to clean the streets by hand when machines were now available to do this job. For all that, he did not state that people should not work on these days. A scene I observed in a small town on Friday, 8 August 2008, is also very revealing. The manager of a residential building summoned the residents to attend a *subbotnik*. They were scheduled to meet at 6 p.m. The aim was to clean up the areas around the building. However, everyone thought that the surroundings were already well maintained. In this case, the criticism took the form of a defection. By 6:30 p.m., the residents were already sitting in front of their television screens to watch the opening ceremony of the Olympic Games in Beijing.

Finally, it should be emphasized that the same people, interviewed on different dates (between 2005 and 2007) and in different situations (face-to-face interactions, family meals, and discussions in the presence of work colleagues), express contradictory opinions. In this way, Irina, in a face-to-face interaction, placed the emphasis on her sense of altruism and on the solidarity expressed within the group during these days. On another occasion, she voiced a different opinion in the presence of her sister Tatiana, insisting on the constraints and on the profits to be made by certain parties. This is her way of challenging the idealized version of *subbotniki* presented by Tatiana as a manifestation of national solidarity. Indeed, not only did Tatiana compel her factory's employees to participate, she also benefited directly from these days, as she was then entitled to send her children to the most prestigious holiday camps. When carried out by other people, such self-interested maneuvering sometimes arouses a certain bitterness, jealousy, and moral reprobation.

These three types of criticisms do not challenge the legitimacy of the organization of *subbotniki*. During a discussion in October 2007, I suddenly ask Irina and her husband Vladimir the following question: "Should the *subbotniki* be abolished?" Vladimir remained silent for a moment. After a pause, he declared, "They are totally pointless if the people just sweep the streets; but they can be beneficial if they keep the factories operating." His wife continued: "It depends. For example, it's a good thing to send the children off to look after elderly people." While the actual reasons for attachment to the *subbotniki* are different from the motivations desired by the political authorities, it can be seen here that the easiest, quickest, and most effective way to answer such a question consists in reproducing the official discourse. These criticisms reflect a detachment in relation to the expectations of the regime, but do not contest the legitimacy of this ritual or the forms of solidarity generated by it.

In fact, the concrete practices involved in participation in the *subbotniki* generate forms of solidarity that could be described as "practical." According to Pierre Bourdieu (2000: 139), "The practical sense is what enables one to act as one 'should' (*ôs dei*, as Aristotle put it) without positing or executing a Kantian 'should', a rule of conduct." By analogy, the practical solidarity generated by the *subbotniki* does not stem from the execution of an explicit order issued from above, but rather the sentiment induced by actions produced in situ in order to adapt to the imposed constraint. Indeed, this ritual seems to take the form of an exchange of good practices. By analyzing this practice over a longer period than the single day on which it takes place, it can be seen that it is consistent with practices involving the pooling of services, undertaken in a circular solidarity context—Alena Ledeneva (1998: 81–83) uses the traditional Russian expression *krugovaja poruka*. Such practices were characteristic of everyday life in the USSR in the 1980s, and are still widespread in post-Soviet Belarus.

Participating in the *subbotnik* is a way to avoid causing problems for the local organizer of the event. If it is not carried out correctly by a sufficient number of people, the person in charge may indeed be punished. As a consequence, he or she becomes indebted to the participants and in return will allow the participants to obtain material benefits from the event, gain access to specific services, or take advantage of certain arrangements in the organization of work, which leads to this occasion being described as the expression of a form of solidarity. It asserts the existence of an "us"—that is, a group of individuals who are highly interdependent at the local level (Yurchak 2006: 108–114). This is the sense in which participation in *subbotniki* is mentioned in discourses as a duty that relates to a practical sense of everyday solidarity rather than a disembodied form of altruism. In the same way, it reflects a solidarity with one's hierarchical superiors that is not dictated by one's unqualified support for a supreme socialist community, but by the common constraints governing individual positions and from which people can partially liberate themselves, together. It is also remarkable to note that the people responsible for organizing the *subbotniki* at the local level also participate in these activities. This is confirmed by the assistant principal of the technical high school, and Irina, the principal of the primary school, now retired. Their insistence on the idea of having to be "exemplary" reflects the importance of pointing out to one's subordinates that they all share a common existence characterized by similar constraints. It is important to note that these reciprocal interests were not clearly verbalized. The exchanges were described in the form of gifts and counter-gifts. Although they are "self-interested donations" (*dons intéressés*; Testart 2007: 161–162), the self-interest must remain concealed or denied in order to ensure that the exchanges appear to be dictated by motivations other than the benefit ultimately obtained (Bourdieu 1994: 94–95). Not only does everyone claim to be acting altruistically, they also genuinely seem to consider these practices morally sound (Ledeneva 1998: 6, 37).

Moreover, this existence of a group, which becomes apparent in these hardly discernible and largely unspoken arrangements, is symbolically reasserted by the organization of exclusive social rituals at certain *subbotniki*. Indeed, participation in these events is often an opportunity for collective socialization. This is borne out by several consistent accounts. People rarely work too hard. "The main point for the organizing official is to show that the *subbotnik* happened, and the only concern of the participants is to be able to say that they participated. Little work tends to get done on these occasions" (Humphrey 2001: 164). It is often an ideal opportunity to organize a picnic for colleagues, who are often neighbors. With the allocation of housing often depending on where one works, it is indeed common for neighbors to be colleagues and vice versa. Sometimes people club together or, alternatively, the participants collectively purchase items to eat and drink together with the money paid—unofficially—by their superiors in exchange for this participation. These days are sometimes described with an air of enchantment. Tatiana recalled how romances had blossomed on such events. She looked back at the history of the factory she joined in 1963, remembering that in the 1960s, the mechanical engineering shop was "full of handsome young workers." The assembly shop was staffed exclusively by young women. There was never any contact between these worlds in the factory's daily routine. Consequently, everyone was keen to take part in the *subbotnik* in order to socialize. She stated that several families were founded in this way. This festive dimension has great resonance in the collective representations, as illustrated by a cartoon published in the third edition of the satirical Belarusian newspaper *Vožyk* (Hedgehog) in 2001. Three strapping lads, dressed in coveralls and wearing a cap or beret, are carrying a cylindrical vessel on their shoulders labeled "Beer." A sign has been erected in the foreground beside the railroad line they are walking on, pointing "To the *subbotnik*." The scene makes a direct reference to Lenin, shouldering a tree trunk with two comrades when cleaning up a construction site at the Kremlin, on the Communist Saturday of 1 May 1920. In this context, these events seem not only to be the manifestation of solidarity-oriented practices, but also a festive celebration of them. This practical solidarity echoes the abstract solidarity promoted by the regime, but it is not a mechanical consequence of the regime's discourse.

For these different reasons, it is easy to understand why people who refuse to take part are frowned upon. They are seen as defying the group, as refusing to allow themselves to join it. They are behaving overly independently, as "free-riders." They are asserting their individuality while ultimately benefiting from the group's efforts, since the performance of the work demanded "from above" enables people to avoid "hassles" (unannounced inspections, sanctions applied to the entire group). Refusers are judged from a moral standpoint as selfish and disdainful. They are suspected of being protected and "sheltered." In this sense, the attitudes adopted by work colleagues and/or neighbors could well be a harsher punishment to bear for failing to participate in a *subbotniki* than any inconvenience the hierarchical superior might impose. The ensuing damage to people's reputations could have a stigmatizing effect and exclude them from a series of everyday networks of material and symbolic exchanges, which are of fundamental importance in contemporary Belarusian life (Hervouet 2009a: 65–95). These are the terms in which Irina's son explained the need for his mother to participate: "If she does not work for free, it's not so much her career or bonuses that she's risking, it's her reputation. Her reputation as a primary school teacher, but also her family's reputation. It's not only on the professional level, it's on the village level. She must be a valuable member of society who is beyond reproach. In general, nobody wants to be the subject of rumors."

However, there are people who do not worry about these informal sanctions. Darya, around thirty years old, was a middle-school teacher. During a meal, her husband mentioned two young sports teachers who used to teach in the same school a few years earlier. After they had graduated, the state had assigned them to the school for two years, and thereafter, they could seek employment wherever they wanted. The teachers in question did not want to remain in this town. Therefore, they were not worried about any sanctions. Consequently, they were prepared to disobey the principal openly and never participated in the *subbotniki*.

Lastly, it can be noted that this practical and symbolic manifestation of solidarity echoes the authorities' stage-managed displays during these rituals. There is a manifest continuity between Lenin's ideological project and the authorities' rhetoric during these events. President Lukashenko maintains that the work carried out on these days must be exemplary precisely because it is carried out for a national cause that surpasses and transcends individual interests. He therefore insists that people must do more than what has been planned and make faster progress than expected. During the national *subbotnik* of 2004, for example, Lukashenko deemed that the rate of work performed at Khatyn was too slow. He said that people needed to increase their efforts. In 2006, he announced that no more time should be granted for the construction of the Minsk-Arena sports complex. He even asked for the duration of the works to be reduced in relation to the initial project.[9] This discourse is stage-managed in a particular manner. The president, in a gesture symbolizing the effacement of the social and political hierarchy, agrees to work personally on a collective undertaking, like all the other citizens. He wears work clothing, dons a hat, cap, or construction hard hat, and works manually on restoring the massacre site at the village of Khatyn, or on the construction of a children's hospital. The photographs displayed on the presidential website show him with shovel in hand, engaged in pouring concrete or cutting thick cables.[10] When *subbotniki* are organized at the regional level, the television cameras are on hand to film the political leaders, equipped with shovels, digging holes to plant trees. The people questioned remain relatively uncritical of these stage-managed actions, without identifying with them or supporting them. This day of solidarity, desired by the authorities, is perceived as such by the participants, but in ways that differ from the manner intended by the authorities.

The ethnographic approach enables the researcher to examine of the ways in which this ritual is commended, criticized, contested, and/or appropriated by ordinary citizens. The participants accomplish this ritual imposed by the authorities according to a logic of "secondary adjustments"

(Goffman 2007: 189). The reasons for their participation in the *subbotniki* differ from those promised and expected by the authorities. The ritual may be reinterpreted, but the meaning instilled in the actions is not independent of the structures and language of power. Although the sense of solidarity experienced as a result of this participation is not a consequence of the authorities' discourse, it nevertheless echoes it. The people negotiate with the prescribed behaviors; they reinterpret them but do not depart from them entirely.

The Principle of Misrecognition

The operation of *subbotniki* is dependent upon powerful systems of horizontal and vertical interdependencies. At the same time, this acceptance of dependency enables the eradication of other types of dependencies, either immediately or subsequently. Participation in these days is therefore a constraint which simultaneously enables the easing of other constraints. Indeed, it allows participants to reduce their economic dependency by obtaining certain material resources and to ease their bureaucratic dependency by obtaining a little room to maneuver in the organization of their daily lives. In this manner, participation in these days is an integral part of the interdependency systems within which the people interviewed further their own interests. In this regard, participation is not pointless, and, furthermore, in the people's perceptions of themselves, it is seen as an action carried out on a moral level. In this regard, it is not illegitimate. These practices generate a sentiment of practical solidarity, which is consistent with the regime's expectations without being a direct product of it. The reasoning for this political and social ritual that emerges from this study can be extended to the general configuration of rural communities.

The description of rural communities has revealed the existence of multiple resources that can be mobilized when one forms part of a network connecting people and groups within interdependency-based relationships. As in the case of the *subbotniki*, the pursuit of personal interests is often carried out and formulated with reference to collective solidarity. While the "structural truth" (Bourdieu 1994: 94), according to which "working for socialism" is "working for oneself" (Kideckel 1993: 101–137), may emerge from the analysis, this cannot be used as a pretext to conclude unilaterally that the "solitude of collectivism" is a formative component of socialist rurality, as the anthropologist David A. Kideckel (1993: xiii) nonetheless proposes with regard to Romania: "The socialist system, though ostensibly designed to create new persons motivated by the needs of groups and of society as a whole, in fact created people who were of necessity self-centered, distrustful, and apathetic to the very core of their beings." Such a conclusion is only meaningful if it is based on one of the following hypotheses: either the interviewees are unprincipled, hypocritical, and lying when they claim to approach these exchanges from a solidarity-based perspective, or they are manifesting a "double consciousness." In this case, this would correspond to "remain[ing] within a philosophy of consciousness and act[ing] as if each agent were inhabited by a double consciousness, a split consciousness, divided against itself, *consciously* repressing a truth which it otherwise knows" (Bourdieu 1998: 97). These two premises fail to account for the feeling of solidarity mentioned by my interviewees who consider themselves to be sincerely altruistic people with a genuine concern for the common good. In fact, "we can only understand the economy of symbolic goods if, from the outset, we [agree to take] this ambiguity seriously, an ambiguity which is not [generated] by the scientist, but which is present in reality itself, a sort of contradiction between subjective truth and objective reality" (Bourdieu 1998: 95).

How can we explain this paradox? Bourdieu (1998: 95) defines the principle of "misrecognition": "This duality is rendered possible, and viable, through a sort of *self-deception* or self-mystification. But this individual *self-deception* is sustained by a collective *self-deception*, a veritable *collective misrecognition*." Alena Ledeneva (1998: 1) takes up this idea and adds a few twists to it in her analysis of the *blat* in the Soviet Union: "*Blat* is the use of personal networks and informal contacts to obtain goods and services in short supply and to find a way around formal procedures." In Russian, this term has negative connotations. It conveys the ability to wheel and deal at the very heart of the system in pursuit of personal gain. It belongs to the semantic field of dishonesty and duplicity. Ledeneva (1998: 60) points out the following paradox: the people interviewed describe personal practices corresponding to the objective definition of *blat*, but refuse to describe them as such. They refer to them as "mutual aid practices," placing the emphasis on the sense of duty and the solidarity-based values binding the people who belong to their network. As in P. Bourdieu's (1998: 95) analysis, misrecognition is made possible by "the fact that through the interposed time interval, those involved in the exchange work, without knowing or planning, to mask or repress the objective truth of their action." The practices are not seen as relating to the transactional logic of quid pro quo arrangements and profit, but rather to the logic of counter-gifts and selflessness. However, when Ledeneva (1998) questions these same people about *blat* in general, they describe analogous practices but interpret them differently. They are perceived to relate to the logic of the quid pro quo principle and are judged negatively. The principle of misrecognition does not govern the entire social world, as in the Kabyle society analyzed by Bourdieu. It does not apply to the practices employed within one's own circle. The criticism of *blat*, systematically related to other people's practices, brings to light the structural truth of the exchanges. It denounces the transactional logic of the quid pro quo principle and exposes the hypocrisy of the practice of counter-gifting lauded by others. Therefore, these reciprocal interests are not verbalized when people are talking about themselves.

When someone does not form part of interdependency networks enabling the mobilization of the rural community's resources and the construction of desirable lives, this person considers the "others" to be society as a whole. When people are isolated, all that emerges is a disenchanted discourse on the unscrupulousness, amorality, or immorality of the members of the village community, and a wistful nostalgia lamenting the old times when people stood together and helped each other out. In this respect, the following testimony is highly significant. In October 2006, I met Ossip, a former student, at her great-aunt's house in a village on the outskirts of Vitebsk. She advised us to visit a friend of hers to discuss life in the village. We knocked on her door, which remained closed. We heard her voice from inside the house. She did not want to open her door to strangers. She was afraid. We explained that her neighbor had sent us to see her. She let us in. Her legs were twisted and deformed. But she did not complain. The conversation started with her telling us why she refuses to talk to people she does not know. She explained that gypsies had recently been bothering her and had tried to extort money from her, and that she had been forced to call the police. She was from the Smoleviči region and came to this village in 1961. Before, people worked hard on the kolkhoz, until nightfall every day. They were paid in *trudodni*. Her husband was a tractor driver and earned a decent wage. She earned "veteran" worker status. She worked at the power plant for many years. Under Brezhnev, everything was cheap, she said. In the 1960s–1980s, there was no corruption like today. She mentioned the director of the kolkhoz at that time. He granted a loan to her husband for reroofing the house. He used to help everyone. He really understood people. She told the story of someone who had drunk too much. The director told him to go home and come back to work later. He dealt with human weaknesses kindly. The leaders today were greedy and selfish. Before, people used to help one another; they were close and concerned about each other. There was the tradition of *talaka*. Now, people no longer supported each other. She then started talking about *Dožinki*. Before, the harvest celebrations were a time for socializing. People used to sing. That also happened on election days. Today, the *Dožinki* had lost their appeal. The directors and managers of the *rajispolkom* (district administration) received televisions as gifts. The tractor drivers got almost nothing, or they were given toys. Before, they received bonuses. Before, the men did not drink as much as they do now. Now, the alcoholics lived off their mothers' pensions. She said that her pension of two million rubles was enough for her. Her son helped out on the plot of land. But he drank too much. Before, they had everything, cows, calves.... Today, young people did not want to stay in the village. Just as we were about to leave, her son came in. He lived nearby. A long silence set in. Ossip gave me a sign that we should leave.

This babushka complained about a world in which everyone is unprincipled. Before, people used to help each other; the workers received real gifts in recognition of their efforts; they were respected because people were aware of everyone's contribution to the accomplishment of the collective undertaking; the director was strict but fair, meaning that he acted in pursuit of the common good. Now, everyone was looking to obtain a personal advantage from every situation. The gifts given at the *Dožinki* did not go to the people who worked the hardest for the community. Listening to her, one could easily conclude that the village has changed radically over recent decades. However, an interview with Maria, my informant's great-aunt, who lived just a few blocks of houses away, did not bear this out at all. Maria told us that she gets by because the residents help each other out.[11] Yet this old woman's perception was very different. She maintained that solidarity had ceased to exist in the situations in which she used to witness it because she had become marginalized in the networks of exchanges. Her household no longer had any tradable resources in the local interdependency system. Her tractor-driving husband was dead; she was sick and disabled; her son was an alcoholic and probably marginalized in the village. Her vision of her environment was formed by demystifying the solidarity lauded by others, and by asserting that people were only thinking of themselves. As she saw it, her village—and by extension, society as a whole—was a world governed not by altruism but by selfishness.

In this way, people's evaluation of the moral dimensions of the social world depend on the configurations in operation. Certain people fail to take advantage of exchanges in the village simply because they have nothing to offer, and then criticize the immorality of those who manage to participate. The distribution of ethical qualities therefore obeys specific social logics. Variable perceptions of morality can be observed according to different contexts, the interviewee's status, the biographical moment of the statement, and the context of the interaction. The boundary of what separates the moral "us" from the immoral "others" is itself fluid. According to the position of the people and their situation, the "us" may include the members of the household, the employees of the kolkhoz, and even the senior managers of agricultural holdings. The "sense of people outside who are not 'Us'" (Hoggart 2009: 57) exists, but it is felt to varying extents, while, at the same time, the boundary separating "us" from "them" is also fluid. Friends and family members are sometimes said to be honest and upstanding, while others are indifferent to the fate of their fellow citizens. Sometimes the distinction is more remote, contrasting the authentically good and altruistic people with the unprincipled and immoral authorities. Sometimes, the whole of society is considered to be corrupted. The same world is both selfish and altruistic.

Therefore, solidarity is not presented as a manifestation of the effectiveness and mechanical performativity of the official discourses. By analyzing the political and social ritual, we observed that although participation in *subbotniki* is imposed, it also opens up new possibilities for the participants. It requires the mobilization of solidarities within a group—with such pleasure being derived from these manifestations of solidarity that certain *subbotniki* become an occasion for festive meals among colleagues and friends. Given the demands imposed by the regime, people implement countermeasures (Goffman 2007: 304) and use "tactics" (Certeau 1988: 36–39) to restore their self-image. Indeed, participation in these days seems to relate to what the German historian Alf Lüdtke (2000: 165) terms *Eigensinn*—"practices of conflictual disengagement which do not come from submission to domination or overt resistance." However, while the "practice of the order constructed by others redistributes its space" (Certeau 1988: 18), the misuses observed do not radically depart from the aims of the authorities. It would be erroneous to see them as a manifestation of the existence of a society of "niches." In fact, this metaphor, which is often used to characterize the communist societies of Europe (e.g., Völker and Flap 1995), suggests that compromise practices are likely to be situated outside the power structure and to exist independently of it. Yet the survey shows that although the meaning attributed by the actors to the actions is not mechanically determined by the authorities, it does directly echo them. Indeed, the effectiveness of the political ritual analyzed stems from the analogical relationship that this ritual maintains with material and symbolic practices that people perceive to be crucially important. This conclusion is consistent with certain analyses carried out on forms of reappropriation of official rituals introduced in the GDR (e.g., Kott 2014: 228–229).

This reasoning can be extended to all rural communities. Although the solidarity encountered is not dictated by orders from above, it does remain a consequence of the adoption of specific behaviors required to cope with the complex system of pressures exerted by the governing authorities. Investment in the system of interdependencies is not a product of the performative effectiveness of the authorities' discourse concerning the power of the group, but rather a product of the dissemination of multiple material, technical, and administrative constraints throughout society as a whole. These problems can only be overcome by the mobilization of numerous interdependent actors. Coping with these difficulties requires mutual aid. In this manner, the regime *indirectly* generates a feeling of practical solidarity that is consistent with its political ideology vaunting the collectivist spirit that is supposed to motivate the members of society.

NOTES

1. This chapter is partially inspired by the following articles: Hervouet and Kurilo 2010; Hervouet 2013a. I would like to thank A. Kurilo for allowing me to include certain analyses that were previously published in a joint article.
2. Consequently, on the official website of the President of the Republic of Belarus, the English expression proposed to designate the *subbotnik* organized throughout the nation is "nationwide day of voluntary work" (retrieved 5 September 2007 from http://www.president.gov.by/en/press15006.print.html). In Russian, *subbotniki* is the plural of *subbotnik*.
3. An ancient unit of mass used in Russia, worth approximately 36,11 pounds. It was abolished in the USSR in 1924.
4. According to the *Soviet Encyclopedic Dictionary* published in Moscow in 1989 (5th ed., p. 619), "Communist Leninist *subbotniki*" have been organized since 1970. According to the *Belaruskaâ èncyklapedyâ* (Belarusian encyclopedia, vol. 15, p. 240), published in Minsk in 2002, they have been held since 1969.
5. This information was reported in the *New York Times* of 5 May 1985.
6. "In contemporary Russia and in other members of the CIS, *subbotnik* is the term used to describe any local or regional improvement work if it is not carried out by specialized organizations. In this manner public and private enterprises carry out the cleaning of buildings and territories with the help of their employees. The administrative bodies of schools and other educational institutions rely on help from their pupils and students" (*Grand Encyclopedia* 2006, vol. 48: 511–512).
7. Inaugurated in 1969, the Khatyn memorial is a monument to the massacre of Belarusian civilians during the Nazi occupation. The 149 inhabitants of this Belarusian village were killed on 22 March 1943. This toponym should not be confused with Katyn, where several thousand Poles were massacred by the NKVD in the spring of 1940 in a forest near Smolensk, in Russia (see chapter 6).
8. These details reveal that this was Lenin.
9. Page of President Alexander Lukashenko's official website (retrieved 5 September 2007 from http://www.president.gov.by/en/press28597.html).
10. For example, the photographs of his participation in the *subbotnik* of 19 April 2003 can be consulted (retrieved 5 November 2020 from http://www.president.gov.by/en/news_en/view/alexander-lukashenko-partakes-in-nationwide-subbotnik-11239/).
11. Chapter 6.

CHAPTER

8

DIGNITY

External perspectives on kolkhozes generally focus on the difficult working conditions, low wages, disorganized production, harsh social relations, alcoholism, and so on. However, ethnographic analysis reveals how the system also generates forms of dignity, which enable the acquisition of social worth in local settings. When the interviewed workers talk about their practices, their projects, or their regrets, they mention the moral motives underlying a meaningful life. These discourses outline a "moral community" (Lamont 2000: 9) that adheres to shared principles and quite explicitly defines the prerequisites for dignity. The collectivized countryside not only generates resources that enable people to satisfy their needs, and bonds that foster adherence to forms of collective life, it also creates places where modes of subjectivation and singularization can be expressed.

WORK

Endurance

The first prerequisite for social worth is an unrelenting commitment to work. A highly regarded worker is, first and foremost, one who performs the tasks expected of him or her in a collective farm. These moral qualities are socially validated by the granting of different bonuses, titles, and official recognition. Alexander, a former kolkhoz director, mentioned these:

There was an entire system of rewards for people who worked well. They were recognized; companies organized celebrations. At the district or party executive committee level, these workers were regularly invited to official meetings where they would receive small bonuses. For Agriculture Day on 20 October—an event that existed in Soviet times—deserving workers could receive rewards such as gifts, etc. There was a whole system in operation to reward people in this way. For example, a flag could be raised in their honor, or their photograph could be put on the honor board, which was displayed in public, and so this also had an impact.... [For housing], these workers obviously had priority. At the time, it was difficult to buy a car, for example. So there was a special list for the kolkhozians who obtained good results. They were able to buy a car more quickly than others. This was also a type of reward. (Alexander, a former kolkhoz director attached to the technical high school, now a teacher in this technical high school. Interview recorded on 21 April 2006)

On several occasions, the people I met showed me medals and decorations they had obtained for their work during their careers. These attributions of honorable distinctions, sometimes embodied in highly regarded material rewards, occasionally take on ritualized forms. I was told about the harvest festival (*prazdnik urožaâ*) organized in certain villages, as in Soviet times. In the cultural center at the kolkhoz headquarters, people congratulate each other as bonuses and rewards are handed out. Everyone is invited to celebrate in the restaurant.

Sergei's trajectory (Hervouet 2009b: 210–213) illustrates how the world of the kolkhoz could generate forms of dignity in Soviet times. I met Sergei and his wife Margarita in November 2007. They were the best friends of Mikhail and his wife Elena, who organized our meeting in their home, over a meal. My friend Vova was present. We took our places around the table. Margarita very quickly told me that Mikhail's father was a great help to her family in the past. This help was all the more precious as her own father was not around. She tersely stated that he had been sent to the gulag "for having survived Stalingrad." Captured by the Nazis in this deadly battle, he returned to the USSR and suffered the same fate as around 360,000 of the 1,545,000 Soviet prisoners who returned from Germany (Werth 1999a: 231). Sergei and Margarita then told me about life in the days before the end of the USSR, when they worked on a sovkhoz located a few dozen kilometers from Minsk. The sovkhozes—state farms—paid their farm workers a fixed wage, while the kolkhozes—collective farms—distributed a share of the common harvest to their members. Wages in the former were higher, and workers received other social benefits, such as housing, but their personal plots of land were smaller than those cultivated by kolkhozians. In practice, the difference between the two forms of collective ownership became "formal" (Maurel 1980: 47) in the 1970s. Sergei and Margarita moved onto this sovkhoz when they were newlyweds. She was an accountant, he was a tractor driver.

I ask Sergei to describe his professional activity. He insisted from the outset that he was considered indispensable. When he was called up for military service in the early 1980s, everyone wanted him to return to the sovkhoz, which he did in 1984. The work was very strenuous. He would start at 8:00 AM and sometimes finish at 10:00 PM. He would then take a shower and not return home until 11:00 PM or even midnight. He did the same again on the next day, at the same pace. But he was well paid. He earned 315 rubles per month and, depending on the quantities harvested, he could receive up to 3,000 rubles in bonuses at the end of the year. It was a time of plenty. Sergei talked about the fuel that never ran short, which people even used for washing their hands. This system encouraged emulation. The tractor drivers were in competition. Some of them used underhand means, such as putting sand in the engines of their competitors' tractors. But others worked honorably, in teams of two. The colleague with whom he shared his tractor quickly became a very close friend, and they continued to see each other regularly now, even though they had not worked together for more than ten years. It was a job that put a strain on your body but allowed you to make a name for yourself and defend your honor as a good worker. Rituals were organized that fostered a sense of belonging to a different group than the others. On the first day of the harvest every year, for example, the machines were lined up together before the start of the working season was declared. Once, the Soviet flag was even raised. This was the Soviet authorities' way of recognizing the figure of the tractor driver, who personified "the application of scientific and technological progress to agricultural production" and, through the work he performed, embodied the "process of eliminating differences between urban and rural life" (Maurel 1980: 88). Sergei remembered these rituals and claimed to have found such practices moving. These carefully staged presentations were simplified as the years went by. He said he regrets this.

Everything changed for him in the early 1990s. The collapse of the USSR was accompanied by an economic crisis that severely affected the country.[1] The sovkhoz often ran out of fuel. Sergei was then unable to work. The machines would break down on a regular basis. He even mentioned that he got angry one day because one of them was immobilized due to a very basic part that was impossible to find. His salary also decreased. But at the time, he was less upset about earning less than working less. The foundations on which the meaning of his social existence was based, which strengthened his body fatigued by working the land, crumbled. He then felt useless, and this pained him. Sergei also talked about the sovkhoz directors appointed to places near the capital, like where he lived. They obtain an apartment there, which quickly increases in value since the place is close to Minsk. He said he considers this real estate speculation scandalous.

He therefore decided on a career change and found a job in the private sector, still underdeveloped in Belarus (Livoskaïa 2001: 107–109). After working for a company that produces soft drinks, he became a driver for a company that sells and installs windows, for which he was now paid a modest salary of one million rubles per month, or about $400. Sergei was appreciated by his work colleagues. He told me that he develops a good reputation wherever he works. When he arrives, nobody knows him. When he wants to leave a place, the employers try to keep him. When he leaves, they tell him that they are willing to take him back whenever he wants. However, Sergei seemed to miss the time when recognition was earned through the travails of very arduous physical work, and when it was manifested by rituals highlighting the importance of his tasks.

At first sight, Sergei's narrative reveals forms of performativity in the state ideology, as if echoing the Stakhanovite figure (Siegelbaum 1988) who marked representations and imaginations in the USSR and Eastern European countries (Bafoil 2016). Yet, while Sergei's pride in his work could be attributed to the fact that it makes him useful to his collective structure, to his company, and more generally to society—he suffered more from being "useless" than from being poorly paid in the 1990s—we can also interpret the situation differently and consider that his position as a tractor driver provided a visible setting for the expression of his strong work ethic, and that other settings also enable this manifestation of a "disciplined self" (Lamont 2000: 4). This would imply that the purpose of the task is less meaningful than the manifestation of arduous physical toil carried out for its own sake. Indeed, other forms of work in the rural world, which are sometimes carefully staged but most often ignored or repressed by official organizations, seem to be equally valued in the discourse of the people I encountered. These forms, induced by the deficiencies of the production system and the inability to satisfy employees by giving them a decent income, are not denounced as scandalous chores. On the contrary, they are seen as complementary modalities that are more or less unofficially authorized by professional or government hierarchies, and which enable people to engage in activities reflecting their endurance and uprightness. Irrespective of the different professional functions performed by the tractor drivers, milkers, sales assistants, teachers, veterinarians and others I encountered, work carried out "on the side" in addition to one's official employment—even though it may be imposed due to short-term economic constraints—is not perceived as a "chore" (F. Weber 1998: 203–204) or as degrading and humiliating "dirty work" (Hughes 1993: 343). It enables people to satisfy their "taste for activity" in its dual active ("appreciation of work performed for its own sake") and productive ("appreciation of the results of the activity") components (F. Weber 2009a: 199). In rural Belarusian communities, as in the world of workers in Montbard

(France) in the 1980s studied by Florence Weber (2009a: 200), "the morality of activity seems to be powerful and shared." As a manifestation of courage, investment in these activities also makes a substantial contribution to forging local reputations and increases the ways in which people can be officially described as "good workers." Indeed, respected people are those who work "around the clock," in both winter and summer, and who never allow themselves to rest. They acquire an "agonistic type of legitimacy," similar to that analyzed by Olivier Schwartz (1990: 293) among workers in the north of France: "Pitting oneself against the elements, putting one's strength to the tests of fatigue and conflict and proving that one is capable of "resisting," are ultimately about expressing oneself in a language in which courage and challenge function as ways of accessing value." Here, working relentlessly means facing up to adversity, the constraints of the kolkhoz, economic fluctuations, and the vagaries of the climate, which inject uncertainty into the functioning of the domestic economy. Several of the people I encountered were praised for their total commitment to both their paid work and their work on the side, thus satisfying their household needs but also preparing for their children's future by building a house, saving a few thousand rubles or a small amount of currency day after day. Mikhail, a retired technical high school teacher, continued to teach classes while tirelessly cultivating his vegetable garden, and spent ten years building a house for his married son, who had two children of his own. This asceticism was also evident among the elderly women I met, who had devoted their lives to work. Thus the theme of endurance becomes a powerful narrative thread in Soviet and post-Soviet daily life (Ries 1997: 59). There is also a significant overlap between the social and institutional qualifications of these qualities, although the former cannot be clearly considered to stem from the latter.

However, two distinctions can be made. First, when the efforts required within a company are perceived as being delegated to subordinates and not shared by the hierarchy, the tasks to be accomplished are seen as unrewarding. Consequently, such tasks are viewed as "dirty work"—not because of the intrinsic characteristics of the activities themselves, but rather due to the social relations they bring into play. For Vladimir, a young mechanic employed by a kolkhoz, the tasks on the kolkhoz are devalued because the management gets rich by taking advantage of informal resources without any consideration and without caring about the group as a whole, leading him to ask, "Why bother working if you can make a living just by stealing?"[2] This implies that "the physically disgusting part of [his] work is directly involved in his relations with other actors in his work drama" (Hughes 1993: 344). Making efforts in this context seems illegitimate and stupid. However, Vladimir still values work itself, failing to turn up for his official work and covering up his absences in order to sell his services to a self-employed carpenter in the village. Second, it should be added that, in reality, two ethics—sometimes contradictory and sometimes complementary—appear in the discourses. Among the vast majority of the oldest people, dignity resides in the efforts made, but sometimes, and especially among the youngest people, it resides in the ability to consume, to acquire everyday consumer items, or even to travel. In some of my encounters, I heard, "If you work for nothing, there's no reason for you to be respected." We can distinguish between a production ethic, in which social worth stems from efforts produced and energy expended, and an acquisition ethic, in which dignity is linked to the ability to possess objects that remain rare. Members of prewar generations expect to consume very little. For members of postwar generations, the production ethic and the acquisition ethic are intertwined and limited. For members of late-twentieth-century generations, the low acquisition capacity associated with hard-earned wages and arduous tasks is considered synonymous with idiocy and a traditional mentality. They attach little importance to the nature of the work as long as it enables them to consume. Consequently, I quite frequently heard of young people wanting to leave the village, not because there are no jobs there, but because the wages are too low. Therefore, the organization of work in rural areas and on the kolkhoz in particular does not mechanically produce forms of investment and arouses recurrent reticence and criticism. However, for the majority of the people I encountered, it also generates forms of dignity based on endurance: directly, due to the physical nature of the efforts required, and indirectly, due to the additional work "on the side" that this requires and allows them to take on. As in the American working classes studied by Michèle Lamont (2000: 4), morality is based on a "caring self" turned toward practices of solidarity but also on a "disciplined self" immersed in a strong sense of effort.

Ingenuity

The second motive for social worth is based on technical expertise and practical intelligence. These discourses are explicit in the comments of the agricultural high school teachers I met. In April 2006 and again in March 2008, I visited a workshop in such a school. Mikhail, a retired teacher who continued to teach there, proudly showed me a lawnmower that his students had made from an electric drill. He showed me machines that the teaching team had designed to teach students how to operate excavators and other mechanical devices. For this reason, the school won various prizes during the Soviet era, not only in Belarus, but also at the national level: the school was honored by the VDNKh (Vystavka Dostiženij Narodnogo Hozâjstva), the Exhibition of National Economic Achievement located in Moscow. An unexpected event occurred during my visit, recorded as follows in my field log:

Mikhail starts up all the machines. A file suddenly flies out from one of them and falls at the feet of his wife and my partner. Mikhail grows pale, apologizes profusely, and keeps saying that he is ashamed, despite our efforts to console him. In his ethos as an upright and responsible man whose workshop mirrors his own qualities, such an incident is perceived as a dramatic event. He then talks about his students who do not concentrate, who are not interested in anything, who do not take care of the machines. He recalls an episode when, behind his back, students put burning paper in a gas tank that was fortunately empty. It contained some oil. In a panic, the pupils poured water on it. "They didn't even know that oil continues to burn in water and that all they had to do was cover the tank to put out the flames." (Field survey log, 4 March 2008)

His students' negligence offended him because it reflected their indifference to his value system. The faulty machine can be seen as a metonymy for his bruised ethos.

This valorization of manual work, engineering, and technical intelligence is promoted by the country's authorities. In March 2008, I accompanied Alexei, Mikhail's son and vice-principal of this same agricultural high school, on a visit to an exhibition, held in Minsk, of objects created by Belarusian technical high school students. Specialists working in this republican center select items sent from different parts of the country. The objects are divided into different categories: electronics, scale models (trucks, planes, boats, etc.), models of buildings (existing or invented), old refurbished motorcycles, and miscellaneous inventions. Andrei explained that to create their models of boats, the students sometimes carry out research in places as far away as Saint Petersburg. The smallest details of these models, such as the thickness of ropes, must be accurate. If string of the right diameter is not sold commercially, the students must make it themselves. Alexei told me about the care, the time, and the patience devoted to the manufacture of these objects. He tried to convey to me his sensitivity to the "aesthetics of production" in evidence there. This "aesthetics of production," as opposed to an "aesthetics of contemplation," "refers to the perceptions of people who are interested in the conditions for production of a sensitive world, i.e. who have both the means to discover its production process and an interest in this knowledge, and who owe their judgment of taste to this very knowledge" (F. Weber 2009a: 216). The technical expertise and aesthetics of production are promoted by the country's authorities. During the previous year, the press, television, and the minister of education were present at the inauguration of the exhibition. This approach, Andrei added, was developed by the Soviets back in 1929, as part of the general movement to glorify Soviet inventors and technology (Sumpf 2013: 642–655). During the communist era, this type of exhibition was held in various countries around the world, including Africa, China, and Austria. It gave the students an opportunity to travel and see the world. Andrei was proud that the agricultural high school, of which he was vice-principal, was taking part in this exhibition for the first time.

Among these teachers in agricultural high schools, the promotion of technical intelligence takes place not only within the school but also in the many activities in which they participate outside it. For example, Mikhail spent ten years building a house for his son.[3] He showed me the fruit of his many years of labor. The "build-it-yourself" process involves multiple competencies that the actors must acquire through imitation, by consulting different publications, through trial and error, with patience, and by acquiring precise knowledge of the qualities of the materials used. The finished house embodies the sum of the project manager's labor and technical qualities, and he thus acquires a certain respectability in the neighborhood.

The valorization of technical performance is not limited to teachers as a group and appears in many of the discourses gathered as a manifestation of a person's qualities. Testimonies often mention universally admired exploits. In 2012, I heard about an uncle who had built a motorized hang glider from different purchased or recycled parts, powered by a car engine. This handyman had no licenses or authorizations and flew his machine illicitly. He was able to assemble and dismantle it quickly, then pack it away in his van. During the same year, Ludmilla told me about the tractor her grandfather had built from an American jeep recovered from the battlefields after the war. A few hours later, a babushka from Polesia, who had had to leave her native village when it was contaminated by the Chernobyl disaster, showed me the tapestries she embroiders herself, based on simple motifs in the tradition of the region she misses. She is self-taught, she told me. She likes to draw. A few weeks earlier, the *sel'soviet* had organized a celebration. This babushka had exhibited her tapestries there, and the television company had sent out a crew to film her. Ingenuity allows those who possess this quality to use different objects—sometimes standardized, sometimes heterogeneous and collected more or less at random—to make and tinker with useful and aesthetically pleasing items. This taste for activity and these ways of valorizing it transcend the boundaries of rural worlds and are not, as in Western societies, essentially confined to popular cultures (F. Weber 2009a: 79–96; Cam 1991; Anteby 2003: 453–471). Also observed in the practices of city dwellers in their dachas (Hervouet 2009a: 130–133), traces of such activities can be found in different social worlds today but also before 1991, in the USSR and Eastern Europe, where they permeated societies. Sometimes attributed to supply constraints, particularly in the construction (Kenedi 1981) and fashionable clothing sectors (Zakharova 2011), this mobilization of manual skills and deployment of material creativity are also the manifestation of a passion that reflects technical, aesthetic, and moral qualities (Haraszti 1976: 138–146; Ries 1997: 56–57).

As such, the following account, published in 1978 by Jean and Nina Kéhayan, is paradigmatic:

> Another extreme case of originality is the touch of madness displayed by a Jew from Leningrad to whom common friends had taken us. . . . At the end of the evening, our hosts, having made sure of our total trustworthiness, decided to tell us about their plans. He worked in an aviation factory and had set his mind on building a helicopter that would enable them to fly to Finland and ultimately make it to Israel. How was he doing this? It was quite simple: for two years now, he had been smuggling parts out of the factory by either recovering them from the stock of defective parts or simply stealing them. We didn't know what to say, having reservations about the feasibility of accomplishing such a crazy project. For Yacha, who liked practising the English that would be useful to him in future, it was *"no problem."* His smile never left his lips; the project couldn't fail and was clearly in his thoughts twenty-four hours a day since he had come up with the idea. Definitely emboldened because we had not made fun of him, he took us by the arm and led us to his lair: a very dark room—the curtains were always drawn—in the middle of which, in an indescribable jumble of scrap metal, tools and plans, stood the skeleton of the monster that one day was supposed to take off from the fifth-floor balcony and whisk this seemingly ordinary little couple up into the air. (Kéhayan and Kéhayan 1978: 202–203)

This account highlights not only a taste for activity for its own sake but also the satisfaction of accomplishing a task, an undertaking, against the injunctions of the hierarchy and beyond the obstacles erected to prevent the accomplishment of the project. The social worth associated with ingenuity is based not only on the material manipulation of the world but also on the ability to bend the rules and to subvert them. This was rarely referred to explicitly in the interviews I conducted in Belarus. Sometimes, by a turn of phrase or in a fleeting smile glimpsed on a person's lips, I understood the pride felt in managing to obtain a given type of material, in having repurposed it, in having managed to gain the trust of a third party and ensure his or her collaboration, or in having managed to convince a particular person to participate in the construction of a house or in harvesting crops on a plot of land. Here, social worth is based on guile. The world is structured around powerful constraints that are perceived as challenges to be overcome. These "banal anabases" (Hervouet 2009a: 31–37)—part of everyday life in communist Europe—sometimes have unfortunate outcomes. For example, Katherine Verdery (1996: 56) talks about a friend of hers who was confronted with the multiple ordinary difficulties that characterized life in communist Romania in the 1980s, and who manages to buy three broken eggs after more than two hours of waiting and heated discussions with a sales assistant in a store; she collapses in tears after leaving the store, feeling "utterly humiliated" at the end of this "ultimate experience of impotence." It is precisely because it is difficult to overcome these obstacles in everyday life that managing to do so produces special forms of contentment. These testimonies echo the words of Alena Ledeneva (1998: 56, 58, 162) when analyzing the emotions aroused by practices of *blat* in the Soviet era: through it, people express their intelligence, efficiency, and creativity—their "ability to get things done." She concludes that when workers manage to "beat the system," they take control of their destiny and the rewards they can gain are not only monetary (Ledeneva 1998: 58). In communist Poland, Janine Wedel (1986: 31) also notes the "satisfaction" of successfully bending the rules of the system. In Belarus today, resourcefulness and cunning are also valued skills.

Enthusiasm

Enthusiasm is a political emotion with an ambiguous status (Mariot 2008), which resonates throughout the revolutionary theories of the twentieth century (Marx 1970; 1972) and recurs in Soviet political discourse. Apparent in Lenin's (1919) texts praising the achievements of *subbotniki* participants, it is presented as an action analysis category in a recent historical account of the postwar reconstruction of Minsk, highlighting the exploits of the city's residents driven by the workers' "enthusiasm" (*na volne trudovogo èntuziazma*; Babkoŭ 2006: 452). This category of the Soviet political and historiographic discourse is also reflected in the village's modes of identification. The figure of the "enthusiast" appears several times in the narratives.

In October 2006, November 2007, and again in March 2008, I met Alexander, an agricultural high school teacher and former director of a small kolkhoz. My friend Vova, who introduced me to him, pointed out that Alexander was an "enthusiast." I asked him to talk about his background, his job, his passions. He did so willingly. I asked few questions, avoided direct references to dysfunctions in the high school and the kolkhoz, and listened to the ways in which he presented his biographical narratives. During these meetings held over quite a lengthy period, he returned to several motivations that gradually revealed why his colleagues, neighbors, and friends considered him an "enthusiast."

He spoke with emotion about his love of beekeeping. A few years ago, the principal of the technical high school in which Alexander taught agronomy purchased some hives for the school and suggested that he look after three of them. As Alexander liked bees, he accepted, hoping that he could place the hives in favorable locations on the several hectares of land managed by the agricultural school. He set them up in a carefully chosen spot between the river and the forest, in the hope of obtaining high-quality honey. He was not willing to settle for a "nondescript" honey with basic aromas; instead, he wanted its flavors to reflect the variety of flora that grew on this land blessed with sufficient sunshine and rainfall. This activity allowed him to remain on good terms with the principal of the agricultural high school—I also learned that Alexander's daughter was an accountant in this school. Beekeeping enabled him not only to satisfy a partner within a local network of interdependencies, but also to earn a valuable additional income. Indeed, part of his production was earmarked for the school canteen and the rest was consumed or sold by Alexander. He told me that "it's hard in winter" because he has to live on a meager salary; however, in summer, he can sell this honey. He also asked me about its production in France: the number of annual harvests, the price per kilogram. But these economic and relational dimensions were played down in his remarks. Above all, he talked about his hives in a passionate way. He could not let a week go by without taking care of them. The buzzing of the bees soothed and relaxed him, and reminded him of his childhood, when a very elderly neighbor with an apiary had asked him for help and, in this way, passed on his know-how to Alexander, who then furthered his knowledge by reading encyclopedias and specialized books. At the end of our first conversation, his wife discreetly retired to a room next to the classroom where we were talking and returned a few moments later with a jar of honey they wanted me to taste. Her husband's face lit up with pride when, taking the spoon out of my mouth, I told him that I found it delicious.

When he first arrived at the technical high school, only his colleague Elena[4] grew plants in her classroom. Elena still continued to cultivate this passion. When we arrived at the school to meet Alexander, she showed me her tall lemon tree, insisted that I smell the scent of its flowers, and then showed me a fruit growing on a branch. The classroom in which Alexander taught was also full of plants and flowers. He did not do this to comply with any hierarchical injunction, and said that he only tends to his plants because he enjoys doing so. In the past, there were only a few old, half-dead cacti. Today, he plants various seeds and attempts to graft certain specimens. "Growing plants is all about experimenting," he said. A few years after his arrival, he and Elena asked the school's management team whether flowers could be grown in the corridors. Their colleagues tried to dissuade them from doing so, explaining that the students would only destroy them. In the end, the plants grew. The enthusiast added that one of his former students had developed the same passion and was now growing plants on her apartment windowsill. They swapped advice when they met in the village. During our conversation, I also learned that fir trees had recently been planted in a park next to the school. It was Alexander who took his students into the forest to collect these saplings and replant them in the park. But relationships with the students were becoming increasingly difficult. He reproached them for having no taste for their studies. For a passionate person like him, it was very difficult to accept that people could have no interest in his expertise, or in what he wanted to pass on.

He also mentioned his vegetable garden. He cultivated the two to three ares of land surrounding his house and twenty-five ares of land managed by the agricultural high school. He grew wheat, which was then used to feed his chickens, and potatoes. He also talked about the experiments he conducted in his garden. Although difficult, the grafting of apples and pears had been a success. He tried to create new hybrids of the varieties in his orchard using wild trees to create fruits with a particular, special, and recognizable taste. Finally, I learned that he was building a house at the bottom of his garden, which he planned to give to one of his daughters. During a third meeting, I was accompanied by my partner, who comes from France. He welcomed us with a glass of wine he had made. He told us that people who never drink wine appreciate his and he asked us for our opinion. Marion and I answered diplomatically and asked questions about how he makes it. He grew two types of grapes: Isabella—in France, this variety was banned in 1935 before its planting was authorized again in 2003—and another that he grew from seeds donated by a Muscovite he met during a stay in a sanatorium.

Alexander kept eighteen hens and one pig. At one time, he used to raise coypus for their fur. He killed one pig a year, in the winter. He drew attention to his original way of slaughtering the animals: he does not force the pig to the ground, as it then squeals, grunts and struggles, and he feels pity for an animal in distress. He instead bleeds the pig while it is still standing. Elena joined the conversation and together they told stories of incompetent villagers. One, in an attempt to electrocute a pig, actually gave his mother an electric shock. Another used a shotgun, aiming at the animal but managing to shoot his colleague in the buttocks, who then had to spend two weeks in the hospital. Elements of tragedy then emerged from Alexander's discourse. When he talked about his expertise, he mentioned his confrontation with the world, but also with history. He explained that kolkhozes did not appear in Western Belarus until 1952. There had been no dekulakization in this region; expertise and know-how had therefore been passed on. In the East, however, where numerous deportations had occurred, the remaining people were those with the least knowledge of how to work the land. His deported stepfather never returned. No one knew what happened to him.

At this point, the expression of his expertise and know-how takes on a new dimension. It reflects the desire to regain forms of dignity that have been destroyed in the past. His discourse is laden with ambiguities. He came back to the idea, echoed by his wife, that because of Stalinist policies, local people here no longer had any connection to the land. They had become, in their own words, "laborers of the land." Then Alexander mentioned President Lukashenko, the heir to Soviet politics, and stated that, thanks to him, the kolkhozes had been reorganized and had grown stronger.

Alexander's anticipation of the honey maturing in his hives, the blooming of the flowers that decorate his classroom, and the ripening of the fruits in his kitchen garden, reflect his sensitivity to the future of the material world that surrounded him. The actual outcomes of his activities—extra income, the satisfaction of a partner in a system of mutual dependency, and the benefits to his reputation—were of minor importance compared with the joy of transforming the world, which he procured from his meticulous interventions. This emotion was based less on ethics than on aesthetics, since it enabled the people in contact with his works, through the way in which they viewed them, to share the beauty of nature with him and banish from their worlds the tendency toward cold calculation and finite perceptions. Thus the enthusiasm driving Alexander was "the feeling of a possible beginning" (Ruby 1997: 7). Because his activities appeared to be selfless and passionate, but also because they benefitted others and aroused vocations, they were perceived as the acts of an "enthusiast."

AUTONOMY

Autarchy

To be worthy, it is not sufficient to be a hard worker blessed with technical skills and cleverness, or even craftiness. To work in a system governed by unstable rules, you must also be able to assert your autonomy. This last quality encapsulates and powerfully expresses the previous ones. It is displayed in many ways, when people are showing me everything they have grown, raised, adapted, or built by themselves (*sam*). Maksim embodies this figure of a self-sufficient utopia, in which the greatest social worth is seen in local representations of reputation.

In my encounters with Maksim, I noticed that he radiated exceptional physical and intellectual energy. We were both about thirty-five years old, but he had already lived several lives. There was a touch of Orwell, Hemingway, Cendrars, and London in Maksim. I met him though friends from Minsk who were friendly with Belarusian artists. He was introduced to me as a visual artist who lived in the countryside. He was a carpenter with a small business based in the small town closest to his village, and he made wooden artworks at his home. After I spent a first day at his house with our mutual friends, he invited me to come back alone a few days later. In November 2012 and October 2013, I traveled by bus from Minsk to the town of 2,500 inhabitants closest to the hamlet where he lived. About eighty people lived in his village. Maksim liked to discuss, exchange opinions, and chat. Adopting a provocative stance, he quickly portrayed himself as an apologist for the Belarusian regime and carefully monitored my reactions. He let me meet some of his friends. He introduced me to Boris, for example, who worked with glass and crystal. Boris had lived in Barcelona and the United States and detested Lukashenko. From the outset, the carpenter was the driving force behind our discussions. When presenting my research activities, I mentioned my survey on dachas—the subject of my doctoral thesis. He asked why, in my opinion, do people visit them so often? I mentioned the products grown there. He immediately interrupted because, as he saw it, I was wrong. He explained that, more often than not, city-dwellers originated from villages: "Growing things is part of their mentality!" Maksim loved to present his arguments. One of his friends had told him about the psychology of crowds, which fascinated him. He added that he would like to study sociology at university. When he was a student teacher, he enjoyed courses on statistics and social analysis.

His testimony, which took on a variety of forms—from personal memories, comments on political and social events, and remarks about manual work, to philosophical questioning or lyrical digressions on art—provides an insight into the motives for autonomy in a stylized manner, and helps to explain the importance of this principle in the moral worlds operating in rural areas. In this way, Maksim is an atypical character. On the one hand, he displayed a strong willingness to engage in verbal sparring, argumentative discussions, and political debates. On the other hand, his background, marked by dependency and the threat of degeneration, graphically illustrates the importance of autonomy in the construction of a personal world.

During our three meetings, Maskim elaborated on personal details of his life. He mentioned the tragic Soviet century in this region. His grandfather was the director of a kolkhoz in the Babruysk region. In 1941, as the Nazis were drawing near, the Bolsheviks began to destroy everything and slaughter the cattle. His grandfather objected to this. They shot him, but he survived and collaborated with the occupying forces. Maksim's great-grandmother, a German from Riga, was deported to Siberia. He mentions his grandmother, who was a "hard woman." At the age of twelve, Maksim was plowing the land, helping in the fields, and earning his first rubles in this way. His parents now lived in Babruysk. For a long time, they worked at the Belšina tire factory, which provided the city's economic lifeblood. At that time, they made a good living. Between them, they earned 600 rubles a month and enjoyed relaxing breaks in the southern USSR. His father, who spent twelve years working for Belšina, now received the same pension as people who worked there all their lives.

In 1995, Maksim spent a year training to be a sports teacher. But his salary was too low. He joined the army as an officer in a detachment of firefighters. He was in charge of maintaining discipline (*zampolit*). His account of his trajectory from that point became somewhat muddled. Here is what I managed to make of it: His marital background was marked by instability. He had been married four times. His first wife, a Tatar and Muslim, "was very beautiful." When he was between twenty-five and twenty-seven years old, he worked in construction (*na strojke*) and became an alcoholic. "When you work on construction sites run by a state-owned company, the workers earn low wages and will inevitably drink," he said. In his work team (*kollectiv*), he drank every day for two years. Then he lost everything in a single month: his job and his family. At twenty-seven years of age, he returned to Babruysk to live with his parents and had to start over from scratch. Maksim then took correspondence courses. After that, he went to work in Leningrad—he insisted on this appellation—for a year. Upon his return to Belarus, he was employed by a private company for one or two years, then moved to the countryside. He became a carpenter. When he decided to move to the village, his mother wept. It was a sign of failure. Then came television reports on his work, and articles in the press, which gave his mother a sense of pride and came as a great relief. Now Maksim worked as a self-employed carpenter and earned $200 a week. It is a private *biznes*. His wife, a manager in a construction company, led a team of five men who respected her. She was the same age as Maksim and had an eighteen-year-old child from a previous union. At the time of our first meeting, they had a several-month-old baby. The carpenter had not drunk a drop of alcohol for several years. He told me vodka puts evil thoughts in his head, making him impatient, dissatisfied, nervous, and angry. He often used to fight after drinking, and lost several teeth in this way.

Maksim was respected in his neighborhood. He worked tirelessly. He was praised and recognized for his technical skills. He knew how to cultivate the land, hunt, and build. Practical knowledge of material things was the motive for his material self-reliance (Crawford 2010: 7). At the same time, the people in the village feared him somewhat and considered him a bad neighbor because he did not drink or fight. His neighbors did not understand him. They laughed about the forest that he rented from the kolkhoz and did not exploit. They describe him as a *čudak*—a "strange guy," an "eccentric." It took him a year to build outdoor latrines, for example, when other villagers are usually happy to nail a few boards together in a single day. He patiently searched the forest for the fine timber he used to create the structure and decorated the interior with mosaics. He also built a small house in a majestic tree. I told him about Italo Calvino, with whom he was not familiar. He was indifferent to mockery and what others might think. He was aware of what made him different. He returned to his interest in statistics and sociology; the villagers wanted the same things as all the other members of society—that is, cars, houses, and opportunities to travel. He mentioned a survey he recently heard about: when asked what they would like to do if they won the lottery, 95 percent of the respondents gave the same answers—buy cars, apartments, holidays—while only 5 percent of the sample expressed different views such as "the desire to build something." He knew he belonged to this minority. Maksim was an artist, a dreamer. Erecting a building with his own hands gave him great pleasure. He took me to a place near his home, at night, and proudly showed me two empty houses that he built entirely using techniques that reflect considerable expertise. The people who commissioned this project never honored their contract and did not pay him for it. He also explained that he has many ideas about architecture in general, that he is gathering information and has a big project in mind: to build a house using techniques employed in the territory of present-day Belarus five thousand years ago. That evening, he showed me a DVD with photographs of the works of a Russian sculptor who uses large wooden buildings to create performances in natural settings.

Maksim showed particular pride in telling me that he lives a self-sufficient life, and that he knows how to obtain everything he needs to live, without recourse to either money or other members of society. This was a recurring theme in his discourses on the three occasions we met. He produced everything. The fruits and vegetables he ate were grown on land he owned or rented from the neighboring kolkhoz. He stored a ton of potatoes in his cellar. He sometimes raised pigs and a few geese. From 1 November each year, he went hunting in the nearby woods, where he shot deer and reindeer. He butchered the animals himself and made his own sausage. He stored meat in his own refrigerator, in a large freezer in Minsk, and also in his parents' freezer in Babruysk. He had planted tobacco which, if necessary, enabled him to avoid buying cigarettes at the village store. He knew about medicinal plants, which he dried in his house, and was familiar with the virtues of certain flowers that he used to make homemade tea. His hives provided him with sugar. For his building projects, he recycled or recovered everything—from bricks found in an abandoned factory to wood from the forest near his home. He told me that he made his *bania* without spending a ruble. In the narration of his robinsonade, he employed motives which were epic and romantic—he was alone in the woods in winter, with a gun in his hand, following the tracks of animals that would feed him or, sitting on the frozen surface of a pond, waiting for the fish to bite—but also apocalyptic. If a major energy crisis were to hit Europe or the world, Belarusians would fare better than Westerners. Here, even without electricity, people could still live, whereas in Western Europe, people were dependent on their objects, technologies, technical processes, and their sophisticated logistics systems. He, Maksim—the village carpenter, a Belarusian Thoreau—could live self-sufficiently, and nothing could touch him.

Independence

As a character, Maksim is enlightening because he is an "ethnographic case study—as we say about clinical cases" (F. Weber 2013: 37). His background and his eloquence make him exceptional. His testimony provides a kaleidoscopic insight into the motives for autonomy in the rural world. In this context, autonomous activity refers to an activity determined by the subject's volition in accordance with his or her personal choices. Indeed, his much-vaunted autarchy reflects his ability to construct a world that follows the rules he has personally laid down. An external perspective on life in or around the kolkhoz points to the powerful heteronomy at work in these social worlds, characterized by hierarchical controls, numerous administrative injunctions, and fragile budgetary resources that make households vulnerable and dependent—in short, a universe characterized by a high degree of uncertainty, which prevents people from projecting themselves into a future that makes sense to them. Maksim's narrative shows that it is possible, in this context, to reappropriate rules and resources for oneself in order to create a personal universe governed by personal rules, and to regain forms of power over one's environment. The carpenter's case is paradigmatic. In several testimonies, personally producing everything required to live well is a recurrent discourse. One person does not need to spend hard-earned rubles to obtain fruits and vegetables; another does not need to buy a house as he can simply build one. This discourse is also present in the testimonies of city-dwellers who garden at their dachas in Belarus (Hervouet 2009a: 65–80) and also in Russia (Ries 2009: 200).

These discourses on autarchy and autonomy very often prompt a shift toward the assertion that these people are not dependent on anyone. However, the notions of autonomy and independence are not strictly synonymous. One can successfully accomplish one's projects in an autonomous manner while relying on resources whose use is dependent on others. Moreover, the autarchic utopias mentioned are populated by people who intervene in order to procure materials, obtain authorization to rent a few hectares of forest from the kolkhoz, or feed the animals when one is busy in the workshop or on a construction site. To construct his world autonomously, Maksim, like the other interlocutors encountered, is entwined in networks of interdependencies that provide him with material, technical, organizational, and administrative support. However, these aspects were ignored, played down, or omitted from his comments. This insistence on independence could be interpreted as the valorization of his inverted biographical trajectory. Long dependent on his employers for successive construction projects, on the vodka that ruined his youth, on his parents with whom he returned to live at the age of twenty-seven, Maksim rebuilt his trajectory by gradually developing a form of autonomy synonymous with regained dignity. In his discourse, this autonomy takes the form of independence: he depends on nobody for work since he is self-employed; he depends on nobody to provide for his needs because he knows how to exploit his natural environment to feed himself; he depends on nobody's way of thinking since he displays an originality that irritates his neighborhood. However, his discourse is ambivalent. Indeed, he asserts his independence but declares his support for Lukashenko, who despises individual freedoms. In this way, he seems to reveal that the system of interdependencies prevailing in rural areas has not prevented him from being himself. On the contrary, he indicates that this system has enabled him to build his autonomy. In my presence as an external observer who, presumably, completely espouses the liberal discourse condemning the incoherence of economic structures established in Belarus, he declares that it is possible, in this context, to assert one's dignity—not by opposing the system, like human rights defenders—but with its help and from within it. Declaring, as Maksim does, that one does not depend on anyone, means declaring that the system is acceptable because one can live with it because it allows people to be autonomous and worthy, provided they have sufficient moral resources to make the efforts required to ensure their autonomy.

Declaring that one does not depend on anyone means simultaneously asserting, through one's actions, that inclusion in networks of interdependencies is not based on ulterior motives—since, theoretically, one could do without them—but on altruism and concern for others. In this way, people claim that they can get by without others, and that they cannot be accused of cynically exploiting them. This is the meaning of the horizon formed by the autarchic utopia. Proving that one could get by on one's own reveals the authenticity of altruism. Moral qualities are validated by other people's perceptions, by one's reputation as an "honest man" earned in and around the village. But for Maksim, this validation of his existence via other people's perceptions appears to be the ultimate obstacle to his proclaimed self-reliance. As Bourdieu (2000: 237) says, "And if God is dead, who can be asked to provide this justification? It has to be sought in the judgement of others, this major principle of uncertainty and insecurity, but also, and without contradiction, of certainty, assurance, consecration." The other solution would be to resurrect this departed God. This enables us to understand and interpret the episode of Maksim's conversion. Early one morning, as we were sharing coffee and tobacco by the stove, he told me the following story. It was the day of *Maslenitsa*, the eve of Great Lent, a few years ago. Everyone had been celebrating throughout the day. In the evening, Maksim went home alone. He felt terrible and thought he was going to die. Then he calmed down. He saw his whole life pass before his eyes and then suddenly felt better. It was a miracle (*čudo*); he had God by his side.

Fairness

The interlocutors state that it is possible to lead a dignified life in the rural world, implying that the existing economic structures enable people—because they have room to maneuver—to create existences associated with values, in their eyes and in the eyes of people around them, or, in other words, which enable them to express their "sense of [self-]worth" (Lamont 2000: 245). By defending themselves against the potential "reduction of oneself" brought about by external injunctions, people can assert themselves "as someone" (F. Weber 2009b: 245–246). Indeed, the people encountered engage in activities that are not pure products of imposed constraints and thus manifest ways of "living as they please" (F. Weber 2009b: 237). These considerations echo Alf Lüdtke's (1990) reflection on workers in Germany during the 1930s. The historian places the "emphasis on the activities and desires through which individuals, alone or in groups, seek to escape the demands and orders from 'above' or 'outside'" (Lüdtke 1990) and uses the term *"Eigensinn"* to qualify them, which is translated into French by F. Weber (2009b: 223) as *"dignité personnelle"*—"personal dignity." More generally, the Belarusian rural world, as described by the people encountered, gives "recognition, consideration, in other words, quite simply, reasons for being" (Bourdieu 2000: 240).

This observation of the possibility of a dignified life is not the result of any performativity in the state ideology that might mechanically shape modes of perception of the world based on discourses that are widely disseminated throughout society, even if, as we have noted, there are resonances between the categories of valorized public intervention and the practical categories used in daily life—sense of effort, technical intelligence, and enthusiasm. The "most salient principles of classification and identification that operate behind workers' evaluations of worth and perceptions of social hierarchies" certainly mobilize the "cultural resources" to which people have access (Lamont 2000: 4, 7). However, while there are insufficient materials to map out these cultural resources, it can be assumed that the state ideology forms only one part of them and that, for example, religious references are also implicitly mobilized. But my interlocutors' *"normative activity"* (Dubet 2016: 5) is, above all, rooted in the "the structural conditions in which they are placed" (Lamont 2000: 7) in their immediate environment. Their perceptions of the world and of themselves are derived from their daily, professional, and domestic practices. This may provide an insight into the "theories that people use to make sense of their lives" and "the taken-for-granted categories they mobilize when interpreting and organizing the differences that surround them" (Lamont 2000: 4). The universe emerging from the three previous chapters is a world where it is possible to support oneself, where the principle of solidarity defines daily relationships, where effort and endurance are rewarded, and where it is possible to live independently by accentuating one's creativity and uniqueness. These valorized forms of life can be considered as relating to "general rules of a syntax that could form the basis—the vocabulary and grammar, as it were—of [my interlocutors'] normative activity" (Dubet 2016: 4). From a pragmatic sociological perspective, we can identify "legitimate forms of the common good, which we call forms of 'worth' [*grandeurs*]" (Boltanski and Thévenot 2006: 19). Indeed, the fair world underlying the collected narratives borrows from the different "polities" (*cités*) identified by Luc Boltanski and Laurent Thévenot. In them, we can identify the importance of "*feelings* and *passions*" (Boltanski and Thévenot 2006: 159) in the "Inspired Polity" (*cité inspirée*), the idea of "renunciation of self-indulgence" (Boltanski and Thévenot 2006: 96) in the "Domestic Polity" (*cité domestique*), and the idea of social utility specific to the "Industrial Polity" (*cité industrielle*). Indeed, the "the ordering of the industrial world is based on the *efficiency* of beings, their *performance*, their *productivity*, and their *capacity* to ensure *normal operations* and to respond usefully to *needs*" (Boltanski and Thévenot 2006: 204). However, the polity model struggles to reveal the foundations of the "moral community" studied in rural Belarusian worlds. The mainsprings of this fair world borrow various elements from different polities without being exclusively embodied by one of them in particular.

However, François Dubet's (2016) sociology of the experience of injustices—albeit with certain adaptations, since there are great differences between the professional and national worlds studied—highlights the essential features of the fair world that permeates discourses without being explicitly reconstructed by my interlocutors. For Dubet (2016: 5), "work is at once *status, exchange value,* and *creative activity*, and each of these 'natures' refers to a principle of justice." The first principle of fairness is equality. "What outrages us, far more than the inequalities themselves, are the vast chasms separating the richest and the poorest" (Dubet 2016: 7). The world described by my interlocutors enables everyone to satisfy their material needs, although there are generational differences in the definition of these needs. Unlike the rural worlds in other countries of the former Soviet Union, in which "proletarianization" (Allina-Pisano 2008: 189) characterizes the rural condition, the Belarusian system provides protection and employment opportunities for all. The second principle of fairness is based on merit. "Assuming that we are all equal, and that every society nevertheless ranks and classifies individuals, the only way to do so is by evaluating the talents, energy, and efforts of free and equal individuals" (Dubet 2016: 8). In the world described by my interlocutors, it is possible, by dint of one's personal energy, to mobilize both authorized and other informal resources, to build desirable life worlds, and thus be rewarded for the efforts made. The third principle of fairness resides in autonomy. "Each of us judges the fairness of his or her work in terms of the freedom, autonomy, and self-fulfillment it affords" (Dubet 2016: 11). In the world described by my interlocutors, it is possible to orient one's actions in accordance with one's own wishes and to express one's uniqueness in certain forms of work. This importance of autonomy in a professional universe seemingly characterized by the dominance of superiors and by varied forms of heteronomy (administrative, bureaucratic, and hierarchical) has also been underlined by François Bafoil (2000). Indeed, when analyzing the motives for the sense of fairness among workers in the GDR, he writes,

> The sense of fairness thus seems to refer to the capacities authorized by the old system within a very constraining environment. Beyond all the constantly denounced injustices, what remains in memories today is the actors' fundamental ability to be autonomous; in other words, the opportunity that is granted to them to bypass a form of control that was generally quite relaxed and to adopt a local management of norms in opposition to it. The ability to challenge norms was a benchmark of individual freedom and fairness, related less to an objective measurement—as recorded by a stopwatch—than to an actual sense of autonomy gained over hierarchical control. (Bafoil 2000: 94–95)

The three principles of justice formulated by Dubet could be accompanied by a fourth principle to reflect the motives of the fair world that emerges from the narratives collected in Belarus. The fourth principle of fairness is based on solidarity. The world described by my interlocutors makes it possible for one's actions to be driven by something other than self-interest. Through experience, moral sentiments such as altruism and generosity are perceived as part of the fabric of everyday life, even if this interpretation is surrounded by profound ambivalence.

In this way, the world of the collectivized countryside can be perceived as a fair world. A distinction must be made between the manner in which external observers evaluate and qualify the environment and that used by the interlocutors I encountered. The analysis does not state that this cosmos *is* fair; it shows why, in the respondents' eyes, it may *appear* to be. It is a world that is not fundamentally unfair, because practical experience of it draws on principles that make sense to the interlocutors: equality, merit, autonomy, and solidarity are possible in this world and enable people to lead dignified and meaningful lives in it.

NOTES

1. In the early 1990s, GDP declined sharply. By 1998, it still had not returned to its 1990 level. In 1998, the annual per capita income was just $1,396—one of the lowest in Eastern Europe (Livoskaïa 2001: 104).
2. Chapter 4.
3. Chapter 6.
4. Elena is married to Mikhail, whose background is presented in chapter 6.

CHAPTER

9

THE FRAGILITY OF THE WORLD

The available resources in rural areas and the ways in which they are mobilized in systems of interdependencies give rise to specific practices endowed with meaning and generating shared values. Through their narratives, the people I encountered paint a picture of moral communities that are unified in relation to identifiable frames of reference: equality, solidarity, merit, and self-reliance, which add up to dignity. Rural communities are therefore governed by norms, rules, and obligations that authorize the expression of forms of fairness. In contrast to the evaluations of "fair and reasonable actions" in rural China characterized by the "plurality of references" (Thireau and Hua 1998: 535), the structuring of norms and morality in this context is based on a stabilized and broadly shared architecture. However, the discussions indicate that these forms of fairness remain fragile. Unfair situations are commented upon, discussed, and denounced in everyday conversations. Examining these experiences and these representations of injustice enables the documentation of the links between the people encountered and everyday politics. In fact, the question of the regime's legitimacy is raised only rarely in the conversations. The system is perceived as a "self-evident fact" (*état de fait*) consisting of "institutions, buildings, machines, tools, texts, categories of perception, of representation, of judgement"—that is, a "an established order of things" (Lahire 2019: 21) enabling the deployment of fair forms of life. Consequently, politics are not discussed, in the sense of exchanges of views about the validity of the rules governing collective life. However, it is mentioned that the system is being undermined by menacing behaviors that are challenging and damaging the foundations on which moral communities are based.

These behaviors are not explained as products of the organization of social and economic life but as a consequence of the lack of morality of the offending people. Therefore, my interviewees refer—sometimes implicitly and sometimes explicitly—to the political mechanisms required to protect or restore the conditions for perpetuating the world as it exists, either by disciplining individuals who are characterized by their moral incompetence with a view to converting them, or by punishing them. The description of the scandalous figures embodied by the "moral offenders" (Lamont 2000: 6) thus enables the observer to understand ordinary citizens' political expectations.

MORAL OFFENDERS

An examination of the informal discussions and "talking situations" (*situations de parole*; Schwartz 1993: 268) that occur during the course of daily life brings to light behaviors mentioned in modes of denunciation and criticism. People who exhibit these behaviors can be divided into three types: profiteers, idlers, and moralists. These types are a researcher's reconstruction proposed on the basis of a compilation of miscellaneous accounts and anecdotes collected in the field. The people interviewed do not use these specific categories, which have no fixed, clearly defined, or established existence in the discussions. These types resemble unofficial countermodels, reconstructed by the sociologist retroactively, to which the inhabitants of rural communities refer more implicitly than explicitly in their verbal exchanges. These three figures, each in their own way, refuse to adhere to the *illusio*, this "fundamental belief in the interest of the game and the value of the stakes which is inherent in that membership" (Bourdieu 2000: 11), that gives meaning to the village cosmogony. They are judged harshly.

Profiteers

Accompanied by my friend Vova, I visited, on 5 November 2007, a poor kolkhoz in Western Belarus with around three hundred employees. "There are lots of old people here and the young ones move away. After a month, and even with free housing, people prefer to leave the village," explained Ekaterina, who was around fifty years old and worked in a service station on the outskirts of the small town. For a long time, she worked in the village grocery store. Her son Denis was around thirty years old. He lived with his mother and stepfather. He did not drink or smoke. Very reserved, he stated that for as long as he could remember, he had always wanted to drive tractors. Ekaterina's daughter graduated from a technical university, married a Frenchman, and now lived in a rural town in northern France. My interviewee's former husband lived just a few kilometers away. He was an alcoholic and never saw his children. Her current husband was a truck driver on the kolkhoz. For a long time, he was the director's personal driver. In winter, he earned no more than $100 per month. During the other months of the year, when there was much more to do, he earned between $300 and $400 per month. Ekaterina, her husband, and son lived very modestly. They raised two pigs in the barn adjoining the house. They would eat one of them and sell the other for a small profit.

Upon my arrival, the vivacious Ekaterina listed all the French presidents elected during the Fifth Republic and proudly declared that she finished her schooling with a nearly perfect score of 4.9 out of 5, but explained that she had not wanted to go into higher education. She was very highly regarded when she worked in the village store. The clients were delighted with the high-quality products she sold in the store. This reputation prompted the owners of the service station to hire her away from the store by offering her a salary of $350 per month. On this Wednesday in November, we visited the grocery store where she used to work. The sales assistant, who was around thirty, worked on the checkout but was struggling with the bookkeeping. Ekaterina told her that she would drop in the evening to help her out. Vova told me that the employee has to manage the store. If there is any unsold stock, she has to boost the cash flow with her own funds. Ekaterina offered to give her replacement some advice. By insisting on her intellectual and moral competencies in this way, she was defining her lofty status in the locality, which legitimized her right to talk about other people. When we sat down to eat lunch together, she, her husband, and her son immediately started criticizing Vlada Borisovna, the director of the kolkhoz, who was sixty-six years old and had been in charge of the collective farm since 1972.

Several different of complaints were made against her. First, she behaved in an unscrupulous manner. She misappropriated the kolkhoz's resources and used them for her own benefit. She took advantage of the institution's driver to attend hospital appointments and used her professional mobile phone for personal calls. This hints at the opacity of certain practices. Another complaint was that the collective farm has its own beehives but "the kolkhozians have never seen a drop of their honey." The director was also accused of lining her pockets at other people's expense. Her house was on the same street as my hosts' home. While strolling through the village, we walked past the director's house, and Ekaterina told me that "people think she also owns apartments in Germany and France." Vova pointed out the terrace on the first floor of the house, stressing that it was an ostentatious sign of wealth. This luxury was all the more scandalous given that her incompetence was ruining the kolkhoz. Denis explained that the collective farm owned two combine harvesters and a few tractors, but the machines were not adapted to the production requirements and it was impossible to plow properly on some of the steep slopes on the farm. His mother also underlined the inconsistencies in the production objectives: carrots are planted one year and beetroot the next, and 15 percent of the harvest is left to rot in the fields because buyers cannot be found at profitable prices. The soil is quickly turned over, to bury what has been grown. Vlada Borisovna was also accused of corrupting the people in power: "She bribes everyone" at the local authority level. She was said to have even more power than the leader of the municipality. Furthermore, she was disrespectful toward the employees and humiliated them. In the village, there were no more than four cows belonging to kolkhozians, and the old people were now too infirm to look after cattle. Yet, I was told, "the director only lets cattle graze in distant fields." My hosts mentioned the potholes and ruts worn in the village's roadways, the handcarts containing mash to feed the cattle that often tipped over, and all the dirty, thankless, and grueling tasks the workers had to perform on a daily basis. Vlada Borisovna also behaved immorally, they said. At Lent during the Soviet era, she used to prevent her own mother, a devout Christian, from following the religious precepts and fasting. Ekaterina's husband, who used to be the director's personal driver, secretly gave fish to the director's mother. Her immorality was compounded by her duplicity. Formerly a zealous atheist, she had since become a devout follower of the Orthodox church. For five years, she had been financing the building of a church by dipping into the kolkhoz's funds, despite the organization being in great difficulty. This church was dedicated to the icon that helps cure alcoholics. Her increasing efforts to display her supposed concern for the moralization of workers publicly through religion were said to be driven more by her desire to access the favors handed out by her superiors than by a desire to promote the redemption and saving of souls. People went almost so far as to suspect her of being evil or devilish. There were also surreptitious murmurings about her former lover, who committed suicide a few years earlier.

Tales of profiteers cropped up repeatedly in the discussions. Ekaterina and her husband also described the case of another kolkhoz. The former director, now the assistant director, was seventy-two years old. He was paid a high salary of $500 to $600 per month. In reality, the agronomist ran the collective farm, but earned much less. "He is young and strong," I was told. "He was picked to do his military service in submarines." In another interview, criticisms were leveled at people who managed to make enough money to buy homes in the city. On this subject, I met the wife of Maksim, the carpenter, in 2012. This urbanite was the senior manager of a real estate construction firm. I talked to her about all the buildings being built so quickly in

Minsk and asked her who was in a position to buy property in this context of crisis. She told me that it is people from rural communities, probably directors of kolkhozes, or high-ranking technicians in the administration of collective farms, who pay cash for apartments costing several tens of thousands of dollars.

In many interviews, criticisms were made of neighbors who enjoyed (a little) more material success than the others. Some of them were denounced for making a profit from their dear mothers' homes and were accused of exploiting unfortunate alcoholics, as in this example from a conversation with Ludmilla, her aunt, and cousin:

> We are talking about our neighbors whose mother was living in the house. She's given it to her children who don't even look after her and she's ninety-six years old. They've built greenhouses to grow flowers in. They pay their employees 25,000 rubles per day, which is less than $3. Only alcoholics are willing to work for that wage. These are people who used to live in Minsk and have returned. (The aunt of Ludmilla, senior manager of a firm in Minsk; her aunt; and cousin, a construction engineer in Minsk. They grow everything the garden of their dacha located in a village. Unrecorded interview, 27 October 2012)

Other people try to do whatever they can to take advantage of the system as they stray from the legitimate path of access to social recognition through hard work and determination.

> In Vova's family, there has been much talk about the neighbors recently. Their children are dirty—they are "wild children." The couple already have four children and the mother has only just turned thirty. She's expecting her fifth. They will then be entitled to subsidized housing. This is frowned upon by Vova's family, who consider that these are people who don't look after their offspring and are still assisted by the state. Vova tells me that they are very cunning people. They have launched an ecotourism project that has actually been presented on the Internet, in the newspapers and even on a tourist map of Belarus. Vova emphasizes the enormous contrast between their lifestyle ("it's the Middle Ages"; "they throw their garbage on the floor") and their ability to communicate via the media. He adds that his late grandfather[1] would have been appalled if he had seen the way these neighbors live. (Field survey log, 29 October 2007)

One year later, this family's case cropped up again in a discussion:

> Vova is talking about the Soutine Museum which has opened in Smiloviči. The family that runs it, which has a poor reputation in the village, keeps an old wardrobe in the museum, which it had "stolen" from a resident of the village, who had then demanded its return but to no avail. (Field survey log, 1 March 2008)

The definition of profiteers is very wide-ranging. With no first-hand knowledge of the alleged offenders' behaviors, the neighbors have to assume or even deduce their potential deviancy from external signs. This visibility is even more noticeable in light of the great conformity that exists in relation to homes, lifestyles, and plots of land. The houses, interiors, and gardens all look alike. When people exhibit signs of success that are not universally shared and not directly the result of manual work that one has carried out in person, they attract suspicion and rumors. In this way, a forest ranger (*lesnik*) whose home is equipped with running water, a water heater, a shower, and indoor toilets is suspected of dishonesty by his neighbors. He is thought to be doing better than everyone else because he is taking unfair advantage of the system. It becomes easier to understand the relationship that is maintained with the idea of equality. When certain people stand out from the others, they are assumed to be taking unfair advantage of the system. Those who fail to benefit from it get the feeling that they are being duped. This attachment to a level playing field is not only the fruit of cultural heritage, even if this attitude is sometimes explained with reference to age-old mentalities shaped by a "culture of envy" or a "tradition of egalitarianism" (Shanin 1972; Van Atta 1993; cited by Hivon 1998b: 34–36). The carpenter Maksim explained to me that people in the villages all want to be alike, and then talked about the era of the *kulaks*, when people who were slightly different were punished. Equality is a focal point that is central to the illusion of the social game. If inequalities become too apparent, people can no longer take comfort in the idea that everyone is pulling together to improve their lot. This suggests that people work until they are worn out solely to be exploited by others.

These stories, anecdotes, and private denunciations constituted gossip and tittle-tattle that are widely incorporated into everyday conversations. This gossiping contributes to "boundary work" (Lamont 2000: 3) between the members of a community and the people who are symbolically excluded from it because they offend the group's recognized values. The discussions concern behaviors, reported statements, and visible signs of a person's status (e.g., a car or the architecture of a house), which are analyzed, interpreted, evaluated, and judged with implicit reference to the moral incompetencies they reflect (unscrupulousness, duplicity, opportunism, insincerity, greed, selfishness, etc.). This gossiping also contributes to maintaining the group's unity, morality, and values (Gluckman 1963: 308). It has "the function of excluding people and of cutting relations. It could serve as a highly effective instrument of rejection" (Elias and Scotson 1994: 94). These behaviors are labeled as deviant. Although they cannot be publicized because they implicate a person in authority, this does not diminish their power to scandalize because they threaten the values upheld by the group. Indeed, the outrage reveals that these values "are not intangible" and leads to a "state of concern, of uncertainty" (Blic and Lemieux 2005: 13). Through its "consuming" and "corrosive" effects, it "reinforces these same values by the very fact that it undermines them" (Dampierre 1954: 335–336). In this way, the gossiping structures the ways in which people evaluate each other at the local level, setting norms to which one must conform or risk denunciation and criticism, and reasserting the principles on which the group is based. The reputations of individuals, who must conform to a given model, are dependent on this gossiping, tittle-tattling, and rumor-mongering. Honest and hardworking citizens are praised, and by describing others in these terms, people—by a mirror effect—identify with this image and consider themselves to be dignified people. Calling into question the level of what is legitimate within the group amounts to challenging the entire ethos that gives meaning to everyone's lives.

Profiteers are people who offend defenders of the values that define the boundaries of the moral community. Because they work only for their own gain and without concern for others, they are assumed to be exploiting the inhabitants of the locality and ignoring the principle of equality that governs social relations. Profiteers, because they use and instrumentalize others, enrich themselves not through their own efforts but by appropriating the work carried out by others. This confiscation of the value produced by other people calls into question the forces of dignity based on merit and self-reliance. But above all, profiteers are people who subvert the principle of solidarity. Most people in a community adopt practices that are presented as a form of mutual aid—described on a moral level as altruistic practices—and in doing so, manage to increase their resources and make their worlds endurable. Admitting that these practices enable the satisfaction of one's own interests would mean having to admit that one is exploiting other people, so this is avoided. Profiteers, however, are people who do not think twice about harming others for their personal gain. They rank their own interests and their self-love above the common morality. They only fulfill their duties if it does not interfere with their own happiness. They only consider others if it imposes no constraints on their own comfort. This defines them as people who opt out of the common morality and who seek to improve their lot in life or satisfy their illegitimate needs by exploiting others. Indeed, "if there is such a thing as morality, it must necessarily link man to goals that go beyond the circle of individual interest" (Durkheim 1961: 65). Profiteers are boundlessly selfish and unscrupulous. They are uninterested in the welfare of others and are devoid of compassion. When everyone lives by pulling together in order to get by collectively, profiteers are seen as people who depart from the common morality, break away from the group and spurn it by riding roughshod over its principles. If certain people in the system operate on an overly personal basis, the others will feel wronged. The illusion of solidarity-based relationships is therefore dispelled, and the world is perceived as corrupted.

The resentment aroused by the figure of the profiteer is exacerbated by conflicting opinions on how to deal with the problem. Profiteers are people who steal and embezzle for their own benefit. Yet people tell me, "Everyone steals." The boundary is blurred between those who portray themselves as altruistic and participate in the flows of goods and services to help others—even if this does not run counter to their own interest—and those who are described as unscrupulous and selfish. There is risk for the whole community, "as government institutions are selective in their compliance with the laws, and in the absence of clear and defined rules of the game, absolutely anyone can be sentenced to prison" (Karbalévitch 2012: 212–213). Consequently, if the authorities intervene, the entire system of village interdependencies, in which a state of equilibrium had previously been maintained, will be jeopardized. As everyone steals, everyone is at risk. This is the principle of suspended punishment, a characteristic of the former Soviet Union (Ledeneva 1998: 77–79) and the former communist bloc (Hibou 2017: 289–295). The feeling of solidarity associated with the flows of gifts and debts within local configurations is reinforced by the diffuse fear that permeates the social entity. The links endure through exchanges of goods and services as a risk of punishment hangs over the different participants. People tell me that "everyone holds everyone else 'in check'"; "everything's tightly controlled"; "the entire system of dependencies rises like a pyramid to the very top." As a consequence, the official rules take on a special meaning. Their very existence is likely to depend on them not being applied to the letter. For people to get by, it would not only be impossible to apply them, but almost immoral. Following them would amount to isolating oneself and breaking the ties of practical solidarity that operate on a daily basis. Exchanges bind individuals to one another and foster a feeling of belonging to an "us" that extends beyond the village boundaries. This increases the animosity toward profiteers, who cannot always be publicly denounced. Not only might they occupy positions of power—like Vlada Borisovna, the director of the kolkhoz—and pose a direct threat to their accusers; denunciation could also jeopardize the informal circuits of local exchanges and compromise honest people whose transgressions can be explained by their desire to help others. Profiteers' behaviors blur the boundaries between genuineness, lies, and insincerity. Therefore, when individual ends prevail over the fragile foundations of a collective life, the local equilibriums are undermined.

Idlers

The second figure is embodied by the idler who lacks the will to work. Profiteers do little work because they exploit other people's labor, but they are reproached more for their unscrupulousness than for their idleness. Alcoholics are the quintessential idlers. Their will to work is destroyed by their dependency on alcohol. The term "alcoholic" is not a medical definition but rather the fruit of a social categorization. These are the people who sell their property (furniture, tools, and sometimes their domestic electrical appliances) in order to consume alcohol. These are the people who fail to work satisfactorily on the kolkhoz, who are dismissed but rehired a few weeks later due to a shortage of labor. These are also the people who might eventually be the beneficiaries of charitable practices. Like the poor person described by Simmel (1965: 140), who is not defined by a "lack of means" but rather as "the individual who receives assistance because of this lack of means," alcoholics are not defined by their excessive alcohol consumption but by the behaviors they adopt and the social reactions they elicit. They are the people who need to be rescued by a form of help that cannot be returned—the kolkhoz director who hires them to give them a final chance, the priest who receives them to support them with prayers, the kolkhoz veterinarian who lends them a mobile phone, the babushka who gives a few clothes to the drunkard who lives on the outskirts of the village.

Alcoholics sometimes arouse sympathy and pity, as recorded in this extract from my field survey log. The scene unfolds in a Western Belarusian village.

> As we arrive, a man passes by. He is under forty years old, with tattoos on his hands indicating that he has probably spent time in prison. He does not want to be photographed by my friend Andrei because the people at the kolkhoz will probably recognize him. He then goes on to talk about his work in a litany of complaints. He is paid less than $250 per month. He used to live in Minsk. We don't know the reasons that brought him to the village with his wife and two children. Perhaps he sold his apartment, spent the money, and was left with no other choice than to find a place on a kolkhoz that would house him in return for his labor. With his horse, he does the rounds of the village collecting privately produced milk and then delivers it to the kolkhoz. He works every day, including weekends, starting very early in the morning. When he arrives, two parcels have already been prepared for him by the women I'm visiting, containing things for the newborn baby, including powdered milk which, for him, is very expensive. He will soon become a grandfather (at first, I thought I had misunderstood). Then I clearly understand that his fifteen-year-old daughter is pregnant, although still at school. What is more, they no longer live in a house but in the former school buildings. His name is Igor. (Unrecorded interview with Ludmilla, her aunt, and cousin, 27 October 2012)

However, such accounts are rare. Here, I pick up a few scraps of information about Igor's life history, his biographical disruptions and ongoing struggles in life. The descriptions are generally very brief. People are labeled as alcoholics without any mention of their backgrounds. There is also talk of the *bomži*, who have no connection with the rural community and wander from one region to another. From rural areas of Belarus to Kiev, the term *bomži* "has . . . moral connotations and is used to describe people who wear old and dirty clothing, drink alcohol, do not work, have no family ties, and are sick and/or dangerous" (Ryabchuk 2010: 353). Their problematic behaviors are mentioned. They steal, carry out thankless and underpaid tasks for the *dačniki* and retired people in return for a bottle of vodka; they wait in line for the grocery store to open in the morning in order to buy vodka or the syrupy 18 percent–proof wine, and so on.

Alcoholics break with the values dear to the local rural community. Their condition prevents them from being considered committed members of the circular solidarity networks that play a fundamental role in village life. Their physical condition and their physiological dependency make their reasons for wanting to join the networks of exchanges clearly apparent to everyone. No one can imagine that they are driven by any other motivation than obtaining a few bottles of vodka. At best, they may form part of local interdependency systems. They are tolerated but cannot pretend—to themselves or to others—that their actions are driven by a sense of moral duty, honesty toward the community, or altruism. Their motivations cannot be misunderstood, kept quiet, concealed, or held back. They cannot belong to the "us" developed by exchanges in the form of gifts and counter-gifts. They are also unable to access dignity, which arises from the idea of access to independence. Yet alcoholics depend on the daily dose of vodka they require to retain control over their bodies. They are dishonest, bone-idle, and selfish. They are unstable people.

The figure of the alcoholic occupies a special place in the collected discourses. As people who are scorned, generate aversion, and bear the "stigma of collective disgrace" (Elias and Scotson 1994: xx), alcoholics are also needed to emphasize the strength of those who resist the lure of drink, whose paradigmatic figure is the real communist worker or the true believer disciplined in mind and body. "Blame gossip" (Elias and Scotson 1994: 105), like the Durkheimian condemnation of crime (Durkheim 1982: 97–104), reinforces the feeling of community. The relationships between residents of the village and alcoholics thus share numerous characteristics with those between the "established" and the "outsiders" in the small British community of Winston Prava, described by Elias and Scotson (1994: xv): the members of the established group "closed ranks against them and stigmatised them generally as people of lesser human worth. They were thought to lack the superior human virtue—the distinguishing group charisma—which the dominant group attributed to itself." At the same time, the character embodies the menacing figure of the village cosmogony who disrupts the social order. He or she personifies the potential downfall of members of the integrated group should they stray from the norms—sense of effort, codified and controlled consumption of alcohol, etc. As a result, "as outsiders are felt to be anomic, close contact with them threatens a member of an established group with 'anomic infection'" (Elias and Scotson 1994: xxiv). Alcoholics are deemed to be untrustworthy and are kept at bay.

Moralists

Profiteers and idlers are characters without morals. The other menacing figure is embodied by anyone who presents an alternative morality that conflicts with the morality shared locally. Moralists do not subvert the system; instead, they invalidate it, delegitimize it, and look down on it. Two characters are perceived as bearers of alternative moralities. In certain cases, urbanites are considered to be bearers of a morality based on materialism. Negative judgments are often directed at urbanites first and foremost, especially the *dačniki*, who visit rural areas. In October 2012, I talked to a French friend who was married to a Belarusian and had lived in Belarus for over ten years. At one time, he had bought a dacha. On the road approaching Rakov, he told me the story of this small house he wanted to develop. The neighbors were jealous as they wanted to graze their goats in the garden and pick the apples. He ended up selling it quickly. In 2013, an old lady in a village in the Vitebsk area told me about her neighbors. They were urbanites. Some of them were born there. In general, they had inherited their deceased parents' *isba*. They were "simple folk" and everything about them was fine. But other neighbors had built a new dacha, which was ostentatious. The owner was the director of a factory. The old lady was shocked because he wanted to live "like a boss-man," without a cow. "How can you live without a cow?" she asked. They never spoke to each other.

The other figures, who are sometimes mentioned directly but often crop up in certain talking situations, are political opponents and human rights activists. In certain cases, they are very simply reduced to the figure of opportunists and unscrupulous profiteers, people who do not believe in what they say but who criticize the regime in order to attract more aid from foreign powers. On a more fundamental level, however, they are seen as scandalous figures who challenge the order on which people's existences are based. By refusing to play by the established rules, and by talking about democracy, Europe, and the market, they are perceived by my interviewees as denying any value to the fundamental dignity to which they themselves lay claim.

In this perspective, the experiences of my friend Yuri are significant. After working as an academic, he entered politics and supported an opponent of Alexander Lukashenko. Yuri came from the rural world. His parents, now retired, were kolkhozians. They lived around fifty kilometers away from Minsk. They had a large kitchen garden, raised a cow, pigs, and hens and covered most of their own needs. His brother worked in the police force.

Thanks to this status, he was able to build his parents' house by mobilizing different networks within the informal economy.² Yuri's family had taken a very dim view of Yuri's change of direction. It was seen as an affront, which not only could directly endanger his family—and, in particular, undermine his brother's position, who could be suspected of failing to support the regime due to his brother's heretical political affiliations—but could also, and above all, call into question the legitimacy of the world they had created for themselves and which they considered to be desirable. What could the opposition, democracy, and Europe possibly offer them? The only conceivable prospect would be instability and to cast doubt upon the desirability of their lives. Yuri's relationship with his brother—with whom he had not spoken in several years—had become strained, and the same applied to his dealings with his father.

The language issue is also revealing in this case. Yuri spoke Belarusian, whereas his parents spoke Trasânka, a mixture of Russian and Belarusian. Trasânka is the equivalent of Surzhyk in Ukraine.

> *Surzhyk* was originally a pejorative word meaning an unrefined mixture of cereals (wheat mixed with rye or barley, and a poor-quality type of bread made from this mixture). Equivalent terms are found in Russian (*suržanka*), Polish (*sqrżyca*) and Czech (*souržice*), but only in Ukraine has this word taken on the pejorative metaphorical meanings of "half-breed" and "mixed language," which have been in use since the start of the twentieth century. The equivalent Belarusian reference to a mixed language is *trasjanka*, a word also of agricultural origin and originally a pejorative term for a mixture of hay and straw (in both cases, the general meaning is that of a confused and disparate mixture, best conveyed by the word 'hodgepodge' [*salmigondis*])." (Sériot 2005: 39)

According to data from the 1999 census, 62.8 percent of the population use Russian for daily communication, and 36.7 percent speak "Belarusian" (Kittel et al. 2010: 47). In this case, Belarusian includes Trasânka, Taraškevica, a language codified by Branislav A. Tarashkyevich in 1918, which is defended by nationalists and used by the intellectuals of the Belarusian Popular Front, and Narkomovka, corresponding to the literary standard established at the time of the Soviet reform of 1933 (Ioffe 2003: 1017, 1026), which is criticized by nationalists for being too similar to Russian. In 1990, Belarusian became the official language of the Soviet Republic of Byelorussia. It is enshrined as the official language in Article 17 of the constitution of the independent republic, adopted in 1994. After becoming president, Lukashenko organized a referendum in 1995 that allowed him to revise the constitution, introduce Russian as the second official language, and effectively restore the primacy of the language of Pushkin. Its use in daily life reflects political and social stances. For certain nationalists like Zianon Pazniak, Russian is perceived as the language of the occupying forces responsible for an "ethnocide"; Trasânka is seen as a "creolized Russo-Belarusian pseudo-language" reflecting the nation's decadence, Narkomovka is considered "impure," and Taraškevica is seen as the "natural" language of the Belarusian nation (Goujon 1999: 668, 671–672). Opponents of the regime, including nationalists of different persuasions who have formed an important political fringe since the country gained independence, stress the democratic dimension of using a form of Belarusian that has been cleansed of its impurities borrowed from Russian. The political scientist Alexandra Goujon summarizes the prevailing logic in the following terms: "'We speak Belarusian and we support democratic values; as a consequence, Belarusian is the language of democracy.' The Belarusian language is contrasted with Russian, which is considered to be the language of persecution and communist ideology" (Goujon 1999: 671). The attachment to Taraškevica is increased by the fact that its creator fell victim to the Stalinian purges of the 1930s. In symmetrical manner, Lukashenko sees Russian as a language inherited from the Soviet Union that is synonymous with "social promotion" and more broadly with "modernization, culture and civilization" (Goujon 1999: 667). Literary Belarusian is the language of anti-Soviet opponents and, by extension, of collaborators during the Nazi occupation. Trasânka is the language of the people, from whom the president himself originates, and which he uses to underline his rural roots and his concern for ordinary citizens' daily lives (Goujon 1999: 666– 668).

Yuri's father, Leonid, spoke Trasânka and understood Russian, which is the commonly spoken Soviet language used in the political and administrative sphere. He also understood the 1933 form of Belarusian employed in certain bureaucratic practices and by certain media. The Taraškevica spoken by his son Yuri, who presented it as the true national language, sounded strange to Leonid. It was an idiom that Leonid did not understand, primarily used by intellectuals from the opposition who claimed to be defenders of democracy and the people's will. Leonid challenged its use, which he did not see as a promotion of his culture, but rather of the imposition of a way of speaking that was devoid of any practical use. "You use a stupid language," he said to his son. It is a reconstructed language that Leonid and others perceived as artificial and a manifestation of the desire to change the order of the world from the top down.

The "conservatism" of rural people can be partly explained from this angle. In this regard, let us return to the discussion I had with the director of a kolkhoz in October 2007. This man in his forties, presenting himself as a modern person, started by telling me that "Kolkhozes have ceased to exist in Belarus, they are now cooperatives," in this way inviting me to forget the term inherited from the Soviet past that was used to designate collective farms. His organization covered six villages with 843 inhabitants and employed 320 employees. Thirty of them worked hard; they were autonomous and dedicated to carrying out their tasks. The others were passive, expecting to be told what to do and waiting until they were given orders. All they wanted was to be paid. The director pointed out why sudden changes were ineffective:

> What is freedom? It's when you can invite your friends to eat at a restaurant and can afford to pay for it. . . . The government is trying to get people used to freedom by laying the foundations for real reforms in the future. But there's no guaranteeing we'll live long enough to see the changes. If a sudden transformation were implemented, only ten employees would cope with it. The others would become homeless people and rebel. (Kolkhoz director, unrecorded interview, 31 October 2007)

Translated into the language of company executives, local contestation of the civil liberties claims made by activists belonging to the opposition appear to be the fruit of a "mentality" that is deeply rooted in the local culture. It implicitly reveals an attachment to worlds reflecting their own consistencies, in which the feeling of creating one's own existence in a self-sufficient manner is detached from the political and constitutional conditions required to exercise freedom of thought. These conditions are not seen as necessary for personal emancipation but rather as heralding the collective downfall of moral rural communities. Proof resides in the post-socialist experiments that have turned rural worlds upside down. The situation in Russia, revealed by the media and especially by accounts from acquaintances or family members, acts as a disincentive.

EVERYDAY POLITICS

The three controversial figures tell us about people's political expectations. They reveal that the world is divided into people who share the values of the moral community and all the others: the profiteers, idlers, and moralists who threaten their world. The contrast between "us" and "them" is not an opposition based on a status-based hierarchy (the dominant/dominated, the powerful/weak), as in the English lower classes described by Richard Hoggart (2009: 57–84), but rather an opposition between moral beings and amoral or immoral beings. In response to this danger, several expectations are implicitly expressed in the discourses, which inform us about everyday politics. What do people expect of the authorities?

Conversion

My interviewees believed that the fundamental problem with the social structure and organization did not reside in the nature of the political and social configurations but in the unequal distribution of morality. The organizational structure of the collectivized countryside was seen as liable to enable the deployment of personal dignities for anyone displaying the approved life ethics but also, and at the same time, as being liable to systematically promote immoral behaviors. The collected discourses are imbued with ambivalence. For example, in November 2012, I asked the carpenter Maksim, an advocate of the collectivist system, why the villagers did not—like him—cultivate more land than their small personal plots by renting land from the kolkhozes. He said (as I recalled in my field notes), "Having more land means having more work and more responsibilities. And why work when you can sell what you've stolen? . . . Nobody's responsible for anything and they couldn't give a damn about anyone else." One gathers that the kolkhoz authorizes forms of honorability but simultaneously permits the development, via system effects, of reprehensible practices. It enables people to be dignified and to adopt contemptible attitudes. It fosters the dignity in work required to circumvent the powerful constraints imposed upon everyone while simultaneously breeding moral baseness by enabling people to steal in order to get by in life. This baseness, if it were extended, could seriously compromise the foundations of the structure on which desirable existences are based. The political system must therefore control the latent immorality that endangers the world.

Let us now explore the sinuous and euphemized narrative pathways taken by my interviewees in relation to politics, in response to a simple question that I often asked them: "What makes a good kolkhoz?" The frequent answer to this question is both simple and enigmatic. "It all depends on the director." How can this figure be characterized? Maksim's response is brief but, for him, self-evident: the most important quality in a director is concern for others (*zabota*). Bad directors are people who do not respect the local balances, who do not consider the dignity of the beneficiaries of these balances, who pursue their own interests to the detriment of the common good. They are often seen as idlers or profiteers who could endanger the fragile configurations on which their worlds are based, or irresponsible managers who allow the profiteers to prosper. Good directors allow everyone to express their qualities without seeking to further their own personal interests. They know how to recognize good workers and reward them with official gifts or by allowing leeway in terms of access to the informal economy and curbing the appetites of profiteers. They recognize the people's dignity, their morality, and recompense them with official or unofficial symbolic or material rewards. They are natural leaders with the ability to generate practical solidarity. Directors give bad workers, who may not spontaneously act according to the expected principles of morality, opportunities to redeem themselves. Therefore, the paternalistic moralization schemes targeting workers, and the forms of control over line managers, seek to transform these people into honest workers.

This makes it essential for the authorities to keep a close eye on the morality of senior managers. If the control mechanisms employed by the authorities are insufficient, the people are allowed to protest against bad directors. It is emphasized that official complaints are possible, as during the Soviet era (Hibou 2017: 272), that people can appeal to the courts, and that this is effective.

> People can submit a complaint to the president and the ministry must respond quickly. A commission can be appointed to verify the statements.... There was a case like this in the Babruysk region. A kolkhoz director had sacked a truck driver, who considered this to be unfair. He won his case, received five times the amount of his wage that had not been paid during the months of proceedings, and got his job back. The complaints may concern the environment, such as the dumping of waste in the river or lake, etc. (Maksim, unrecorded interview, 28 October 2012)

The authorities see this opportunity for citizens to submit complaints as the manifestation of the democratic nature of the regime.

> In 2000, Mikhail Miasnikovich, the head of the president's office, came out with a classic example of ideological reasoning: "Hundreds of thousands of our fellow citizens can contact different executive bodies, which will understand and support them. Isn't that clear proof of their rights?" This, for the authorities, is the "optimal form of democracy": a serf's right to petition.... The population contacts the president's office directly for any problem that can be resolved locally. Every month, the Head of State receives nearly 30,000 complaints from citizens, and thousands of people patiently wait their turn to be received by Lukashenko in person. (Karbalévitch 2012: 191, 200)

For this mechanism to work, there needs to be a supreme figure to judge the morality of the lower levels of the system. The world of kolkhozes is not governed by anonymous forces like market mechanisms, but by an attentive leader—Lukashenko—who is concerned about the fate of each of his fellow citizens. As the state, embodied by the president, is doing everything it can to help individuals, there is no reason to complain about the system. Only the incompetent dare to do so. The arbiter of morality himself must be exemplary and irreproachable. Consequently, Lukashenko comes across in certain discourses as a sincere character. The criterion of support for his policies does not relate to his economic choices or his decisions, but to the fact of being genuine. On 2 November 2012, Maksim told me about a younger distant relative who had studied in Washington. Upon his return, he became the president's official interpreter. This relative is supposed to have said that "Lukashenko was really concerned about the people, that he was upset by the difficulties experienced by the inhabitants of the country, and that he really was a sincere person." This caused Maksim to change the image he had formulated about him. If he is honest, in a world full of unscrupulous profiteers with no concern for the common good, he must be supported at all costs. He is sometimes compared, more or less explicitly, with a historic leader of the country: the figure of Pyotr Masherov cropped up in my interviewees' declarations on several occasions. He governed the Socialist Soviet Republic of Byelorussia in the 1970s. On 28 October 2007, during a meal at Vova's parents-in-law, I was told how sincere he really was. He always kept rubber boots in his limousine, and the ministers were obliged to follow his lead when mowing the grass. One day, his helicopter broke down. He landed in the stadium of the agricultural high school and took the opportunity to meet local residents. He enjoyed immense popularity, which was unusual for the communist leaders of that time. In my field survey log (21 December 2009), I note that "Vova tells me he clearly remembers the day Masherov died. It was on a Sunday; his father returned home from work, very sad. He was a very popular and beloved figure. There were spontaneous gatherings on that day. This recollection contrasts sharply with the analyses of 'Soviet manifestations' by Alexandra Goujon" (see Goujon 2009: 37–39).

Other testimonies insist that Lukashenko could be likened to Leonid Brezhnev or Mikhail Gorbachev—an unscrupulous leader accused of enriching himself at the citizens' expense. The scale of judgment used to assess the leaders' qualities, at the national or local level, revolves around this question of transparency and sincerity. In this respect, the majority of my interviewees do not call for a change in the rules of the game, as they consider that if the system is not working, it is because certain people do not conform to the rules of morality required for it to survive.

Punishment

Consequently, the threat of disorder appears to reside in a lack of morality that can only be corrected by control and conversion. If the paternalistic practices motivated by the benevolence of the state are insufficient, then recourse to punishment seems legitimate. This expectation vis-à-vis the authorities appears either in the form of explicit justifications for coercive measures adopted by the regime, or as an attitude of indifference regarding these measures when they target "offenders of morality."

This type of discourse primarily concerns idlers. As the system runs schemes to offer repentant alcoholics a chance to redeem themselves, there is no outcry if a director uses violence to demonstrate his or her authority should these measures fail. The use of physical force to subdue behaviors was mentioned in several interviews, most commonly in recollections of certain directors during the Soviet era. While the illegality of such practices makes it difficult to ascertain whether such forms of corporal punishment are still used and if so, to what extent, the collected discourses reveal that these ultimate forms of violence are not condemned. In this regard, the zootechnician at a kolkhoz in the vicinity of Minsk complained about the behavior of alcoholics and mentioned the desired and justified recourse to violence, while smashing his fist into the palm of his hand. The leader must also have the ability to punish people who are dishonest or bone-idle, sometimes physically.

> What methods are used to tackle the problem of alcoholics? Sometimes they are dismissed, but we're then obliged to re-hire the same people two days later due to the lack of available labor in the region. What's more, they're not really worried about being fired because they are frequently hired by the *dačniki* for odd jobs, and paid in vodka. The salary doesn't motivate them to work any better. In three days, they've spent their entire wage on vodka. Sometimes, you can do this [he smashes his fist into the palm of his hand]. If I had the best workers, I could significantly increase productivity.... I'd only need five people rather than the twelve I have now. Then I could put on a shirt and tie and walk around all day watching the workers do their jobs. (Veterinarian on a small kolkhoz, Minsk region. Unrecorded interview, 16 April 2006)

Therefore, violence at work, even physical, does not cause outrage. A babushka recalled a kolkhoz director in these terms, who was highly appreciated by the villagers and ran the collective farm with an iron fist for several decades after the Great Patriotic War.

> If somebody was drinking, the director wouldn't think twice about beating him with his fists. He considered himself a *hozâin* [a master, a patriarch] and behaved like one. But everyone appreciated him because he was fair. If you asked him for an advance on your wages, he'd give you one if you were a good worker. Everyone wanted him to stay on and his contract was renewed at each new election. (Babushka, a retired kolkhozian, in her *isba* near Rakov. Unrecorded interview, 28 October 2012)

Also during the Soviet era, President Lukashenko himself, then the director of a sovkhoz, is said to have used physical force on his workers.

> Two criminal investigations were opened against him. In particular, Alexander Lukashenko was accused of repeatedly punching a tractor driver on the Gorodets sovkhoz he ran, which was confirmed by three witnesses. During the inquiry, the local outpost of the Ministry of the Interior received a similar complaint from another tractor driver on the same sovkhoz. Physical assaults were apparently methods used by the director to maintain order on his farm. If the inquiries had gone to trial, Lukashenko could have been sentenced to prison for between three and eight years. (Karbalévitch 2012: 47)

In the same manner, the carpenter Maksim sang the praises of new labor organization methods currently implemented in certain regions of Russia. If the idlers could be forced to work, then at least they could be prevented—by recourse to physical force—from causing any disruption.

> People need to be aware that they have to work. There are interesting experiments going on in Russia. I've heard about a place where it's going very well, near Orel. People shared the land, then some of them bought shares. Over there, there are armed guards [*ohrana*] whose job is to keep an eye on things in order to prevent theft. (Maksim and his friend, a glassblower, unrecorded interview, 1 November 2012)

These discourses then target the profiteers. If the direct hierarchy does not defend the common good and acts only in pursuit of its own interests by diverting public property for its own profit, the system, in a hierarchical manner, guarantees the restoration of discipline exactly where the morality was lacking. In such cases, the methods used to punish profiteers are of little importance. The use of physical violence is seen as self-evident. The fact that kolkhoz directors and administrative managers are regularly punished, imprisoned, and sentenced after being interrogated by the police or security services clearly shows that the system must defend itself against those who act in pursuit of their own interests. It is important for people to avoid being overwhelmed by the others, and for everyone to find a way of coping in life by appropriating something for themselves in this world. People want the rules to be maintained so that they can continue to use the strategies which, through experience, they have been able to implement. To this end, nobody should be allowed to dominate completely. If the wrongs are not put right, it will no longer be in the interest of morally upstanding people to behave righteously. Without discipline, the profiteers and idlers will prevail. Only fear and violence can keep the system intact, and, while they are not always acknowledged, they do not cause outrage. Consequently, when the president in his different speeches insists on the use of force to maintain order in the country, it becomes apparent that his declarations reflect the representations of countryfolk.

> Lukashenko is convinced that any problem can be solved through force, punishment, threats, intimidation, etc. The conviction that you can achieve anything through toughness and decrees leads to Utopian projects, like "relaunching industry" and "eliminating corruption." . . . In 2006, he told Russian journalists how he had tackled the shortage of sugar in the capital: "I invited the head of the president's office—that was Miasnikovich—and the mayor of Minsk, Yermoshin, to visit me and I told them: 'If tomorrow morning, there's no sugar in any of the stores I visit, you're going to jail.' And guess what? They found some sugar, and they carried it in bags with the workers, on their shoulders, to stock up the stores." . . . [And this] warning [was] issued to the Prime Minister, Vladimir Yermoshin, to the president of the Committee of State Control, Anatoli Tozik, and to the head of the president's office, Mikhail Miasnikovich, in 2001, prior to the sowing campaign: "If you mess up this campaign, I'll send you off

to dig with a shovel behind the barbed wire at Chernobyl!" (Karbalévitch 2012: 193, 199, 219).

This casts the strong state in a protective light, whereas, from an objective perspective, it poses a threat to everyone. As a consequence, Lukashenko is defended because he has the power to bring down anyone, including powerful people; in this way he is regarded as a last resort and a "Grand Inquisitor"–type figure. The absence of a powerful, centralized regulatory authority could lead to radical disorder because there would no longer be any opportunity to express moral sentiments, which would be annihilated by unscrupulousness and self-interest. Without violence, the profiteers and their radical figures—the "bandits"—would reign supreme, as in Russia. In the 1990s, growing inequalities showed that only certain people had managed to prosper in an anomic climate. The idea of solidarity was ruined by these transformations. In Belarus, the limitation of inequalities shows that it is still in everyone's interest to work together in order to do better individually. Maksim touched on this in one of our conversations:

> What do they expect from politics? They couldn't give a damn about other people. They want stability. In Russia, there were bandits. Here, we want security and we want roads to be built. . . . Kolkhozians often talk about politics and they all support Lukashenko. Why? Because he ensures stability, makes sure that there are no bandits like in Russia and that if people aren't happy, they can complain. . . . [I talk to him about the parliamentary elections held recently. He tells me that] the people in charge took the ballot box from house to house, including to his and his neighbor's homes. Initially, there had been two candidates, but in the end, one of them pulled out, leaving just a single candidate. The people vote as they are expected to vote. The only thing that interests them is finding out when the road that leads to the village will be properly paved. (Maksim and his friend, a glassblower, unrecorded interview, 1 November 2012)

These considerations are finally applied to those we have referred to as "moralists." Clear comments against them were rarely made in my presence. I was assumed to side with human rights advocates, and this subject was avoided in my presence. Only Maksim, who liked to goad me and get me to react to his provocations, commented on current events and made judgments against opponents repressed by the regime. Coming from him, this rejection of alternative forms of political life embodied by opposition activists was expressed by comments of a gender-oriented nature. In October 2012, his wife took part in the discussion. She mentioned events in the Arab world broadcast on Russian and Belarusian television channels. Here, the fight against authoritarianism was seen through the lens of Belarusian forms of life. She was indignant that people in Egypt and Tunisia were protesting in public and spending their time doing nothing when they should be working. "Why are they out on the streets every day? What's the point? They have families and must work at all costs; you have to work to feed your family." She came back to this subject several times. The only morality there is consists in protecting one's family, using the socially acceptable means at one's disposal: work. Protesting is seen as complaining in a feminine and devirilizing manner, and this echoes certain discourses conveyed by the Belarusian media (Ousmanova 2008). The carpenter also mentioned protests by the opposition on 19 December 2010, after the disputed presidential election in Belarus, which met with severe repression, saying that if the people had really been angry, they would have made mincemeat out of the security forces (*omon*), which were just scared young lads. Incidentally, the carpenter repeated that he wanted to live in the country in order to become a real man. Defending one's dignity puts the emphasis on a form of masculinity that is associated with virility and a strong and capable body, built by working with unforgiving materials and overcoming technical obstacles. Hardship is not just an ordeal that one suffers; it is also an experience to be endured, in which one can take pride (Shevchenko 2009: 81, 108). In a certain manner, the authoritarian regime and its constraints do not stand in the way of self-realization. On the contrary, it is the very harshness of the world that makes this possible. In the discussions we had in October 2012, Maksim asked me about my academic work and gender studies. He then explained to me that the people around there did not want any part of it. "We should live as people lived before, in the past," he said; "My first wife, a Muslim, served men their meals, didn't remain with them, and when her friends came, the men didn't need to make conversation. And that worked out just fine." For workers who have a local reputation and a status, the authoritarian regime does not inhibit the expression of their personal dignity. On the contrary, the rigors of the world require individuals to exhibit their power in order to succeed. Conversely, democracy hinders complete self-realization. When life is too easy or too superficial, when it lacks trials and hardship, it becomes impossible to distinguish real men from the others. Maksim also talked to me about the rights of homosexuals in France—the debates on "marriage for all" are widely reported by the Russian and Belarusian media—while denouncing the feminization of the male world. There is no scandal in certain opponents rotting in the prisons of the Belarusian security services, or sometimes being subjected to torture. However, it is scandalous for homosexuals to gain the right to get married in France, he said. He continued in this vein by employing cultural references such as the Slavic soul and Belarusians being destined to gain redemption by overcoming suffering. The arbitrary violence employed by the state against certain citizens was of no importance as long as these people did not belong to the "us"—to those who defend their ethos through their work and their daily labor. Maksim accepted the world as it was, and simply wanted it to remain unchanged, precisely because he had managed to construct himself as a person within it. "I couldn't care less who's in charge—Lukashenko, Putin, or the European Union," he said; "the only thing that counts for me is that they leave me alone to do the work I'm interested in." In general, I heard few real complaints about the system of constraints on individuals. Regrets were sometimes expressed about being unable to take better advantage of the system, as some people do. People might possibly want things to change for themselves, but demand that they do not change for others. It is a world that fundamentally aspires to its own reproduction. The stability of the rules and their modes of application enable individuals to find their bearings and construct viable, and even desirable, worlds for themselves.

My open discussions with Maksim were an exceptional occurrence in my field of investigation—reflections on opposition activists are generally nonexistent or take on sinuous and loosely structured forms. Leonid's attitude is highly significant. He did not understand why his son Yuri had adopted Taraškevica as a language, which conveys a worldview that calls into question the very foundations of his social existence and posed a direct threat to the status of his other son, a policeman. Indeed, the latter could be suspected, due to his brother's political activities, of having links with opponents of the regime. As a young man, Leonid endured suffering in the century of Soviet rule. His own father, convicted on grounds of being a *kulak*, never returned from deportation. On the day of our conversation, however, when Leonid and Yuri were discussing politics, the father claimed to be a follower of Stalin, which antagonized his son, who was an ardent advocate of individual liberties. How should we interpret this reference to a period that brought suffering to his own family?

In this context, the only way for Leonid to defend his world is to take shortcuts. How can a kolkhozian convey the universe of meaning that this book has set out to portray? In a world in which the expression of his worldview is kept strictly to himself, the only way to defend himself is not to explain the merits of the kolkhoz, whose economic incoherence would be demonstrated by an expert in that field, and which would be denounced by a political scientist as a dominating institution that alienates the inhabitants of rural areas. Stalin, the USSR, and the past are present as an allusion, in an unexplained shortcut, to the coherence of the life world that the person is seeking to defend. This is a practical form of metonymy used, as Bourdieu (1994: 98) puts it, to designate the "language of denial" and of "practical euphemisms," which reflects a form of politicization. This opinion is not a mechanical product of propaganda but rather the discursive extension of a world that has been experienced and which has its own coherence. The regime is based on violence but disseminates the belief throughout society that it is possible for everyone to construct a desirable life without being imperiled by the security services. Therefore, repressed opponents are not seen as victims but rather as unscrupulous people who refuse to behave like the rest of the population. As they are aware that they run the risk of repression, they have no reason to complain if this should actually happen. In the countryside but also in towns, I rarely detected sympathy or compassion toward opponents. On the contrary, they tended to be seen as responsible for their—sometimes dire—fates.

The Moral Economy

In this way, we see the emergence of forms of everyday politics that are not structured by theoretical constructs and "deliberative choices," and that are far from the "ordinary conception of the political game, surveys and political intellectuals" (Collovald 2004: 124; cited by Pudal 2011: 918). They are an extension of moral judgments linked to the coherence of people's own worlds constructed in the rural areas of Belarus. The notion of "moral economy" highlights the importance of everyday values associated with "a series of networks of obligation" (*réseaux d'obligations en cascade*; Fontaine 2014: 4) in political expectations. Reflecting on the food riots in seventeenth-century England, Edward P. Thompson (1991: 188) describes "a consistent traditional view of social norms and obligations, of the proper economic functions of several parties within the community, which, taken together, can be said to constitute the moral economy of the poor." James C. Scott (1976) revisits this notion when analyzing the subsistence economy of Southeast Asia. The interest of the notion of moral economy is, first, that it articulates "the popular conceptions of what is fair and unfair in economic matters" (Siméant 2010: 145), what is tolerable and intolerable (Scott 1976: 3), what "should be done and what should not be done"—that is, "the principles of a good life, justice, dignity and respect, which could be said to amount to recognition according to Axel Honneth" (Fassin 2009: 1243–1244); and, second, that it conveys the "relationship between the leaders and the led" (Siméant 2010: 145), "the vertical dimension of the links between elites and the people" (Siméant 2010: 150), the idea of the "responsibility of the great toward the small" (Siméant 2010: 147), "the interdependency relationships binding 'the governors and the crowd'" (Cerutti 2015: 936), and the idea of "a particular balance of class or social forces" (Thompson 1991 : 340). The moral economy "therefore implies the serious consideration of expectations which, although focusing without exception on subsistence, never relate precisely to subsistence alone, but to a sense of fairness and unfairness that is attached to it—a sense that is itself derived from what seems reasonable to expect from the authorities" (Siméant 2010: 151).

This notion prompts reflection on forms of everyday politics (Thompson 1991: 345). In the contemporary Belarusian context, forms resembling the situation in seventeenth-century England or twentieth-century Southeast Asia can be identified. The countryfolk encountered defend their right to lead meaningful lives. On the one hand, they expect the authorities to tolerate the minor illegalities that enable honest people to live decently (this is not a question of survival but of an acceptable existence) in return for a minimal engagement in work on the kolkhoz, at the agricultural high school, or in the factory. On the other hand, they expect the authorities to convert, or possibly punish, the figures who jeopardize this social order—in short, to protect these righteous worlds. Therefore, these expectations do not solely concern the material conditions of ordinary existence but also, and above all, its moral conditions. The regular economic fluctuations during the course of my investigative research did not cause any particular anger among the families encountered precisely because the configurations enabling people to lead a dignified existence were not called into question. This "patience"—also described in the Russian context of the 1990s (Coenen-Huther 1997)—should not, therefore, be attributed to the atavistic conservatism of countryfolk, nor to the mechanical efficiency of the regime's ideological discourse. As Didier Fassin (2009: 1248) stated when analyzing Scott's theses, "The moral economy provides an understanding of how a system of exploitation can survive even when local principles of justice prevail."

NOTES

1. This grandfather is described in Hervouet 2007.
2. I described his experiences in Hervouet 2009: 83–95.

CHAPTER

10

LEVELS OF SOCIAL ORDER

In this political ethnography of rural worlds in Belarus, I started by analyzing modes of rural government from a "top-down" perspective. I then shifted my focus to observe the resources scattered throughout these territories and the ways in which they are mobilized within networks of interdependencies. Next, I sought to understand the types of moral sentiments (equality, solidarity, dignity) generated by these worlds. Finally, I set out to analyze everyday politics in this authoritarian regime, with reference to materials that remain incomplete, by showing how the people I met expect the authorities to protect these fragile worlds from the potential, or alleged, threats posed by moral offenders—profiteers, idlers, and moralists. In this manner, I have defined a "moral economy of the collectivized countryside." This process is based on a "discrete" ethnography. Traveling from one region to another, I have sought to use fragmented materials to piece together specific types of relationships with the world.

This final chapter presents fewer additional arguments.[1] Instead, it presents a detailed analysis of a single village and, based on a partial monograph, sets out to analyze the imposed order of things by highlighting the interconnections between its different dimensions—social, moral, political, and memorial. It is therefore an epilogue, in the sense of the "'resolution' (of a complicated case)" (*Dictionnaire historique* 2000), in which the scattered threads encountered in previous chapters come together to make sense of the story of a concrete and clearly defined place. This approach provides an insight into the levels of order that persist in Belarus, by moving not only from one field of activity to another (domestic, economic, religious, administrative, political, judicial), but also from one territorial dimension to another (local, national), and from one historical focus to another (from the present day to the Great Patriotic War), to reflect the "multi-layered structure [*structure feuilletée*] of the social sphere" (Revel 1996: 13).

The village of Mosar is the main focus of this investigation. Here, an elderly Catholic priest named Ûsaf Bul'ka, who died in 2010, launched a policy of combating alcoholism and set up a vast park that attracts followers and tourists alike. The priest's work was recognized by the country's highest authorities: he was decorated by President Lukashenko himself for his work. A few months before his death, Bul'ka was accused by the Lithuanian courts of having participated in the "genocide" of members of the resistance against the Soviet occupation in Lithuania after the Great Patriotic War of 1941–1945. Examining the case of the village of Mosar sheds light on the modes of government in an authoritarian regime. It shows how political, professional, and spiritual institutions work together to establish an order that tolerates no challenge. Each type of order that seeks to establish itself echoes the others rather than contradicting them. The establishment of a spiritual order promotes the stability of the social order, which, in turn, guarantees political order. The case of Mosar is all the more interesting in that it provides an insight into how the legitimization of the regime unfolds according to modalities that appear to be clearly disciplinary, but which, at the same time, outline configurations from which forms of dignity can emerge. Indeed, describing the imposition of this order would paint a very bleak picture if it concerned only processes of subjection. The project implemented in this village eases certain constraints, although it contributes, through its influence, to the reproduction of a liberticidal political order on a larger scale.

This chapter draws on different types of materials. I visited the Mosar region on four occasions between 2008 and 2011 and was able to meet Bul'ka in person during my first two visits. However, in our discussions, I soon realized that it would be difficult to gather meaningful statements about the history of the site. As the priest expressed himself only in metaphysical or religious terms and showed no interest whatsoever in my factual questions, I opted to base my presentation of the political and social logics at work in this territory on a systematic reading of the press. An analysis of readers' comments and discussion forums supplemented this written corpus. This information was correlated, on the one hand, with the observations collected in this village and, on the other hand, with the statements reported by people encountered in this region of Belarus: one of Bul'ka's associates, who was remarkable for his silences and elliptical responses; an old woman picked up when she was hitchhiking thirty kilometers from Mosar and whose remarks contained some significant information; the librarian in Pariž, a village near Mosar, in which the priest also worked; and, finally, the mother of a friend from Minsk who knows the region well because she grew up there and because her own mother, who was on friendly terms with the priest, lived there until her death in May 2011.

PROSELYTISM AND MORAL ORDER

Spatial Planning

According to the *Belarusian Encyclopaedia* (2002), the Catholic church in the village of Mosar was built in 1792. This land was Polish until 1793 and then became Russian, returned to Polish rule in 1921, and was sovietized in 1939. It has belonged to independent Belarus since 1991. As a direct legacy of this turbulent history, Mosar is now a Catholic village. Almost 90 percent of the inhabitants claim to belong to this faith (Zenina 2003). In 1999, the village had 489 inhabitants. In 2008, Bul'ka told me that 200 people were living there. Over the years, this tiny village came to be held up as an example by the country's authorities in the 1990s.

The priest arrived in Mosar in 1986. A journalist from the official press organization *Belarus' Segodnâ* (Zenina 2003) recounts his arrival in the parish. At that time, the graves in the surrounding area were neglected. Bul'ka tidied up the cemeteries, moved vegetable gardens, installed sculptures, and cut down old trees to make these places brighter. His projects were far from confined to people's final resting places. The church's estate covers twenty-four hectares. He drained the marshlands around the church, planted birches, dug two symmetrical ponds connected by a "lovers' bridge," erected small *kurgans* on the fields, and laid out a path leading to a spring and a sports ground behind the presbytery. Several hundred meters from the church stands a hill on top of which Bul'ka erected a twenty-three-meter cross, weighing ten tons, which is visible from twenty-five kilometers away in any direction (Bogdanov 2010). On the path leading to it, he invited anyone who wished to do so to erect a cross and write their name on it. He told me that "as history is written over time, crosses will one day line the path all the way to the top of the hill." This long path—a Belarusian version of Mount Calvary—was supposed to embody the repentance of the parish's faithful, who have chosen to live temperate lives in accordance with the holy scriptures. In the end, Bul'ka created an estate whose symbolic topography and manifest order were supposed to reflect the inhabitants' moral conversion. The well-kept cemeteries show respect for the dead; the path to the spring—lined with biblical representations—indicates the self-improvement efforts required to attain purity; the ponds and flower beds show the beauty of divine creation, provided that people, through their labor, are willing to reveal it.

These earthly manifestations of beauty were intended to reflect the moral qualities of the parish's faithful. Sinners were redeemed in the eyes of the community by the beauties they had helped reveal. Here, Bul'ka had deployed a "theodicy of happiness," where virtue is rewarded by contemplation of the work accomplished collectively (F. Weber 2001a: 187). This material order is the revelation of a spirituality incarnated in the community and guided by the priest, who stepped aside in favor of these beauties. Imposing plaster statues representing the great biblical figures are scattered throughout the area. The sacred texts are always present in interpretations of the place's beauty. When contemplating nature, viewers cannot escape the reminders provided by these monuments, which occupy carefully chosen positions throughout the estate: the Virgin, a monumental Christ standing in the middle of the cemetery, Moses and the table of the Ten Commandments, John the Baptist, King David, etc. This landscape is always described as exceptional in the newspapers. Pilgrims, tourists, and people passing through express the emotion felt in this place and describe it as a "mini-Versailles." Journalists, especially in the official press, praise the exceptionality of the place with its "flowery oases, which delight the eyes and soul with their beauty" (Ulitënok 2003).

Moral Reform

The priest's discourse suggested that his word, and the Word of God transmitted through him, had performative virtue. However, a thorough reading of the press reveals that the inhabitants, to a certain extent, were partly coerced into participating in this project. The priest had a monopoly on "salvation goods" in the region and gainfully exploited them. In one of the very rare critical comments made by newspaper readers about the work in Mosar, an Internet user wrote that "in the morning, Bul'ka turns up at someone's house and shouts: 'Today, you'll weed here and there.'" Anyone who refused ran a great risk—that the priest would refuse them the sacrament during an important ritual. Therefore, according to a local government official, "people [were] willing to tidy up the cemetery, even at night if necessary" (Zenina 2003). Like the "ruling organisations" that Weber describes as "hierocratic," Bul'ka used "psychic coercion through the distribution or denial of religious benefits" (M. Weber 2019: 136). He was thus described as an "authoritarian priest," but without any derogatory overtones (Zenina 2003). Moreover, he only agreed to perform burial services, marriages, and christenings if alcohol was totally banned from the ceremony.

The priest was not only seeking to develop harmony in nature; he was also striving to create healthy bodies that are spared the torments of alcohol. Upon his arrival in the parish, he embarked on his long crusade against alcoholism. Like the "prototype of the rule creator" defined by Howard Becker (1997: 147), he became a "crusading reformer." This obsession was a central theme in what he told me at our two meetings, one on 6 March 2008 and the other on 19 July 2009. In 2008, I arrived unannounced, accompanied by my partner and my Belarusian friend Vova. We talked about his fight against alcoholism, which we had heard about in the press. "They drink everywhere!" he said, raising his voice. He talked about alcohol, drugs, cigarettes, and the women who indulge in these vices and pass on the problem to their children through their genes. He explained how he advises people to stop drinking. Traditions should be changed and the ritual of making toasts with vodka should be banned, he said. He had also built what he called a "temperance museum." When I visited, it was located in a small building near the church. It occupies an area of about fifteen square meters. To the right of the entrance hung a sign denouncing the practice of abortion. Below it stood a baby carriage containing two dolls. Other wooden panels were affixed to the three sides of the main room, displaying various texts (a quotation from Saint Luke, another from Jack London, and extracts from alcoholism prevention manuals) and paintings depicting Christ, the Devil, and the alcoholic. The room also contained an old still and a coffee table on which an empty bottle, a full ashtray, and a dirty can of food had been placed. These items were presented as condemning evidence of the alcoholic's degenerate lifestyle. Near a samovar, alcoholics themselves, or their relatives, left their vows and ex-votos expressing predictable sentiments: "Help us recover," "Save my son," "Thank you, Lord."

I also had the opportunity to observe Bul'ka in action. On Sunday, 19 July 2009, I returned to Mosar with my partner, my eldest son—who was three years old at the time—and my Belarusian friend Vova. After Mass, my colleague and I knocked on the door of the room at the back of the church. Bul'ka told us to come in. We introduced ourselves; he blessed us and invited us to sit down on two of the four chairs in front of his desk. "Stay here, I'll show you how I work," he said. A skinny man of indeterminate age with a careworn face then entered the room. He might have been twenty years old or he might have been thirty. A woman in her fifties was with him. Calmly, the priest asked him: "Do you drink?"

"Yes," the man replied before mumbling a few details about his family situation. He was previously married, had one child, and lived with his mother and this child. His father and uncle were dead. The woman with him, who happened to be his aunt, pointed out that the young alcoholic's mother was very devout, and that she had worked for the church for a while, selling candles there.

Bul'ka addressed the woman formally, telling her, "Thank you for helping this boy." Then he addressed the man as if they were on familiar terms and abruptly asked him, "Are there times when you drink for several days in a row?" He used the Russian term *zapoj*, which means a long and extreme state of inebriation.

The man replied that he was capable of drinking for an entire month.

"How many days can you go without drinking?"

"Two."

"Do you have a job?"

The answer was muddled—he sometimes worked on a neighboring kolkhoz.

The priest explained that he would tell his employer that he had come to see him in an effort to stop drinking. Five minutes went by in this way, and the discussion came to an end. "Here is a special prayer." He handed the man a small printed image in color. A picture of Christ was printed on one side and a prayer was written on the other. "You must pray every day, then come back and see me in a week so I can see whether you are cured."

The alcoholic scribbled a few words on a small form that the priest asked him to leave in the church—probably a vow to the Lord. The woman wanted to kiss the priest's hand, but he refused. This entire scene exuded a muted violence, first related to the destructive pathology affecting this person but also due to the unease caused by our presence, which turned the manifestation of this misery into a spectacle. Although it was impossible to assess the effects of this meeting, it nevertheless reflected the immense social despair confronting the priest, and gave us an idea of the gratitude shown to him by the people who had come through this ordeal, and by their entourage, who attribute their redemption to his intervention.

The landscape bore witness to the successes of his crusade against alcoholism. A few months earlier, around forty groups of Alcoholics Anonymous (AA) from different cities in Belarus, but also from Russia and Lithuania, had traveled to Mosar to attend a mass dedicated to them. At the end of the service, each group planted a tree along "Temperance Alley." A sign stating the origin of each AA group was placed at the foot of every tree.

Bul'ka even tried to impact children's lives. A few ostriches lived in an enclosure near the church. They were given to Bul'ka by a "friend" who owned a farm in the area. Maxims denouncing tobacco and alcohol were written in large letters on the wooden fences around the enclosure. The priest explained that children liked to come and see these birds and were then exposed both to nature and messages about the harmful effects of cigarettes and vodka.

COLLUSION AND POLITICAL ORDER

Local Networks

Bul'ka's crusade was not solely based on the differentiated and adroitly managed distribution of salvation goods. It also relied on support from the local bureaucracy and police. On 10 April 2008, the official press published an article entitled "Mosar's priest shares his experience in the fight against alcoholism with the local police in Vitebsk Oblast" (*Belarus' Segodnâ* 2008a). In fact, back in the hard times of the early 1990s when alcohol was obtained in exchange for coupons, Bul'ka asked parishioners who sought his help to provide a certificate from the local authorities proving that they had refused these "vodka vouchers" from the *sel'soviet* (rural council). "At first, we didn't understand," admitted a representative of the *sel'soviet*. "Then we realized that the new priest would do nothing if he wasn't convinced of the absence of vodka, so we started drawing up these certificates" (Zenina 2003). Later, he convinced the authorities to define the territory of Mosar as an alcohol-free zone. Following this proposal, alcoholic beverages were initially banned from sale in the *sel'soviet* of Udelovskij's stores until 31 December 2009 (*Charter 97* 2009c). This measure was subsequently extended. Although it is very difficult to assess the full extent of his endeavors, and despite the jokes about the extent of clandestine distillation still told on the Internet, different testimonies have suggested that his actions were not in vain: villagers were said to be drinking less.

Descriptions of the Mosar region reveal the existence of tightly knit networks in this rural part of Belarus. They show how religious, professional, and bureaucratic institutions work together, in collusion, to ensure the stability of social order in the rural world. Bul'ka, through his actions, promoted virtues—temperance and a disciplined local labor force—that are appreciated in the world of work, which is essentially composed of kolkhozes. Employees, who were inclined to be more docile and self-controlled due to the partial conversion carried out by the priest, would be more productive. Back in the 1980s, collective farm managers in the USSR could rarely count on having a sober workforce for more than half a day (White 1996: 46). Regular articles on vodka consumption in the press suggest that this issue continues to be a major challenge for the management of kolkhoz workforces. In addition, the extra-local reputation acquired by this village—as both a place of pilgrimage and a tourist destination—pleased the local administration, which benefited substantially from Bul'ka's work. The priest even strove to influence the local labor market directly. During our first meeting, for example, he mentioned the economic activity of Pariž, a neighboring municipality. Its main factory had shut down. The priest was wanting to "give people work." He asked me, quite seriously, whether I knew any investors in France. He was clearly trying to mobilize his networks in an effort to revive economic activity in the municipality. The different actors were well aware of their common interests and collaborated closely in the governance of this territory. Bul'ka cooperated with the directors of neighboring kolkhozes, who in turn provided material support for the performance of different tasks. In this way, the infrastructures that helped to promote the parish were looked after by the local authorities, as the head of the information department at the Glubokoe *rajispolkom* (district administration) explained: "Of course, there are more difficult jobs, such as draining swamps and paving roads, which people cannot do without help from the local authorities. We help, because we can see that our workforce and resources make a real difference" (*Charter 97* 2009c). This interweaving of the religious, political, and economic worlds in the region became strongly apparent during Bul'ka's convalescence in December 2009, as Česlava Lavrinovič, who was involved in the church at Mosar, testified: "Everyone came to see him in hospital. Three weeks ago, his blood pressure was very high. Everyone—the police, a representative of the *rajispolkom*, and a representative of the *sel'soviet*. Everyone seeks advice from him, everyone respects him" (Strižak 2009b).

National Recognition

Bul'ka was so successful that he established a nationwide reputation. In 2006, he was awarded the Francisk Skorina Medal—named after the sixteenth-century humanist born in Polotsk who first translated the Bible into the Eastern Slavic language and whose work profoundly influenced the Belarusian language and literature. According to the president's press office, Bul'ka received this award for "his many years of sustained efforts to strengthen spiritual value and promote a healthy lifestyle" (*Belarus' Segodnâ* 2006). The year before, he became the first Catholic priest to receive the "For Spiritual Rebirth" award, presented by Lukashenko himself. Through his "honorary State management" initiative (Ihl 2004: 5), the autocrat rewards those who recognize the legitimacy of his ideology and his government practices. The "For Spiritual Rebirth" award ceremony was held at the Palace of the Republic on 7 January 2005, after the Orthodox Christmas Mass at the Cathedral of the Holy Spirit in Minsk. A journalist from the official press was present alongside the priest at this event and reported his comments. Bul'ka had already decided to use the financial part of the award to fulfill one of his long-standing ambitions: to pave the beautiful lane leading to the cemetery in his parish. These words were spoken a few minutes after the president—invited to deliver a message of peace at the invitation of the Metropolitan Bishop Filaret—had given his speech: "In Belarus, there will be no revolution of any kind—'pink,' 'orange' or 'banana.' ... Live in peace, placidly. The President's great task is to ensure peace and security for you, your children, members of your family and friends" (Krât 2005). This speech alluded to the "Orange Revolution," which started in Ukraine in November, and, in retrospect, heralded the brutal repression, in March 2006, of the Belarusian opposition's protests against the results of the presidential election when Lukashenko was credited with a first-round score of 82.6 percent (Goujon 2009: 208–226). This simultaneity—Bul'ka's award and Lukashenko's speech—clearly shows the elective affinities between the local policies implemented by the clergyman and the authoritarian policy adopted by the regime since 1996. Although Mosar is not a representative case—even if some people have tried to imitate the priest (Golesnik 2008)—it is nonetheless significant, or "typical" in the Weberian sense, as it clearly shows the relationship between the institutional practices adopted at the national level and disciplinary procedures implemented locally. While Bul'ka's policy did not mechanically generate docility toward the regime, it did favor the possibility of not only accepting it, but of actually approving of it. The discipline he expected of his parishioners increased "the *Chance* that, because of practised disposition, a command will find prompt, automatic, and schematic obedience among a definite number of persons" (M. Weber 2019: 134). If, as Foucault (2001: 1337) and Bourdieu (2000: 169) assert, consent to order is disseminated by bodies, Bul'ka's work contributed to domination insofar as it increases "the Chance" that "a command will meet with compliance" (M. Weber 2019: 135). His statements did not contradict this interpretation. He told a journalist from the official press who came to interview him a few years earlier that he categorically refused to talk about politics. In the discussion, however, he praised the qualities of Belarusians, calling them "disciplined," before slipping in a few of his personal opinions:

> There are so many problems in the world: alcoholism, drug addiction .... Why don't politicians think about that? Unfortunately, there are very few believers among them. Most of them are careerists. Many people talk about democracy and other similar things. Yes, democracy is good, I do not dispute that, but who said that democracy should mean a lack of discipline? (Babenko 2005)

These words echo de Tocqueville's (2019: 16) maxim: "The love of order is confounded with a taste for oppression."

Finally, Bul'ka not only promoted the emergence of the conditions for consent to domination through his work; he also agreed to act as an instrument that could be mobilized by the authorities in order to pursue their political opponents. In this way, his position and prestige on both the local and national scenes has made him a useful tool, in the authorities' eyes, for the public management of the Polish minority, whose activists are sometimes close to the opposition. Lukashenko regularly accuses its representatives of seeking to destabilize or even overthrow his regime. In 2005, a crisis broke out between Minsk and Warsaw over the appointment of a new representative of these minorities in Belarus (Lepesant 2007: 508). Threats, searches, and arrests soon followed. In this context, and to challenge allegations that Poles were being bullied and Catholics treated worse than members of the Orthodox Church in Belarus, the official press exploited Bul'ka's declarations that there was no problem of this kind in the country (Babenko 2005). Moreover, the statue of Pope John Paul II at the entrance to the Church of Mosar—the first of its kind in Belarus—is not there to remind people of the subversive force that religion may have played in the Eastern bloc, but to celebrate the rigor of a pope who was a passionate believer in order. Here, the challenge posed by the Catholic religion—potentially a vehicle for the expression of ideological and political oppositions—is ostensibly defused. It contributes to a broader program of ideological neutralization. Ultimately, for our protagonist, only social, political, moral, and spiritual order counted, providing fertile ground for his proselytism.

However, it would be simplistic to see Mosar's world solely in terms of the deployment of a disciplinary program that subjugated parishioners—in short, as a simple cog in the dictatorship's "machinery" (Lallemand and Symaniec 2007). Observations made in the field and villagers' testimonies suggest that Bul'ka's popularity at the local level was due not only to "psychological coercion" but also to the distribution of various "psychological rewards" in return. These "rewards" related to obtaining "salvation goods," such as a religious experience, healing, in the case of repentant alcoholics, or pride, for the members of a parish that had established a national reputation. They were also of a material nature—when the priest enabled a repentant alcoholic to keep his job on the kolkhoz, for example. In this way, Bul'ka increased the material and symbolic resources that could be mobilized in this territory, enhancing the parishioners' "autochthonous capital" (*capital d'autochtonie*; Renahy 2005: 264). More broadly, in a world characterized in the 1990s by a certain anomie, confusion, and challenges to the living environment that was gradually developed by the Soviet authorities, the prelate's work enabled the reintroduction of a certain coherence and the construction, in his own way, of "a meaningful 'cosmos'" (M. Weber 1958: 281). By practicing a form of politics, he was also contributing to the effacement of politics and, consequently, to the effacement of political domination. Unilaterally interpreting his actions in terms of subjection would prevent us from understanding the roles of composition and ambivalence in this symbolic universe. For certain parishioners, the conditions established in Mosar over the past fifteen years have provided moments of respite and created places with a sense of otherness. This problem of interpretation becomes particularly acute when we examine Bul'ka's links to historical events.

PAST LIVES AND MEMORIAL ORDER

Patrimonialization

During our first visit, Bul'ka showed us the ethnographic museum he had created in Mosar. It occupied an old barn located a few steps away from the church and contained an eighteenth-century billiard table, an old clock made in Paris, traditional tools, handmade rugs, and more. He emphasized the fact that these different items were brought in by inhabitants of the village and surrounding areas. He had asked them to seek out these abandoned objects so that he could exhibit them and thus show visitors traces of the parish's past. This museum also exhibited documents associated with the village's history, including the personal belongings of a man born in Mosar, which are meaningfully displayed. During the Great Patriotic War of 1941–1945, this soldier was captured by the Germans, escaped, and, after fighting for the French Resistance, went to England at the end of the war, studied at Cambridge, and then emigrated to Australia to work in the nuclear industry. He returned to visit his birthplace in the early 1990s. It is interesting to note that this trajectory does not correspond to the stereotype of the valiant Soviet Belarusian, and that in another era it would have been associated with an "enemy of the people" who betrayed his homeland. Bul'ka nevertheless turned the spotlight on this character, a person suspended in the historical ether, unwittingly buffeted by the winds of history, but whose roots were in this village. It was apparent that the "history" presented there remained silent about the collectivization and deportations that accompanied the sovietization of a region that belonged to Poland until 1939 (Applebaum 2003). The knowledge and traditions on display are, like those meticulously recorded by the amateur historians in the Rybinsk region encountered by the anthropologist Elisabeth Gessat-Anstett (2007: 49), "aproblematic." By proceeding in this way, Bul'ka was granting "psychological rewards" to the villagers—enhancing their destinies and mummifying their history. Their everyday objects and handicrafts were traces of the existence of simple folk considered worthy of interest. By promoting these objects, he was simultaneously promoting the people who lived with them.

However, the priest's ambitions were not confined to this museum. The village of Pariž (Paris in Russian) is located a few kilometers away from Mosar (Golesnik 2010). According to local legend, this toponym probably dates back to the passage of Napoleonic troops through this region in 1812 (*Belarus' Segodnâ* 2008b). This is not the only place nearby to bear this name. As the historian Juliette Denis (2010: 141) points out, "Clearings [in the Belarusian and Latvian countryside] are dotted with hamlets called "*Parizh*"— founded by deserters from the Great Napoleonic Army in honor of their native country." In the case of the village near Mosar, the Soviet authorities decided to abandon this name in 1967, and to rename Pariž as Novodruck. In the 1990s, Bul'ka lent his support to certain residents and journalists who wanted to reinstate the village's former name. In 2006, the Toponymic Commission under the authority of the Council of Ministers of Belarus and the Council of Deputies for the *rajon* (district) gave its approval. The priest then had an Eiffel Tower built in Pariž. Constructed "for free," he told me, by the Glubokoe power supply company, it is made of metal and stands thirty meters tall, but differs significantly from its French counterpart in one respect: "On this one, there is a cross!" He opened the John Paul II Museum on a site near this tower, which exhibits photographs, books on the Pope's life, and a white cassock that is said to have belonged to him.

This was the priest's manner of celebrating the past, echoing those "entomologist monks who devote their wonder-struck vigils to cataloging the 'riches' of popular culture, shutting out any noise from the world of symbolic domination" (Grignon and Passeron 1989: 37). Place names must retain the traces of this past, but erase its disruptions and conflicts, in order to access a temporality where only people are present before God: sinners, repenters, and saints. Bul'ka strove to resurrect a buried past, composed of ancient place names, sundry items harking back to a prerevolutionary life that was looked down upon as "uncivilized" in Soviet times, Catholic rituals long banned by the Kremlin, and previously unknown destinies such as that of the Australian émigré attached to his native land. This patrimonialized past, possessing certain "dignifying" virtues for the inhabitants of the surrounding area—the descendants of people who possessed know-how and values—is an inert past, without power relations and without enemies. It is an orderly past whose only impact on the present is to indicate what must be accomplished in daily life: working (for oneself and for God) and obeying (the priest, the kolkhoz director, and the government). It is a past that guarantees the locality's links with an identity that predates communism, an identity that seeks to reconnect with the long history of tradition—that is, the repetition of actions bequeathed by the ancestors. It is a dehistoricized past, in the sense that it makes no mention of conflicts, personal choices, biographical upheavals, or politics. In this case, John Paul II is not the symbol of resistance to communism in Poland, but rather the incarnation of a pope who was fiercely attached to the Catholic tradition.

Criminal "Affairs"

These issues took on great memorial importance in 2009. The "Bul'ka Affair," revealed by Andrzej Poczobut in the Polish newspaper *Gazeta Wyborcza*, hit the headlines on 3 March. In the weeks that followed, it was taken up by the independent Belarusian press. During the late 1940s, Bul'ka had been a member of resistance fighters called the Forest Brothers, combating the Soviet invader in Lithuania. Then, after joining what would become the KGB, he was accused of having committed at least fifty-six murders. The journalist published his conclusions following proceedings initiated by the Lithuanian judicial authorities. In early 2009, Prosecutor Valdemaras Baranauskas issued a European arrest warrant for Bul'ka, accusing him of participating in the Soviet "genocide" of Lithuanians. If he had appeared before a Lithuanian court, he would have been sentenced to a maximum of twenty-five years in prison, under Article 99 of the Lithuanian Criminal Code (*Charter 97* 2009a, 2009b). It should be recalled that following the Molotov-Ribbentrop Pact signed on 23 August 1939, Soviet troops entered Lithuania on 15 June 1940. The sovietization of the country then began, even before its official annexation on 3 August (Anušauskas 2001: 323). Despite the ensuing deportations—12,562 people (7,439 families) between 15 and 17 June 1941 (Wolff and Moullec 2005: 26)—the Soviet authorities were confronted, after the Great Patriotic War and the German occupation, with a "war waged by partisans" (Anušauskas 2001: 328), who considered the Soviets, and particularly the Russians, to be "occupying" Lithuania. The order was given to quell the nationalist rebellion without delay. From 1945 to 1959, the security bodies (successively called NKVD/NKGB, MVB/MGB, and then the KGB) entrusted the repression of the Lithuanian resistance to "groups of combatants" defined, according to a top-secret KGB publication dated 1972, as having the authority "in complete independence, to capture or liquidate intelligence and sabotage units and gangs" (Anušauskas 2001: 332). Their methods included torture, looting, summary execution, and operations staged to deceive the enemy. In total, between 1945 and 1959, nearly five hundred partisans were executed by these special forces and 220 were taken prisoner. Seven hundred members of the anti-Soviet opposition were interrogated, leading to the arrest of five thousand supporters, liaison officers, and reservists of the armed underground movement (Anušauskas 2001: 354). Other estimates indicate that, during this period, "tens of thousands" of these Forest Brothers were killed (Wolff and Moullec 2005: 6).

Journalist Andrzej Poczobut stated he had carefully studied documents from the KGB archives and met witnesses (Strižak 2009b). He reconstructed the course of events in the following manner. After his initial arrest, Bul'ka gave the names of twenty fighters, their pseudonyms, and places of residence. He then managed to escape. A few years later, the MGB arrested him again. His brother and mother appear to have been killed during this operation. After his arrest, he agreed to collaborate with the KGB, and from then on he was known to the security services under the pseudonym "Bimba." Between 1951 and 1954, he worked with groups of agents responsible for tracking down the Forest Brothers. According to Poczobut, the documents reviewed indicate that Bul'ka was an irreproachable chekist who was allegedly responsible for the deaths of at least fifty-six people. The journalist gave details of the methods used:

> For example, Bul'ka once laid a mine in a bunker where a partisans' meeting was in progress. He came out and the mine exploded. Some of the partisans were killed. Another proven fact is known. Bul'ka personally killed at least one person. It happened in the following way. To arrest the partisans, a product called "Neptune" was used. Bul'ka used to mix it with the partisans' food and drink. They would fall into a deep sleep and wake up in an MGB prison. Bul'ka once exceeded the dose and a partisan died. (Strižak 2009b)

In an article published by a leading French academic journal several years before this media controversy, the historian A. Anušauskas (2001: 349) had already mentioned Bul'ka's involvement in different operations:

> On 11 April 1951, in Strazdai, a village in the Utena *rajon*, four combatants started shooting at the Balis Vaičėnas-Liubartas detachment of the brigade for the *okrug* of Vytautas. Six partisans were killed along with the [five] witnesses who were there.... The recruited partisan Juozas Bulka-Skrajūnas acted as the guide for this top-secret operation. (This man, known under the *agentura* pseudonym of 'Bimba,' is now living in Belarus).

Anušauskas (2001: 351) subsequently adds further details. "Several bogus partisan organizations were active in the MGB until the summer of 1953, such as the unit operating in the Vytautas region, led by Juozas Bulka-Skrajunas (Special Agent 'Bimba')."

Thereafter, his life is shrouded in mystery. He is said to have received technical training in agronomy, and to have worked in a factory manufacturing electric meters in Vilnius before retiring. Some people suspect him of having been married (*Charter 97* 2009b). In 1987, he was ordained as a priest in Poland. The Catholic hierarchy is not thought to have looked into his past (*Charter 97* 2009b). This does not seem to be an isolated case, since historian Aléna Lapatniova (2006: 761) writes that "in January 2000, the Lithuanian Catholic Church publicly apologized on behalf of the priests who had collaborated with the KGB, [but] neither the overall number of these priests nor even the percentage were disclosed." Some even argue that Bul'ka was ordained as a priest with the help of the special services and that when his case came to light, the KGB continued to protect him (Strijak 2009a). Although born in Lithuania, he decided to obtain Belarusian nationality. It also transpired that he spent a long period of time in Kazakhstan (Zaval'nûk 2007). In 2008, the Lithuanians asked the Belarusian authorities to question him. The press department of the Belarus General Prosecutor's Office told Euroradio journalists, "We are aware of the case, but we will not comment on it in any way." Bul'ka denied the accusations.

This case illustrates the "iron curtain of memory" (Droit 2007: 103) separating the two territories. With the USSR's victory over the Nazi enemy and its collaborators largely contributing to the definition of the Russian (Denis 2010: 146) and Belarusian (Goujon 2010) identities, today Lithuania, like the other Baltic countries, assesses the Soviet occupation essentially from the victim's perspective, thus distancing itself from the official Soviet memory, even if it means ignoring its citizens' participation in the Shoah (Droit 2007: 107). Lithuania thus uses the term "genocide" to describe the crimes committed by the Soviet occupiers. The Vilnius Museum of Genocide Victims (Droit 2007: 110; Denis 2010: 149) and the Genocide and Resistance Research Center of Lithuania, where the aforementioned historian Anušauskas formerly worked, both set out to address the issue of the suffering endured by the country's population during the Soviet occupation. This dividing line between memorial cultures is not only defined by official "memory entrepreneurs" (Droit 2007: 102), it is also reflected in individual evocations of the past. For example, comments posted on the press websites and on various Belarusian forums highlight the involvement of Lithuanians in the massacre of Jews in the region. In this context, the Belarusian authorities did not deny the accusations leveled at Bul'ka, but their silence was indicative of their different interpretation of his possible collaboration with KGB services. Far from committing "genocide," the Soviet forces pacified a territory in which their enemies were operating, enemies who had collaborated with the Nazis. In Belarus, Soviet action during the Great Patriotic War was not called into question. The people demonstrated their greatness and sacrificed themselves to defend their homeland and the world (Goujon 2010). During this conflict, 2.2 million people died in Belarus—a quarter of the total population (Drweski 1993: 103).

The "Bul'ka Affair" emerged at around the same time as other similar controversies. This clash of memorial cultures is also apparent in the way the official press handled the Kononov case, for example. Imprisoned by the Latvian authorities for war crimes from August 1998 to April 2000, this man was convicted of murdering nine innocent citizens while leading a group of partisans. He countered that these people had been collaborating with the Nazis. When, on 17 May 2010, the Grand Chamber of the European Court of Human Rights annulled the court's decision of 24 July 2008, ruling that the conviction handed down by the Latvian court was illegal, the Russian authorities immediately reacted strongly. Two days after Kononov's death at the age of eighty-nine on 31 March 2011, the official Belarusian press devoted an article to him, titled "He lived and died like a soldier," and denounced the "contemporary Nazi revisionism" promoted by "European bureaucrats" (Belyh 2011). This affair reflects other, less publicized, cases. Consequently, the historian Juliette Denis (2010: 150) observes that "the prosecution for crimes against humanity, by the Lithuanian judiciary, of ghetto survivors who joined the partisans and fought the collaborators, has very recently aroused contrasting reactions and has once again revived the debate on the assimilation of Nazism and Stalinism." The Bul'ka case thus revealed a past composed of enemies, executioners, and victims, in which the actors have had to grapple with their history, been forced to make choices, and sometimes committed terrible acts. As it resurfaces, this past raises the question of individual responsibility and the collective choices that determine the course of history, with the implication that this course can be considered to unfold in varied ways. The present could amount to more than the docile repetition of ancient acts, and could be a place of innovation, novelty, and questioning—what Bul'ka considered as the disorder of democracy, in short. In this manner, it can be seen that someone who based his reputation on the orderly representation of a patrimonialized past was eventually caught up by the realities of history and his biographical past. This past threatened not only Bul'ka personally but more fundamentally the order of the world he had gradually created in Mosar. It is clear that this politicized past contrasted with the patrimonialized and orderly past that was embodied in a place described as paradisiacal by its visitors.

In the end, what remains of these two different pasts in Mosar? Did the revelations about the clergyman ultimately change the course of events? At this point, it is interesting to consider the reactions to this affair. While the official press remained silent on this subject, the opposition press initially published several articles specifying the issues raised by the controversy. Calling the Soviet forces' actions into question enabled the legitimacy of the current political regime, which lays claim to this heritage, to be tacitly challenged. However, a few months later, when Bul'ka died on 9 January 2010 (*Belarus' Segodnâ* 2010), the opposition press itself failed to mention this affair and paid tribute to the man who had created the "mini-Versailles" of Belarus (*Charter 97* 2010). More than one year later, when the newspaper *Naša Niva* (2011)—a recurrent target of repressive measures—reported on activities in Mosar, it no longer even mentioned Bul'ka. These silences seem to point toward a certain embarrassment and, basically, to the success of the priest's venture. Forming a hybrid ideological universe, a palimpsest of varied and intertwined traditions combining messages of the gospel, the cult of John Paul II, the defense of tradition, attachment to nature, and the promotion of order, and embodying this symbolic universe in an orderly and renowned territory embellished by flowers, it somehow smooths out the glaring ideological differences between political groups and blurs party affiliations. The priest himself—on 6 April 2009, a few days after the Lithuanians' accusation—told the Belarusian news agency Interfax, "They don't want Belarus to be beautiful." The reactions to his death—unanimous in the press—reflected his ability to disarm his opponents, probably because, in addition to the disciplinary measures he implemented, he also distributed different psychological and material rewards to the people around him. Upon his death, the charisma associated with his role, combined with his personal charisma, made any questioning of his actions seem impossible. Some felt that even if he had murdered fifty-six Lithuanians, he could be considered to have redeemed himself through his work in Mosar. It was all the more difficult to be critical because, both in the press and in the different testimonies gathered, it was claimed that he died as a result of the accusations made against him. Reversing the roles of the villain and victim, Bul'ka acquired a "saintly" dimension post mortem. This has been alluded to on numerous occasions in the press, in readers' comments, and on forums, in claims that he was killed by the soiling of his reputation by a part of humanity, and that he served with devotion and asceticism by creating the "paradise of Mosar." And this sociologist can only remain silent, with the "affair" rendering any fieldwork impossible and highly sensitive, since a Frenchman could no longer innocently ask questions about parish life without being suspected of passing judgment, yet again, on the man who had done so much for the villagers' wellbeing.

Today, near the church in Mosar, people can visit the tomb of Bul'ka, who was born in 1925 and died in 2010. The following words, in Belarusian, are engraved in the marble: "He loved God, Nature and the Belarusian people." His successors are now perpetuating his legacy (Korbut 2011). Honoring the inhabitants with his policy of intensive local development (support for alcoholics, enshrinement of local popular traditions in a museum, construction of a tourist site whose reputation reflects favorably on parishioners, etc.), he simultaneously contributed to the establishment of moral, social, political, and memorial order in this territory. Studies show that the procedures used to impose a certain order in everyday life are all the more effective if they are linked to a certain representation of the past. Far from being independent processes, there are homologies in the imposition of order on bodies, morals, practices, territories, and memory that reflect the systematic efforts to promote discipline and order in this locality. The careful orchestration of the past must provide reminders that after the upheavals of history, people only find true value in respect for traditions, order, and the sacred, timeless scriptures. Consequently, the Mount Calvary in Belarus reflects the mountain climbed by Christ twenty centuries ago; the statues of biblical characters remind people living today of the atemporality of their condition as sinners in search of redemption. The spiritualization of souls and bodies traumatized by today's history—harsh working conditions, economic crisis, poverty, and the violence wrought by alcohol—is accompanied by the depoliticization of individual destinies. If the world is an ordeal, it is not because politicians organize social relations in a particular way, but because this has always been the case and people can overcome adversity only if they display their moral qualities—first and foremost, their respect for discipline.

As his reputation extended far beyond the boundaries of the local scene, Bul'ka also helped to legitimize the current regime, either incidentally (through his methodical approach to instilling discipline in bodies and souls, and through the silence that prevailed following the revelation of his collaboration with the KGB), or explicitly (by claiming that Polish minorities were free in Belarus, or by accepting honorary and material awards from the president himself). But the analysis of his trajectory also shows that order, while based on physical and psychological constraints, is also favored by the distribution of different types of rewards—most certainly material, but also psychological.

Although this is not a representative case, it is not an isolated one. It ultimately encapsulates different practices observed in the Belarusian countryside between 2006 and 2013, and which are particularly apparent in Mosar, where paternalism, tutelary power, and philanthropic overtones are combined, in different configurations, with what could be described as dignifying mechanisms, or which are at least perceived as such. In fact, by specifying that "the concept of 'power'" is merely "sociologically amorphous," M. Weber (2019: 134) invites us to consider the precise mechanisms that domination relies on, besides violence and material rewards. As Grignon and Passeron (1989: 63) write, "Sociology begins when historical forms, instruments and configurations of domination are defined." Consequently, life under a system of authoritarian rule, such as the regime in place in Belarus since 1996, would appear to be an appropriate setting for analyzing the diverse ways in which a political group can obtain docility and "the plasticity of the authoritarian exercise of power" (Hibou 2017: 303). The case of Mosar illustrates how the political regime can benefit from actions carried out locally, outside any clearly pre-established program, and—by recognizing the value of these unanticipated initiatives and absorbing them into the government's operating procedures—how it can hold up these individual behaviors as an example for others to follow. By the same token, the authorities indicate that good deeds, far from being the result of a manufactured ideology, are guided by the nature of things. This shows the meticulous work of "dehistoricization" that is required to maintain the current state of moral, social, and political order (Bourdieu 2000: 160). This study, as it unfolds, also shows how the sociologist can be overwhelmed, during the investigation period, by the occurrence of events that disrupt the course of life and the world that could previously be observed. On the one hand, this disruption required the suspension of the study carried out in the village. On the other hand, it gave insight into the extent to which the imposition of social and political order in the territory studied was intrinsically linked to the imposition of a memorial order whose ultimate aim was to erase history—its disorders and its conflicts—and thus enable the exclusive emergence of souls threatened by the specter of evil and cowed by questions of salvation and redemption.

NOTE

1. This chapter is based on elements published in a previous article (Hervouet 2014), but with a somewhat different demonstrative thread.

CONCLUSION

DOMINATION

In Belarus, rural governance remains consistent with the practices employed during the Soviet era. It is based on the collectivist matrix, associated with forms of administrative pressure, coercive management of the labor force, and paternalistic mechanisms. Kolkhozes are clearly paradoxical in that they are both a controlled and an uncertain world. Living conditions depend on many factors: the quality of the land, which varies according to geographical location; the director's personality, partly determined by his or her background and professional ambitions; investments decided on at hierarchical levels outside the kolkhozians' control; vagaries of the weather; erratic market developments that depend on both economic and geopolitical factors; and so on. Although it displays a particularly strong disciplinary dimension, in practice this closed world tolerates many illegalisms that, without calling into question the general directives handed down from above, ease certain constraints on countryfolk at the local level and make their future more predictable. These illegalisms include the private use of collective resources (theft, robbery, misappropriation, accounting fraud), the distillation and distribution of home-made alcohol, and, in a more residual manner, poaching or prostitution. They also complement the authorized resources that people can obtain in rural areas. Indeed, countryfolk can legally increase their resources by cultivating their personal plots of land. Some of this production is destined for self-consumption, with the surplus being sold on markets. They can also perform transactions with urbanites who live in the country, engage in cross-border activities, or make profits from more marginal practices, such as exchange-rate speculation and the misappropriation of humanitarian aid or the gifts and remittances of foreign currency made possible in contexts of social mobility resulting from transnational marriages. These practices can be accurately documented by conducting a "discrete ethnography" over an extended period. These resources are mobilized within systems of horizontal and vertical interdependencies implying relatively stable configurations of reciprocities and obligations.

First, the use of these resources enables the satisfaction of certain material expectations, which differ according to generational affiliations. Their modes of appropriation and mobilization then produce forms of practical solidarity. Finally, they allow people to lead dignified and meaningful lives, since they enable the manifestation of socially recognized qualities: endurance, ingenuity, enthusiasm, and a sense of independence. Individuals thus negotiate with the imposed constraints in order to decompartmentalize their life worlds. These constraints are not seen as the embodiments of an oppressive system, but rather as an order of things that must be appropriated in order to construct one's own universe. They may therefore seem "enabling" (Giddens 1986: 169). They close some worlds while simultaneously opening up others. This research thus shows that, from the perspective of the political economy of domination, "economic relations, which are also power relations, can indeed allow control and normalization, but are simultaneously spaces of freedom, spaces of relaxation of discipline, or quite simply autonomous spaces" (Hibou 2017: 288). For those who are loyal to the hierarchy and the authorities, the system provides unwritten, unspoken, and unstated rules, within which everyone knows how to maneuver in order to exert a small and tenuous but real hold over their existence. To this end, people must not exploit their position unreasonably, although the judgment of what is reasonable varies, since the differentiated management of illegalisms relates to diverse configurations defined by several dimensions, including the general political context, the economic results of the region in question, and local power relations in the administration. The fact that everyone is involved in these systems of illegalisms allows the political authorities to maintain order in these rural areas where everyone can potentially be repressed. However, the arbitrariness of these practices is not perceived as unjust since everyone—even the most powerful people—can be punished. On the contrary, this arbitrariness could reveal a form of "poetic justice" by embodying "a wish for negative reciprocity, a settling of scores when the high shall be brought low and the last shall be first" (Scott 1990: 41–42). This world is ultimately perceived as a moral universe. Admittedly, the people encountered denounce the dysfunctions linked to the organization of work, as in the Soviet era. I am told that the tractors coming out of the Minsk factory are defective. A veterinarian complains that the director of his kolkhoz is a former sports teacher whose personal connections got him the job, and laments the fact that he knows nothing about agriculture. Criticism is leveled at alcoholics—a category of interpretation of the social world that is particularly prevalent in everyday discussions—who do not work when they are needed. Superiors are denounced for requiring their subordinates to work hard for a few thousand rubles while they themselves misappropriate substantial volumes of diesel fuel originally intended for equipment used on the kolkhoz. However, while this system is subject to various types of criticism, it is not fundamentally called into question. This moral world revolves around three principles of justice that define the organization of life universes: solidarity, equality, and dignity. If one does not openly challenge this mode of regulation, if one complies with certain hierarchical expectations, if one works hard and manages to seize the opportunities offered, one can attain an honorable status in terms of material success and social recognition. In return, the state is expected to quell the threats embodied by three major figures: the idler, the profiteer, and the moralist. The aim is to maintain a predictable, orderly, stable, and familiar universe that has been tamed. The imposition of social, political, economic, and religious control thus ensures the perpetuation of this order.

By inducing specific practices through the circumvention of official constraints, the system thus *indirectly* generates a specific moral economy. This concept refers to the values shared by a population, values on which are based its conceptions of what is fair or unfair, tolerable or intolerable, acceptable or scandalous. The moral economy of a social group is firmly rooted in everyday practices. It configures its organization, but also the emotions, moral feelings, indignation, resentment, and the modalities of action or protest that must be deployed when its principles are not respected. In this way, the dominated "see themselves as endowed with qualities and logics that guide them in their evaluation of what is good and what is fair and on which they rely to act in the world" (Fassin 2009: 1238). This notion thus makes it possible "to envisage domination without presupposing the unconditional internalization of consent" (Siméant 2010: 145). Indeed, from this perspective, "the structural determinations of domination are never 'determinisms,' that is, they never negate the actors' reflexive consciousness or their critical capacity" (Tarragoni 2017: 118). In the Belarusian case, people—by mobilizing various resources and exercising their moral qualities—open up the field of possibilities, construct their worlds, and gain recognition. This enables them not to prevent domination, but to help shape and alter it (Hibou 2017: 304). However, as these are fragile balances, the populations develop expectations of the political authorities—expectations that the regime meets by repressing threatening figures.

IDEOLOGY

This moral economy reflects the ideological foundations of the regime without mechanically reproducing them. It is claimed that "market socialism" develops an efficient economy while controlling the growth of inequalities and defending the egalitarian principle inherited from the Soviet century, and also counters the individualistic effects of the market by promoting collectivism. Its other alleged benefits include enabling the expression of forms of popular dignity prohibited in capitalist systems of exploitation, and combating the deleterious effects of globalization and "cosmopolitanism" by defending tradition (Mel'nik 2010). Countryfolk recognize themselves in this top-down discourse. However, attachment to these principles and the legitimacy of the regime that stems from them are not the consequence of a performative official discourse, but the symbolic extension of practices firmly rooted in everyday life. Adopting an ethnographic approach to the study of worlds under the dictatorship can therefore reveal that this everyday existence is not reduced to a simple projection of the authorities' views. Countryfolk, in order to create lifestyles that they consider acceptable or even desirable, adopt practices (illegalisms, mutual aid) that are supposed to help them adapt to constraints imposed from above (rules, injunctions, controls). These practices generate worldviews and feelings of justice (solidarity, equality, and dignity) that directly echo the official discourses without automatically being a product of them. They reflect what Alexei Yurchak (2006: 26) calls a "heteronymous shift," referring to the heterogeneous, unpredictable, shifting and constantly reinvented meanings underlying the reproduction of ideological forms. Local accounts of power and the economy are congruent with the authorities' propaganda and narratives, without any implication that the people encountered might be "cultural dopes" manipulated by the regime. Ideology is therefore not the primary explanatory principle for their behavior, nor is it the yardstick outside local situations by which reality is evaluated and judged, unlike the case of the Polish and Hungarian working classes during the communist era, analyzed by Michael Burawoy and János Lukács (1992: 139):

> Out of this divergence of ideology and reality there develops a distinctive working-class consciousness. State socialism becomes the brunt of critique for failing to live up to its own pretensions, pretensions that assume an independent force because they are repeatedly enacted in orchestrated, compulsory rituals and because they correspond to unrealized aims and aspirations embedded in the lived experience of work.

In the contemporary Belarusian context, however, ideology—caught up in the "surreptitious paths of domination" (Hibou 2017: 275)—takes on a form similar to that analyzed by Béatrice Hibou (2017: 318) in her comparative approach to authoritarian regimes:

> Ideology does not define social functions; it does not set out one rationality but multiple rationalities that are themselves mobile and fluid. What we find is more a concatenation of rationalities than the application of one rationality uniquely and unambiguously determined by ideology; this is why there are often contradictions between ideology and the dispositifs that rely upon it. The unintentional aspect of domination also appears in those practices that "vampirize" the proclamations of ideology.

Indeed, the system disseminates numerous constraints linked to its ideological agenda, and in this way induces systematic circumventions of the rules, which themselves generate a morality reminiscent of the authorities' views. Consequently, the system indirectly produces forms relating less to adherence to a doctrinal corpus than to acceptance of an existing situation that is interpreted as being neither unfair nor illegitimate. This shows that obedience, docility, and consent are not synonymous with adhesion. The people I encountered accept the authoritarian regime without espousing its aims and values. Behaviors that do not conform to the rules handed down from above still accommodate them and cannot, therefore, be considered as a conflicting form of resistance to the official line. They are marked by cooperation and conflict, adherence and misgivings, subjugation and subtle or tenuous forms of insubordination.

This perspective diverges from the binary reasoning that characterizes a number of analyses of everyday life under authoritarian regimes: victim/offender, dissident/activist, adherence/opposition, resistance/collaboration (Yurchak 2006: 4–8, 102–108). Indeed, the specific study of Belarusian rural worlds indicates that the "unspectacular" behaviors identified cannot be classified according to "the bipolarity of 'obedience-or-resistance'" (Lüdtke 2015: 50). This is at odds with approaches endorsing the performativity of the state discourse, and the existence of "ideological hegemony" and "involuntary subordination" (Scott 1990: 82), but also with "infrapolitical" interpretations that focus on "a wide variety of low-profile forms of resistance that dare not speak in their own name" (Scott 1990: 19), tending to consider any deviation from the rule as an oppositional practice. Admittedly, certain discursive traces gathered in the field, such as the use of irony and humor, may stem from a hidden transcript, "the privileged site for nonhegemonic, contrapuntal, dissident, subversive discourse" (Scott 1990: 25). However, the comments I collected reflect more of an intertwining than a dissociation of the hidden and public transcripts. They do not manifest a "somewhat schizophrenic way" of existing that would be characteristic of "double people" (Dimov 1980), wearing "masks" (Scott 1990: 55), driven by a "double consciousness" (Scott 1990: 44), or systematically guided by "cynical disbelief" (Scott 1990: 66), duplicity, and pretense, but rather "proliferating meanings" (Hibou 2017: 308) in which local principles of justice and state ideology are reflected.

Different concepts bear witness to the incompleteness of dominating practices. Some of them originate from the historiography of communist regimes in Europe. The notion of *Eigensinn* developed by Alf Lüdtke (Lüdtke and Oeser 2015) reflects "the varied forms of ideological positions [that] can coexist in the same person" (Oeser 2015: 10) and sheds light on the forms of "morose loyalty" (Lüdtke 2000: 189) of ordinary citizens observed under totalitarian and authoritarian regimes. Nicolas Werth (2001a, 2001b) highlights two other notions. The German term *"resistenz"* refers to "any social behavior revealing a limit to the total hold exerted by the regime (as opposed to the notion of *widerstand*, indicating a radical and determined resistance)" (Werth 2001a: 132). The Russian term *"stihiâ,"* which is "hard to translate," is "very often used by the Soviet authorities to simultaneously designate spontaneity, disorder, chaos, the force of natural or social elements opposing the 'regulatory' action of political power," and is distinct from the term *"soprotivlenie,"* meaning action taken "against" (*protiv*) attacks on society and presupposing a real commitment (Werth 2001b: 883). The anthropologist Alexei Yurchak (2006: 127–133) uses the Russian term *"vnye"* to describe behavior that is neither obedient nor compliant, thereby referring to ways of being both inside and outside the system. He also uses the expression "internal emigration" (Yurchak 2006: 132), specifying that this expression implies not closure but rather a variable and ambivalent position. Other concepts developed in different contexts help to capture the range of attitudes that we are seeking to qualify here. In his analysis of the "arts of doing" (*arts de faire*) practiced in the consumer society, Michel de Certeau (1998: 38) places the emphasis on "tactics" and "poaching" when qualifying the "cross-cuts, fragments, cracks and lucky hits in the framework of a system." In his sociology of psychiatric institutions, Erving Goffman (2007: 171, 189) emphasizes the existence of "underlives" and "secondary adjustments" structuring the daily functioning of hospitals, in order to emphasize the deviations and discrepancies vis-à-vis the expectations and norms of a social organization. To some extent, these different terms relate to the "tricks of the mind" known as *mètis* in the ancient Greek world.

> There is no doubt that *mètis* is a type of intelligence and of thought, a way of knowing; it implies a complex but very coherent body of mental attitudes and intellectual behaviour which combine flair, wisdom, forethought, subtlety of mind, deception, resourcefulness, vigilance, opportunism, various skills, and experience acquired over the years. It is applied to situations which are transient, shifting, disconcerting and ambiguous, situations which do not lend themselves to precise measurement, exact calculation or rigorous logic. (Détienne and Vernant 1991: 3–4)

Semantic inflation, the instability of notions, and the use of foreign terms that are difficult to translate to qualify the spectrum of ordinary behavior in an authoritarian regime indicate that this field of conceptual construction remains fallow.

NOSTALGIA

The political ethnography of rural Belarus prompts reflection on the links between nostalgia, ideology, and everyday life. A feeling of nostalgia has spread throughout countries that are no longer communist states. In her polyphonic literary form devoted to "the end of the red man," Svetlana A. Alexievich (2017b) sifts through interwoven testimonies gathered from citizens who grew up and lived in the USSR, expressing their nostalgia for past times and memories of food products, smells, objects, architecture, space conquests, military power, order, love of culture, dreams and horizons, rituals and festivals, films and songs, etc. Academic analyses have identified different forms, modalities, and intensities of nostalgia in former Eastern bloc countries (Bartmanski 2011; Todorova and Gill 2012), which are reflected in neologisms referring to national situations (*Ostalgie* in Germany, *Yugonostalgia*) and in the heterogeneous vehicles for these aspirations, such as museums (Bach 2017) or television programs (Oushakine 2007). These reflections also reveal the "polysemy of nostalgic practices" (Nadkarni and Shevchenko 2004). Svetlana Boym (2001) thus distinguishes between restorative nostalgia promoting the restoration of the past, which is instrumentalized by the implementation of memorial policies striving to re-establish forms of national greatness, and reflective nostalgia, which is represented as a personal and melancholic sense of escaping from time.

How can the political ethnography of rural Belarus help to explain this phenomenon? It can be observed that in regions and countries from which "traditional" *subbotniki* have disappeared, they are sometimes missed. For example, Sarah Ashwin (1995: 1375) and Anne White (2000: 686), in their studies of changes in two small towns in the Russian province of Vishnovka in the Kuzbass basin and Zubtsov in the Tver region in the 1990s, both observed a certain nostalgia for the *subbotniki* organized during the Soviet era. Similarly, the anthropologist Olga Shevchenko (2009: 41) recorded the following remark made by Maria, a 37-year-old nurse from Moscow, in the 1990s: "Life is joyless.... Before, there were meetings; the Pioneer and Komsomol meetings, and even the *subbotniki*, were enjoyable in the end. There was more sociability." This feeling is not simply the expression of an idealized reconstruction of the past. It reflects clearly assumed forms of attachment to this practice. How can this link be explained while considering the interviewees not to be pure products of the ideological apparatus of the Soviet regime? Attachment to *subbotniki* in post-Soviet Belarus cannot be explained by the effectiveness of the ideology but rather by the forms of practical solidarity adopted to cope with the constraints, directives, and pressures imposed by the hierarchy. To some degree, the system fortuitously necessitates solidarity.

These considerations enable the interpretation of certain manifestations of nostalgia without overpoliticizing the reasons for its emergence. Different literary accounts contain nostalgic references to parades and the enthusiasm that would appear to have accompanied public celebrations. These include the Belarusian artist Artur Klinau's (2015: 133–135) recollections of his childhood in Minsk:

> Revolution Day—November 7—also coincided with the school holidays. . . . Every once in a while, my mother would take me with her to the march. . . . We were marching with the delegation from the shoe factory. When we arrived at the agreed place, we found people who radiated a genuine joy: this really was a celebration for them. . . . As the stands came into view, the crowd's roars became even louder. When we were finally right up against the stands, they filled the whole space around us and enveloped us too: "Hu-u-u-urrra-a-a-y!," yelled the participants toward the stands on which the big shots of Sun City were standing with smiles on their lips. This was the highlight of the day, the height of the enthusiasm, a feeling of infinite happiness. Then, while marching toward Victory Square, the columns of people would scatter, returning to their homes where tables sagging under the weight of scarce products that had been tracked down for the festivities awaited them. By the evening, practically the entire city would be drunk. The revels continued on the next day, but the euphoria gradually waned. Calm returned after the celebrations.

Other researchers underline the recurrent expressions of nostalgia for a time when people relied on each other, as distinct from the contemporary era in which "everyone has become greedy" (Paxson 2005: 93). They miss the days when solidarity was supposedly stronger. In the former GDR, Michel Streith (2005: 163) notes that "during interviews, the women willingly recall the social benefits, solidarity, mutual aid and the dynamism of village life." Here are other testimonies concerning Russia in the 1990s:

> Rimma (now 50 years old) looks back nostalgically on her first years as an instructor: "We all knew each other; we used to meet at my house on Sundays—fifteen of us in our two-roomed apartment; we would tell each other everything, we shared everything—the joys and the sorrows." Perhaps without realizing it, Rimma had recreated the communal atmosphere she had loved as a child in Polegorodok and later in the Communist Youth movement. The nostalgia that Rimma expresses in 1992, after the fall of the regime, cannot be reduced to nostalgia for her youth; it expresses a much deeper malaise, caused by the irretrievable loss of a cultural model that forged social bonds, that integrated society through a system of values shared, if not by all, then at

least by the vast majority. Her husband Viktor says the same thing more succinctly: "I still do the same job, I go to the (trolley) depot every morning, but the atmosphere has changed. Today, no one needs anyone anymore." (Bertaux and Malysheva 1994: 205)

On the face of it, there could be a temptation to attribute this feeling to an ideological cause, as if the dissemination of the official doctrine had mechanically produced adhesion, as if the discourse had been genuinely performative. Field research in contemporary Belarus casts doubt on this way of reconstructing the past, without considering it groundless. This research shows that several intertwined worlds shaped everyday life under communism, that this system *indirectly* produced forms of happiness, and that this lost happiness is reconstructed a posteriori as if it had originated *directly* from the official discourse: power, equality, and a radiant future. This explanatory model makes it possible to understand some of the reasons for the nostalgia felt toward the Soviet regime without assuming that those who express such sentiments are pure victims of propaganda or retrospective illusions. People are nostalgic for a system that, although it directly produced contested worlds (repression, oppression, shortages, etc.), also *indirectly* produced worlds that were appreciated (for their forms of solidarity, forms of dignity, forms of justice). The ethnographic survey has revealed how the regime's expectations intersect, in a nonmechanical way, with those of the people it governs. The acceptance of domination does not simply stem from the performativity of the authorities' discourse, but from the interaction between a political project and life plans that are indirectly and, more often than not, unintentionally produced by the regime itself. Seen from within, this world offers a number of possibilities providing limited but diverse opportunities at the individual level and a type of order that both public authorities and individuals are calling for at the collective level. The fall of the Wall ushered in a new era in which these meaningful universes collapsed. Individual destinies are heterogeneous, but this sense of loss sometimes generates resentment, anger, and violence—against oneself, against others, against the world. In Belarus, however, these worlds—wiped out elsewhere—continue to exist.

Consequently, in this country, this nostalgia for a bygone era is sometimes manifested by a concertinaing of temporalities. S. A. Alexievich (2017b: 466) recorded this significant testimony by Tania Kulechova, a 21-year-old student who had taken part in the demonstrations of 19 December 2010, which took place a few hundred meters from the building I was living in with my family at the time. She was arrested, spent a month in prison, and then returned to her village to see her mother.

> I bought a ticket home. When I'm in the city, I miss my village. Although I'm not quite sure which village I miss; it's probably the village of my childhood. The village where

Papa would take me along to watch him take out the frames from the beehives, heavy with honey. First, he would fill them with smoke so that the bees would fly away and wouldn't sting us. When I was little, I was funny . . . I thought that bees were little birds. . . . On the bus, one of our neighbors sat down next to me. He was drunk. He talked about politics: "I would beat every moron democrat's face in myself if I could. They let you off easy. I swear to God! All among them ought to be shot. I wouldn't have given it a second thought. America is behind all this, they're paying for it . . . Hillary Clinton . . . But we're a strong people. We lived through perestroika, and we'll make it through another revolution. One wise man told me that the kikes are the ones behind it." The whole bus supported him. (Alexievich 2017b: 466)

While some young opponents are striving to bring in a new era, as in other countries where communism has been replaced by democratic systems, other social groups are seeking to keep the past alive in the present, and to perpetuate coherent cosmoses that have been wiped out elsewhere, along with the ideology that, without defining them, used to accompany them. In seeking to preserve their worlds, they are hoping to maintain the regime that indirectly produces them. Without really adhering to the ideology, they nevertheless believe that it guarantees the structures of their everyday lives. Fearing the demise of the opportunities offered to their members, as has happened in other postcommunist countries, they defend the system that claims to protect them by oppressing members of other social groups, to which belong some of the students and their relatives whom I met in Belarus, whose desires for alternative futures the authorities are seeking to destroy.

REFERENCES

BOOKS AND JOURNAL ARTICLES

Ackerman, Galia. 2006. *Tchernobyl, retour sur un désastre*. Paris: Buchet-Chastel.
———. 2016. *Traverser Tchernobyl*. Lamecy: Premier Parallèle.
Alexievich, Svetlana. (1997) 2005. *Voices from Chernobyl: The Oral History of a Nuclear Disaster*. Translated by Keith Gessen. Normal, IL: Dalkey Archive Press.
———. (2004) 2017a. *The Unwomanly Face of War: An Oral History of Women in World War II*. Translated by Richard Pevear and Larissa Volokhonsky. New York: Random House.
———. (2013) 2017b. *Secondhand Time: The Last of the Soviets*. Translated by Bela Shayevich. New York: Random House.
Allina-Pisano, Jessica. 2008. *The Post-Soviet Potemkin Village: Politics and Property Rights in the Black Earth*. Cambridge: Cambridge University Press.
Alymov, Sergei. 2011. "On the Soviet Ethnography of the Soviet Life: The Case of the 'Village of Viriatino.'" *Histories of Anthropology Annual* 7: 23–48.
Amalrik, Andrei. 1970. *Involuntary Journey to Siberia*. Translated by Manya Harari and Max Hayward. New York: Harcourt Brace Jovanovich.
Ambrosio, Thomas. 2006. "The Political Success of Russia-Belarus Relations: Insulating Minsk from a Color Revolution." *Demokratizatsiya: The Journal of Post-Soviet Democratization* 14(3): 407–434.
Amin, Samir. 2004. "On China: 'Market Socialism,' a Stage in the Long Socialist Transition or Shortcut to Capitalism?" *Social Scientist* 32(11–12): 3–20.
Anteby, Michel. 2003. "La 'perruque' en usine: approche d'une pratique marginale, illégale et fuyante." *Sociologie du travail* 45(4): 453–471.
Anušauskas, Arvydas. 2001. "La composition et les méthodes secrètes des organes de sécurité soviétiques en Lituanie, 1940–1953." *Cahiers du monde russe* 42(2–4): 321–356.
Applebaum, Anne. 2003. *Gulag: A History*. London: Doubleday.
Arendt, Hannah. 1951. *The Origins of Totalitarianism*. New York: Harcourt, Brace and Company.
Arutiunian, Yuri. 1973. "Social Mobility in the Countryside." In *Social Stratification and Mobility in the USSR*, edited by Murray Yanowitch and Wesley Fisher, 320–353. White Plains, NY: International Arts and Sciences Press.

Ashwin, Sarah. 1995. "'There's No Joy Any More': The Experience of Reform in a Kuzbass Mining Settlement." *Europe-Asia Studies* 47(8): 1367–1381.
Augustins, Georges. 1998. "La perpétuation des groupes domestiques. Un essai de formalisation." *L'Homme* 148: 15–45.
Babkoŭ, Uladzimir A., ed. 2006. *Istoriâ Minska*. Minsk: Belaruskaâ èncyklapedyâ imâ Petrusâ Broŭkì.
Bach, Daniel C. 2012. "Patrimonialism and Neopatrimonialism: Comparative Receptions and Transitions." In *Neopatrimonialism in Africa and Beyond*, edited by Daniel C. Bach and Mamoudou Gazibo, 25–45. New York: Routledge.
Bach, Jonathan P. 2017. *What Remains: Everyday Encounters with the Socialist Past in Germany*. New York: Columbia University Press.
Bafoil, François. 2000. "La classe ouvrière post-communiste. Des 'héros au pouvoir' à l'exclusion des 'petites gens.'" *Genèses. Sciences sociales et histoire* 39: 74–97.
———. (2012) 2014. *Emerging Capitalism in Central Europe and Southeast Asia: A Comparison of Political Economies*. Translated by Michael O'Mahony and John Angell. New York: Palgrave Macmillan.
———. 2016. "Adolph Hennecke. Le Stakhanov de la RDA." *Ethnologie française* 46(3): 495–506.
Bartmanski, Dominik. 2011. "Successful Icons of Failed Time: Rethinking Post-Communist Nostalgia." *Acta Sociologica* 54(3): 213–231.
Batisse, Cécile, and Monique Sélim. 2008. "Du socialisme (de marché) au post-communisme. Singularités et unicité dans la globalisation du capitalisme." *Autrepart* 48: 3–12.
Bayart, Jean-François. 1985. "L'énonciation du politique." *Revue française de science politique* 35(3): 343–373.
Beaud, Stéphane, and Florence Weber. (1997) 2010. *Guide de l'enquête de terrain: produire et analyser des données ethnographiques*. Paris: La Découverte.
Becker, Howard S. (1963) 1997. *Outsiders: Studies in the Sociology of Deviance*. New York: The Free Press.
———. 1998. *Tricks of the Trade: How to Think about Your Research While You're Doing It*. Chicago: University of Chicago Press.
Belaruskaâ èncyklapedyâ [Belarusian Encyclopedia]. 2002. Minsk.
Benett, Brian M., 2011. *The Last Dictatorship in Europe: Belarus under Lukashenko*. London: Hurst & Company.
Bensa, Alban, and Éric Fassin. 2002. "Les sciences sociales face à l'événement." *Terrain* 38: 5–20.
Beresford, Melanie. 2008. "*Doi Moi* in Review: The Challenges of Building Market Socialism in Vietnam." *Journal of Contemporary Asia* 38(2): 221–243.
Bertaux, Daniel, and Véronique Garros. 1998. *Lioudmilla: une Russe dans le siècle*. Paris: La Dispute.
Bertaux, Daniel, and Marina Malysheva. 1994. "Le modèle culturel des classes populaires russes face au passage à l'économie de marché." *Revue d'études comparatives Est-Ouest* 25(4): 197–228.
Bertaux, Daniel, Anna Rotkirch, and Paul Thompson, eds. (2004) 2005. *Living through the Soviet System*. New Brunswick, NJ: Transaction Publishers.
Bigday, Maria. 2017. *L'Engagement intellectuel sous régime autoritaire: les* think tankers *biélorusses entre expertise et dissidence*. Paris: Dalloz.
Bikbov, Alexander. 2009. "Is Sociology the Same Discipline in Russia and France? A Brief Political Micro-history." *Laboratorium* 1: 124–139.

Binns, Christopher. 1980. "The Changing Face of Power: Revolution and Accommodation in the Development of the Soviet Ceremonial System: Part II." *Man* 15(1): 170–187.
Blic, Damien (de), and Cyril Lemieux. 2005. "Le scandale comme épreuve. Éléments de sociologie pragmatique." *Politix* 71: 9–38.
Boltanski, Luc, and Laurent Thévenot. (1991) 2006. *On Justification: Economies of Worth*. Translated by Catherine Porter. Princeton: Princeton University Press.
Bonnet, François. 2008. "La distance sociale dans le travail de terrain: compétence stratégique et compétence culturelle dans l'interaction d'enquête." *Genèses. Sciences sociales et histoire* 73: 57–74.
Boumaza, Magali, and Aurélie Campana. 2007. "Enquêter en milieu 'difficile.'" *Revue française de science politique* 57(1): 5–25.
Bourdieu, Pierre. (1994) 1998. *Practical Reason: On the Theory of Action*. Stanford: Stanford University Press
———. (1997) 2000. *Pascalian Meditations*. Translated by Richard Nice. Stanford: Stanford University Press.
———. (2002) 2008. *The Bachelor's Ball: The Crisis of Peasant Society in Béarn*. Translated by Richard Nice. Cambridge: Polity Press
Boym, Svetlana. 2001. *The Future of Nostalgia*. New York: Basic Books.
Braux, Adeline. 2015. "Au-delà des 'Natacha': les migrations féminines postsoviétiques à Istanbul." *Revue européenne des Migrations Internationales* 31(1): 81–102.
Bridger, Susan. 1987. *Women in the Soviet Countryside: Women's Roles in Rural Development in the Soviet Union*. Cambridge: Cambridge University Press.
Brutel, Chantal. 2014. "Les immigrés récemment arrivés en France. Une immigration de plus en plus européenne." *Insee Première* 1524.
Burawoy, Michael, and János Lukács. 1992. *The Radiant Past: Ideology and Reality in Hungary's Road to Capitalism*. Chicago: University of Chicago Press.
Caldwell, Melissa L., 2011. *Dacha Idylls: Living Organically in Russia's Countryside*. Berkeley: University of California Press.
Cam, Pierre. 1991. "Le bricolage: un art pour l'art." *Critiques sociales* 1: 32–38.
Casas, Joseph, and François Labouesse. 1983. *Monographie de deux kolkhozes soviétiques: octobre 1981*. Montpellier: INRA.
Castel, Robert. 1968. "Présentation." In *Asiles: études sur la condition sociale des malades mentaux et autres reclus*, edited by Erving Goffman, 7–35. Paris: Éd. de Minuit.
———. 2003. *L'Insécurité sociale: qu'est-ce qu'être protégé?* Paris: Éd. du Seuil.
Castel, Robert, and Claudine Haroche. 2001. *Propriété privée, propriété sociale, propriété de soi: entretiens sur la construction de l'individu modern*. Paris: Fayard.
Castelain, Jean-Pierre. 1989. *Manières de vivre, manières de boire: alcool et sociabilité sur le port*. Paris: Éd. Imago.
Céfaï, Daniel, ed. 2003. *L'enquête de terrain*. Paris: La Découverte.
Cerovic, Masha. 2018. *Les Enfants de Staline: la guerre des partisans soviétiques (1941–1944)*. Paris: Éd. du Seuil.
Certeau, Michel (de). (1980) 1988. *The Practice of Everyday Life*. Translated by Steven Rendall. Berkeley: University of California Press.
Cerutti, Simona. 2015. "*Who is below?* E. P. Thompson, historien des sociétés modernes: une relecture." *Annales. Histoire, Sciences Sociales* 70(4): 931–956.
Chaléard, Jean-Louis. 2010. "Notre planète: atouts et contraintes naturels pour l'agriculture." In *La question agricole mondiale: enjeux économiques, sociaux et envi-

ronmentaux, edited by Thierry Doré and Olivier Réchaudière, 39–56. Paris: La Documentation française.
Chase, William. 1989. "Voluntarism, Mobilisation and Coercion: *Subbotniki* 1919–1921." *Soviet Studies* 41(1): 111–128.
Christian, Michel, and Sandrine Kott. 2009. "Introduction. Sphère publique et sphère privée dans les sociétés socialistes. La mise à l'épreuve d'une dichotomie." *Histoire@ Politique. Politique, culture, société* 7. Retrieved 13 February 2018 from https://www.histoire-politique.fr/documents/07/dossier/pdf/HP7-Introduction-Kott-Christan-pdf.pdf.
Coenen-Huther, Jacques. 1997. "La patience russe entre stratégies et impuissance: quelques remarques complémentaires." *Archives européennes de sociologie* 38(2): 291–298.
Cohen, Yves. 2012. *Le Siècle des chefs: une histoire transnationale du commandement et de l'autorité, 1890–1940*. Paris: Éd. Amsterdam.
Collovald, Annie. 2004. *Le Populisme du FN, un dangereux contresens*. Bellecombe-en-Bauges: Éd. du Croquant.
Crawford, Matthew B. (2009) 2010. *Shop Class as Soulcraft: An Inquiry into the Value of Work*. New York: Penguin Books.
Creed, Gerald W. 1998. *Domesticating Revolution: From Socialist Reform to Ambivalent Transition in a Bulgarian Village*. University Park: Pennsylvania State University Press.
Crowley, David, and Susan E. Reid, eds. 2002. *Socialist Spaces: Sites of Everyday Life in the Eastern Bloc*. Oxford: Berg.
Crozier, Michel, and Erhard Friedberg. 1977. *L'Acteur et le système: les contraintes de l'action collective*. Paris: Éd. du Seuil.
Cuin, Charles-Henry. 1991. "Durkheim et l'inégalité sociale: les avatars et les leçons d'une entreprise." *Recherches sociologiques* 22(3): 17–32.
Dampierre, Éric (de). 1954. "Thèmes pour l'étude du scandale." *Annales ESC* 9(3): 328–336.
Darley, Mathilde. 2007. "La prostitution en clubs dans les régions frontalières de la République tchèque." *Revue française de sociologie* 48(2): 273–306.
Dean, Martin. 2000. *Collaboration in the Holocaust: Crimes of the Local Police in Belorussia and Ukraine, 1941–44*. New York: St. Martin's Press.
Denis, Juliette. 2010. "Violences en URSS: chantiers historiographiques et enjeux mémoriels." *Tracés* 19: 141–153.
Depretto, Jean-Paul. 2001. "Pour une histoire sociale de la dictature soviétique." *Le Mouvement social* 196: 3–19.
Desreumaux, Vincent. 2013. "Équilibre général et justice sociale: la théorie néoclassique comme philosophie politique?" *Cahiers d'économie politique / Papers in Political Economy* 64(1): 75–110.
Détienne, Marcel, and Jean-Pierre Vernant. (1974) 1991. *Cunning Intelligence in Greek Culture and Society*. Translated by Janet Loyd. Chicago: University of Chicago Press.
Dictionnaire historique de la langue française / Le Robert. (1993) 2000. Paris: Dictionnaires Le Robert.
Dimov, Alexandre. 1980. *Les Hommes doubles: la vie quotidienne en Union soviétique*. Paris: Éd. J.-C. Lattès.
Droit, Emmanuel. 2007. "Le Goulag contre la Shoah. Mémoires officielles et cultures mémorielles dans l'Europe élargie." *Vingtième siècle. Revue d'histoire* 94: 101–120.

———. 2009. *Vers un Homme nouveau?: l'éducation socialiste en RDA, 1949–1989*. Rennes: Presses universitaires de Rennes.
Drweski, Bruno. 1993. *La Biélorussie*. Paris: Presses universitaires de France.
Dubet, François. (2006) 2016. *Injustice at Work*. New York: Routledge.
Dufy, Caroline, and Ronan Hervouet. 2017. "Introduction. Mondes ruraux et marchés dans l'Europe postcommuniste." *Revue d'études comparatives Est-Ouest* 48(1): 9–20.
Dufy, Caroline, and Florence Weber. 2007. *L'Ethnographie économique*. Paris: La Découverte.
Duprat-Kushtanina, Veronika. 2013. "Remembering the Repression of the Stalin Era in Russia: On the Non-transmission of Family Memory." *Nationalities Papers: The Journal of Nationalism and Ethnicity* 2: 225–239.
Duprat-Kushtanina, Veronika, and Lisa Vapné. 2015. "'De drôles d'années.' Les événements de la période transitionnelle (1985–1993) au prisme de deux corpus de récits de vie." *Temporalités* 22: 2–16.
Durkheim, Émile. (1895) 1982. *The Rules of Sociological Method*. Translated by W. D. Halls. New York: The Free Press.
———. (1897) 2002. *Suicide: A Study in Sociology*. Translated by John A. Spaulding and George Simpson. London: Routledge.
———. (1925) 1961. *Moral Education: A Study in the Theory and Application of the Sociology of Education*. Translated by Everett K. Wilson and Herman Schnurer. New York: The Free Press of Glencoe.
Eaton, Katherine. 2004. *Daily Life in the Soviet Union*. Westport, CT: Greenwood Press.
Ehrenburg, Ilya, and Vasily Grossman. (1993) 2009. *The Complete Black Book of Russian Jewry*. Translated by David Patterson. New Brunswick, NJ: Transaction Publishers.
Eke, Steven, and Taras Kuzio. 2000. "Sultanism in Eastern Europe: The Socio-political Roots of Authoritarian Populism in Belarus." *Europe-Asia Studies* 52(3): 523–547.
Elias, Norbert. (1969) 2006. *The Court Society*. Translated by Edmund Jephcott. Dublin: University College Dublin Press.
———. (1970) 1978. *What Is Sociology?* Translated by Stephen Menell and Grace Morrissey. New York: Columbia University Press.
Elias, Norbert, and John L. Scotson. (1965) 1994. *The Established and the Outsiders: A Sociological Enquiry into Community Problems*. London: Sage.
Engelking, Anna. 2001–2002. "The Mentality of Kolkhoz Inhabitants: Research Notes from the Grodno Region of Belarus." *International Journal of Sociology* 31(4): 64–78.
EBRD (European Bank for Reconstruction and Development). 2013. *Transition Report 2013: Stuck in Transition*. Retrieved 30 March 2016 from www.ebrd.com/documents/comms.../pdf-transition-report-2013-english.pdf.
Fassin, Didier. 2009. "Les économies morales revisitées." *Annales. Histoire, Sciences Sociales* 64(6): 1237–1266.
Favarel-Garrigues Gilles. 2007. *La Police des mœurs économiques: de l'URSS à la Russie, 1965–1995*. Paris: CNRS Éd.
Fehér, Ferenc, Agnes Heller, and György Márkus. 1983. *Dictatorship over Needs: An Analysis of Soviet Societies*. Oxford: Blackwell.
Field, Deborah A. 2007. *Private Life and Communist Morality in Khrushchev's Russia*. New York: Peter Lang.
Figes, Orlando. (1996) 1997. *A People's Tragedy: The Russian Revolution 1891–1924*. London: Pimlico.

---. 2007. *The Whisperers: Private Life in Stalin's Russia*. London: Allen Lane/Penguin Books.
Fitzpatrick, Sheila. 1999. *Everyday Stalinism, Ordinary Life in Extraordinary Times: Soviet Russia in the 1930s*. Oxford: Oxford University Press.
Flavier, Hugo. 2017. "La propriété foncière en Biélorussie. Entre hybridation et ambiguïtés juridiques." *Revue d'études comparatives Est-Ouest* 48(1-2): 179-208.
Fontaine, Laurence. (2008) 2014. *The Moral Economy: Poverty, Credit, and Trust in Early Modern Europe*. New York: Cambridge University Press.
Foucault, Michel. (1973) 2001. "La société punitive." In *Dits et écrits, 1954-1988*, vol. 1: *1954-1975*, 1324-1338. Paris: Gallimard.
---. (1975) 1995. *Discipline and Punish: The Birth of the Prison*. Translated by Alan Sheridan. New York: Vintage Books.
Friedrich, Carl J., and Zbigniew K. Brzezinski. (1956) 1961. *Totalitarian Dictatorship and Autocracy*. New York: Praeger.
Gajduk, Kirill, Elena Rakova, and Vitalij Silickij, eds. 2009. *Social'nye kontrakty v sovremennoj Belarusi* [Social contracts in contemporary Belarus]. Minsk: IPM.
Gessat-Anstett, Élisabeth. 2001a. "Du collectif au communautaire. À propos des réseaux familiaux dans la Russie post-soviétique." *L'Homme* 157: 115-136.
---. 2001b. "Les mots/maux de l'etnografiâ. À propos d'une discipline et de ses attendus, l'ethnologie russe post-soviétique." *Journal des anthropologues* 87: 65-78.
---. 2007. *Une Atlantide russe: anthropologie de la mémoire en Russie post-soviétique*. Paris: La Découverte.
Giabiconi, Dominique. 2005. "Les mariages mixtes franco-polonais. Contours et enjeux." *Revue européenne des migrations internationales* 21(1): 259-273.
Giddens, Anthony. (1984) 1986. *The Constitution of Society: Outline of the Theory of Structuration*. Cambridge: Polity Press.
Giustino, Cathleen M., Catherine J. Plum, and Alexander Vari, eds. 2013. *Socialist Escapes: Breaking Away from Ideology and Everyday Routine in Eastern Europe, 1945-1989*. New York: Berghahn Books.
Gluckman, Max. 1963. "Gossip and Scandal." *Current Anthropology* 4(3): 307-316.
Goffman, Erving. (1961) 2007. *Asylums: Essays on The Social Situation of Mental Patients and Other Inmates*. New Brunswick, NJ: Aldine Transaction.
Goujon, Alexandra. 1999. "Language, Nationalism, and Populism in Belarus." *Nationalities Papers* 27(4): 661-677.
---. 2002. "Le 'loukachisme' ou le populisme autoritaire en Biélorussie." *Politique et sociétés* 21(2): 29-50.
---. 2008. "Kurapaty (1937-1941): NKVD Mass Killings in Soviet Belarus." *Online Encyclopedia of Mass Violence*. Retrieved 13 April 2017 from http://www.massviolence.org/Kurapaty-1937-1941-NKVD-Mass-Killings-in-Soviet-Belarus.
---. 2009. *Révolutions politiques et identitaires en Ukraine et en Biélorussie, 1988-2008*. Paris: Belin.
---. 2010. "Memorial Narratives of WWII Partisans and Genocide in Belarus." *East European Politics and Societies* 24(1): 6-25.
---. 2011. "La mémoire des villages brûlés pendant la Seconde Guerre mondiale: l'exemple de Khatyn en Biélorussie." In *Commémorer les Victimes en Europe: XVIe-XXIe siècle*, edited by David El Kenz and François-Xavier Nérard, 77-90. Seyssel: Champ Vallon.
Grand Encyclopedia (62 volumes). 2006. Moscow: Ed. Terra.

Graziosi, Andrea. 2010. *Histoire de l'URSS*. Paris: Presses universitaires de France.
Grignon, Claude, and Jean-Claude Passeron. 1989. *Le Savant et le populaire: misérabilisme et populisme en sociologie et en littérature*. Paris: Gallimard/Le Seuil.
Grossman, Gregory. 1977. "The 'Second Economy' of the USSR." *Problems of Communism* 26(5): 25–40.
Gueslin, André. 1992. "Le paternalisme revisité en Europe occidentale (seconde moitié du XIXe siècle, début XXe siècle)." *Genèses. Sciences sociales et histoire* 7: 201–211.
Guliyev, Farid. 2011. "Personal Rule, Neopatrimonialism, and Regime Typologies: Integrating Dahlian and Weberian Approaches to Regime Studies." *Demokratizatsiya: The Journal of Post-Soviet Democratization* 18(3): 575–601.
Guriev Sergei, and Andrei Rachninsky. 2005. "The Role of Oligarchs in Russian Capitalism." *Journal of Economic Perspectives* 19(1): 131–150.
Gusakov, Vladimir. 2014. "Nekotopye principial'nye voprosy tekuŝego i dolgosročnogo rasvitiâ APK [Key questions concerning the APK's current and long-term development]." *Agrarnaâ èkonomika* 5: 2–9.
Hann, Chris. 1980. *Tázlár: A Village in Hungary*. Cambridge: Cambridge University Press.
———. 1985. *A Village without Solidarity: Polish Peasants in Years of Crisis*. New Haven: Yale University Press.
———. 1994. "After Communism: Reflections on East European Anthropology and the 'Transition.'" *Social Anthropology* 2(3): 229–249.
Haraszti, Miklós. (1975) 1977. *A Worker in a Worker's State: Piece-Rates in Hungary*. Translated by Michael Wright. New York: Penguin Books.
Havel, Václav. (1978) 1985. "The Power of the Powerless." Translated by Paul Wilson. In *The Power of the Powerless: Citizens against the State in Central-Eastern Europe*, edited by Stephen Lukes, 23–96. Armonk, NY: Sharpe.
Heller, Michel. (1985) 1988. *Cogs in the Soviet Wheel: The Formation of Soviet Man*. Translated by David Floyd. London: Collins Harvill.
Hervouet, Ronan. 2006. "L'économie du potager en Biélorussie et en Russie." *Études rurales* 177: 25–42.
———. 2007. "Datchas et mémoires familiales en Biélorussie." *Ethnologie française* 37(3): 533–540.
———. (2007) 2009a. *Datcha blues: existences ordinaires et dictature en Biélorussie*. Paris: Belin.
———. 2009b. "Biélorussie. Mémoires et ruptures de vie de citoyens soviétiques." In *1989 à l'Est de l'Europe: une mémoire controversée*, edited by Jérôme Heurtaux and Cédric Pellen, 203–227. La Tour d'Aigues: Éd. de l'Aube.
———. 2013a. "La tradition soviétique des *subbotniki* dans la Biélorussie de Loukachenko." *La Revue russe* 41: 25–36.
———. 2013b. "Le 'socialisme de marché' dans la Biélorussie de Loukachenko: égalitarisme, néopatrimonialisme et dépendance extérieure." *Revue internationale de politique comparée* 20(3): 97–113.
———. 2013c. "La Biélorussie de Loukachenko, dernière dictature d'Europe. [Review of] Benett Brian, *The Last Dictatorship in Europe: Belarus under Lukashenko*; Karbalévitch Valeri, *Le Satrape de Biélorussie: Alexandre Loukachenko, dernier tyran d'Europe*; Wilson Andrew, *Belarus: The Last European Dictatorship in Europe*." *Revue française de science politique* 63(3–4): 690–693.
———. 2014. "Usages du passé et ordre social en Biélorussie. L'histoire d'un prêtre charismatique aux prises avec son passé criminel." *Ethnologie française* 44(3): 409–419.

———. 2019. "A Political Ethnography of Rural Communities under an Authoritarian Regime: The Case of Belarus." *Bulletin de méthodologie sociologique / Bulletin of Sociological Methodology* 141: 85–112.
Hervouet, Ronan, and Alexandre Kurilo. 2010. "Travailler 'bénévolement' pour la collectivité: les *subbotniki* en Biélorussie postsoviétique." *Genèses. Sciences sociales et histoire* 78: 87–104.
———. 2016. "The Heritage of Soviet Paternalism in the Belarusian Countryside: The Moralization and Folklorization of the Social World." *Mir Rossii* 25(4): 30–51.
Hervouet, Ronan, Alexandre Kurilo, and Ioulia Shukan. 2017. "Socialisme de Marché et Gouvernement des campagnes en Biélorussie." *Revue d'études comparatives Est-Ouest* 48(1–2): 85–120.
Hervouet, Ronan, and Claire Schiff. 2017. "Des épouses dominées? Mariages transnationaux, inégalités dans le couple et parcours de vie en France de femmes russes, biélorusses et ukrainiennes." *Recherches familiales* 14: 95–106.
Hibou, Béatrice. (2011) 2017. *The Political Anatomy of Domination*. London: Palgrave.
Hivon, Myriam. 1994. "Vodka: The 'Spirit' of Exchange." *Cambridge Journal of Anthropology* 17(3): 1–18.
———. 1998a. "'Payer en liquide.' L'utilisation de la vodka dans les échanges en Russie rurale." *Ethnologie française* 28(4): 515–524.
———. 1998b. "The Bullied Farmer: Social Pressure as a Survival Strategy?" In *Surviving Post-Socialism: Local Strategies and Regional Responses in Eastern Europe and the Former Soviet Union*, edited by Sue Bridger and Frances Pine, 33–51. London: Routledge.
Hobsbawn, Eric. (1983) 2000. "Introduction: Inventing Traditions." In *The Invention of Tradition*, edited by Eric Hobsbawn and Terence Ranger, 1–14. Cambridge: Cambridge University Press.
Hoggart, Richard. (1957) 2009. *The Uses of Literacy: Aspects of Working-Class Life*. London: Penguin Books.
Hughes, Everett C. (1984) 1993. *The Sociological Eye: Selected Papers*. New Brunswick, NJ: Transaction Publishers.
Humphrey, Caroline. (1983) 2001. *Marx Went Away – But Karl Stayed Behind*. Rev. ed. of *Karl Marx Collective: Economy, Society and Religion in a Siberian Collective Farm*. Ann Arbor: University of Michigan Press.
Ihl, Olivier. 1996. *La Fête républicaine*. Paris: Gallimard.
———. 2004. "Gouverner par les honneurs. Distinctions honorifiques et économie politique dans l'Europe du début du xixe siècle." *Genèses. Sciences sociales et histoire* 55: 4–26.
ILO (International Labour Organization). 2004. *Trade Union Rights in Belarus: Report of the Inquiry Committee*. Retrieved 11 February 2008 from http://www.ilo.org/public/french/standards/relm/gb/docs/gb291/pdf/ci-belarus.pdf.
Ingrao, Christian. (2006) 2013. *The SS Dirlewanger Brigade: The History of the Black Hunters*. Translated by Phoebe Green. New York: Skyhorse Publishing.
Ioffe, Grigory. 2003. "Understanding Belarus: Questions of Language." *Europe-Asia Studies* 55(7): 1009–1047.
———. 2004. "Understanding Belarus: Economy and Political Landscape." *Europe-Asia Studies* 56(1): 85–118.
———. 2014. *Understanding Belarus and How Western Foreign Policy Misses the Mark*. Lanham, MD: Rowman and Littlefield.

Jarausch, Konrad. 2003. "Au-delà des condamnations morales et des fausses explications. Plaidoyer pour une histoire différenciée de la RDA." *Genèses. Sciences sociales et histoire* 52: 80–95.

Kaplan, Frederick. 1965. "The Origin and Function of the Subbotniks and Voskresniks." *Jahrbücher für Geschichte Osteuropas* 13(1): 30–39.

Karbalévitch, Valeri. 2012. *Le Satrape de Biélorussie: Alexandre Loukachenko, dernier tyran d'Europe*. Paris: F. Bourin.

Kasperski, Tatiana. 2020. *Les politiques de la radioactivité: Tchernobyl et la mémoire nationale en Biélorussie contemporaine*. Paris: Pétra.

Katsenelinboigen, Aron. 1977. "Colored Markets in the Soviet Union." *Soviet Studies* 29(1): 62–85.

Kéhayan, Jean, and Nina Kéhayan. 1978. *Rue du prolétaire rouge: deux communistes français en URSS*. Paris: Éd. du Seuil.

Kenedi, János. 1981. *Do It Yourself: Hungary's Hidden Economy*. London: Pluto Press.

Kerblay, Basile. 1985. *Du Mir aux agrovilles*. Paris: Institut d'études slaves.

Kideckel, David. 1993. *The Solitude of Collectivism: Romanian Villagers to the Revolution and Beyond*. Ithaca, NY: Cornell University Press.

Kisseliova, Evguenia. (1996) 2000. *Une femme russe dans le siècle: journal de Evguenia Kisseliova: 1916–1991*. Paris: A. Michel.

Kittel Bernhard, Diana Lindner, Sviatlana Tesch, and Gerd Hentschel. 2010. "Mixed Language Usage in Belarus: The Sociostructural Background of Language Choice." *International Journal of the Sociology of Language* 206: 47–71.

Klinau, Artur. (2006) 2015. *Minsk. Cité de rêve*. Paris: Éd. Signes et balises.

Kocka, Jürgen. 1995. "L'histoire sociale de la RDA." *Actes de la recherche en sciences sociales* 106–107: 80–84.

Kodeks Respubliki Belarus' o zemle [Land Code of the Republic of Belarus]. 2008. 23 July, No. 425-3 [z], art. 36. Retrieved 18 January 2016 from http://etalonline.by/?type=text&regnum=Hk0800425#load_text_none_1_.

Koleva, Daniela, ed. 2012. *Negotiating Normality: Everyday Lives in Socialist Institutions*. New Brunswick, NJ: Transaction Publishers.

Kollontaj, Alexandra. 1978. "La dictature du prolétariat: la révolution des mœurs." In *Conférences sur la libération des femmes*. Dijon: Éd. La Brèche.

Kott, Sandrine. (2001) 2014. *Communism Day-to-Day: State Enterprises in East German Society*. Translated by Lisa Godin-Roger. Ann Arbor: University of Michigan Press.

———. 2002a. "Pour une histoire sociale du pouvoir en Europe communiste: introduction thématique." *Revue d'histoire contemporaine et moderne* 49(2): 5–23.

———. 2002b. "[Review of] Alf Lüdtke, *Des Ouvriers dans l'Allemagne du XXe siècle. Le quotidien des dictatures*." *Revue d'histoire contemporaine et moderne* 49(2): 226–229.

Krakovský, Roman. (2014) 2018. *State and Society in Communist Czechoslovakia: Transforming the Everyday from World War II to the Fall of the Berlin Wall*. Translated by Jennifer Higgins. London: Bloomsbury Academic.

Kryzhanouski, Yauheni. 2017. "Gouverner la dissidence. Sociologie de la censure sous régime autoritaire: le cas du rock contestataire biélorusse." *Critique internationale* 76: 123–145.

Kusin Vladimir. 1978. *From Dubček to Charter 77: A Study of Normalization in Czechoslovakia, 1968–1978*. Edinburgh: Q. Press.

Labica, Georges, and Gérard Bensussan, eds. 1982. *Dictionnaire critique du marxisme*. Paris: Presses universitaires de France.
Laferté, Gilles. 2010. "Théoriser le crédit de face-à-face: un système d'information dans une économie de l'obligation." *Entreprises et histoire* 59(2): 57–67.
Lagrave, Rose-Marie, ed. 2011. *Fragments du communisme en Europe centrale*. Paris: Éd. de l'EHESS.
Lahire, Bernard. 2012. *Monde pluriel: penser l'unité des sciences sociales*. Paris: Éd. du Seuil.
———. (2015) 2019. *This Is Not Just a Painting: An Inquiry into Art, Domination, Magic and the Sacred*. Translated by Helen Morrison. Cambridge: Polity Press.
Lallemand, Jean-Charles. 2006. "Biélorussie: un régime autoritaire en quête d'une idéologie d'État." *Esprit* 2: 200–209.
Lallemand, Jean-Charles, and Virginie Symaniec. 2007. *Biélorussie: mécanique d'une dictature*. Paris: Les Petits matins.
Lamont, Michèle. 2000. *The Dignity of Working Men: Morality and the Boundaries of Race, Class, and Immigration*. Cambridge, MA: Harvard University Press.
Lampland, Martha. 1991. "Pigs, Party Secretaries, and Private Lives." *American Ethnologist* 18(3): 459–479.
Lane, Christel. 1981. *The Rites of Rulers: Ritual in Industrial Society; The Soviet Case*. Cambridge: Cambridge University Press.
Lapatniova, Alena. 2001. *Biélorussie: les mises en scène du pouvoir*. Paris: L'Harmattan.
———. 2006. "Administrer la religion en URSS. Le cas de la Biélorussie et de la Lituanie." *Cahiers du monde russe* 47(4): 749–780.
Laruelle, Marlène. 2012. "Discussing Neopatrimonialism and Patronal Presidentialism in the Central Asian Context." *Demokratizatsiya: The Journal of Post-Soviet Democratization* 20(4): 301–324.
Le Velly, Ronan. 2012. *Sociologie du marché*. Paris: La Découverte.
Ledeneva, Alena. 1998. *Russia's Economy of Favours: Blat, Networking and Informal Exchange*. Cambridge: Cambridge University Press.
Lenin, Vladimir. 1919. "A Great Beginning: Heroism of the Workers in the Rear; 'Communist *subbotniks*.'" Retrieved 10 March 2020 from https://www.marxists.org/archive/lenin/works/1919/jun/28.htm.
———. 1920. "From the First Subbotnik on the Moscow-Kazan Railway to the All-Russia May Day Subbotnik." Retrieved 11 March 2020 from https://ww.marxists.org/archive/lenin/works/1920/may/02.htm.
Lepesant, Gilles. 2007. "La Pologne et son voisinage oriental." In *La Pologne*, edited by François Bafoil, 498–521. Paris: Fayard/CERI.
Leshchenko, Natalia. 2008. "The National Ideology and the Basis of the Lukashenka Regime in Belarus." *Europe-Asia Studies* 60(8): 1419–1433.
Lewin, Moshe. 2005. *The Soviet Century*. Edited by Gregory Elliott. London: Verso.
Linz, Juan. 2000. *Totalitarian and Authoritarian Regimes*. Boulder, CO: Lynne Rienner Publishers.
Livoskaïa, Nadia. 2001. "Évolution de la situation économique en Biélorussie de 1991 à 1999." In *Chroniques sur la Biélorussie contemporaine*, edited by Alexandra Goujon, Jean-Charles Lallemand, and Virginie Symaniec, 109–126. Paris: L'Harmattan.
Lüdtke, Alf. 1990. "La domination au quotidien. 'Sens de soi' et individualité des travailleurs avant et après 1933 en Allemagne." *Politix* 13: 68–78.

———. 1998. "La République Démocratique Allemande comme histoire. Réflexions historiographiques." *Annales. Histoire, Sciences Sociales* 53(1): 3–39.
———. 2000. *Des Ouvriers dans l'Allemagne du xxème siècle: le quotidien des dictatures.* Paris: L'Harmattan.
———. 2015. "La domination comme pratique sociale. Traduction d'Alexandra Oeser avec la collaboration de Fabien Jobard." *Sociétés contemporaines* 99-100: 17–63.
Lüdtke, Alf, and Alexandra Oeser. 2015. "L'Histoire comme science sociale. Entretien avec Alf Lüdtke, par Alexandra Oeser." *Sociétés contemporaines* 99-100: 169–191.
Luehrmann, Sonja. 2004. "Mediated Marriage: Internet Matchmaking in Provincial Russia." *Europe-Asia Studies* 56(6): 857–875.
Mainguy, Glenn. 2016. "L'Économie du quotidien: une étude de la précarité à travers l'exemple des pratiques agricoles domestiques dans le monde rural russe." PhD thesis, University of Bordeaux.
Malia, Martin. 1994. *The Soviet Tragedy: A History of Socialism in Russia, 1917-1991*. New York: The Free Press.
Marcou Jean, and Sergueï Pankovski. 2003. "Le phénomène biélorusse." In *Le Bélarus: L'état de l'exception*, edited by François Dépelteau and Aurélie Lacassagne, 13–32. Sainte-Foy, Québec: Presses de l'Université Laval.
Marin, Anaïs. 2010. "La guerre médiatique, nouvel outil de pression russe sur le régime biélorusse." *Regards sur l'Est*. Retrieved 14 January 2013 from http://www.regard-est.com/home/breve_contenu.php?id=1142.
Mariot, Nicolas. 1995. "Le rite sans ses mythes: forme rituelle, temps et histoire." *Genèses. Sciences sociales et histoire* 21: 148–162.
———. 2008, "Qu'est-ce qu'un 'enthousiasme civique'? Sur l'historiographie des fêtes politiques en France après 1789." *Annales. Histoire, Sciences Sociales* 63(1): 113–139.
Marples, David. 1994. "Kuropaty: The Investigation of a Stalinist Historical Controversy." *Slavic Review* 53(2): 513–523.
Martinovich, Viktor. 2010. *Paranoia*. Saint Petersburg: Astrel SPB.
Marx, Karl. (1843) 1970. *Critique of Hegel's "Philosophy of Right."* Translated by Annette Jolin and Joseph O'Malley. New York: Cambridge University Press.
———. (1871) 1972. *The Civil War in France*. Edited by Hal Draper. New York: Monthly Review Press.
Matsuzato, Kimitaka. 2004. "A Populist Island in an Ocean of Clan Politics: The Lukashenka Regime as an Exception among CIS Countries." *Europe-Asia Studies* 56(2): 235–261.
Mauger, Gérard. 1991. "Enquêter en milieu populaire." *Genèses. Sciences sociales et histoire.* 6: 125–143.
Maurel, Marie-Claude. 1980. *La Campagne collectivisée: société et espace rural en Russie*. Paris: Éd. Anthropos.
———. 1985. "La petite agriculture en URSS et en Europe de l'est." *Études rurales* 99–100: 157–178.
Mauss, Marcel. (1924–1925) 2002. *The Gift: The Form and Reason for Exchange in Archaic Societies*. Translated by W. D. Halls. London: Routledge.
McMahon, Margery. 1997. "Aleksandr Lukashenka, President, Republic of Belarus." *Journal of Communist Studies and Transition Politics* 13(4): 129–137.
Médard, Jean-François. 1992. "Le 'big man' en Afrique: esquisse d'analyse du politicien entrepreneur." *L'Année sociologique* 42(1): 167–192.
Medvedev, Roj. 2010. *Aleksandr Lukašenko. Kontury belorusskoj modeli*. Moscow: BBPG.

Mel'nik, V. A. 2010. *Osnovy ideologii belorusskogo gosudarstva* [The foundations of Belarusian ideology]. Mink: Vyšèjšaâ škola.
Memmi, Albert. (1979) 1993. *La dépendance: esquisse pour un portrait du dépendant: suivi d'une lettre de Vercors*. Paris: Gallimard.
Merle, Pierre, and Bertrand Le Beau. 2004. "Alcoolisation et alcoolisme au travail. Ethnographie d'un centre de tri postal." *Revue française de sociologie* 45(1): 3–36.
Mischi, Julian, and Nicolas Renahy. 2008. "Pour une sociologie politique des mondes ruraux." *Politix* 83: 9–21.
Moine, Nathalie, and John Angell. 2011. "Defining 'War Crimes against Humanity' in the Soviet Union: Nazi Arson of Soviet Villages and the Soviet Narrative on Jewish and Non-Jewish War Victims, 1941–1947." *Cahiers du monde russe* 52(2–3): 1–32.
Mondon, Hélène, ed. 2004. *Nous Autres, paysans: lettres aux Soviets, 1925–1931*. Lagrasse: Verdier.
Mourão, Paulo. 2015. "The Complex Relation between Belarusian Trade Openness and the Agricultural Sector." *Land Use Policy* 43: 74–81.
Muldrewn, Craig. 1998. *The Economy of Obligation: The Culture of Credit and Social Relations in Early Modern England*. New York: St. Martin's Press.
Nacou, Démosthène. 1958 *Du Kolkhoze au sovkhoze, commune, artel, toze, kolkhoze, M.T.S., sovkhoze*. Paris: Éd. de Minuit.
Nadkarni, Maya, and Olga Shevchenko. 2004. "The Politics of Nostalgia: A Case for Comparative Analysis of Post-Socialist Practices." *Ab Imperio* 2: 487–519.
National Statistical Committee of the Republic of Belarus. 2014. "Sel'skoe hozâjstvo Respubliki Belarus'" [Agriculture in the Republic of Belarus]. Retrieved 16 December 2015 from http://belstat.gov.by/bgd/public_compilation/index_438/.
Neculau, Adrian, ed. 2008. *La Vie quotidienne en Roumanie sous le communisme*. Paris: L'Harmattan.
Oeser, Alexandra. 2015. "Introduction. Penser les rapports de domination avec Alf Lüdtke." *Sociétés contemporaines* 99–100: 5–16.
Olivier de Sardan, Jean-Pierre. 2000. "Le 'je' méthodologique. Implication et explicitation dans l'enquête de terrain." *Revue française de sociologie* 41(3): 417–445.
Oushakine, Serguei. 2007. "'We're Nostalgic but We're Not Crazy': Retrofitting the Past in Russia." *Russian Review* 66(3): 451–482.
Ousmanova, Almira. 2008. "Pouvoir, sexualité et politique dans les médias biélorusses." *Raisons politiques* 31: 47–63.
Palairet, Michael. 1995. "'Lenin' and 'Brezhnev': Steel Making and the Bulgarian Economy, 1956–90." *Europe-Asia Studies* 47(3): 493–505.
Parfionov, Leonid. 2009. *Namedni. Naša era. 1961–1970*. Moscow: Kolibri.
Paxson, Margaret. 2005. *Solovyovo: The Story of Memory in a Russian Village*. Washington, DC: Woodrow Wilson Center Press/Indiana University Press.
Perchoc, Philippe. 2006. "L'enseignement supérieur biélorusse en exil." *Le courrier des pays de l'Est* 1057: 79–83.
Pesmen, Dale. 1995. "Standing Bottles, Washing Deals, and Drinking 'for the Soul' in a Siberian City." *Anthropology of East Europe Review* 13(2): 65–74.
———. 2000. *Russia and Soul: An Exploration*. Ithaca, NY: Cornell University Press.
Pétric, Boris. (2013) 2015. *Where Are All Our Sheep? Kyrgyzstan, A Global Political Arena*. Translated by Cynthia Schoch. New York: Berghahn Books.
Petryna, Adriana. 2002. *Life Exposed: Biological Citizens after Chernobyl*. Princeton, NJ: Princeton University Press.

Pialoux, Michel. 1992. "Alcool et politique dans l'atelier. Une usine de carrosserie dans la décennie 1980." *Genèses. Sciences sociales et histoire* 7: 94–128.
Pollack, Michael. 1993. *Une Identité blessée: études de sociologie et d'histoire.* Paris: Métailié.
Popkov, Vjačeslav. 2004. "Arbeitsbeziehungen in der Sowjetunion. Realitäten und Wahrnehmungen am Beispiel der Stadt Kaluga." In *Arbeit im Sozialismus – Arbeit im Postsozialismus: Erkundungen zum Arbeitsleben im östlichen Europa*, edited by Klaus Roth, 167–177. Münster: Lit Verlag.
Pouliquen, Alain. 1982. "L'organisation du travail collectif et le contrôle social de l'activité économique en URSS." *Revue d'études comparatives Est-Ouest* 13(3): 5–48.
Pudal, Bernard. 2009. "Le soviétisme." In *Nouveau Manuel de science politique*, edited by Antonin Cohen, Bernard Lacroix, and Philippe Riutort, 162–172. Paris: La Découverte.
Pudal, Romain. 2011. "La politique à la caserne. Approche ethnographique des rapports à la politique en milieu pompier." *Revue française de science politique* 61(5): 917–944.
Ragaru, Nadège, and Antonela Capelle-Pogăcean, eds. 2010. *Vie quotidienne et pouvoir sous le communisme: la consommation revisitée.* Paris: Karthala.
Rausing, Sigrid. 1998. "L'impossible retour: dons, aides et échanges dans le nord-ouest de l'Estonie." *Ethnologie française* 28(4): 525–531.
Regamey, Amandine. 2007. *Prolétaires de tous pays, excusez-moi!: dérision et politique dans le monde soviétique.* Paris: Buchet-Chastel.
Renahy, Nicolas. 2005. *Les Gars du coin: enquête sur une jeunesse rurale.* Paris: La Découverte.
Rennes, Juliette. 2006. "Une université biélorusse en son exil lituanien. EHU: périple européen, entre résistances et innovation." *EspacesTemps.net.* Retrieved 8 July 2015 from http://www.espacestemps.net/articles/une-universite-bielorusse-en-son-exil-lituanien.
Republic of Belarus. 2011. *Četvert' veka posle černobyl'skoj katastrofy: itogi i perspektivy preodoleniâ. Nacional'nyj doklad Respubliki Belarus'* [A quarter of a century after the nuclear accident at the Chernobyl power plant: appraisal and prospects for recovery. A national report of the Republic of Belarus]. Minsk: Institute of Radiology.
Revel, Jacques. 1989. "Préface. L'histoire au ras du sol." In *Le Pouvoir au village: histoire d'un exorciste dans le Piémont du XVIIe siècle*, by Giovanni Levi, i–xxxiii. Paris: Gallimard.
———, ed. 1996. *Jeux d'échelles: la micro-analyse à l'expérience.* Paris: Gallimard/Le Seuil.
Revuz, Christine. 1980. *Ivan Ivanovitch écrit à la "la pravda."* Paris: Éd. Sociales.
Richard, Yann. 2002. *La Biélorussie: une géographie historique.* Paris: L'Harmattan.
Ries, Nancy. 1997. *Russian Talk: Culture and Conversation during Perestroika.* Ithaca, NY: Cornell University Press.
———. 2009. "Potato Ontology: Surviving Postsocialism in Russia." *Cultural Anthropology* 24(2): 181–212.
Rowell, Jay. 1999. "L'étonnant retour du 'totalitarisme.' Réflexions sur le 'tournant' de 1989 et l'historiographie de la RDA." *Politix* 47: 131–150.
———. 2006. *Le Totalitarisme au concret: les politiques du logement en RDA.* Paris: Économica.
Ruby, Christian. 1997. *L'Enthousiasme: essai sur le sentiment en politique.* Paris: Hatier.

Rudling, Per Anders. 2012. "The Khatyn Massacre in Belorussia: A Historical Controversy Revisited." *Holocaust and Genocide Studies* 26(1): 29–58.
Ryabchuk, Anastasiya. 2010. "La culture du 'BOMJ.' Réponse critique à l'approche culturaliste à partir d'une étude ethnographique en Ukraine." In *L'Arrière-cour de la mondialisation: ethnographie des paupérisés*, edited by Patrick Bruneteaux and Daniel Terolle, 353–375. Bellecombe-en-Bauges: Éd. du Croquant.
Sampson, Steven. 1984. *National Integration through Socialist Planning: An Anthropological Study of Romanian New Town*. Boulder, CO: Columbia University Press.
———. 1987. "The Second Economy of the Soviet Union and Eastern Europe." *Annals of the American Academy of Political and Social Science* 493(1): 120–136.
———. 1991. "Is There an Anthropology of Socialism?" *Anthropology Today* 7(5): 16–19.
Sapir, Jacques. 1984. *Travail et travailleurs en URSS*. Paris: La Découverte.
Schatz, Edward, ed. 2009. *Political Ethnography: What Immersion Contributes to the Study of Power*. Chicago: University of Chicago Press.
Schwartz, Olivier. 1990. *Le Monde privé des ouvriers: hommes et femmes du Nord*. Paris: Presses universitaires de France.
———. 1991. "Sur le rapport des ouvriers du Nord à la politique. Matériaux lacunaires." *Politix* 13: 79–86.
———. 1993. "Postface. L'empirisme irréductible." In *Le Hobo: sociologie du sans-abri*, Nels Anderson, 265–305. Paris: Nathan.
———. 1998. "La Notion de 'classes populaires.'" Thesis, Habilitation à diriger des recherches (Higher doctorate with accreditation to supervise research), Université de Versailles-Saint-Quentin en Yvelines.
Scott, James. 1976. *The Moral Economy of the Peasant: Rebellion and Subsistence in Southeast Asia*. New Haven, CT: Yale University Press.
———. 1990. *Domination and the Arts of Resistance: Hidden Transcripts*. New Haven, CT: Yale University Press.
Selk'skoe hozâjstvo Respubliki Belarus'. Ministerstvo sel'skogo hozâjstva i prodovol'stviâ Respubliki Belarus' [Agriculture in the Republic of Belarus. Ministry of Agriculture and Food of the Republic of Belarus]. 2015. Minsk: Belorusskoe sel'skoe hozâjstva.
Sériot, Patrick. 2005. "Diglossie, bilinguisme et mélange des langues: le cas du *suržyk* en Ukraine." *La linguistique* 41(2): 37–52.
Shanin, Teodor. 1972. *The Awkward Class: Political Sociology of Peasantry in a Developing Society; Russia 1910–1925*. Oxford: Clarendon Press of Oxford University Press.
Shevchenko, Olga. 2009. *Crisis and the Everyday in Postsocialist Moscow*. Bloomington: Indiana University Press.
Shukan, Ioulia. 2005. "La Biélorussie: stratégies présidentielles de domination personnelle." *Critique internationale* 28: 37–45.
Shukan, Tatyana. 2008. "Le flash-mob: forme d'action privilégiée des jeunes contestataires en Biélorussie." *Raisons politiques* 29: 9–21.
Siegelbaum, Lewis. 1988. *Stakhanovism and the Politics of Productivity in the USSR, 1935–1941*. Cambridge: Cambridge University Press.
Silitski, Vitali, and Alexei Pikulik. 2011. "Belarus." In *Nations in Transit 2011. Democratization from Central Europe to Eurasia*, edited by Freedom House, 104–124. New York: House/Rowman & Littlefield Publishers.
Siméant, Johanna. 2010. "'Économie morale' et protestation – détours africains." *Genèses. Sciences sociales et histoire* 81: 142–160.

Simmel, Georg. (1907) 1965. "The Poor." Translated by Claire Jacobson. *Social Problems* 13(2): 118–140.
Smirnova, Rozaliâ, ed. 2009. *Čelovečeskij potencial belorusskoj derevni* [The human potential of rural Belarus]. Minsk: Belorusskaâ Nauka.
Smith, Adam. (1759) 1976. *The Theory of Moral Sentiments*. New York: Oxford University Press.
Smith, Hedrick. 1977. *The Russians*. New York: Ballantine Books.
Snyder, Timothy. 2003. *The Reconstruction of Nations: Poland, Ukraine, Lithuania, Belarus 1569–1999*. New Haven, CT: Yale University Press.
———. 2010a. *Bloodlands: Europe between Hitler and Stalin*. New York: Basic Books.
———. 2010b. "In Darkest Belarus." *New York Review of Books*, 28 October 2010, 34.
Sommer, Stefan, ed. 2002. *Das grosse Lexikon des DDR-Alltags: von Aktivist und Altstoffsammlung über Dederon, Kaufhalle, Rondo und Subbotnik bis zum Zirkel schreibender Arbeiter*. Berlin: Schwarzkopf und Schwarzkopf.
Soviet Encyclopedic Dictionary. 1989. 5th ed. Moscow.
Southworth, Caleb. 2006. "The Dacha Debate: Household Agriculture and Labor Markets in Post-Socialist Russia." *Rural Sociology* 71(3): 451–478.
Stewart, Susan, Margarete Klein, Andrea Schmitz, and Hans-Henning Schröder. 2012. "Introduction." In *Presidents, Oligarchs and Bureaucrats: Forms of Rule in the Post-Soviet Space*, edited by Susan Stewart, Margarete Klein, Andrea Schmitz, and Hans-Henning Schröder, 1–11. Farnham: Ashgate.
Streith, Michel. 2005. *Dynamiques paysannes en Mecklembourg: survie d'un savoir-faire*. Münster: Lit Verlag.
Studer, Brigitte. (2000) 2004. "Totalitarisme et stalinisme." In *Le Siècle des communismes*, edited by Michel Dreyfus, Bruno Groppo, Claudio Sergio Ingerflom, Roland Lew, Claude Pennetier, Bernard Pudal, and Serge Wolikow, 33–63. Paris: Éd. du Seuil.
Sumpf, Alexandre. 2013. *De Lénine à Gagarine: une histoire sociale de l'Union soviétique*. Paris: Gallimard.
Symaniec, Virginie. 2006. "Le théâtre en Biélorussie. L'officiel et le dissident." *Le courrier des pays de l'Est* 1058: 47–55.
Tarragoni, Federico. 2017. "La méthode d'Edward P. Thompson." *Politix* 118: 183–205.
Testart, Alain. 2007. *Critique du don: études sur la circulation non marchande*. Paris: Syllepse.
Thireau, Isabelle, and Linshan Hua. 1998. "Une analyse des disputes dans les villages chinois: aspects historiques et culturels des accords concernant les actions justes et raisonnables." *Revue française de sociologie* 39(3): 535–563.
Thompson, Edward. 1991. *Customs in Common*. London: Merlin Press.
Tinguy, Anne (de). 2004. *La Grande migration: la Russie et les Russes depuis l'ouverture du rideau de fer*. Paris: Plon.
Tocqueville, Alexis (de). (1835–1840) 2019. *Democracy in America*. Vols. 1 and 2. Translated by Henry Reeve. Wroclaw: Independently Published.
Todorova, Marij, and Zsuzsa Gille, eds. (2010) 2012. *Post-Communist Nostalgia*. New York: Berghahn Books.
Traverso, Enzo (texts chosen and presented by). 2001. *Le Totalitarisme: le XXe siècle en débat*. Paris: Éd. du Seuil.
Urban, Michael. 1989. *An Algebra of Soviet Power: Elite Circulation in the Belorussian Republic, 1966–86*. Cambridge: Cambridge University Press.

Van Atta, Donald, ed. 1993. *The "Farmer Threat": The Political Economy of Agrarian Reform in Post-Soviet Russia*. Boulder, CO: Westview Press.

Vaissié, Cécile. 1999. *"Pour votre Liberté et pour la nôtre": le combat des dissidents de Russie*. Paris: R. Laffont.

———. 2010. "[Review of] Ronan Hervouet, *Datcha blues: existences ordinaires et dictature en Biélorussie*." *Vingtième siècle. Revue d'histoire* 106: 287–288.

Vanderhill, Rachel. 2013. *Promoting Authoritarianism Abroad*. Boulder, CO: Lynne Rienner.

Verdery, Katherine. 1983. *Transylvanian Villagers: Three Centuries of Political, Economic, and Ethnic Change*. Berkeley: University of California Press.

———. 1991. "Theorising Socialism: A Prologue to the 'Transition.'" *American Ethnologist* 18(3): 419–439.

———. 1996. *What Was Socialism, and What Comes Next?* Princeton, NJ: Princeton University Press.

———. 2013. "An Anthropologist in Communist Romania, 1973–1989." *Problems of Post-Communism* 60(4): 35–42.

———. 2018. *My Life as a Spy: Investigation in a Secret Police File*. Durham, NC: Duke University Press.

Verdery, Katherine, and Justine Faure. 2011. "Les échanges universitaires, la logique de bloc et l'esprit de guerre froide." *Vingtième siècle. Revue d'histoire* 109: 201–212.

Vichnevski, Anatoli. 2000. *La Faucille et le rouble: la modernisation conservatrice en URSS*. Paris: Gallimard.

Visson, Lynn. (1998) 2001. *Wedded Strangers: The Challenges of Russian-American Marriages*. New York: Hippocrene Books.

Völker Beate, and Henk Flap. 1995. "Amitié et inimitié sous communisme d'État. Le cas de l'Allemagne de l'est." *Revue française de sociologie* 36(1): 629–654.

Weber, Florence. 1996. "Réduire ses dépenses, ne pas compter son temps. Comment mesurer l'économie domestique?" *Genèses. Sciences sociales et histoire* 25: 5–28.

———. 1998. *L'Honneur des jardiniers: les potagers dans la France du XXe siècle*. Paris: Belin.

———. 2001a. *Max Weber*. Paris: Hachette.

———. 2001b. "Settings, Interactions and Things: A Plea for Multi-Integrative Ethnography." *Ethnography* 2(4): 475–499.

———. 2002. "Pour penser la parenté contemporaine. Maisonnée et parentèle, des outils de l'anthropologie." In *Les Solidarités familiales en question: entre aide et transmission*, edited by Danièle Debordeaux and Pierre Strobel, 73–106. Paris: LGDJ/Maison des sciences de l'homme.

———. (1989) 2009a. *Le Travail à-côté: une ethnographie des perceptions*. Paris: Éd. de l'EHESS.

———. 2009b. *Manuel de l'ethnographe*. Paris: Presses universitaires de France.

———. 2013. *Penser la parenté aujourd'hui: la force du quotidien*. Paris: Éd. Rue d'Ulm/Presses de l'École normale supérieure.

Weber, Max. (1921) 2019. *Economy and Society*. Translated by Keith Tribe. Cambridge: Harvard University Press.

———. 1958. *From Max Weber: Essays in Sociology*. Translated by H. H. Gerth and C. Wright Mills. New York: Oxford University Press.

Wedel, Janine. 1986. *The Private Poland: An Anthropologist's Look at Everyday Life*. New York: Facts on File.

Werth, Nicolas. (1997) 1999a. "A State against Its People: Violence, Repression, and Terror in the Soviet Union." In *The Black Book of Communism: Crimes, Terror, Repression*, edited by Stéphane Courtois, Nicolas Werth, Jean-Louis Panné, Andrzej Paczkowski, Karel Bartosek, Jean-Louis Margolin, translated by Jonathan Murphy and Mark Kramer, 33–268. Cambridge, MA: Harvard University Press.

———. 1999b. "L'historiographie de l'U.R.S.S. dans la période post-communiste." *Revue d'études comparatives Est-Ouest* 30(1): 81–104.

———. 2001a. "Le stalinisme au pouvoir. Mise en perspective historiographique." *Vingtième siècle. Revue d'histoire* 69: 125–135.

———. 2001b. "Totalitarisme ou révisionnisme? L'histoire soviétique, une histoire en chantier (1996)." In *Le Totalitarisme: le XXe siècle en débat*, compiled by Enzo Traverso, 878–896. Paris: Seuil.

———. 2012. *Histoire de l'Union soviétique: de l'Empire russe à la Communauté des États indépendants: 1900–1991*. Paris: Presses universitaires de France.

White, Anne. 2000. "Social Change in Provincial Russia: The Intelligentsia in a Raion Centre." *Europe-Asia Studies* 52(4): 677–694.

White, Stephen. 1986. "Economic Performance and Communist Legitimacy." *World Politics* 38(3): 462–482.

———. 1996. *Russia Goes Dry: Alcohol, State and Society*. Cambridge: Cambridge University Press.

Wilkinson, Stephen. 2012. "Neither Beijing nor Hanoi but a Cuban Market Socialism?" *International Journal of Cuban Studies* 4 (3–4): 260–268.

Wilson, Andrew. 2011. *Belarus: The Last European Dictatorship in Europe*. New Haven: Yale University Press.

Wolff, David, and Gaël Moullec. 2005. *Le KGB et les pays baltes: 1939–1991*. Paris: Belin.

Yurchak, Alexei. 2006. *Everything Was Forever, Until It Was No More: The Last Soviet Generation*. Princeton, NJ: Princeton University Press.

Yvert-Jalu, Hélène. 2007. *Femmes et familles en Russie: d'hier et d'aujourd'hui*. Paris: Éd. du Sextant.

Zadora, Anna. 2015. "Le modèle paysan à l'échelle nationale ou la pesanteur des conditions socioéconomiques sur la construction d'une nation." *L'Homme et la société* 195–196: 175–196.

Zakharova, Larissa. 2011. *S'Habiller à la soviétique: la mode et le dégel en URSS*. Paris: Éd. du CNRS.

———. 2013. "Le quotidien du communisme: pratiques et objets." *Annales. Histoire, Sciences Sociales.* 68(2): 305–314.

Zaytseva, Anna. 2008. "La légitimation du rock en URSS dans les années 1970–1980. Acteurs, logiques, institutions." *Cahiers du monde russe* 49(4): 651–680.

Zlotnikov, Anatolii. 2006. "Agrarian Transformations and Public Opinion." *Sociological Research* 45(2): 81–101.

PRESS AND MEDIA

Agence France Presse (AFP). 2012. "Belarus: un opposant torturé en prison?" *lefigaro.fr*, 25 January. Retrieved 11 July 2017 from http://www.lefigaro.fr/flash-actu/2012/01/25/97001-20120125FILWWW00513-belarus-un-opposant-torture-en-prison.php.

Alachnovič, Aleś. 2015. "Why Belarusians Stay Away from the Belarusian Rouble." *Belarus Digest*, 28 September. Retrieved 31 October 2016 from http://belarusdigest.com/story/why-belarusians-stay-away-belarusian-rouble-23293.

Ânuševskaâ, Anastasiâ. 2012. "Každyj tretij belorus – p'ânica" [One third of Belarusians are drunkards]. *Naviny.by*, 13 December. Retrieved 15 February 2017 from http://naviny.by/rubrics/society/2012/12/13/ic_articles_116_180201.

Astapenia, Ryhor. 2013. "Vilnius: the New Mecca for Belarusian Shoppers and Activists." *Belarus Digest*, 6 March. Retrieved 31 October 2016 from http://belarusdigest.com/story/vilnius-new-mecca-belarusian-shoppers-and-activists-13258.

Avril, Pierre. 2010. "L'Occident dénonce l'élection et la répression biélorusse." *lefigaro.fr*, 19 December 2010. Retrieved 11 July 2017 from http://www.lefigaro.fr/international/2010/12/19/01003-20101219ARTFIG00198-bielorussie-loukachenko-etrille-l-opposition.php.

Babenko, Anatolij. 2005. "Žit' v soglassi" [Living harmoniously]. *Belarus' Segodnâ*, 5 August. Retrieved 28 August 2009 from http://www.sb.by/print/post/45698.

Barthet, Elise. 2012. "Femen, les activistes aux seins nus." *lemonde.fr*, 22 February. Retrieved 11 July 2017 from http://www.lemonde.fr/europe/article/2012/02/22/femen-les-activistes-aux-seins-nus_1644775_3214.html.

Belaâ Rus'. 2008. "Programma vozroždeniâ i razvitiâ sela v dejstvii" [The rural revitalization and development program in action]. 2–3 (26).

Belarus' Segodnâ. 2006. "Soobŝeniâ press-slušby Prezidenta. Prezident podpissal râd ukazov o nagraždenii" [Information provided by the President's Press Office. The President signs a series of *ukases* on decorations]. 24 February. Retrieved 28 August 2009 from http://www.sb.by/print/post/50102.

———. 2008a. "Ksëndz iz Mosara podelitsâ s učastkovymi Vitebskoj oblasti opytom borby s p'ânstvom" [Mosar's priest shares his experience in the fight against alcoholism with the local police of Vitebsk Oblast]. 10 April. Retrieved 28 August 2009 from http://www.sb.by/post/65921.

———. 2008b. "V belorusskoj derevne Pariž otkrylis' muzej Ioanna Pavla II, novyj kostël i ocvâŝena 'Ejfeleva bašnâ'" [A new church has been consecrated in the Belarusian village of Pariž, where the John Paul II museum has also opened, and an 'Eiffel Tower' has been built]. 20 October. Retrieved 28 August 2009 from http://www.sb.by/post/75603.

———. 2010. "Skončalsâ izvestnyj v Belarusi ksëndz Ûozas Bul'ka" [The priest Ûozas Bul'ka, famous in Belarus, has died]. 9 January. Retrieved 22 March 2011 from http://www.sb.by/post/95576.

———. 2012. "Belorussiâ pri Lukašenko 1994–2001" [Belarus under Lukashenko from 1994 to 2001]. 6 June. Retrieved 14 January 2016 from http://www.sb.by/luchshee-iz-interneta-vybor-redaktsii-portala/article/belorussiya-pri-lukashenko-1994-2011.html.

Belarus Today. 2000. "Belarussians Drink More Vodka than Russians." 17–23 October.

Belorusskij Partizan. 2012. "Lukašenko prostil svoego lûbimčika – bombardira" [Lukashenko pardons his pet – the top scorer]. 1 April. Retrieved 14 January 2013 from http://www.belaruspartisan.org/print/?ID=207762.

Belyh, Vika. 2011. "Žil i umer kak soldat" [He lived and died like a soldier]. *Belarus' Segodnâ*, 2 April. Retrieved 10 June 2011 from http://www.sb.by/print/post/114741.

Bogdanov, Vladimir. 2010. "Mosarskij stil'" [The style of Mosar]. *Hartiâ 97*, 11 January. Retrieved 11 January 2010 from http://www.charter97.org/ru/news/2010/1/11/25260.

Bohdan, Siarhei. 2011. "Belarusian 'Terrorists' on Trial: Any Hope for Justice?" *Belarus Digest*, 22 November 22. Retrieved 11 July 2017 from http://belarusdigest.com/story/belarusian-terrorists-trial-any-hope-justice-6592.

———. 2012. "Faces of Belarusian Politics: Viktar Lukashenka." *Belarus Digest*, 9 March. Retrieved 14 January 2013 from http://belarusdigest.com/story/faces-belarusian-politics-viktar-lukashenka-8203.

Borovoj, Artur. 2013. "Raspredelenie bez prikras: zarplata 300 dollarov, dom bez otopleniâ i dumy o buduŝem molodogo specialista" [Disorderly distribution: A salary of 300 dollars, a house without heating and a young specialist's thoughts on the future]. *people.onliner.by*, 29 November. Retrieved 16 December 2015 from http://people.onliner.by/2013/11/29/spec-4/.

Borowska, Paula. 2013. "Belarus Wants to Keep Its Western Border Locked Shut." *Belarus Digest*, 29 March. Retrieved 31 October 2016 from http://belarusdigest.com/story/belarus-wants-keep-its-western-border-locked-shut-13511.

BT. 2016. "V Belarusi otpuskaûtsâ ceny na social'no značimye produkty pitaniâ" [The prices of socially significant foods are deregulated in Belarus]. 14 January.

Charnysh, Volha. 2015. "Why Do So Few Tourists Visit Belarus?" *Belarus Digest*, 14 January. Retrieved 29 October 2016 from http://belarusdigest.com/story/why-do-so-few-tourists-visit-belarus-21079.

Charter '97. 2009a. "Genprokuratura ne kommentiruet situaciû s razyskivaemym ksëndzom Bul'koj" [General Prosecutor's Office makes no comment on the situation of the indicted priest Bul'ka]. 6 April. Retrieved 23 March 2011 from http://www.charter97.org/ru/news/2009/4/6/16968.

———. 2009b. "Litva vydala order na arest izvestnogo belorusskogo ksëndza Ûozassa Bul'ki" [Lithuania issues an arrest warrant for the famous Belarusian priest Ûossas Bul'ka]. 6 April. Retrieved 23 March 2011 from http://www.charter97.org/ru/news/2009/4/6/16936.

———. 2009c. "V regionah poâvlâûtsâ zony trezvosti" [Temperance zones exist in the regions]. 27 August. Retrieved 23 March 2011 from http://www.charter97.org/ru/news/2009/8/27/21437.

———. 2010. "Skončalsâ ksëndz Ûzaf Bul'ka" [The priest Ûzaf Bul'ka has died]. 9 January. Retrieved 23 March 2011 from http://www.charter97.org/ru/news/2010/1/9/25216.

———. 2012a. "Korrupcionnyj skandal v upravlenii delami Lukašenko" [A corruption scandal in the Lukashenko administration]. 11 June. Retrieved 14 January 2013 from http://charter97.org/ru/news/2012/6/11/53577/.

———. 2012b. "Korrupciâ v Belarusi – na urovne afrikanskih stran" [Corruption in Belarus – on a par with African countries]. 5 December. Retrieved 13 January 2013 from http://charter97.org/ru/news/2012/12/5/62336/.

Elder, Miriam, and Luke Harding. 2010. "WikiLeaks cables describe Belarus leader as 'bizarre' and 'disturbed.'" *The Guardian*, 17 December. Retrieved 14 January 2013 from http://www.guardian.co.uk/world/2010/dec/17/wikileaks-belarus-leader-bizarre-disturbed.

Galinovskij, Dmitrij. 2012. "Planirovanie 'Dožinok' – zakonodatel'noe oformlenie" [The planning of '*Dožinki*' – legislative presentation]. *Eurobelarus*, 18 December. Retrieved 16 December 2015 from http://eurobelarus.info/news/society/2012/12/18/dmitriy-galinovskiy—planirovanie-dozhinok-zakonodatel-noe-oformlenie.html.

Golesnik, Serguej. 2008. "Zavâzyvaem! V Verhnedvinske rešili aktivno borot'câ protiv vrednoj privyčki" [We are stopping! In Verkhnedvinsk, we have decided to actively combat bad habits]. *Belarus' Segodnâ*, 19 July. Retrieved 28 August 2009 from http://www.sb.by/post/70615.

———. 2010. "Okno v Pariž" [Window on Pariž]. *Belarus' Segodnâ*, 6 April. Retrieved 22 March 2011 from http://www.sb.by/post/98833.

Grablevski, Oleg. 2011. "Rabstvo v trude" [Slavery at work]. *Naše mnenie*, 7 September. Retrieved 12 November 2012 from http://nmnby.eu/news/analytics/3270.html.

Gubarevich, Igar. 2016. "Chernobyl as Belarus' foreign policy priority." *Belarus Digest*, 26 April. Retrieved 31 October 2016 from http://belarusdigest.com/story/chernobyl-belarus-foreign-policy-priority-25481.

Harris, Mike. 2010. "A Death in Minsk Should Sound the Alarm Bells." *Belarus Digest*, 9 September. Retrieved 11 July 2017 from http://belarusdigest.com/2010/09/09/a-death-in-minsk-should-sound-the-alarm-bells.

Kachurka, Raman. 2014. "Cargo Trains Smuggle Cigarettes from Belarus into the European Union." *Belarus Digest*, 17 December. Retrieved 31 October 2016 from http://belarusdigest.com/story/cargo-trains-smuggle-cigarettes-belarus-european-union-20830.

Korbut, Viktor. 2011. "Gorodok na vsû žizn'" [A small town for life]. *Belarus' Segodnâ*, 8 February. Retrieved 22 March 2011 from http://www.sb.by/post/112228.

Kozlovič, Nikolaj. 2013. "Imitaciâ: kak vyžit' v obrazcovom agrogorodke, kotoryj postroil Nacbank" [Imitation: how to survive in an exemplary agritown built by the National Bank]. *people.onliner.by*, 6 November. Retrieved 30 March 2016 from http://people.onliner.by/2013/11/06/agro-2.

Krasnova, Hanna. 2003. "Students refuse to work on subbotnik." *Viasna*. Retrieved 21 May 2008 from http://spring96.org/en/news/11864/.

Krât, Dmitrij. 2005. "Vremâ mira" [Time of peace]. *Belarus' Segodnâ*, 11 January. Retrieved 28 August 2009 from http://www.sb.by/print/post/41104.

Kryvoi, Yarik. 2011. "Cheap Booze for the People of Belarus." *Belarus Digest*, 2 September. Retrieved 15 February 2017 from http://belarusdigest.com/story/cheap-booze-people-belarus-5528.

Kuzina, Anastasiâ. 2015. "Zapret na kodirovanie ot alkogolizma: čto my terâem?" [Ban on therapeutic coding to treat alcoholism: What are we losing?]. *zdorov'e mail.ru*, 31 August. Retrieved 26 January 2017 from https://health.mail.ru/news/kodirovanie/.

Lashuk, Nadine. 2012. "How to Survive on 200 Dollars a Month." *Belarus Digest*, 3 February. Retrieved 30 October 2016 from http://belarusdigest.com/story/how-survive-200-dollars-month-7591.

Le Figaro. 2015. "Depardieu joue au paysan en Biélorussie." 24 July. Retrieved 12 January 2016 from http://www.lefigaro.fr/cinema/2015/07/24/03002-20150724ARTFIG00048-depardieu-joue-au-paysan-en-bielorussie.php#2.

Leshchenko, Natalia. 2011. "The Sound of Clapping." *Belarus Digest*, 24 June. Retrieved 11 July 2017 from http://belarusdigest.com/2011/06/24/sound-clapping.

Levšina, Irina, and Serguej Pul'ša. 2012. "Belorusskij rabotnik v les ne ubežit" [No escape for the Belarusian worker]. *Naviny.by*, 7 December. Retrieved 14 January 2013 from http://naviny.by/rubrics/society/2012/12/07/ic_articles_116_180144/.

Lukashenko, Alexander. 2015. "Obrašenie s Poslaniem k belorusskomu narodu i Nacional'nomu Sobraniû" [Address with a message to the Belarusian people and the National Assembly]. 29 April. Retrieved 16 December 2015 from http://president.gov

.by/ru/news_ru/view/obraschenie-s-poslaniem-k-belorusskomu-narodu-i-natsio nalnomu-sobraniju-11301/.

———. 2016. "Doklad Prezidenta Belarusi na pâtom Vsebelorusskom narodnom sobranii" [Address to the Fifth Belarusian People's Assembly]. 22 June. Retrieved 25 January 2017 from http://president.gov.by/ru/news_ru/view/uchastie-v-pjatom-vsebelorusskom-narodnom-sobranii-13867/.

Naša Niva. 2011. "Letniaâ sustreca 'Legiëni Maryi'" [Summer meeting of the "Legion of Mary" / in the Belarusian language]. 13 June. Retrieved 29 July 2011 from http://nn.by/?c=ar&i=55662.

Naviny.by. 2006. "Prokuratura Belarusi prokommentirovala delo latvijskogo diplomata" [The Belarusian Public Prosecutor's Office has commented on the case of the Latvian diplomat]. 1 August. Retrieved 13 July 2015 from http://naviny.by/rubrics/society/2006/08/01/ic_news_116_256958/.

———. 2013. "Užestočenie kontraktnoj sistemy usilit želanie belorusov skazat' rodine 'proŝaj'" [Tougher contractual conditions are making Belarusians more willing to say 'farewell' to their homeland]. 24 November. Retrieved 8 January 2016 from http://naviny.by/rubrics/economic/2013/11/24/ic_articles_113_183746/.

Nečapajka, Tat'âna. 2005. "'Diskreditaciâ gosudarstva' stanet v Belorussii prestupleniem" [In Belarus, "discrediting the state" becomes a crime]. *BBCRUSSIAN.com*, 2 December. Retrieved 13 July 2015 from http://news.bbc.co.uk/hi/russian/news/newsid_4492000/4492182.stm.

New York Times. 1985. "Another Day of Work Is Donated in Soviet." 5 May. Retrieved 5 September 2007 from http://www.nytimes.com/1985/05/05/world/another-day-of-work-is-donated-in-soviet.html.

Plaschinsky, George. 2012. "Why Young Belarusians Go to Russia, not Europe." *Belarus Digest*, 10 January. Retrieved 31 October 2016 from http://belarusdigest.com/story/why-young-belarusians-go-russia-not-europe-7260.

———. 2012. "Political Prisoners as Part of Belarus Electoral Process." *Belarus Digest*, 20 February. Retrieved 11 July 2017 from http://belarusdigest.com/story/political-prisoners-part-belarus-electoral-process-7852.

Preiherman, Yauheni. 2012. "Sex Tours Save the Belarusian Tourist Industry." *Belarus Digest*, 13 June. Retrieved 31 October 2016 from http://belarusdigest.com/story/sex-tours-save-belarusian-tourist-industry-9664.

———. 2012. "The New Serfdom in Belarus." *Belarus Digest*, 12 December. Retrieved 16 December 2015 from http://belarusdigest.com/story/new-serfdom-belarus-12400?utm_source=Belarus+Digest+Newsletter&utm_campaign=c3dfe7343b-mailchimp&utm_medium=email.

Proleskovskij, Ruslan. 2013. "Iz tranšej – v festival', ili kak Žlobin gotovitsâ k 'Dožinkam'" [From trench to festival, or how Žlobin is preparing for the '*Dožinki*']. *tut.by*, 14 August. Retrieved 16 December 2015 from http://news.tut.by/society/361428.html.

Rusyj, Mihail. 2011. "Report of the Minister for Agriculture." *Belorusskaâ Niva*, 28 November.

Sahalin i Kurily. 2016. "Na ûge Sahalina pristupili k sozdaniû pervogo agrogorodka" [Work has begun on building the first agri-town in the south of Sakhalin]. 16 March. Retrieved 30 March 2016 from http://www.skr.su/news/257130.

Schreck, Carl. 2015. "Western Scholars Alarmed by Russian Deportations, Fines." *Radio Free Europe/Radio Liberty*, 31 March. Retrieved 6 July 2015 from http://www.rferl.org/content/russia-western-scholars-alarmed-deportations/26929921.html.

Smok, Vadzim. 2015. "Dealing with Slavery and Human Trafficking in Belarus." *Belarus Digest*, 9 February. Retrieved 16 February 2017 from http://belarusdigest.com/story/dealing-slavery-and-human-trafficking-belarus-21502.

———. 2013. "Hrodna Region: The Land of Catholics and Smugglers." *Belarus Digest*, 28 May. Retrieved 31 October 2016 from http://belarusdigest.com/story/hrodna-region-land-catholics-and-smugglers-14163.

———. 2014. "Why Belarusians Turned to Shopping Abroad?" *Belarus Digest*, 9 December. Retrieved 31 October 2016 from http://belarusdigest.com/story/why-belarusians-turned-shopping-abroad-20682.

———. 2015. "Hunting Tourism and Corruption in Belarus." *Belarus Digest*, 9 January. Retrieved 30 October 2016 from http://belarusdigest.com/story/hunting-tourism-and-corruption-belarus-20937.

———. 2016. "Poland Lures 'the Best Migrants in the World' from Belarus." *Belarus Digest*, 23 February. Retrieved 31 October 2016 from http://belarusdigest.com/story/poland-lures-best-migrants-world-belarus-24674.

Smolar, Piotr. 2012. "Biélorussie. Inventaire avant liquidation." *Le Monde*, 19–20 February.

Strižak, Danila. 2009a. "Bul'ka mog byt' rukopoložen v svâŝenniki s pomoŝ'û specslužb?" [Bul'ka could have been ordained a priest with the help of the special services]. *Euradio/Evropejskoe radio dlâ Belarusi (ERB)*, 10 April. Retrieved 26 August 2009 from http://www.euroradio.fm/ru/815/reports/31087/?tpl=208.

———. 2009b. "V resultate skandala Ûosas Bul'ka popal v bol'nitsu" [Following the scandal, Bul'ka ends up in hospital]. *Euradio/Evropejskoe radio dlâ Belarusi (ERB)*, 8 April. Retrieved 26 August 2009 from http://www.euroradio.fm/ru/813/reports/30960/?tpl=208.

Sturejko, Stepan. 2012. "Dožinki i arhitekturnoe nasledie" [*Dožinki* and architectural heritage]. *Eurobelarus*, 21 December. Retrieved 15 December 2015 from http://eurobelarus.info/news/society/2012/12/21/stepan-stureyko-dozhinki-i-arhitekturnoe-nasledie.html.

Šanski, A. 2003. "Navuka pra dačnikav" [A scientific approach to the activity of the *dačniki* / in the Belarusian language]. *Naša Niva*, 16 May.

Taras, Anton. 2011. "Vengriâ ne poterpit 'travli svoih diplomatov'" [Hungary does not tolerate any "harassment of its diplomats"]. *Naviny.by*, 27 June. Retrieved 10 July 2015 from http://naviny.by/rubrics/politic/2011/06/27/ic_articles_112_174162.

Tkačenko, E. 2002. "'Postavil' na daču" [He "banked" on the dacha]. *Belorusskaâ Delovaâ Gazeta*, 16 May.

Ulitënok, Galina. 2003. "Episcop-ogon'" [The bishop with the sacred fire]. *Belarus' Segodnâ*, 13 August. Retrieved 22 March 2011 from http://www.sb.by/print/post/30128.

Vitkine, Benoît. 2007. "La 'verticale du pouvoir', ligne directrice du poutinisme." *Le Monde*, 29 November. Retrieved 8 April 2013 from http://www.lemonde.fr/europe/article/2007/11/29/la-verticale-du-pouvoir-ligne-directrice-du-poutinisme_983668_3214.html.

Vodolažskaâ, Tat'âna. 2012. "Dožinki kak faktor razvitiâ belarusskih gorodov" [*Dožinki* as a factor in the development of Belarusian cities]. *Eurobelarus*, 19 December. Retrieved 15 December 2015 from http://eurobelarus.info/news/society/2012/12/19/tat-yana-vodolazhskaya-dozhinki-kak-faktor-razvitiya-belarusskih-gorodov.html.

Volkova, Veronika. 2014. "Smert' kolhozam. U belorusskoj agrarnoj reformy est' načalo, no net konca" [The death of kolkhozes. In the reform of Belarusian agriculture, there is a beginning, but no end]. *Belgazeta*, 24 March. Retrieved 16 December 2015 from http://www.belgazeta.by/ru/2014_03_24/economics/28628/.

Zajac, Aliaksandr, and Siarhiej Jakaulieu. 2012. "The Government Alcoholises the Belarusians." *Belarus Digest*, 30 November. Retrieved 15 February 2017 from http://belarusdigest.com/story/government-alcoholises-belarusians-12306.

Zaval'nûk, Vladislav. 2007. "Slovo o prelate Bul'ko. Neraskrytaâ tajna Mosara" [A few words about prelate Bul'ko. Mosar's unspoken secret]. *Belarus' Segodnâ*, 4 November. Retrieved 28 July 2011 from http://www.sb.by/post/62303.

Zenina, Tamara. 2003. "Kanonik iz Mosara" [The canon of Mosar]. *Belarus' Segodnâ*, 22 November. Retrieved 22 March 2011 from http://www.sb.by/print/post/32816.

INDEX

access to public resources, 98, 100
accounting fraud. *See under* theft
administrative pressure, 14–15, 24, 222
agriculture, 12–14, 15, 19, 28, 36, 38, 59, 94–95, 98, 100, 104, 124, 128, 158
    small-scale agriculture, 50
agri-town, 17–21
alcohol, 21–23, 43, 48, 77–78, 100, 171, 206–208, 209, 220, 222
    alcoholics, 13, 22, 23, 78–84, 85, 94, 95, 102, 131, 132, 153, 157, 180–189, 195–196, 204, 207–208, 209, 211, 212, 219, 224
    distillation, 84–85
    drunkenness, 43
    samogon, 43, 68, 84, 85, 103
    vodka, 7, 22, 43, 44, 56, 68, 77–86, 123, 144, 171, 173, 188, 196, 207, 208, 209
    wine, 7, 42, 80, 123, 168, 188
Alexievich, Svetlana A., 79, 118, 122, 228, 230–231
altruism. *See under* solidarity
Amalrik, Andreï, 84, 137
anekdot. See under jokes
anthropology, 28, 31
    of socialism, 4
arrhythmia (of socialist temporality). *See under* time
autarchy. *See under* autonomy
autonomy, 169–177
    autarchy, 85, 169–172, 173
    See also independence
authoritarian, 1, 2, 3, 5, 6, 7, 16, 24, 26, 27, 31, 38, 39, 40, 44, 45, 46, 90, 133, 199, 203, 204, 206, 211, 220, 228
    dictatorship, 1, 3, 6, 24, 26, 27, 31, 37, 225

bandits, 118, 198
bania, 7, 44, 58, 59, 72, 73, 83, 88, 97, 112, 172
beat the system, 166
Becker, Howard S., 27, 207
blat, 126, 152, 166
Boltanski, Luc, 176
bomži, 56, 82–83, 187
Bourdieu, Pierre, 39, 71, 147, 148, 151, 152, 174, 175, 180, 200, 211, 221
Boym, Svetlana, 228
bribery. *See under* corruption
Bulgaria, 4, 98, 136
Burawoy, Michael, 4, 47n2, 136, 225
bureaucracy, 45, 146, 209

Certeau, Michel de, 155, 227
Chernobyl, 59, 66, 86, 122, 164, 198
church, 22, 32, 102, 146, 182, 205, 207, 208, 210, 212, 213, 216, 219. *See also* religion
collectivization, 49, 67, 114, 115, 119, 120, 121, 129, 130, 213
competition, 19, 22, 100, 159
communist Saturday. *See under subbotnik*
configurations, 7, 9, 38, 61, 90, 99, 105, 110, 111, 151, 154, 186, 193, 202, 204, 220, 223. *See also* interdependencies
consumption, 4, 76, 77, 125, 133
    consumption abroad, 63, 64
    own consumption, 48–54
    self-consumption, 54, 222
conversion, 174, 192–195, 205, 209
corruption, 98, 99, 101, 153, 197
    bribery, 99
    crony capitalism, 101
Creed, Gerald W., 98

crony capitalism. *See under* corruption
cross-border activities, 62–65, 222
Cuba, 6, 10, 60
cunning, 166, 183

dachas, 34, 50, 51, 65, 71, 80, 183, 189
democracy, 23, 113, 129, 189, 190, 191, 194, 199, 211, 218
devaluation, 53, 61–62, 131
dictatorship. *See under* authoritarian
dignity, 7, 88, 125, 157–178, 179, 185, 188, 189, 193, 199, 201, 203, 204, 224, 225, 230
    dignifying practices, 21, 214, 220
Dirlewanger unit. *See under* Nazis
dissidence. *See under* opposition
distillation. *See under* alcohol
Dožinki, 18–21, 22, 24, 49, 153, 154
drunkeness. *See under* alcohol
Dubet, François, 175–177
Durkheim, Émile, 112, 113, 185, 188
Dzerzhinsky, Felix, 2, 60, 87

elections, 2, 18, 53, 98, 110n5, 127, 128, 132n3, 198
Elias, Norbert, 90, 110, 184, 188, 189
elites, 1, 59, 94, 98, 103, 104–110, 201
    nomenklatura, 100
endurance, 157–162, 176, 223
enthusiasm, 23, 60, 135, 139, 145, 166–169, 175, 223, 229
    enthusiast, 130, 139, 166, 167, 169
entrepreneurs, 57, 58, 60
ethic, 160, 162, 169, 193. *See also* morals
ethnography
    discrete ethnography, 26–47, 203, 223
    informal discussions, 32, 62, 180
    intimacy, 45, 46
    legitimacy of ethnographic knowledge, 45
    political ethnography, 5–9, 203, 228
everyday politics, 179, 192–202, 203
exchange rates, 53, 61–62

fair. *See under* justice
fairness. *See under* justice
farmer, 13, 55
fear, 2, 23, 39, 40, 95, 101, 109, 126, 186, 197
    paranoia, 33
Fassin, Didier, 129, 201, 202, 224
FEMEN, 35
Figes, Orlando, 118, 140
folklore, 18–21, 26, 28, 29
Foucault, Michel, 70, 211

German Democratic Republic (GDR), 3, 4, 125, 136, 138, 155, 177, 229
gender, 31, 52, 198, 199
generation, 113, 114, 122–132, 142, 162, 176, 223
gifts, 22, 42, 49, 66, 68, 84, 154, 158, 186, 193, 222
    gifts and counter-gifts, 74, 148, 152, 153, 188
God, 83, 85, 112, 128, 174, 206, 214, 219, 231
godfather, 110n5
Goffman, Erving, 151, 155, 227
gossip, 184, 185, 188
gulag, 130, 158
gulash socialism, 133. *See also* social contract

happiness, 6, 26, 32, 125, 185, 206, 229, 230
Hibou, Béatrice, 3, 5, 7, 8, 133, 186, 194, 220, 223, 224, 225, 226, 227
Hivon, Myriam, 77–78, 184
Hobsbawn, Eric, 20
Hoggart, Richard, 154, 192
homosexuals, 199
honest, 71, 111, 154, 185, 195
    honest labor, 93
    honest life, 132
    honest person, 123, 125, 174, 186, 202
    honest worker, 194
    honesty, 43, 71, 188
human rights, 140, 174, 189, 198, 218
humanitarian aid, 65–66, 222
humor. *See under* jokes
Humphrey, Caroline, 4, 28, 29, 73, 77, 93, 95, 97, 102, 137, 144, 148
Hungary, 4, 47n2, 136, 225

ideology, 2, 3, 20, 139, 155, 210, 220, 225–228, 229, 231
    communist ideology, 191
    state ideology, 2, 18, 160, 175
illegalisms, 48, 70–90, 93, 96, 96, 103, 222, 223, 225. *See also* informal
independence, 85, 90, 173–177, 188, 215, 223
    economic independence, 55
    national independence, 1, 191
    See also autonomy
inequality, 176, 184, 198, 225
informal
    informal economy, 98, 190, 193
    informal networks, 62, 109, 126, 152, 186
    informal practices, 40, 72, 97, 139, 150
    informal resources, 109, 111, 161, 177

second economy, 70
unwritten rules, 87, 223
See also illegalisms
ingenuity, 162–166, 223
interdependencies, 22, 90, 91–110, 111, 142, 148, 151, 153, 154, 155, 167, 173, 174, 179, 186, 188, 201, 203, 223
mutual dependencies, 98, 104, 169
See also configurations
intimacy. *See under* ethnography
Iron Curtain, 4, 27, 32, 47n2

Jews, 116–117, 165, 217
John Paul II, 212, 214, 219
jokes, 130, 142
anekdot, 141
humor, 226
justice, 11, 176, 177, 201, 202, 223, 224, 225, 227, 230
fair, 8, 111, 154, 176, 177, 179, 196, 201, 224
fairness, 175–177, 179, 201
unfair, 8, 111, 177, 179, 184, 194, 201, 224, 226

KGB, 2, 31, 33, 34, 35, 60, 86, 100, 101, 103, 106, 215–217, 220. *See also* security services
Khatyn, 117, 137, 150, 156n7
Kideckel, David A., 4, 29, 98, 151
kinship, 8, 28, 29, 91
kinship network, 92
practical kinship, 92
Komsomol, 57, 228
krugovaja poruka, 147
kulaks, 114, 115, 184
Kurapaty, 115
Kyrgyzstan, 62

Lamont, Michèle, 157, 160, 162, 175, 180, 184
Ledeneva, Alena, 40, 126, 147, 148, 152, 166, 186
Lenin, Vladimir, 36, 134–138, 140, 142, 144, 146, 149, 150, 156n8, 166
legitimacy, 5, 24, 34, 112, 129, 133, 139, 145, 147, 161, 179, 190, 210, 225
legitimate, 5, 37, 111, 113, 132, 176, 183, 185, 195
legitimation, 2, 5
Lithuania, 53, 63, 64, 65, 204, 208, 215, 217
loyalty, 2, 15, 16, 39, 95, 99, 101, 106, 109
morose loyalty, 227
Lüdtke, Alf, 3, 4, 155, 175, 226, 227
Lukács, János, 4, 47n2, 136, 225

market
administered market, 54
free market, 54
labor market, 16, 67, 209
market economy, 10, 11, 19, 24, 189, 194, 225
market socialism, 1, 10, 11, 23–24, 225
market transactions, 54, 73, 222
marketplace, 54, 57, 144
Russian market, 14
marriages, 30, 68, 91, 199, 206
transnational marriages, 67–68, 223
Masherov, Pyotr, 195
Mauss, Marcel, 74
memory, 2, 118, 124, 131, 203, 219
collective memory, 8, 118
Iron curtain of memory, 217
memorial complex, 117, 137, 156n7
memorial order, 213–221, 228
memories, 118, 130, 141, 177, 228
memory entrepreneurs, 217
official memory, 217
private memory, 118, 170
underground memory, 20
misappropriation. *See under* theft
misrecognition, 151–155
moral, 18, 21, 23, 24, 40, 48, 71, 90, 125, 132, 133, 142, 148, 149, 151, 154, 157, 185, 188, 192, 193, 197, 201, 202, 203, 205, 212, 219, 221, 224
moral authority, 102
moral community, 176, 179, 180, 185, 192
moral competencies, 181
moral duty, 188
moral incompetence, 180, 184
moral offenders, 180–191, 203
moral order, 205–208
moral pressure, 106
moral qualities, 157, 164, 174, 206, 220, 224
moral reform, 206–208
moral reprobation, 147
moral resources, 174
moral satisfaction, 134
moral sentiments, 40, 47n4, 111, 177, 198, 203
moral worlds, 170, 223, 224
See also ethic
moral economy, 9, 201–202, 203, 224, 225. *See also* moral
moralists, 9, 180, 189–192, 198, 203, 224

morality, 87, 88, 154, 161, 162, 179, 180, 184, 185, 189, 193, 194, 195, 197, 199, 226. *See also* moral
moralization, 21–24, 25n10, 102, 182, 193. *See also* paternalism
museums, 2, 36, 60, 87, 183, 207, 213, 214, 217, 219
mutual assistance, 40, 52, 92, 93, 146
    mutual aid: 107, 152, 155, 185, 225, 229
    mutualization: 92

Nazis, 59, 110, 114, 117, 118, 129, 130, 136, 156n6, 158, 170, 191, 217, 218
    Dirlewanger unit, 117
neopatrimonialism, 20, 101
networks, 35, 64, 65, 66, 83, 93, 104, 106, 122, 190
    circular solidarity networks, 188
    interdependency networks, 22, 142, 153, 173, 174, 203
    local networks, 209–210
    mutual acquaintances networks, 40
    networks of exchanges, 109, 149, 154, 188
    networks of obligation, 201
    personal networks, 62, 126, 152
NKVD, 115, 156n7, 215
nomenklatura. *See under* elites
norms, 43, 104, 105, 113, 145, 177, 179, 185, 188, 201, 227
    normal, 5, 23, 37, 131, 135, 176
    normalization, 129, 223
    normative activity, 175–176
nostalgia, 86, 153, 228–231
    Ostalgie, 228
    Yugonostalgia, 228

obligation, 13, 16, 64, 72, 74, 91, 140, 145, 179, 201, 223
    economy of obligation, 91–98, 104
oligarchs, 61, 98–99
opposition, 2, 5, 16, 34, 63, 76, 107, 110n8, 142, 145, 190–192, 198–199, 200, 212, 215, 226
    dissidence, 2, 45
    opposition press, 113, 218

paranoia. *See under* fear
Parfionov, Leonid, 136
partisans, 36, 59, 116–118, 215–218
paternalism, 17–25, 220. *See also* moralization
perestroika, 54, 108, 126–130
pilfering. *See under* theft
plan (economy), 17, 77, 109

spatial planning, 205–206
personal plot of land, 48–50, 52, 53, 74, 85, 92, 95, 112, 113, 119, 122, 124, 153, 165
poaching, 86–87, 117, 222, 227
Poland, 1, 4, 53, 54, 58, 62, 65, 114, 115, 166, 213, 214, 216
property, 82, 83, 96, 117, 126, 183, 187
    personal property, 49
    private property, 13, 99, 100, 108
    public property, 100, 197
prostitution, 87–90, 222
punishment, 21, 83, 145, 149, 186, 195–201. *See also* sanctions
purges, 99, 191

reciprocities, 92, 95–98, 223
religion, 102, 182, 212. *See also* church
ritual, 79, 133–156, 206, 207. *See also subbotnik*
robbery. *See under* theft
Romania, 4, 28, 29, 47n4, 73, 74, 98, 109, 151, 165
room for maneuver, 5, 89

Sampson, Steven, 4, 70, 109
samogon. *See under* alcohol
sanctions, 22, 33, 106, 139, 141, 149, 150. *See also* punishment
scandalous, 87, 159, 160, 180, 181, 189, 199, 224
schizophrenia, 226
Schwartz, Olivier, 8, 37, 44, 45, 46, 161, 180
Scott, James C., 201, 202, 223, 226, 227
second economy. *See under* informal
security services, 33, 35, 60, 100, 101, 199, 201, 216. *See also* KGB
self, 40, 160, 162
    self-interest, 145, 148, 177, 198
    self-ownership, 7
    self-reliance, 171, 179, 185
    self-sufficiency, 7, 12, 85, 169, 172, 192
    self-worth, 175
selflessness, 143–145, 152
Shevchenko, Olga, 199, 228
shopping, 64
shortages, 50, 122, 124, 197, 230
    shortage economy, 70, 73, 91
    shortage of labor, 13, 22, 94, 187
Simmel, Georg, 187
smuggling. *See under* theft
Snyder, Timothy, 1, 33, 114, 115
social contract, 133. *See also* gulash socialism
social mobility, 122, 125, 223
social order, 2, 188, 202, 203–221

socialism, 10, 29, 47n2, 135, 151, 225
  anthropology of socialism, 4
  post-socialist, 192
  real socialism, 89
  socialist, 1, 11, 20, 23, 28, 70, 97, 98, 109, 117, 132n2, 134, 135, 148, 151, 195
  See also gulash socialism; market socialism
solidarity, 107, 108, 111, 133–156, 162, 176, 177, 179, 185, 186, 188, 193, 198, 203, 223, 224, 225, 229, 230
  altruism, 40, 66, 138, 146, 147, 148, 152, 154, 155, 174, 177, 185, 186, 188
spy, 29
Stakhanovite, 160
Stalin, Joseph, 39, 115, 119, 121, 130, 200
subbotnik, 20, 41, 74, 133–156, 166, 228, 229
surveillance, 28–35, 37, 100
suspended punishment, 186

tactics, 42, 44, 155, 227
talaka, 146, 153
theft, 56, 72, 74, 83, 85, 103, 186, 197, 188, 193
  accounting fraud, 75–77, 222
  misappropriation, 75, 100, 101, 222
  petty theft, 82, 83
  pilfering, 73, 77
  robbery, 82, 99, 222
  smuggling, 64, 65, 165
Thompson, Edward P., 201, 202
time, 73–75
  arrhythmia (of socialist temporality), 74
Tocqueville, Alexis de, 211
torture, 35, 115, 199, 215
totalitarianism, 3, 4, 227
tourism, 25n7, 36, 56, 57, 59, 86, 104, 105

Trasânka, 118, 190–191
trudoden, 119–122, 153
trust, 7, 37, 42, 45, 46, 76, 95, 97, 128, 165

Ukraine, 18, 35, 39, 63, 86, 101, 114, 116, 128, 131, 190, 211
uncertainty, 4, 29, 44, 61, 66, 74, 89, 94, 104, 105, 130, 161, 173, 174, 184, 222
unfair. *See under* justice
unwritten rules. *See under* informal
"us" vs. "them," 148, 154, 186, 188, 192, 199
use of collective resources, 71, 77, 83, 93, 95, 96, 97, 108, 130, 181, 222
utopia, 169, 173, 174, 197

Verdery, Katherine, 4, 5, 23, 28–29, 73, 74, 165
verticality of power, 2, 14, 98–102, 110n3
violence, 3, 4, 82, 99, 109, 114–117, 195–200, 208, 220, 230
  domestic violence, 79
  mass violence, 117, 118
  police violence, 2
  state-sponsored violence, 34
vodka. *See under* alcohol
Vietnam, 10, 60

Weber, Florence, 7, 8, 38, 44, 45, 52, 53, 54, 92, 139, 160, 161, 163, 164, 173, 175, 206
Weber, Max, 2, 92, 139, 206, 211, 212, 220
Wedel, Janine, 4, 166
Werth, Nicolas, 3, 4, 20, 140, 158, 227
Wilson, Andrew, 1, 2, 24, 99
wine. *See under* alcohol

Yurchak, Alexei, 4, 136, 148, 225, 226, 227

www.ingramcontent.com/pod-product-compliance
Lightning Source LLC
Chambersburg PA
CBHW051533020426
42333CB00016B/1901